BACH

1. JOHANN SEBASTIAN BACH

BACH

A BIOGRAPHY, BY
CHARLES SANFORD
TERRY

Second Edition

OXFORD UNIVERSITY PRESS

LONDON   NEW YORK   TORONTO

Oxford University Press, Ely House, London W. 1

GLASGOW NEW YORK TORONTO MELBOURNE WELLINGTON
CAPE TOWN SALISBURY IBADAN NAIROBI LUSAKA ADDIS ABABA
BOMBAY CALCUTTA MADRAS KARACHI LAHORE DACCA
KUALA LUMPUR HONG KONG TOKYO

FIRST PUBLISHED 1928
SECOND AND REVISED EDITION 1933
SIXTH IMPRESSION 1967

PRINTED IN GREAT BRITAIN
AT THE UNIVERSITY PRESS, OXFORD
BY VIVIAN RIDLER
PRINTER TO THE UNIVERSITY

PREFACE

THE intention of this work is exactly declared by its title: it is a record of Bach's career, not a critical appreciation of his music. His personality has been so buried under the towering pyramid of his manuscript that, for most of us, he is but faintly visible on a background of the Bachgesellschaft folios. The fault lies with his biographers. Forkel, born seventeen months before Bach died, missed a precious opportunity. He knew Bach's eldest sons intimately; one of their sisters was living seven years after his monograph was published. Bach was still a vivid memory at Arnstadt, Mühlhausen, Weimar, Cöthen, where, had he been so minded, Forkel could have sought materials. Of Bach's schooldays at Lüneburg none was better instructed than himself to draft an intimate record, for, like Bach, he had been a chorister there. And several of Bach's pupils were accessible: Gottfried August Homilius died at Dresden in 1785; Christoph Transchel in the same city in 1800; Johann Gottfried Müthel, who was with Bach when he died, survived till about 1790; Johann Christian Kittel, until 1809. Bach's relatives held responsible situations at Eisenach, Schweinfurt, Ohrdruf, Werningshausen, Langenberg, Michelbach, Eisfeld, Wechmar, Meiningen, and elsewhere, sources of intimate detail. Forkel disregarded these opportunities, and his monograph, as a biography, is consequently little more illuminating than Mizler's obituary notice published in 1754. We owe him much: he was the first to claim a place for Bach among the divinities and to clear the clouds that dimmed his brilliance. Yet, though he placed the word on his title-page, his book is not a 'Life' in the biographic sense, but a critical appreciation, based on incomplete materials, of his hero as teacher, player, and composer.

Forkel set an example monotonously followed. In 1850 C. L. Hilgenfeldt, a Hamburg lawyer, published his *Sebastian Bach's Biographie*, devoting twenty pages to 'Die Familie Bach', fifty-one to Bach's characteristics as player and composer, sixty-two to his compositions, twenty to his system as a teacher, and nine to his career, a chapter which added nothing to Forkel's information. For a generation these two writers held the field. In 1869 Edward Francis Rimbault published a little volume, 'adapted from the German of Hilgenfeldt and Forkel', to acquaint English readers with 'the admirable *Life of Bach*' by the latter and 'the more elabo-

rate work' of the former, with 'additions from original sources'
which are negligible; Bach's career fills 10 pages in a volume of
122. Meanwhile there had appeared in Germany a work whose
merits Spitta's later volumes obscured. Carl Hermann Bitter, born
in 1813, was Prussian Finanzminister from 1879 to 1882 and died
at Berlin in 1885. Until official duties diverted his pen, he was an
active investigator of sources neither Forkel nor Hilgenfeldt had
explored, and, to supply the lack of 'eine geordnete und vollständige Biographie dieses merkwürdigen Mannes', published his
Johann Sebastian Bach in two volumes in 1865. The achievement
is notable: the archives of Arnstadt, Mühlhausen, Halle, Cöthen,
Leipzig, had been laid under contribution and a large proportion
of the materials later exposed by Spitta was assembled. Bitter, in
fact, was the first biographer to approach Bach by modern methods,
though his analytical and critical chapters are much inferior to
Spitta's.[1] Three years later (1868) Bitter produced a study of
Bach's sons not yet superseded, while in 1881 a 'zweite umgearbeitete und vermehrte Auflage' of his earlier work was issued in
four volumes; the Preface is dated 'Berlin, im Juni 1880'.

Bitter was introduced to English readers by Janet E. Kay-
Shuttleworth in 1873, *The Life of J. Sebastian Bach. An abridged
translation from the German of C. H. Bitter*, to which Julius Benedict added a platitudinous Preface. But Spitta's more brilliant
sun already had eclipsed Bitter's effulgence: the first volume of
his *Joh. Seb. Bach* is dated 'Sondershausen, im März 1873', the
second appeared in the winter of 1879–80, and the English edition
is dated 'Berlin, Summer of 1880', though publication was delayed
till 1883-5. Only those who have travelled closely and critically
over the same ground can fully realize the stupendous task Spitta
set himself to achieve, the various qualities its accomplishment
required, and their astonishing combination in himself. But the
result is familiar: his *Bach* is at once the best and the worst of the
classic biographies of the Masters; its fabric grew to such proportions that Bach fades out of sight, a nebulous figure in an eclipsing
frame, obliterated under a pitiless avalanche of exposition.

Since Spitta published his volumes Bach has attracted the pens
of more writers than any other composer. Yet their pages have
advanced our knowledge of his personality hardly at all. Philipp
Wolfrum dedicated his *Johann Sebastian Bach* to Richard Strauss
in 1906, and of 401 pages devoted 66 to Bach's career. Two years
later (1908) Albert Schweitzer published an expanded version of

[1] It is disagreeable to read Spitta's ungenerous remarks in the Preface to his
English edition, p. iv.

a monograph originally issued in French (1905), with whose merits every student of Bach is familiar. It has opened the eyes of thousands, as it did Charles-Marie Widor's, to a composer whose idiom they previously but faintly understood. But Schweitzer's illumination is upon the art, indirectly upon the man. Four chapters out of thirty-five, 90 pages out of 844, develop Bach's career, and, with infrequent additions, restate the facts already set out in Spitta. Both works have been reprinted more than once; neither has been corrected or expanded, and later writers have been content baldly to re-echo them.

France holds a distinguished place in Bach literature through the labours of Albert Schweitzer and André Pirro. The latter, working on the lines of the Alsatian author, but with wider scholarship, published his remarkable *L'Esthétique de Jean-Sébastien Bach* in 1907, a work whose inaccessibility in an English text is to be deplored. As its title declares, it approaches Bach from Schweitzer's standpoint and makes no profession of a biographical purpose. Pirro, in fact, had already published (1906) a monograph on Bach, only 80 of whose 237 pages, however, are devoted to his career. Twelve years earlier (1894) he had issued a small work not less distinguished, *L'Orgue de Jean-Sébastien Bach*, now out of print, of which an English translation by Wallace Goodrich was published at New York in 1902. English readers are so familiar with Schweitzer's exposition of Bach's aesthetic that it is proper to remark Pirro's labour in the same field ten years before Schweitzer published his original volume. To an earlier generation belongs Félix Grenier's translation (1876) of Forkel's monograph, the fruit of an interest roused by Charles Lamoureux's performances of the 'Matthäuspassion' at Paris in March and April 1874. Writing eight years later (1882), however, Ernest David admitted candidly: 'En réalité, sauf son *Clavecin bien tempéré*, ses Suites pour le Clavier et quelques Concertos, le monde musical français ignore tout ce qu'a écrit Bach, et Dieu sait cependant si le nombre de ses compositions est considérable!' To introduce his countrymen to this vast and unknown literature David published (1882) his *La vie et les œuvres de Jean-Sébastien Bach, sa famille, ses élèves, ses contemporains*. Based upon German materials then available, he relied chiefly on Spitta, whom indeed he had at first proposed to translate, but, discovering in his author 'aussi bien des hors-d'œuvre qui n'intéresseraient que médiocrement les lecteurs français', concluded merely to extract 'les détails essentiels'. His book in effect is a judicious compendium of Spitta. The second centenary of Bach's birth in 1885 was marked by the appearance of

William Cart's *Étude sur J.S.Bach*, 'l'artiste que nous aimons plus que tout autre'. Professor Th. Gérold's *J.-S. Bach: biographie critique* (1925) completes the tale of biographic material published in France; on the historical side its scholarship is not appreciably in advance of 1882.

Among English books Hubert Parry's *Johann Sebastian Bach: the story of the development of a great personality* (1909) not only holds the first place, but stands among the best on its subject in any language. It owes its pre-eminence to its interpretation of Bach's genius by a writer singularly in tune with it, illuminating in his judgements, and extraordinarily penetrating in his criticism; there is not another book from which we receive a more satisfying impression of Bach's moral and artistic grandeur. But the portrait is not biographical; the 'great personality' that interested Parry was not the individual, but the artist; he was content to take his history from Spitta, whose researches, he declared, left little for those who followed him 'but to confess their obligations'. Dr. Reginald Lane Poole acknowledged a similar indebtedness in his *Sebastian Bach* (1882), which holds a place of its own as the first considerable work on Bach in English not translated from a German original. Excepting a few facts gleaned during a visit to Germany, C. F. Abdy Williams's *Bach* (1900) takes us no farther than its predecessors.

Are we, then, to infer, to quote Dr. Lane Poole, that, 'thanks to the devotion of Professor Spitta, we can congratulate ourselves on the possession of absolutely all the attainable facts' of Bach's life? If we turn to the official *Bach-Jahrbuch*, which for twenty-three years has published the researches of Bach scholars, it would almost appear that Spitta's indefatigable pursuit had run to earth every recoverable detail of Bach's career and circumstances. Expositions of his technique, aesthetic appreciations of his art, spring from a fount of inexhaustible fluency; contributions that approach him from the historical side are rarely encountered. Yet, in the past quarter-century the *Bach-Jahrbuch* has published valuable work in that field. The veteran Professor Bernhard Fr. Richter has contributed articles on the conditions of Bach's service at Leipzig. Rudolf Bunge has explored the circumstances of his career at Cöthen, and Dr. Werner Wolffheim has corrected Spitta's errors regarding 'Hans der Spielmann'. Important papers have been published elsewhere by Dr. Max Seiffert and others in the 'Neue Zeitschrift für Musik', 'Monatshefte für Musikgeschichte', 'Internationale Musik-Gesellschaft', 'Die Musik', 'Archiv für Musikwissenschaft', and 'Allgemeine Musikalische Zeitung'. Also from parochial sources new information is forthcoming; for instance, Wilhelm Heimann's article in the 'Arnstädter Anzeiger'. In every town with which Bach was associated investigators have explored local archives or plumbed local tradition to salvage some record of him. I name in this connexion particularly Diakonus Weissgerber in Arnstadt, Herren Bethge, Götze, and Robert Schulze in Cöthen, Dr. Junghans and Pastor Reuter in Lüneburg, Professors Thomas and Burckas in Ohrdruf, Professor Jordan and Archidiakonus Thiele in Mühlhausen, Herr Paul von Bojanowski in Weimar, Dr. Adolf Werner in Weissenfels, and Drs. Werner Wolffheim and Wäschke in Celle. These and similar sources of information I have not neglected. I have also searched the Thuringian Staatsarchiv at Weimar and Sondershausen, the Anhalt Staatsarchiv at Zerbst (to whose Director I am otherwise under an obligation), the Stadtarchiv at Leipzig, and the Archiv des Ministeriums für Volksbildung in Sachsen at Dresden. While the search has demonstrated the thoroughness of Spitta's winnowing, it has discovered materials he overlooked.

I have referred to the valuable work accomplished by local antiquaries in the various towns Bach frequented. I made it my agreeable task to get into touch with them and cannot too cordially acknowledge the friendly welcome and assistance I everywhere received in Germany. In particular I name Professor Bernhard Fr. Richter, Professor Dr. Karl Straube, and Herr Bibliothekar Kessler, of Leipzig; Pastor Hoppe and Geheimer Studienrat Dr. Grosse of Arnstadt; Dr. Albert Neukirch, Director of the Bomann Museum, Celle; Herr Kreis-Schulrat Bethge, Chairman of the Vereins-Heimatmuseum, Cöthen; Herr Conrad Freyse, Director of the Bachmuseum, Eisenach; Professor Dr. Walther Schubring, Hamburg; Herr Wilhelm Stahl, of Lübeck; Pastor prim. Reuter of Lüneburg; Superintendent Palme and Archidiakonus Thiele, of Mühlhausen; the late Professor Dr. Victor Burckas, Ohrdruf; Professor Dr. Köhler, Director of the Weimar Schlossmuseum, and Pfarrer Otto Michaelis, Weimar; and Pfarrer Schmalck of Wechmar. Others to whom I am indebted are named in association with the facts contributed by them. But I must mention in particular three who have aided my endeavour to correct the Bach genealogy and to extend it to the present generation: Herr Oberlehrer Hugo Lämmerhirt, of Leipzig; Herr Carl Oscar Bach, of Berlin; and Herr Postinspektor Paul Bach, of Weimar.

With the generous encouragement of the Oxford University Press, the following pages are decorated with a large number of illustrations which permit the reader to visualize Bach's surroundings from the beginning to the end of his career, as well as many of the persons with whom he associated. Many are photographs taken by myself, others were made under my direction. In the latter category I mention particularly the Schlosstheater at Celle and the exquisite chapel there; the interior of the Bonifaciuskirche at Arnstadt, showing the disposition of the organ and choir gallery in Bach's time; the view of Mühlhausen in 1707 and the Untermarktkirche there; the interior of the church at Dornheim in which Bach was married; the pictures of the Wilhelmsburg and Gelbes Schloss at Weimar, as well as the ducal portraits; the Cöthen pictures of Prince Leopold and his wife; and the photographs of the Leipzig churches. I must also acknowledge the permission accorded me to picture the interiors of the Catharinenkirche at Hamburg and Marienkirche at Lübeck. Herr Louis Pernitzsch allows me to reproduce the photograph of the Thomasschule before its destruction, and Herr Robert Schulze has conferred a similar favour in the drawing of the Schloss from his *Köthen in Anhalt*. To Ministerial Councillor Dr. Norbert Kovács I am much indebted for the drawing of a hussar livery such as Bach probably wore at Weimar.

The proofs of these pages have been read, to their advantage, by Mrs. Esther Meynell, author of that delicate work *The Little Chronicle of Anna Magdalena Bach* (1925), and by Mr. F. T. Arnold; to both I tender sincere thanks.

C. S. T.

King's College,
Old Aberdeen.
February 1928.

NOTE TO THE SECOND EDITION

I HAVE taken advantage of the present opportunity to make a complete revision of the book, and to test once more its statements and references. A few minor errors have come to light, and two of a more serious nature. Relying on a minute quoted *verbatim* by Bitter, I accepted 29 July 1750 as the date of Harrer's appointment in Bach's room. The Leipzig archives, which I have since consulted, reveal that Bitter's minute relates to the Cantorship of the Nikolaischule, and that Harrer was not appointed to the Thomasschule until August 7, a week after Bach's funeral. The second matter that called for correction relates to Bach's widow. In the first edition I stated that Anna Magdalena died in an almshouse in the Hainstrasse, and scolded the indecent apathy of the community. That she died an almswoman ('Almosenfrau') and was buried with the ritual accorded to the indigent are established facts; but, as the result of inquiries on the spot, it does not appear that the recipients of public charity were segregated in an almshouse. Anna Magdalena died in the Hainstrasse, and the fact that her sometime curator and Bach's old friend, Dr. Graf, had a house in that street encourages the hope that she passed her last years in one of the humbler tenements under its roof. The charity she received has been represented to me as an honourable pension accorded to the widow of a valued public servant. I find it hard to reconcile this opinion with the circumstances of her funeral.

Since the first edition was published, the investigations of Herr Fritz Rollberg, Eisenach, have clearly proved that the house on the Frauenplan was at no time in Johann Ambrosius Bach's occupation, and therefore cannot be accepted as Sebastian's birthplace. For a photograph of the actual site (Lutherstrasse 35) I am indebted to Herr Rollberg.

C. S. T.

KING'S COLLEGE,
OLD ABERDEEN.
October 1932.

CONTENTS

ILLUSTRATIONS

[1] From a photograph by the Author.

[1] From a photograph by the Author.

AUTHORITIES AND ABBREVIATIONS

Archiv f. M.W.='Archiv für Musikwissenschaft' (Bückeburg).

Aug.=Augener's ed. of Bach's organ music.

B.C.T.='Joh. Seb. Bach: Cantata texts sacred and secular. With a reconstruction of the Leipzig Liturgy of his period. By Charles Sanford Terry.' London: 1926.

B.-G.=Publications of the Bachgesellschaft, 1850–1900.

B.-J.='Bach-Jahrbuch: Herausgegeben von der Neuen Bachgesellschaft.' Leipzig: issued annually since 1904.

Barth='Johann Sebastian Bach. Ein Lebensbild von Hermann Barth. Mit elf Bildern.' Berlin: [1901].

Beier='Tausend Jahre deutscher Vergangenheit in Quellen heimatlicher Geschichte insbesondere Leipzigs und des Leipziger Kreises. Herausgegeben von K. Beier und A. Dobritzsch, Lehrern in Leipzig.' 2 vols. Leipzig: 1911.

Bethge='Johann Sebastian Bach 1685–1750 und sein Wirken in Cöthen 1717–1723. Ein Führer durch die Bachabteilung des Cöthener Heimatmuseums. Im Auftrage des Arbeitsausschusses des Heimatmuseums in Cöthen bearbeitet von W. Bethge und W. Götze.' Cöthen: 1925.

Beyer='Bach. Eine Kunde vom Genius. Von Oskar Beyer.' Berlin: 1924. 2nd ed. 1928.

Bi.='Johann Sebastian Bach. Von C. H. Bitter, königlich Preussischem Finanzminister. Zweite, umgearbeitete und vermehrte Auflage.' 4 vols. Berlin: 1881.

Bojanowski='Das Weimar Johann Sebastian Bachs. Zur Erinnerung an den 8. April 1703. Von Paul von Bojanowski. Mit einem Bilde: Die Schlosskirche zur Zeit Bachs.' Weimar: 1903.

Bunge='Johann Sebastian Bachs Kapelle zu Cöthen und deren nachgelassene Instrumente. Nach urkundlichen Quellen von Rudolf Bunge, Geh. Hofrat in Cöthen (Anhalt).' In B.-J. 1905, pp. 14–47.

Cart='Étude sur J. S. Bach 1685–1750. Par William Cart.' Paris: 1885.

Dahms='Johann Sebastian Bach. Ein Bild seines Lebens zusammengestellt von Walter Dahms.' Munich: 1924.

David='La vie et les œuvres de Jean-Sébastien Bach, sa famille, ses élèves, ses contemporains. Par Ernest David.' Paris: 1882.

D.J.F.L.='Das jetzt lebende und jetzt florirende Leipzig, welches die Nahmen, Characteren, Chargen, Professionen und Wohnungen . . . allhier zu finden.' Leipzig: 1736.

Fischer='Musik in Hannover. Von Dr. med. Georg Fischer, Hannover. Zweite, vermehrte Auflage von "Opern und Concerte im Hoftheater zu Hannover bis 1866".' Hannover and Leipzig: 1903.

Flade='Der Orgelbauer Gottfried Silbermann. Ein Beitrag zur Geschichte des deutschen Orgelbaues im Zeitalter Bachs.' By Ernst Flade. Leipzig: 1926.

Flossmann='Picander (Christian Friedrich Henrici). Inaugural-Dissertation . . . Von Paul Flossmann.' Liebertwolkwitz: 1899.

For.='Ueber Johann Sebastian Bachs Leben, Kunst und Kunstwerke. Von J. N. Forkel. Nach der Originalausgabe von 1802 neu herausgegeben mit Einleitung und ausführlichem Nachwort von Josef M. Müller-Blattäu.' Augsburg: 1925.

Forkel='Johann Sebastian Bach, his life, art, and work. Translated from the German of Johann Nikolaus Forkel, with notes and appendices, by Charles Sanford Terry.' London: 1920.

Genealogy='Ursprung der musikalisch-Bachischen Familie. Nachrichten über Johann Sebastian Bach von Carl Philipp Emanuel Bach. Herausgegeben von Max Schneider.' N.B.G., Jahrgang xvii, Heft 3. See also p. 3 n. 4.

Gerber='Historie der Kirchen-Ceremonien in Sachsen. Von Christian Gerber.' Dresden and Leipzig: 1732.

Gerhardt='Friedrich Gerhardt, Pastor zu Weissenfels. Geschichte der Stadt Weissenfels a. S. mit neuen Beiträgen zur Geschichte des Herzogtums Sachsen-Weissenfels.' Weissenfels: [1907].

Gérold='J.-S. Bach. Par Th. Gérold, Professeur à l'Université de Strasbourg. Biographie critique illustrée de douze reproductions hors texte.' Paris: 1925.

Gesner='E. E. Hochweisen Raths der Stadt Leipzig Gesetze der Schule zu S. Thomae.' Leipzig: 1733.

Also a Latin edition:
'Leges scholae Thomanae alumnis ab amplissimo Senatu Lipsiensi scriptae et promulgatae 1733.'

Görges='Die Schulen des Michaelisklosters in Lüneburg. II. Die Michaelis-schule. Vom Professor Wilhelm Görges. Jahresbericht des Johanneums zu Lüneburg. Ostern 1902.' Lüneburg: 1902

Grace='The Organ works of Bach. By Harvey Grace.' London: [1922].

Graff='Geschichte der Auflösung der alten gottesdienstlichen Formen in der evangelischen Kirche Deutschlands. Von Paul Graff, Pastor in Kleinfreden.' Göttingen: 1921.

Grenier='Vie, talents et travaux de Jean-Sébastien Bach, ouvrage traduit de l'allemand de J. N. Forkel, annoté et précédé d'un aperçu de l'état de la musique en Allemagne aux xvie et xviie siècles. Par Félix Grenier. Nouvelle édition.' Paris: n.d.

Grove='Grove's Dictionary of Music and Musicians.' Third edn. 1927. Revised 1928. Ed. Henry Cope Colles.

Hashagen='Johann Sebastian Bach als Sänger und Musiker des Evangeliums und der lutherischen Reformation. Skizzen von D. Fr. Hashagen, Professor der prakt. Theologie und Universitäts-Prediger zu Rostock.' Wismar: 1909.

Heimann='Die Bache in Arnstadt,' by Wilhelm Heimann, in the 'Arnstädter Anzeiger' for 15 June 1924.

Heiss='Das Ohrdrufer Schloss "Der Ehrenstein". Mit Zeichnungen und Rekonstruktionen von Dr. phil. Ernst Heiss, herzoglich Sächs. Baurat.' Ohrdruf: n.d.

Hertel='Arnstadt und seine Umgebung. Herausgegeben von Richard Hertel. 2. Auflage.' Arnstadt: 1924.

Hilgenfeldt='Johann Sebastian Bach's Leben, Wirken und Werke. Ein Beitrag zur Kunstgeschichte des achtzehnten Jahrhunderts. Von C. L. Hilgenfeldt. Als Programm zu dem am 28. Julius 1850 eintretenden Säculartage des Todes von Johann Sebastian Bach. Mit einer genealogischen Tabelle und Notenbeilagen.' Leipzig: [1850].

His='Johann Sebastian Bach. Forschungen über dessen Grabstätte, Gebeine und Antlitz. Von Prof. Wilhelm His.' Leipzig: 1895.

Hoppe='Die Pflege der Musik in Naumburg a. S. Von Friedrich Hoppe.' Naumburg: 1914.

Ihle=Paul Ihle's Bach family tree (see p. 4 *infra*).

I.M.G.=Sammelbände der Internationalen Musik-Gesellschaft.

J.C.K.=Johann Christian Kittel's copy of the Bach family tree (see p. 4 *infra*).

J.L.B.=The Bach family tree compiled by Joh. Lorenz Bach (see p. 4 *infra*).

J.M.K.=Joh. Matthias Korabinsky's 'Beschreibung der königl. ungarischen Haupt-, Frey- und Krönungsstadt Pressburg', Pressburg : 1784.

Jöde='Fritz Jöde: Die Kunst Bachs dargestellt an seinen Inventionen.' Wolfenbüttel: 1926.

Jordan='Aus der Geschichte der Musik in Mühlhausen. Von Prof. Dr. Jordan. Zur Geschichte der Stadt Mühlhausen i. Thür. Heft 5.' Mühlhausen: 1905.

Jürgens='Die Lande Braunschweig und Lüneburg. Fortsetzung zu der Übersicht über die ältere Geschichte Niedersachsens II. Von Dr. O. Jürgens. Veröffentlichungen zur niedersächsischen Geschichte. 13.Heft.' Hannover: n.d.

Junghans='Johann Sebastian Bach als Schüler der Partikularschule zu St. Michaelis in Lüneburg, oder Lüneburg eine Pflegstätte kirchlicher Musik. Von Professor W. Junghans, Programm des Johanneums zu Lüneburg, Ostern 1870.' Lüneburg: 1870.

Kemmerling='Die Thomasschule zu Leipzig, eine kurze Geschichte von ihrer Gründung 1212 bis zum Jahre 1927, von Franz Kemmerling.' Leipzig: 1927.

Kretzschmar='Bach-Kolleg: Vorlesungen über Johann Sebastian Bach gehalten an der Universität zu Berlin von Hermann Kretzschmar.' Leipzig: 1922.

Kroker='Bachs Berufung in das Kantorat der Thomasschule. Von Ernst Kroker.' In 'Leipzig: eine Monatsschrift herausgegeben vom Rate der Stadt Leipzig. Erster Jahrgang, Heft 2,' June 1924.

La Mara=' Johann Sebastian Bach. Von La Mara [Marie Lipsius]. Neubearbeiteter Einzeldruck aus den musikalischen Studienköpfen. 8.u.9.Auflage.' Leipzig: 1921.

Liliencron='Festschrift zum 90. Geburtstage Sr. Excellenz Rochus Freiherrn von Liliencron.' Leipzig: 1910.

Marconnay='Ernst August, Herzog von Sachsen-Weimar-Eisenach (1688–1748). Kulturgeschichtlicher Versuch von Carl Freiherrn von Beaulieu Marconnay.' Leipzig: 1872.

Mattheson='Grundlage einer Ehren-Pforte . . . Von Mattheson, Hamburg. 1740. . . . Herausgegeben von Max Schneider.' Berlin: 1910.

Meyer='Johann Sebastian Bach. Vortrag von Dr. Paul Meyer.' Basel: 1887.

Monatsh. f. M.G.='Monatshefte für Musikgeschichte.'

N. = Novello's edition of Bach's organ music.

N.B.G. = Publications of the Neue Bachgesellschaft, 1900 ff.

Nekrolog = 'Der Nekrolog auf Seb. Bach vom Jahre 1754. Neudruck.' In B.-J. 1920, pp. 11–29.

P. = Peters edition of Bach's instrumental music.[1]

Parry = 'Johann Sebastian Bach. The story of the development of a great personality. By C.Hubert H.Parry. Illustrated.' New York and London:[1909].

Pi. = 'Bach, sein Leben und seine Werke. Von André Pirro. Vom Verfasser autorisierte deutsche Ausgabe von Bernhard Engelke. 14. und 15. Tausend.' Berlin: 1924.

Pirro (1) = 'J. S. Bach. Par André Pirro. Avec Portrait hors texte et citations musicales dans le texte. Quatrième édition.' Paris: 1913.

Pirro (2)='L'esthétique de Jean-Sébastien Bach. Par André Pirro.' Paris: 1907.

Pirro (3) = 'Johann Sebastian Bach, the Organist, and his works for the Organ. By A. Pirro. With a Preface by Ch.-M. Widor. Translated from the French by Wallace Goodrich.' New York: 1902.

[1] The references to it throughout conform with Dörffel's Thematic Catalogue.

Poole='Sebastian Bach. By Reginald Lane Poole. New edition.' London: [1882].

Reimann='Johann Sebastian Bach. Von Heinrich Reimann. Zweite Auflage, neu bearbeitet und erweitert von Bruno Schrader.' Berlin: [1921].

Reuter='Die St. Michaeliskirche in Lüneburg. Ein Rückblick auf ihre tausendjährige Geschichte am fünfhundertjährigen Jubeltage, dem 11. Juli 1918. Pastor prim. H. Reuter.' Hannover and Leipzig: 1918.

Richter='Das Innere der alten Thomasschule. Von Bernhard Friedrich Richter. Schriften des Vereins für die Geschichte Leipzigs. 7 Band.' Leipzig: 1904.

Riemann='Hugo Riemanns Musik-Lexikon. Elfte Auflage, bearbeitet von Alfred Einstein.' Berlin: 1929.

Robinson='Handel and his orbit. By P. Robinson.' London: 1908.

Rudloff='Geschichte des Lyceums zu Ohrdruf. Von J. Chr. Rudloff.' Arnstadt: 1845.

Sachse='Die ältere Geschichte der Thomasschule zu Leipzig. Nach den Quellen dargestellt von Dr. Richard Sachse, Konrektor. Mit 31 Tafeln.' Leipzig: 1912.

Schering='Musikgeschichte Leipzigs. In drei Bänden. Zweiter Band: von 1650 bis 1723. Von Arnold Schering.' Leipzig: 1926.

Schulordnung 1723='E. E. Hochw. Raths der Stadt Leipzig Ordnung der Schule zu S. Thomæ.' Leipzig: 1723.

Schulze='Köthen in Anhalt. Ein Führer durch die Stadt und ihre Geschichte. Von Robert Schulze. Bildschmuck von Martin Theuerjahr.' Cöthen: [1923].

Schw.='J. S. Bach. Von Albert Schweitzer, Professor, Dr. theol., phil. et med., Strassburg i. E. Vorrede von Charles Marie Widor. 4. u. 5. Auflage.' Leipzig: 1922.

Schweitzer='J. S. Bach. By Albert Schweitzer, Dr. philos., Privatdozent at the Kaiser Wilhelm University at Strassburg, Organist to the Bach Society of Paris. With a Preface by C. M. Widor. English translation by Ernest Newman.' 2 vols. London: 1911.

Sitte='Johann Sebastian Bach als "Legende" erzählt. Von Heinrich Sitte.' Berlin: 1925.

Söhle='Sebastian Bach in Arnstadt. Ein musikalisches Kulturbild aus dem Anfang des 18. Jahrhunderts. Von Karl Söhle. Neue Ausgabe. Sechstes bis elftes Tausend.' Leipzig: 1922.

Sp.='Joh. Seb. Bach. Von Philipp Spitta. Dritte unveränderte Auflage.' 2 vols. Leipzig: 1921.

Spitta='Johann Sebastian Bach. His work and influence on the music of Germany, 1685–1750. By Philipp Spitta. Translated from the German by Clara Bell and J. A. Fuller-Maitland.' 3 vols. London: 1899.

Stahl='Franz Tunder und Dietrich Buxtehude. Ein biographischer Versuch von Wilhelm Stahl, Lübeck. Mit 19 Abbildungen.' Leipzig: 1926.

Stein='Johann Sebastian Bach. Ein Künstlerleben. Von Armin Stein.' Halle: 1896.

Stiehl='Die Organisten an der St. Marienkirche und die Abendmusiken zu Lübeck. Von C. Stiehl. Zeitschrift des Vereins für Lübeckische Geschichte und Alterthumskunde. Bd. 5, Heft 2.' Lübeck: 1887.

Stuart='Johann Sebastian Bach. Av Elsa Marianne Stuart.' Stockholm: [1922].

T.B.C.='Bach's Chorals. By Charles Sanford Terry.' 3 vols. Cambridge: 1915–1921.

Thiele='Die Familie Bach in Mühlhausen. Von Archidiakonus Georg Thiele, Mühlhäuser Geschichtsblätter, Jahrgang 21, 1920–1921.' Mühlhausen: 1921.

Thomas='Stammbaum des Ohrdrufer Zweiges der Familie von Joh. Seb. Bach.
Jahresbericht des Gräflich Gleichenschen Gymnasiums, Progymnasium und
Realprogymnasium.' Ohrdruf: 1899.
Thomas (2)='Einige Ergebnisse über Johann Sebastian Bachs Ohrdrufer Schul-
zeit, aus der Matrikel des Lyceums geschöpft von Prof. Dr. Fr. Thomas.
Jahresbericht des Gräflich Gleichenschen Gymnasiums, Progymnasium und
Realprogymnasium (Letzteres in Umwandlung in eine Realschule begriffen)
zu Ohrdruf für das Schuljahr 1899–1900.' Ohrdruf: 1900.
Wäschke='Die Hofkapelle in Cöthen unter Joh. Seb. Bach. Von Archivrat
Dr. Wäschke in Zerbst.' In Zerbster Jahrbuch, Jahrgang iii, 1907, pp.
31–40. Zerbst: 1907.
Weissgerber='Johann Sebastian Bach in Arnstadt. Festrede zur Feier des
73. Geburtstages Sr. Durchlaucht des regierenden Fürsten, gehalten von
Diakonus Weissgerber. Fürstliche Realschule in Arnstadt (Fürstentum
Schwarzburg-Sondershausen). Jahresbericht über das Schuljahr von Ostern
1903 bis Ostern 1904.' Arnstadt: 1904.
Werner='Städtische und fürstliche Musikpflege in Weissenfels bis zum Ende
des 18. Jahrhunderts. Von Arno Werner.' Leipzig: 1911.
Williams='Bach. By C. F. Abdy Williams. With Illustrations and Portraits.'
London: 1921.
Wolffheim='Mitteilungen zur Geschichte der Hofmusik in Celle (1635–1706)
und über Arnold M. Brunckhorst. Von Werner Wolffheim. Festschrift
zum 90. Geburtstage Rochus Freiherrn von Liliencron.' Leipzig: 1910.
Wolfrum='Johann Sebastian Bach. Von Philipp Wolfrum.' 2 vols. Leipzig:
1910.
Wotquenne='Thematisches Verzeichnis der Werke von Carl Philipp Emanuel
Bach (1714–1788). Herausgegeben von Alfred Wotquenne.' Leipzig: 1905.
Zahn='Die Melodien der deutschen evangelischen Kirchenlieder, aus den
Quellen geschöpft und mitgeteilt von Johannes Zahn.' 6 vols. Gütersloh:
1889–1893.
Z. f. M.='Zeitschrift für Musik.'
Zor='The Origin of the Family of Bach Musicians.' By Charles Sanford
Terry. London: 1929.

To the above list the following may be added:

Gustave Robert, 'Le Descriptif chez Bach'. Paris: 1909.
Peter Epstein, 'Der Schulchos vom 16. Jahrhundert bis zur Gegenwart.'
Leipzig: 1929.
Rutland Boughton, 'Bach'. London: 1930.
Erich Schwebsch, 'Die Kunst der Fuge'. Stuttgart: 1930.
Charles Sanford Terry, 'Bach: the historical approach'. New York: 1930.
Charles Sanford Terry, 'Bach's Orchestra'. Oxford: 1932.
Charles Sanford Terry, 'The Music of Bach'. Oxford: 1932.
Albert Dreetz, 'Johann Christian Kittel, der letzte Bach-Schüler'. Leipzig: 1932.

Also the following biographies of Bach's children:

Martin Falck, 'Wilhelm Friedemann Bach', second edn. Leipzig: 1919.
Otto Vrieslander, 'Philipp Emanuel Bach'. Munich: 1923.
Heinrich Miesner, 'Philipp Emanuel Bach in Hamburg': 1919.
Charles Sanford Terry, 'John Christian Bach'. Oxford: 1929.

CHAPTER I
THE FAMILY

THE story of the Bachs records a musical apostleship extraordinarily prolonged, abnormally fruitful, and incidentally
gilds the shields of the petty principalities of Thuringia, 'das alte
Kulturland'. Himself of that soil, Luther was frequenting its
oldest University when the earliest Bach appears in its neighbourhood. Bismarck was thirty years old when the last male of Sebastian's lineage passed unremarked to his rest. Seven generations
separate these distant relatives, and of the many Bachs recorded
by name and profession in the long interval all but few were
Cantors, organists, or town's musicians, some of high eminence.
So synonymous were the name and the craft that Erfurt's musicians
were named 'the Bachs' long after a Bach ceased to fiddle among
them. Kinship and a common profession linked the scattered Bach
septs in a union close and intimate. Indeed, their corporate friendliness was among Sebastian's cherished traditions; from none
other can Carl Philipp Emanuel have received the picture he passed
on to Forkel:[1] 'The Bachs not only displayed a happy contented-
ness, indispensable for the cheery enjoyment of life, but exhibited
a clannish attachment to each other. They could not all live in the
same locality, but it was their habit to meet once a year at a time
and place arranged beforehand. These family gatherings took
place at Erfurt, Eisenach, and, naturally, at Arnstadt. Even after
the family had grown very large, and many of its members had left
Thuringia to settle in Upper and Lower Saxony and Franconia,
the Bachs continued their annual festivals. On these occasions
music was their sole recreation. As those present were Cantors,
organists, or town's musicians, employed in the service of the
Church and accustomed to preface the day's work with prayer,
their first act was to sing a hymn. Having fulfilled their religious
duty, they spent the rest of the day in frivolous recreations. Best
of all they liked to extemporize a chorus out of popular songs,
comic or jocular, weaving them into a harmonious whole while de-
claiming the words of each. They called this hotchpotch a "Quodlibet", laughed uproariously over it, and roused equally hearty and
irrepressible laughter in all who listened to it.'

Racy of their soil, the Bachs come first into view in the Thurin-

[1] A Quodlibet by Bach himself is published by the N.B.G.

B

gian uplands round Arnstadt as the sixteenth century opens. It is a country of broad hedgeless farmlands dotted with little clusters of red-roofed houses sheltering under white-walled spired churches, oases in a landscape sparsely timbered save on the slopes of the Wald, a flat expanse of arable soil over which patient oxen pull the plough, where the women hoe, dig, guide the lumbering wains heavy with market produce, or lead the straining dogs that drag their miniatures. Sheltering picturesquely in a hollow under the wooded heights of the Wald, Gräfenroda[1] discloses the earliest member of the Bach lineage, a peasant characteristically named Hans, a tenant of Count Günther of Schwarzburg-Arnstadt-Sondershausen, who in February 1509 afforded him protection in a suit at the instance of the See of Mainz. His descendants lived in Gräfenroda[2] for generations thereafter;[3] one of them, another Hans (Johannes), was Diakonus in neighbouring Ilmenau in 1676, nine years before Sebastian was born. Northward from Gräfenroda, and nearly midway between Gotha and Arnstadt, another Bach sept is revealed in the same period at Wechmar. Here was living in the middle years of the sixteenth century a third Hans, prominent in his community, whom, as will be shown, we identify as the great-great-great-grandfather of Sebastian. South-westward from Wechmar lies Ohrdruf, whose register records the marriage of Margaret Bach 'von Wechmar' on 13 February 1564,[4] the first of her name in a community which knew it continuously thereafter till the middle of the nineteenth century. She may have been Hans of Wechmar's daughter, if so, a remote aunt of Sebastian, who more than a century later was a schoolboy in that township. At Wölfis, again, hard by Ohrdruf on the south-east, Kunz Bach was a bridegroom in 1568,[5] and Barbara Bach of the same village was married two years later.[6] Also of the Wechmar stock, probably, was Caspar Bach, Stadtpfeifer[7] of Gotha, with whom Sebastian's great-grandfather Hans served his apprenticeship in the tower of the old Rathaus on the Hauptmarkt.[8] Taking the familiar road through Wechmar, Caspar journeyed in later years to Arnstadt, first of the Bachs in that capital of their name, where from 1620 to 1640 he served the Count as Hausmann, lived in the still-

---

[1] Now Gräfenroda-Süd. Cf. B.-J. 1931, p. 107.   [2] Illus. No. 2.
[3] The name has long since died out there, as I was informed by the Church Küster. See generally Sp. Bk. I, ch. i.   [4] Thomas, p. 18.
[5] Bi. i. 7.   [6] Thomas, p. 18.   [7] i.e. town's musician.
[8] Caspar is also described as 'Thürmer'. His duties are defined: 'sollte er die Stunden schlagen und Tag und Nacht auf Reiter und Kutschen und auf alle Wege, wo mehr denn zwei Reiter sind, zu achten haben, zugleich auch melden, da er in der Nähe oder Ferne Feuer sehe' (Heimann). The north portal of the old Gotha Rathaus bears the date 1574. The tower is of later construction.

standing clock-tower of Schloss Neideck,[1] carolled the hours, raised an alarm when fires broke out, and bent a suspicious eye on strangers approaching the town. In this leisurely occupation he throve, married his kinswoman, Catharine Bach, bought himself a house in the Jakobsgasse, whose narrow thoroughfare presses close on the old town-wall, and passed on his office to his sons.[2] Meanwhile, between Arnstadt and Erfurt, some twelve miles distant to the north, two more Bach families come into view. At Rockhausen in the second half of the sixteenth century lived Wolf Bach, a man of substance whose progeny did not long survive. At Molsdorf, a neighbouring village to the west, the church register reveals the second Bach sept, whose origins date back at least to the sixteenth century; it probably counted among its members Johann Bach, 'Musicant' to General Gustav von Wrangel (d. 1676). Nikol Bach of this Molsdorf line, also in Swedish service, was stabbed in a drunken brawl at Arnstadt in 1646. A third, Jakob Bach, was the parent of a branch that carried the family name to Bindersleben, near Erfurt, and subsequently produced Johann Christoph Bach (1782–1846), an organist and composer of Thuringian repute.

All of these rivulets but one are quickly lost in the sands of oblivion. The Wechmar stream alone flows in a widening and recorded channel to Sebastian and beyond, pre-eminently exhibiting in its members the 'Stätigkeit' characteristic of their lineage—a conservative attachment to the old homeland, the familiar family names, the hereditary craft, along with a clannish sense which, in the culminating period of its distinction, declared itself in family trees and genealogies recording its continuity and registering its achievement. The most authoritative of the latter, compiled by Sebastian himself,[3] survives, with annotations by Carl Philipp Emanuel, who sent it to Forkel about 1775.[4] A small quarto of eighteen pages entitled *Ursprung der musicalisch-Bachischen Familie*, it contains brief notes upon fifty-three of the name. The latest date recorded in it (No. 50) is 5 September 1735, the birthday of Sebastian's youngest son, the 'English Bach'. Another son, Johann Gottfried Bernhard (No. 47), is described as organist at Mühlhausen, a position he held in 1736, to which year the completion of the Genealogy may be assigned.[5] Two copies of it survive; the earlier, compiled about 1739–43, passed (1873) into the hands of

---

[1] Illus. No. 5.   [2] Heimann.
[3] The statement is authorized by his son Carl Philipp Emanuel: 'den ersten Aufsatz [of the Genealogy] machte mein seel. Vater vor vielen Jahren.'
[4] It is now in the Preuss. Staatsbibliothek. A facsimile, edited by the present writer, is published by the Oxford University Press (1929).
[5] It does not record Bach's own appointment as Hofcomponist in that year.

Fräulein Emmert of Schweinfurt, since deceased, and was probably made by Johann Elias Bach during his residence in Sebastian's house.[1] The second, probably copied from it rather than the Leipzig original, belonged to Johann Elias's elder brother Johann Lorenz Bach (*d*. 1773), and was published in 1843.[2]

Along with Carl Philipp Emanuel's Genealogy Forkel received a family tree which has disappeared, but of which traces probably are detected in Johann Matthias Korabinsky's *Beschreibung der königl. ungarischen Haupt-, Frey- und Krönungsstadt Pressburg* published in 1784. Another tree belonged to Johann Christian Kittel (1732–1809), of Erfurt,[3] a third to Fräulein Emmert of Schweinfurt, which Spitta dated *c*. 1750–60;[4] a fourth, compiled between 1773 and 1782, with Wechmar associations, has recently been discovered.[5] Three other tables exist which carry the record to our own time: one, made by Carl Volkmar Bach (*d*. 1910) of Weimar, is now owned by his son Carl Oskar Bach, Rechnungsrat in the Reichsversicherungsamt, Berlin; the second belonged to Alfred Wilhelm Bach, chemist, of Witten (Prussia),[6] a descendant of Sebastian's eldest brother, and is now preserved by his son Bernhard.[7] Herr Paul Bach of Weimar owns a pedigree table which brings the genealogy of the Meiningen Bachs to the present generation.

'Vitus[8] Bach, ein Weissbäcker[9] in Ungarn' heads Sebastian's tree. He founded a prolific and famous progeny as well as the fiction of a Hungarian origin. Misguided by the existence of a Johann Bach at Pressburg in his own period,[10] Korabinsky lightly assumed Veit to have plied his trade in that city; he has misled later writers. The Genealogy neither confirms nor confutes the heresy: it states that Veit left Hungary as a Lutheran dissident, sold his business, settled at Wechmar in Thuringia, and there resumed his

---

[1] The inference is supported by the full particulars regarding himself which supplement the original's meagre note, and also by his addition of a brother's name not entered in it. The document is now owned by Herr Hermann Wucherer, of Würzburg, to whose cousin, Herr Oberlehrer Karl Freytag, of Munich, I am indebted for information regarding it. Continued to 1815 by a later hand, it records fifty-six names and closes with Simon Friedrich Bach (1755-99).
[2] In 'Allgemeine Musikal. Zeitung', Jhrg. 45, Nos. 30 and 31.
[3] Printed in 'Allgem. Musikal. Zeitung', 1823, No. 12, with additions by Christian Fr. Michaelis.   [4] Sp. i, p. xvi.
[5] It was owned by Herr Paul Ihle of Gotha in 1915. There is reason to suppose that it is the Stammbaum sent by C. P. E. Bach to Forkel about 1775.
[6] Thomas, p. 17.
[7] I am indebted to both gentlemen for placing their genealogies at my disposal.
[8] Veit is the German form.
[9] The word may be translated 'miller' or 'baker'.
[10] B.-J. 1910, p. 83. See note 2, p. 8 *infra*.

occupation as a miller. His Hungarian exodus is not dated, but occurred, no doubt, in the reign of the semi-sane Rudolf II (1576–1612), whose Counter-Reformation in Hungary was ruthless and drastic. Veit's choice of Wechmar for his German domicile certainly was not fortuitous. Others of his name were already resident there: Hans Bach was a leading member of its community fifteen years before Rudolf began his reign; Margaret Bach of Wechmar was married at Ohrdruf in the same decade. Both may confidently be regarded as Veit's relatives, Hans probably was his father. His name, too, is significant. Ever since the relics of St. Vitus were laid to rest in the Saxon Abbey of Corvey (836) the saint was venerated as Patron of that province. The church of Wechmar is dedicated to him, and Veit clearly owed his name to the fact. We may therefore regard him as a native of Wechmar.[1] What inclination drew him to Hungary? Attachment to Lutheran dogma brought him home, but cannot explain his exile. Nor need a miller have fared so far to make a livelihood. 'What he most delighted in', his great-great-grandson records, 'was his lute,[2] which his habit was to take with him into the mill and play while it was grinding. A pretty noise the pair of them must have made! However, it taught him to keep time, and that apparently is how music first came into our family.' The conclusion may be hazarded that Veit's lute and the Wanderlust of youth carried him so far afield.

With particular piety the pilgrim approaches the acknowledged source of Bach's lineage. Modern Wechmar is a straggling village of 1,350 inhabitants, lying some three English miles along the dusty road that threads the ploughlands between Gotha and Arnstadt. It is a cluster of red-gabled houses grouped in tortuous streets round the church whose patron gave Veit his name, a circular building, whose star-spangled ceiling covers white walls, an unpretentious altar, and the curtained pulpit above it. The east window adds a note of colour to whitewashed monotony. Within it Luther stands defiant at Wittenberg, and in an upper panel St. Vitus with attendant fowl is vigilant over his foundation. The hatchments of Gleichen and Hohenlohe, flanking the altar, declare a secular allegiance less ancient than the saint's. From the church-tower a wide prospect opens. To the north-west, Schloss Friedenstein's domes loom distant above Gotha. South-eastward, the Drei Gleichen point the way to Arnstadt, ancient strengths, the midmost of which, the Wachsenburg, stands, like the more famed Wartburg, poised upon a steeply wooded peak. Embracing the village on the north, the little Apfelstädt, a clear and hurrying stream, flows from the

[1] Cf. Hilgenfeldt, p. 1; Bi. i. 6.   [2] 'Cythringen' (little zither).

Thuringian highlands, shepherded here to drive the mills which, as when Veit Bach lived, grind the harvest of the adjacent fields. The most easterly of the three, the 'Nieder-Mühle' or 'unterste Mühle', once had Veit[1] as tenant. The mill-race still turns the great wheel in its ancient masonry, bulging sacks of flour encumber the floor, and a jolly miller is visible amid the clatter. Veit himself looked out on a picturesque yard bounded with ancient barns. A few paces distant lies the Bachstrasse, where, in a substantial two-storied house whose ample gateway admits to an inner yard, he and Hans the Spielmann dwelt.[2] It is distinguished by a tablet thus inscribed:

Gedenktafel der Musikerfamilie Bach in Wechmar.

In diesem Hause betrieben Veit Bach um das Jahr 1600 und später sein Sohn Hans Bach das Bäckergewerbe. Hans hatte auch in Gotha die Musik gelernt und darneben mit Meisterschaft fortgesetzt. Mehr als 100 Nachkommen dieser Familie Bach haben in sieben Generationen der Welt grosse Tonkünstler und Musikgelehrte und in Johann Sebastian Bach einen der ausgezeichnetsten Tonsetzer, die je gelebt haben, den grössten Kontrapunktisten und Orgelspieler aller Zeiten gegeben.

Ehre ihrem Andenken.

Gestiftet von der Gemeinde Wechmar und dem Böhner-Verein in Gotha.

From the village inn—was it the 'Gasthof zum weissen Ross', that still invites the traveller?—Hans took his wife, Anna Schmied, and here were born the three sons, Johannes, Christoph, Heinrich, from whom in three expanding channels the Bach stream flowed.

In this quiet spot Veit Bach died on 8 March 1619 and was buried the same day. Groping through the Wechmar registers, we come on other Bachs who may have called Veit father. But the Genealogy allots him only two sons. One, a carpet-maker unnamed,[3] is memorable as the ancestor of a lineage that survives to-day in male succession and, in the lifetime of Sebastian, began a musical association with the Court of Sachsen-Meiningen which continued for a century. Sebastian particularly admired Johann Ludwig, first of these Meiningen Bachs, and performed his music.[4] His son Samuel Anton was Sebastian's pupil at Leipzig, but not an alumnus of the Thomasschule.[5] The last of the Meiningen Court organists, Johann Philipp, who outlived Sebastian's last surviving grandson, is represented to-day by his grandson Postinspektor Paul Karl Bernhard Bach, of Weimar. Veit's unnamed son is declared by the Genealogy to have been the father of three

---

[1] Illus. No. 3.   [2] Illus. No. 4.
[3] The church register names Lips, a son of Veit, who died 10 Oct. 1620. The Meiningen tree accepts him as its ancestor. Korabinsky names him Friedrich. Another Lips died of the plague and was buried 21 Sept. 1626.
[4] Seventeen Cantatas by him owned by Sebastian are catalogued in B.-G., Jhrg. XLI.   [5] B.-J. 1907, p. 68.

sons whom the Count of Schwarzburg-Arnstadt-Sondershausen sent to pursue their musical studies in Italy, an adventure not repeated in the history of the family until Sebastian's youngest son took that road more than one hundred years later.

Veit's other, and perhaps elder, son Hans preferably claims our interest: he was Sebastian's great-grandfather, and the first of his direct lineage to make music a livelihood. 'Brought up to the trade of baker,' says the Genealogy, Hans exhibited such evident talent that his father apprenticed him to Caspar Bach, town's musician of Gotha, who may have been the lad's uncle. Living together in the Rathaus [1] on the Hauptmarkt there, master and apprentice fulfilled the duties Caspar afterwards performed at Arnstadt, till Hans, now a master of his craft, returned to Wechmar on his father's death, married Anna Schmied, the innkeeper's daughter, and thereafter was in popular request as a player in Gotha, Arnstadt, Eisenach, Erfurt, even in distant Suhl and Schmalkalden. He died of the plague on 26 December 1626, and was followed in 1635 by his widow, herself a victim of that recurring scourge, which in that year carried off 503 of Wechmar's inhabitants: their names fill ten closely written black pages of its church register.

Hans the Spielmann, most popular and picturesque of Sebastian's forebears, owes his distinction to a confusion lately unravelled,[2] whose detection robs him of a beard and much of his fame. Carl Philipp Emanuel probably inherited from his father two portraits which Spitta and Bitter assumed to represent Sebastian's great-grandfather. One, a folio engraving now in the Preussische Staatsbibliothek, reveals a middle-aged man, close-cropped saving an affectionately nurtured wisp of hair plastered on his forehead, bearded, be-ruffed round the neck, and very unprepossessing. He carries a viol in his left hand, a bow in his right, and a jingling bell on his right shoulder declares him a jester. A fool's cap is sketched in the left-hand corner, and on a panel above it one reads the following doggerel:

Here at his fiddling see Hans Bach!
Whatever he plays, he makes you laugh:
For he scrapes away in a style all his own,
And wears a fine beard by which he is known.[3]

[1] Not in Schloss Grimmenstein, as the Genealogy asserts. The Schloss was demolished in 1567 and was succeeded by the present Schloss Friedenstein.
[2] Dr. Werner Wolffheim was the first to expose the error. See his article in B.-J. 1910, p. 70.
[3] Hie siehst du geigen Hannsen Bachen,
Wenn du es hörst so mustu lachen.
Er geigt gleichwol nach seiner Art,
Unnd tregt ein hipschen Hanns Bachen Bart.

Hans of the Beard was notorious: for the other picture in Carl Philipp's possession [1] is a print of the same person, older, but similarly cropped, bearded, and equipped, and round him the inscription:

> Morio celebris et facetus: fidicen ridiculus: homo laboriosus simplex et pius.

To the right of the face is a note: 'obijt Sexagenarius penult. Nov. 1615', and at the bottom 'M. W. S. fecit Nirtingae anno 1617'. Surrounding the picture eighteen tools such as a carpenter uses in his trade are sketched. As the inscription declares, the original of the two portraits died in 1615, eleven years before Sebastian's ancestor, and the Nürtingen register confirms his burial on 3 December 1615, revealing his identity as a servant of the widowed Duchess of Württemberg, then resident in the castle there. Thus there existed two contemporary Hans Bachs, one at Wechmar in Thuringia, the other at Nürtingen by the Black Forest. The possibility, indeed the probability, of their relationship cannot be excluded, but Hans of the Beard and Bells may no longer be admitted to the gallery of Sebastian's direct ancestors.[2]

As we reach the third generation of Sebastian's ancestry the call to music becomes irresistible. Hans of Wechmar was survived by three sons. Johannes, the eldest, was born at Wechmar on 26 November 1604, the first of Sebastian's forebears whose birthday the Genealogy precisely dates. So precocious was his musicianship that his father was wont to take him on his professional tours, on one of which Christoph Hoffmann, musician at Suhl, impressed by the lad's precocity, persuaded Hans to let him learn the craft. Seven years Johannes spent at Suhl as apprentice and assistant to Hoffmann, and thereafter was briefly organist at Schweinfurt, where his nephew Georg Christoph, Sebastian's uncle, followed him a generation later and founded the Franconian branch of the family. Old Hans's death recalled his son to Wechmar, whence he migrated to Erfurt to direct the town's musicians and become organist of the Predigerkirche there. He was the first of his lineage in a town which learnt to know a Bach and a musician as identical. As 'Musicus designatus' there he married (June 1636) Barbara Hoffmann, daughter of his 'dear master', and after her death took

---

[1] Now in the Bibliothèque Nationale, Paris.
[2] Dr. Wolffheim (p. 82) finds no other Bach in the Nürtingen register until 1719, when a Thomas Bach is recorded as a native of Neuweiler (Alsace). Two of his grandsons are named (sons of Christian Friedrich Bach, d. 1784 at Ofen), one of whom (Johann) married in Hungary. Can this be the Johann Bach whose existence moved Korabinsky to insert the Bach pedigree?

as his second wife Hedwig Lämmerhirt, whose family gave Sebastian his mother thirty years later.[1] For nearly forty troubled years Johannes practised his profession at Erfurt and died in 1673, competent alike in the sacred and secular tasks of his art. His eldest son, Johann Christian (1640–82), the first Bach musician in Eisenach, later succeeded his father in Erfurt, where his brothers were similarly employed. At Eisenach, Erfurt, and elsewhere in Thuringia, succeeding generations of Johannes' lineage continued to practise his profession, two of them of pre-eminent talent: his grandson Johann Bernhard (1676–1749), Sebastian's contemporary, who carried the family name to Magdeburg and was later in ducal service at Eisenach, a composer of high merit;[2] and his son Johann Ernst (1722–77), who inherited his ability and held at Weimar the Capellmeistership which Sebastian, whose pupil he was, coveted nearly forty years earlier. Excepting these two, none of Johannes' lineage rose to distinguished eminence, though his descendants consistently exhibited musical talent which only ceased to manifest itself in its latest generations.

It is a curious fact that, before his advent, Sebastian's branch of the family least revealed genius for composition. His contemporary Johann Ludwig of Meiningen (1677–1741) was descended from a brother of his great-grandfather. Johann Bernhard (1676–1749) and Johann Ernst (1722–77) are traced to his great-uncle Johannes. And, turning to the youngest of old Hans's (d. 1626) children, we discover a composer of an older generation than those already named, himself the father of two sons who carried the fame of the Bachs to an altitude only Sebastian surpassed. Heinrich Bach, third and youngest of Hans's sons, was almost exactly ten years younger than his eldest brother Johannes, to whom he owed the training the elder received from Hoffmann of Suhl. He was the first Bach organist at Arnstadt, served its beautiful Liebfrauenkirche and less ancient Oberkirche from 1641 to 1692, and linked the local Bach tradition, founded by old Caspar, with Sebastian and the younger generation. He long outlived his brother Christoph, also of Arnstadt, and died when Sebastian was a lad of seven. A man of weight in his community, his character and piety were eulogized in a funeral sermon at his death, and Carl Philipp Emanuel, annotating the Genealogy, called him 'a good composer'.[3] His eldest son Johann Christoph (1642–1703), brought up at Arn-

---

[1] The family survives in Herr Oberlehrer Hugo Lämmerhirt, Sedanstrasse 28, Leipzig. For Hedwig see *infra*, p. 15.
[2] See a list of his compositions in the 3rd edition of *Grove's Dictionary*, i. 151.
[3] See a list of his compositions in the 3rd edition of *Grove's Dictionary*, i. 152, and a thematic catalogue of them in B.-J. 1907, p. 105.

stadt, married the town-clerk's daughter there, and in 1665, twenty years before Sebastian's birth in the same town, became organist of the St. Georgenkirche at Eisenach. Housed near the ducal buildings close to the southern aisle of the great church, he there penned music which evoked in the Genealogy a eulogy of him as ' a great and expressive composer'. Forkel[1] records Carl Philipp Emanuel's astonishment at Johann Christoph's unconventional employment of the augmented sixth. His most important works are vocal, several of his motets are published, and examples of his organ music are extant.[2]

Heinrich's second son, Johann Michael (1648–94), was organist and parish clerk at Gehren, some fifteen miles south of Arnstadt, very skilful as a musical instrument-maker, prolific as a composer, but inferior to his brother in ability.[3] He was the father of Maria Barbara, Sebastian's first wife, the 'stranger maiden' whose fresh voice ringing from her lover's organ-loft in Arnstadt's Bonifaciuskirche scandalized the worshipful Consistorium there. She brought from her branch of the family, as we see, a weighty contribution to the genius which distinguished Sebastian's eldest sons. The second generation of Heinrich's lineage produced four musicians, sons of Johann Christoph and first cousins of Sebastian's wife. One of them, Johann Friedrich (d. 1730), succeeded him at Mühlhausen. The rest fared farther afield: one carried the family name to England as a clavier-player; another settled in ' the North '; the eldest, Johann Nikolaus (1669–1753), became town and university organist at Jena, an employment which inspired his comic opera, 'Der Jenaische Wein- und Bierrufer', a tuneful and spirited work contemporary with his cousin Sebastian's secular compositions at Leipzig. A *Missa* by him also is extant, and both works are in print.[4] Outliving his sons, Johann Nikolaus's death in 1753, three years after Sebastian, brought the musical record of his branch to an end.

Johannes and Heinrich, eldest and youngest of the Spielmann's sons, have passed before us. Their brother Christoph asks for closer acquaintance: he was Sebastian's grandfather, but is obscured somewhat by his tremendous father, on whose brows rest the applause of Thuringia and the unearned bays of Nürtingen. Christoph was born at Wechmar on 19 April 1613 in the Spiel-

---

[1] Forkel, p. 4.
[2] See the 3rd edition of *Grove's Dictionary*, i. 152, for his compositions. Sp. i. 71 analyses his motets; B.-J. 1907, p. 132, affords a thematic catalogue of them.
[3] See *Grove's Dictionary* (3rd edit.), i. 153, for his compositions; Sp. i. 53 analyses his motets; B.-J. 1907, p. 114, affords a thematic catalogue of them.
[4] Breitkopf und Härtel publish them.

mann's comfortable house. Old Veit survived in the mill hard by; Johannes, the elder brother, was already precociously skilful in music; and the Spielmann's viol was popular over the countryside, from Gotha and Erfurt in the north to Suhl and Schmalkalden in the south. He was Christoph's master in ' musica instrumentalis'; the Genealogy names no other. The Spielmann's early association with Gotha gained his son his first employment at Weimar, whose Duke Wilhelm (*d.* 1662) was brother to Duke Ernst the Pious (*d.* 1679) of the other duchy.[1] Probably still in his teens, Christoph was received into the ducal household, though the Schloss, agreeably situated on the western bank of the Ilm, had recently (1618) been destroyed by a fire that spared only the Bastille and lofty tower familiar to Sebastian a century later and visible to-day.[2] Christoph was employed as 'fürstlich. Bedienter', ducal lackey or footman, a menial situation in which, as was customary, he functioned also as a member of the ducal Capelle.[3]

Only a faint memory of Christoph's career descended to his grandson, who records his marriage to Maria Magdalena Grabler (or Krabler), a native of Prettin in the north-eastern corner of Saxony. As the eldest child was born in September 1642, the marriage took place towards the end of 1641. But the conjecture that Christoph had found employment in his bride's birthplace is probably incorrect: Prettin did not support a 'Stadtmusicus'

[1] In view of Bach's connexion with Eisenach and Weimar the following table will be useful:

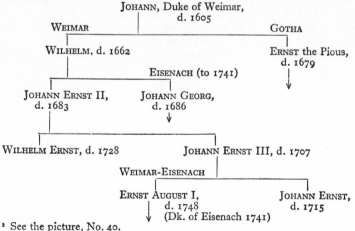

JOHANN, Duke of Weimar,
d. 1605

WEIMAR

GOTHA

WILHELM, d. 1662

ERNST the Pious,
d. 1679

EISENACH (to 1741)

JOHANN ERNST II,
d. 1683

JOHANN GEORG,
d. 1686

WILHELM ERNST, d. 1728

JOHANN ERNST III, d. 1707

WEIMAR-EISENACH

ERNST AUGUST I,
d. 1748
(Dk. of Eisenach 1741)

JOHANN ERNST,
d. 1715

[2] See the picture, No. 40.

[3] In the Weissenfels Court we find a 'Reisefourier' who also served as trumpeter; an oboist, ' Bockpfeifer ', and 'Grenadierpfeifer', each of whom was also a 'Lakai'. Cf. Werner, pp. 91, 97, 98.

(town's musician), and among its 'Spielleute' the name Bach is not found. Probably Christoph met his wife at Weimar, though her family was settled in Prettin as early as 1586, and as late as 1651 is found there.[1] Concluding his Weimar employment, Christoph joined the town's musicians of Erfurt, where, as at Weimar, Hans the Spielmann's familiar personality opened a path to his son. At Erfurt three sons were born to him, Sebastian's father among them, before he transferred his household to Arnstadt and came among relatives. Old Caspar, his father's master, was still living there, or but recently deceased; the veteran had resigned (1640) his office as Hausmann to the Count and, quitting his tower, was admitted a burgess and owner of the house in the Jakobsgasse, where presumably he died.[2] His sons, who had assisted him in his office,[3] predeceased him; his widow died in 1651 (buried 15 July). It may be that Christoph came from Erfurt to fill the vacant office; certainly from 1654[4] he was musician both to the Count and the town. His brother Heinrich was a not distant neighbour in the Kohlenmarkt or the Kirchgasse,[5] near the Oberkirche, of which, with the Liebfrauenkirche, he was organist for fifty years (1641–92), a veteran near 80 when he died, the patriarch of twenty-eight grandchildren and greatly honoured in his community. He outlived Christoph by a generation, and died[6] only a few years before his great-nephew Sebastian came to a town which, for nearly a century, had chosen its musicians from his family.[7]

Christoph died at Arnstadt on 12 September 1661.[8] His widow, surviving him twenty-four days, followed him to the grave on October 6. Georg Christoph, the eldest son (b. 6 September 1642), was already, or soon after, usher at Heinrichs near Suhl, whose proximity explains his preferment. Later he was Cantor at Themar, and subsequently at Schweinfurt, where he died on 24 April 1697, ancestor of the Franconian Bachs. The high esteem in which

---

[1] So I am informed by Herr Superintendent Leisegang, of Prettin.

[2] See the picture, No. 6.

[3] Two are mentioned in the church register: Melchior, buried 7 Sept. 1634, aged 31, and Nikolaus, buried 1 Oct. 1637, aged 19.

[4] Sp. i. 140 notes that documents prove him connected with Erfurt on 16 April 1653, but with Arnstadt on 13 Nov. 1654.   [5] Illus. No. 7.

[6] In his declining years his son-in-law Christoph Herthum was associated with him in his offices, and with him Heinrich lived in the Kohlenmarkt in the little house (No. 18) now occupied by Glasermeister Ulrich. In it thereafter apparently lived the successive organists of the two principal churches. A picture of it is given, No. 7. Herthum received appointment as organist-substitute on 5 Feb. 1692. See Bi. i. 16.

[7] For the Arnstadt Bachs see Heimann. Christoph's receipts are among the town's archives.

[8] Hoppe, p. 14, prints a letter dated 22 June 1661, in which Christoph applied for the vacant post of Stadtpfeifer at Naumburg.

he and his two brothers were held was declared at the funeral of their sister Dorothea Maria, a half-witted girl to whom Sebastian's father gave a home at Eisenach till death called her on 6 February 1679, six years before Sebastian was born. 'Our sister now with the Lord', said the preacher of her funeral sermon, 'was as simple as a child, knowing not her right hand from her left. Yet her brothers are men of understanding and skill, respected, hearkened to in our churches and schools, esteemed by all the community, men in whom the Master's work is glorified.' [1]

By the side of Georg Christoph at his sister's Leichenpredigt in the great church at Eisenach sat his brothers Johann Christoph and Johann Ambrosius, Sebastian's father. Four years his junior, they were born at Erfurt on 22 February 1645, twins of a remarkable resemblance, 'ein Wunder für grosse Herren und jedermann', Sebastian's son added to his father's entry in the Genealogy. In appearance, habits, speech, as in their musical tastes, they were so bewilderingly alike that their very wives were believed unable to distinguish them. Even bodily ailments scourged them in common, and both died in the prime of life, holding similar positions in neighbouring Thuringian towns. Johann Christoph, coming to Arnstadt, became Hofmusicus on 17 February 1671,[2] and maintained the family reputation there for nearly a quarter of a century, comfortably quartered in the Kohlgasse, in the corner house prominent as one descends from the Neutorthurm, now a Schul-Zahnklinik near the Bürgerschule.[3] His acquisition of it, and a previous entanglement,[4] suggest him an engaging fellow. Sophie Elisabeth Kannewürs, a well-to-do baker's widow, made over to him the house in the Kohlgasse, her garden in the Berggasse, and half her fields outside the town, stipulating (presumably) lodging in return, and (specifically) two quarts of beer and a hot 'roast' daily. How long she survived to enjoy this immoderate diet is not recorded.[5] Certainly, Johann Christoph, in the spring of

---

[1] The sermon, preached by Valentin Schrön, was printed at Eisenach (1679), and a copy is in the ducal library at Gotha. The title-page declares it 'Zum täglichen Memorial und güldenen Regel vorgestellet bey der Leichbestattung Dorotheen Marien Bachin des weiland wohl Ehrengeachten und kunsterfahrenen Herrn Christoph Bachens gewesenen Stadt-Musici zu Arnstadt seel. nachgelassener Tochter, welche den 6 Febr. anno 1679 allhier in Eisenach im Herrn seelig entschlaffen und folgendes Tages auf unsern Gottes Acker in ihr Ruhestättlin versetzt worden'.
Of another sister, Barbara Maria (bapt. 2 May 1651), nothing is known.
[2] He was already in service at Arnstadt as Musicus.
[3] See the picture of it, No. 8. Heimann states that after Johann Christoph the house was the regular abode of the Arnstadt Bach organists, whose address is given as 'uff der Kohlgasse'. The house itself is not positively identified.
[4] Sp. i. 156 details the circumstances at length and Johann Christoph's eventual triumph in a breach of promise suit.   [5] Heimann.

1679, when over thirty, brought Martha Elisabeth Eisentraut, of Ohrdruf, to the house as his bride. She was then a woman of twenty-four or twenty-five, who lived (buried 16 January 1719) to entertain Sebastian in the home so curiously acquired. She bore Johann Christoph six children, of whom the eldest son, Johann Ernst, eventually succeeded his cousin Sebastian at the Bonifacius-kirche.

Less prolific than his twin-brother, Johann Christoph's household was still a large one ; for, as was customary, it included his two apprentices (Lehrjungen) and two assistants (Gesellen), who aided his service to the Count. His obligations are detailed in a document which illuminates equally those of Sebastian's father at Eisenach. He might not leave the town without permission, was pledged to make himself proficient in his profession, and to show himself 'willing' to his employer. The Council of the municipality, lying at the Schloss gates and within the same protecting walls, was bidden on occasions of solemnity calling for music to associate its Cantor and town's musician with Hofmusicus Bach, failing him, with the 'Thürmer'—formerly Caspar—or with Bach's assistant. The injunction was issued to allay contentions and rivalries, but induced a catastrophe. The Stadtmusicus Gräser, pursuing Johann Christoph with rancour, waxed so vituperative against the whole of his clan, that the Bachs of Arnstadt and Erfurt instituted proceedings. Enraged at their bickering, the Count (7 January 1681) dismissed both parties as quarrelsome good-for-nothings, a sentence which placed Johann Christoph in hard straits till the new Count Anton Günther composed the strife by combining the two inharmonious offices (1682). Till his death in 1693 Johann Christoph functioned as Hofmusicus and Stadtpfeifer, and lived to see Arnstadt a vigorous musical centre, Sebastian's entry into which ten years later Count Anton Günther (d. 22 December 1716) also survived to witness.

The career of Sebastian's father Johann Ambrosius[1] is not so fully documented as his twin brother's. Born at Erfurt on 22 February 1645, he there laid the foundations of the violin and viola technique he passed on to his son. Before he was ten, Erfurt was exchanged for Arnstadt on his father's migration thither in 1654, and seven years later (1661) the home was broken up by his father's death. After an unrecorded interval, during which he probably assisted his father's successor, we find him in 1667 a member of the Erfurt 'Compagnie' of musicians in room of his cousin Johann Christian. Within a year Ambrosius took his wife from a family with which his Erfurt relatives already were connected.

---

[1] See B.-J. 1927, pp. 133–52.

The Lämmerhirt Pedigree [1]

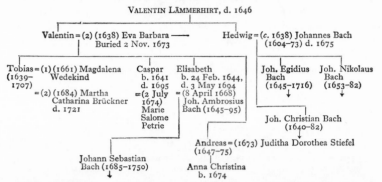

VALENTIN LÄMMERHIRT, d. 1646

Valentin = (2) (1638) Eva Barbara —— Hedwig = (c. 1638) Johannes Bach
Buried 2 Nov. 1673   (1604–73) d. 1675

Tobias = (1) (1661) Magdalena   Caspar   Elisabeth   Joh. Egidius   Joh. Nikolaus
(1639–   Wedekind   b. 1641   b. 24 Feb. 1644,   Bach   Bach
1707)   d. 1695   d. 3 May 1694   (1645–1716)   (1653–82)
= (2) (1684) Martha   = (2 July   = (8 April 1668)
Catharina Brückner   1674)   Joh. Ambrosius
d. 1721   Marie   Bach (1645–95)
Salome   Joh. Christian Bach
Petrie   (1640–82)

Andreas = (1673) Juditha Dorothea Stiefel
(1647–75)

Johann Sebastian   Anna Christina
Bach (1685–1750)   b. 1674

Like the Bachs, the Lämmerhirts were of Thuringian peasant stock. Holding opinions akin to those of the persecuted Anabaptists, they migrated to Schlesien in the sixteenth century, whence they returned on the outbreak of the Thirty Years War, and about 1620 settled in Erfurt, among whose old patrician families therefore they cannot be counted, though within a generation of their arrival they ranked among its ruling plutocracy. Interpretations [2] of Sebastian's genius based upon a suppositional admixture of plebeian and patrician blood in his immediate ancestry are therefore unfounded. Nor from his mother did he inherit any augmentation of his paternal genius for music, though the fact that two women of her house wedded musicians may indicate a family inclination towards that art.

Sebastian's mother, Elisabeth Lämmerhirt, was almost exactly a year older than her husband, with whose fortunes she linked herself on the threshold of his career. She was the daughter of a municipal councillor (Ratsherr), 'eines Ehrbaren Rathsverwandten Valentin Lämmerhirt', as he appears in the Genealogy, whose name is found in the roll of Erfurt councillors (Transitus Senatorum; Ratsliste) in 1648, 1658, and 1663.[3] A furrier by trade, he resided at 'Die drei Rosen' on the Junkersand,[4] where Elisabeth

---

[1] Cf. B.-J. 1925, pp. 114, 128.
[2] See, for instance, Dr. Stephan Kekule von Stradonitz in 'Der Deutsche Herold', 1920, No. 1: 'Festrede zum Gedenktage des fünfzigjährigen Bestehens des "Herold".'
[3] Sp. i. 789 states inaccurately that Valentin's name is not found in the Council before 1658. For notes on the Lämmerhirt pedigree I am greatly indebted to Herr Hugo Lämmerhirt. Cf. B.-J. 1925, pp. 101–37.
[4] Sp. i. 171 describes the house as 'now No. 1285'. In fact, the Lämmerhirt house was burnt down about 1855. The modern one on its site is numbered Junkersand No. 3.

was born. Valentin did not survive to witness her marriage: he
was buried on 19 November 1665. Tobias, his son, later betook
himself to the Breitenstrasse, died in 1707, and bequeathed an
opportune legacy to his sister's children.[1] Elisabeth herself would
not be left penniless by her father, and was free to wed as her
inclination dictated. She probably met her future husband under
the roof of Aunt Hedwig, two of whose sons were already members
of the 'Compagnie', of which Johann Ambrosius was the latest
recruit. The wedding took place on 8 April 1668, but Erfurt remained briefly the home of the young couple. In 1669 or 1670
a short-lived son was born to them, and on 16 June 1671 Elisabeth
gave birth to Johann Christoph, to whom in after years the
orphaned Sebastian owed a home and schooling. Four months
later (October 1671) Ambrosius received a call to Eisenach, where
Heinrich's son Johann Christoph, most eminent of that branch,
was organist.

Eisenach since 1662 and until 1741 was the capital of a
separate duchy, whose sovereign dwelt in the Schloss near the
Marktplatz and picturesque Rathaus, and behind the St. Georgenkirche, before whose western door the statue of Bach to-day stands
sentinel. According to the Genealogy, Ambrosius, like his twin
brother at Arnstadt, was Hofmusicus to Duke Johann Georg and
also town's musician. He did not name the former office, however,
when he petitioned the municipality[2] in 1684 (2 April) for permission to return to Erfurt to direct her 'musicalische Compagnie', giving his reasons in inverse order of urgency: already
six children filled his house—the youngest and greatest of them
was not yet born; he entertained, besides, three Gesellen and
apprentices (Lehrknaben), 'welches ein Jahr lang viel kostet'; his
'accidentia'[3] were disappointingly small, for recurring seasons of
public mourning caused quiet weddings at which his services were
not in request, and even in normal times fees were not easily
earned. He had moreover been prejudiced in his income by
the competition of unofficial and unprivileged musicians (Bierfiedler)[4] in their less distinguished occupation. So he begged
permission to accept the call to Erfurt, where he could live more
cheaply, needed no assistants, and would be more remote from the
scourgings of the plague. He repeated his petition (21 April 1684),
but vainly. In courteous language the Eisenach Council (26 April

---

[1] See p. 76, *infra*.   [2] The documents are printed in Bi. i. 36, 38.
[3] i.e. fees other than his fixed salary, usually earned at weddings.
[4] His twin brother at Arnstadt had a similar experience. See Sp. i. 161. For
'Bierfiedler' see Schering, p. 286.

1684) informed Erfurt that the Duke and whole community were too content with 'unser Statt-Haussmann und Stadt-Musicus Johann Ambrosius Bach' to surrender him. Less insistent than his son in similar circumstances, Ambrosius bowed to the decision. So the wise fingers that spin the web of destiny contrived that in Eisenach, with its vivid memories of Luther and the Minnesinger, Sebastian should be born.

Meanwhile, he was the heir of a tradition not localized. Barely sixty years had passed since Hans the Spielmann was gathered to his fathers, an interval in which Germany had been sucked down in a maelstrom of strife, her cities defaced, her fields wasted, her population destroyed by war and plague. Throughout the turmoil of the Thirty Years War one German family of inconspicuous origin had never ceased to administer comfort, whether in the fanes of the Church or in the homes of princes and people, keeping alive the spirit of a nation battered by the ruder instruments of war. As Cantors and organists in how many churches the name Bach was familiar! If princely service was the hall-mark of primacy, it was conceded to a family whose members in Gotha, Meiningen, Arnstadt, and Eisenach were furthering the musical Renaissance the war's cessation invited, moulding it in forms less brilliant, but less shallow, than contemporary Italy preferred.[1] What a fund of inherited experience informed Sebastian's young fingers as they spread over the keyboard of organ and clavier or clasped the viol's finger-board! How closely it brought him to the Reformation's heritage of hymnody! Yet it is the Bach of the clavier and instrumental suites, the Cöthen Bach, who was the heir of his immediate ancestry. His father, grandfather, and great-grandfather all displayed Veit Bach's preference for secular music; not one of them dedicated his art upon the altar of religion. Still, the indirect urge was imperative in one who called the veteran Heinrich, Johann Christoph, Johann Michael, and the Meiningen Bachs his kinsmen! Individual as was Bach's genius, there is none among the Masters on whom his ancestry made a call so urgent, none who showed himself so responsive and yet so superior to the obligation.

[1] Many of their compositions are calendared in the Catalogue (Hamburg: 1790) of the 'Alt-Bachisches Archiv' formerly in Carl Philipp Emanuel's possession. See Bi. i. 44.

CHAPTER II

SCHOOL

JOHANN SEBASTIAN, youngest child of Johann Ambrosius Bach and Elisabeth Lämmerhirt, was born at Eisenach on Saturday, 21 March 1685,[1] and two days later was baptized in the St. Georgenkirche on the Marktplatz. The register names his godfathers: Johann Georg Koch, an official of the ducal woods and forests, and Sebastian Nagel. The latter, whose high distinction is to have named an immortal, is entered in the register as 'Haussmann zu Gotha', the office once filled by Caspar Bach. That Ambrosius should have invited him to godfather his son suggests an intimacy formed at Erfurt, between whose Bach colony and the Gotha musicians a link is found in the town's organist Egidius Funck, a pupil of Johannes Bach (1604–73). Nagel did not long survive to admire his godson's career.[2]

It would be difficult to propose a spot more fitting than Eisenach for Sebastian's birthplace. In the heart of Germany, sheltered under the tree-clad summits of the Thuringian Wald, Nature had dowered it with beauty of location. Religion, Romance, and Music charged its atmosphere with poetry. Towering precipitously on the south, the stately Wartburg once sheltered Luther. Within the castle, to whose beckoning walls Sebastian often must have climbed, the chamber was accessible in which the German Bible had its birth and the valiant hymn-tunes were conceived which bear the Reformation on their virile phrases. Here lived the saintly Elisabeth, here the famous Tourney of Song was held (1207), and here German minstrelsy prolifically flowered. The town below reacted to these urgent inspirations. 'Claruit semper urbs nostra musicâ', wrote its historian [3] thirteen years after Sebastian's birth, and devised convincing anagrams: 'Isenacum *en musica*' (Here, sirs, find music), and '*en canimus*' (listen! we are singing). Like Luther before him, Sebastian was active in the school Currenden to which the town was accustomed since the fifteenth century, of

[1] Sp. i. 179 states that we have no direct evidence of the date. Bach, in fact, gives it himself in the Genealogy. The date is Old Style. Protestant Germany did not accept the Gregorian Calendar till 1701. A facsimile of the entry in the baptismal register is in Reimann, p. 12. A godmother is not named.
[2] B.-J. 1908, p. 110.
[3] Christianus Franciscus Paullinus, *Annales Isenacenses*, published at Frankfurt am Main, 1698.

a standard notable for more than fifty years before his birth.[1] Moreover, musicians of eminence had served the town. Since 1665 and till his death in 1703 Johann Christoph Bach was organist of the St. Georgenkirche, in whose loft, high on the western wall, Sebastian must often have sat beside his relative, or, in the ample gallery below, sung the music of one whom in after years he recalled as 'ein profonder Componist'.[2] In 1677 the famous Johann Pachelbel came from Vienna to hold the post of Hofmusicant before passing on (1678) to the Predigerkirche at Erfurt. The brief transit of this luminary was not without effect upon Sebastian's development; for Pachelbel stood godfather to one of his sisters[3] and later received as his pupil at Erfurt their elder brother Johann Christoph, through whom the young genius learnt at second-hand the technique of one of the foremost organists of his period, a composer whose example also guided his early pen.

Collateral relatives of Sebastian, prominent in Eisenach's municipal life till the end of the nineteenth century, maintained a seemingly well-founded tradition [4] that he was born in the house on the Frauenplan now (since 1907) the Bachmuseum. It fronts a wide cobbled street rising steeply towards the distantly towering Wartburg, a quaint, two-storied, homely exterior, with three dormers projecting from its red-tiled roof. The front doorway, wide and baroque, opens to disclose a medieval interior, a red-brick floor, black beamed walls and ceiling, and the glimpse of a garden beyond. Dark oak doors within, on the right, conceal two small chambers devoted to domestic uses. On the left a large room is entered which now houses a valuable collection of musical instruments, but in Sebastian's youth probably served as a barn, detached from the fabric which claims to be his birthplace. The living-rooms are on the upper floor, accessible from below by a solid oaken stairway, sharply angled as it rises to a half-landing. In the front, over the doorway, we enter the tiny room where tradition held Sebastian to have been born. A heavy four-poster overfills it, a wooden cradle, such as rocked his infancy, stands at its side, and Hans Sachs smiles approvingly from the wall.

[1] In 1698 about forty boys of the Gymnasium formed the Currende choir, which proceeded through the town at stated seasons singing and gathering pence.
[2] The fine motet *Ich lasse dich nicht*, formerly attributed to Sebastian, is now recognized as Johann Christoph's composition and may have been familiar to the younger composer at Eisenach.   [3] Johanna Juditha Bach, *b*. 26 Jan. 1680.
[4] Conrad Freyse, *Das Bachhaus in Eisenach*, relies on 'eine erhaltene alte Familienchronik' which identifies the house as 'am Frauenplan 303'. Its reliability has recently been challenged. For Fritz Rollberg (B.-J. 1927, p. 134, and 'Mitteilungen des Eisenacher Geschichtvereins', 4 and 5 Hefte, 1928–9) has disproved the tradition of the town's records. So far, Herr Freyse has failed to produce any rebutting evidence.

But it is now established that from 1679 until his death Johann Ambrosius was a 'Hausbesitzer' in the Fleischgasse (the present Lutherstrasse No. 35).[1] The site was conveniently near his duties in the Schloss, though the house was small. Still, it must be presumed to have been adequate to shelter his considerable household, and the supposition that Sebastian was born on the Frauenplan must therefore be abandoned. But the traditions of a conservative community are not easily dissipated, and if the pilgrim to the Frauenplan no longer views the building with confident veneration, he can at least approach it with interest.

Sebastian's Eisenach years pass almost unrecorded. His father's avid pupil, we picture him practising violin and viola with patient concentration, sharing his father's rehearsals, sitting beside Johann Christoph in the St. Georgenkirche, pulling out the lumbersome stops, or turning the thumbed manuscript on the organ desk.[2] We follow him to school, hastening westward along the Lutherstrasse, near the gabled house where (?) Frau von Cotta entertained the Reformer as a boy, along the leafy Esplanade by the ancient Schloss, past the St. Georgenkirche, its present tower[3] alone unfamiliar to him, and so to the Predigerplatz, which takes its name from a Dominican foundation, whose church formed the north side of the convent quadrangle and to-day houses the Thüringer Museum. Its western wing no longer stands, but those of the south and east rise from ancient foundations, whose cloisters, stone-flagged vaulted corridors with mural inscriptions and sculptured memorials, still echo youthful voices as when Sebastian frequented them as a schoolboy.[4]

Sebastian entered the Gymnasium in 1692 or 1693, shortly before or after his eighth birthday. He was forty-seventh in Quinta (Fifth Class) at Easter of the latter year, his brother Johann Jakob, three years his senior, standing immediately below him. At Easter 1694 he was placed fourteenth in Quinta, yet had lost fifty-nine school hours, and with his brother was promoted to Quarta. At Easter 1695 the two were respectively twenty-third and twenty-fifth in the new class, though Sebastian's absences totalled one hundred and three hours. At Eisenach he laid the foundations of a sound education,[5] as his letters of later years

---

[1] Illustration No. 9.
[2] Fr. Commer in 'Musica sacra', Bd. 1, published four little organ choral preludes by Sebastian from the Voss-Buch collection. Perhaps they evidence Johann Christoph's influence; the first three are very elementary.
[3] The tower was built in 1902.
[4] See the picture of the quadrangle, facing east, with the church on the left, No. 10.
[5] Professor Ludwig Weniger (Weimar) furnishes notes on the Eisenach curriculum and on Sebastian's school record in 'Mitteilungen der Gesell. f. deutsche

attest. In Quinta he studied the Catechism, Psalms, and Bible, history, writing, and reading, particularly the Gospels and Epistles in German and Latin. He learned the elements of Latin from the *Latinitatis vestibulum: sive primi ad Latinam linguam aditus* of Johann Amos Komensky (Comenius, 1592–1671), whose novel pages afforded in parallel columns practical information in German and Latin. For, in place of the pedantic methods that teased his own youth, Comenius prescribed that the manual should impart useful facts, and also inserted illustrations to stimulate and assist the memory. In Quarta Sebastian studied the German Catechism and Psalter, Latin declensions, conjugations, and vocabulary. School began at six a.m. in summer, at seven from autumn till spring, and continued till nine or ten, according to the season. The afternoon hours were from one till three, and Wednesday and Saturday were half-holidays. Under the Cantor, Andreas Christian Dedekind, the school furnished the St. Georgenkirche with its choir and sang at weddings and funerals. Its periodical Currenden gratified the citizens and were a source of income to staff and scholars, who at the New Year were accustomed to display their talent also in the neighbouring villages, an exodus whose prohibition provoked a petition to the Rector which Sebastian may have signed (18 January 1693): 'Te etiam atque oramus, ut pro benignitate tua nobis concedas, ut in pagis quibusdam nobis canere liceat. Necessitas enim, ut hoc faciamus, nos monet, siquidem animus nobis est aliquos parare libros.'

Sebastian's schooldays at Eisenach were darkened by bereavements which perhaps explain his irregular attendance. On 3 May 1694 he lost his mother, whose premature death removed from Ambrosius's household its only member competent to order it. For four years past her eldest son Johann Christoph had been earning a livelihood at Ohrdruf; a few months after his mother's death he brought a wife to his modest household there. Two sisters intervened between him and his younger brothers, the elder of whom was about to leave her father's roof, while the younger had barely turned fourteen. So, a few weeks after his son's wedding, Ambrosius married Barbara Margaretha Keul,[1] an Arnstadt woman of good position: her father was Bürgermeister of the town. Comely, or well dowered, she had already been twice married, first (28 November 1682) to Johann Günther Bach, fourth son and assistant of the veteran Heinrich at the Oberkirche and Liebfrauenkirche. Their union was short-lived: the bridegroom died

Erziehungs- und Schulgeschichte', 15. Jhrg. 1905; I.M.G. vii. 505; B.-J. 1906, p. 137; 1930, p. 49.   [1] Not Krül, as in Sp. i. 34 and Heimann.   Keul = Keil.

five months (10 April 1683) after his marriage, apparently without issue. A year later the widow wedded (1 April 1684) Diakonus Jacobus[1] Bartholomäi, one of the Arnstadt clergy, who was buried four years later (16 December 1688), being then, the register records with precise accuracy, sixty-nine years, four months, two weeks, and two days old. One supposes him considerably senior to his widow. Their daughter Christiana Maria (baptized 28 September 1685) had just passed her third birthday when her father died;[2] she added a step-daughter to Ambrosius's family when on 27 November 1694 her mother took him for her third husband. Again and swiftly Frau Barbara Margaretha was widowed: on 24 February 1695,[3] little less than three months after his marriage, Johann Ambrosius was carried to the grave.

Sebastian bore a strong likeness to his father, as is evident from the portrait of Ambrosius that became Carl Philipp Emanuel's possession.[4] It shows a man of forty years or so, brown-haired and moustached, wearing a coat or wrap drawn loosely over his chest, and under it a white camisole carelessly fastened about the neck. Ambrosius stands by a window that gives a distant glimpse of the Wartburg. His left arm, concealed in the folds of the cloak, rests upon a table; his right, with open palm and indicative finger, seems to make such a gesture of control as conductors use. The easy pose, wigless chevelure, unceremonious costume, and the Wartburg distantly seen, suggest that the picture was painted in a chamber from which its lofty and impressive outline was visible. The ample throat, the massive chin and jaw, the prominent nose, its somewhat leftward inclination, are features so clearly reproduced in the son, that in the Ambrosius of 1685 we can picture the Sebastian of 1723. Character, too, we may suppose him to have drawn from his father, if Ambrosius and his twin were so closely similar as tradition related. The pertinacity that carried Johann Christoph to a superior jurisdiction from Anna Cunigunde Wiener's pursuit of him at Arnstadt, winning a verdict after more than two years' litigation, is matched by the nephew's defiance of his Weimar master and stubborn controversies with his Leipzig employers. As his musical instructor, Sebastian's debt to his father certainly was considerable, though his first formal lessons on the

---

[1] Not Johann, as in Heimann.
[2] Her existence has not been observed by previous writers.
[3] B.-J., 1927, p. 149.
[4] In the Hamburg catalogue (1790) it is entered as: 'Bach (Ambrosius), Hofmusicus in Eisenach, des folgenden J. S. Vater, in Oel gemalt, 3 Fuss 2 Zoll hoch, 2 Fuss 9 Zoll breit. In goldenen Rahmen' (Bi. i. 50). The picture is now in the Preuss. Staatsbibliothek. See a reproduction of it, No. 11.

clavier were received from Johann Christoph at Ohrdruf.[1] But his
remarkable skill as a string player, an accomplishment that won
him his first professional income, must be attributed to his
father, himself the heir of a lengthy tradition of excellence. Probably Sebastian's preference for the viola was similarly derived.
With authority behind the statement, Forkel records:[2] 'At musical
gatherings, where quartet or other instrumental music was performed, Bach preferred to play the viola, an instrument which put
him, as it were, in the midst of the harmony, in a position to hear
and enjoy it on both sides.' Fate ordained that Sebastian, unlike
Mozart, should lack the inspiration and control of a father's pride
and experience; yet his purpose was so clearly seen, the call of
his genius so compelling, that guidance was the less needed. His
untimely orphaning, moreover, put him on a path which otherwise
he might not have trodden, a course which led him into surroundings that fired and formed his genius. Lüneburg, Hamburg,
Celle, were brought within his orbit before he reached his
twentieth year, a sequence of experiences consequent upon the
untimely break-up of the Eisenach home and the compulsion
which sent him to his brother's care at Ohrdruf.

Ohrdruf lies some thirty miles south-east from Eisenach, a quiet
community, numbering to-day seven thousand souls, on the fringe
of the Thuringian plain, where Brandkopf, Steinkopf, and others
of the Wald's moderate heights, build a woody barrier on the west,
where fir, beech, and birch rise from beds of heather. The little
Ohra, flowing from the Schwarzwald, moves sluggishly through the
town to its junction with the Apfelstädt near Wechmar. Here, in
the eighth century, St. Boniface set up an altar by the spring that
bubbles at the foot of the Michaeliskirche and swiftly tumbles into
the Ohra hard by. Till the close of the Middle Ages Ohrdruf was
an open village, whose straggling streets merged without a boundary
into the encircling ploughlands. But, towards the end of the fifteenth century, the Counts von Gleichen, whose lofty castles are
visible north-eastward towards Arnstadt, claimed allodial possession from the Abbey of Hersfeld, and, being confirmed in it in
1563, built Schloss Ehrenstein across the Ohra, opposite the
Michaeliskirche. The Schloss,[3] a building in the Italian style with
decorated gables, standing on the site of a conventual building and
in part reared from its quarrying, was erected by Count Georg II

---

[1] The Nekrolog (B.-J. 1920, p. 15) makes the positive statement that Sebastian
'legte unter desselben [J. C. B.] Anführung den Grund zum Clavierspielen'.
[2] Forkel, p. 108.
[3] See Heiss, a minute historical and architectural study of the Schloss.

(*d.* 1570), his widow and her sons, on the death of the last of whom (Johann Ludwig) the allodial lands passed to the related house of Hohenlohe-Langenburg, whose work upon the fabric is evidenced by an inscription dated 1665 over the main (western) entrance. The Schloss stands to-day[1] substantially as Sebastian viewed it from the Michaelisplatz opposite, protected from the town's intrusion by the shallow Ohra, over which a stone bridge, no longer standing, gave access to the courtly edifice, the monotony of whose elevation is broken by the lofty sixteenth-century clock-tower in its south-eastern angle. Raised to the dignity of a Residenzstadt, Ohrdruf enclosed herself within sheltering walls,[2] and built an imposing Renaissance Rathaus[3] befitting her dignity on the Marktplatz, where St. Michael, then as now, guards his fountain. Eastward from it on the roomy Michaelisplatz rose the Michaeliskirche,[4] served by so many generations of Bachs, a solid quadrangular fane looking down on the Ohra from amid cobbled streets and gabled vine-clad houses, the heart of a placid community.

Into this semi-pastoral society the death of their father introduced Sebastian and his elder brother Johann Jakob, apparently in February 1695; the sisters probably remained with their thrice-widowed step-mother. For four years[5] Ambrosius's eldest son Johann Christoph had lived in Ohrdruf as organist of the Michaeliskirche, and three months before his father's death married an Ohrdruf maiden, Dorothea von Hofe.[6] Tradition identifies, but not with certainty, the house he lived in, the home of Sebastian for five years; it stands in the Bachstrasse, close to its junction with the Kirchstrasse, and not distant from the church itself, an unpretentious two-storied cottage[7] suited to a couple whose moderate income totalled forty-five gulden, three measures of corn, and firewood.[8] Though Ohrdruf offered few attractions to a musician of ability, Sebastian owed as much to his brother's teaching as to his hospitality. Johann Christoph learnt his art from Pachelbel, whose

---

[1] It is used partly for administrative offices, partly as school premises.
[2] Considerable stretches are still visible.   [3] It was burnt down in 1808.
[4] The church was burnt in 1753, rebuilt in 1760, and again destroyed in 1808. Only the present tower, concealed behind modern stucco, remains of the church Sebastian frequented, though the structure is similar and its situation identical. See the picture of it, No. 13. An article on ' Das Orgelwerk in St. Michaelis zu Ohrdruf zur Zeit des Aufenthalts J. S. Bachs daselbst, 1695–1700 ' is in B.-J. 1926, p. 145.   [5] Since 17 June 1690 (Bi. i. 51).
[6] Her father was a Rathsherr. The name is variously spelt: Hof, Hofe, Hoff.
[7] To-day it is a greengrocer's shop; the sign above the door reads, 'Gemüse, Obst, Kartoffeln, Spezialität Erfurter Blumenkohl'. See a picture of it, No. 12. Johann Christoph's grandson Johann Christoph Georg (*d.* 1814) lived in the Neugasse, in a house (No. 129) burnt down in 1808. It does not follow that his grandfather also lived there.   [8] Bi. i. 52.

high opinion of his pupil is probably declared in a call to Gotha as organist in 1696.[1] The careers of his five sons, every one of whom followed his profession and received instruction at his hands, clearly attest his competency. That he was Sebastian's first master for the clavier is the more probable, seeing that Sebastian's own son Wilhelm Friedemann began his lessons on that instrument at the age of nine. Probably he also directed his precocious pupil in the art of composition. Among Sebastian's youthful exercises is a four-part fugue whose stiffness, tonal monotony, and lack of contrapuntal invention suggest that it may date from his Ohrdruf days:[2]

The Nekrolog is responsible for a picturesque story which, if it admirably illustrates Sebastian's character, does injustice to his brother. Forkel repeats it:[3] 'Bach's inclination and talent for music must already have been pronounced, for hardly had his brother given him one piece to learn than he would demand another more difficult. The most acclaimed clavier composers of that day were Froberger, Fischer, Johann Caspar Kerll, Pachelbel, Buxtehude, Bruhns, and Böhm. Johann Christoph owned a volume containing many pieces by these masters, and Bach begged earnestly for it, but without effect. Refusal increasing his determination, he laid his plans to get the book without his brother's knowledge. It was kept on a book-shelf with a latticed front; but Bach's small hands got hold of it, rolled it up, and drew it out. As he was not allowed a candle, he could copy it only on moonlight nights, and six months passed before he finished the heavy task. Having completed it, he looked forward to the secret enjoyment of a treasure won by so much toil. But his brother found the copy and unkindly took it from him, nor did Bach recover it till his brother's death soon after.' Johann Christoph, in fact, lived more than twenty years after Sebastian left his roof, and his action, if correctly recorded, can be attributed less to harshness than the need to control the ways of genius. Certainly the innuendo that the brothers were consequently estranged cannot be sustained. One of Sebastian's earliest clavier compositions, the Capriccio in

[1] An increase of stipend by ten gulden and double measures of corn and wood decided Christoph to remain (Bi. i. 52). His letters regarding his stipend at Ohrdruf are printed in Bi. iv. 40–7; they date from 1691 to 1714.
[2] B.-G. XXXVI, No. 29; P., Bk. 212, p. 16.
[3] B.-J. 1920, p. 15 ; Forkel, p. 10.

E major, was dedicated to Johann Christoph,[1] to whose short-lived youngest son he stood godfather and gave his name in 1713, while twelve years later (1725) he requited his brother's early hospitality by inviting to Leipzig his fourth son Johann Heinrich,[2] who passed later into Hohenlohe service at Oehringen.

Ohrdruf's ancient school was reputed throughout Thuringia. An old Klosterschule, its buildings had been more than once destroyed by fire before the erection of those Sebastian frequented on the Schulstrasse, hard by the Michaeliskirche and Johann Christoph's house. Opened on 26 October 1655,[3] they survived till 1753, when fire again destroyed them.[4] When Sebastian entered them, the school numbered rather less than three hundred scholars,[5] of ages varying from twenty-one to five and a half, about half of whom came from other communities, Wechmar, Arnstadt, Gehren, Gotha, Gräfentonna, Gräfenhain, Hohenkirchen, Emleben, Schwabhausen, and even places so distant as Eisenach, Cassel, and Jena, whose patronage attests its efficiency. The staff numbered six masters, one of whom taught the lowest two classes, Sexta and Septima, whose pupils formed about one-third of the school. Sebastian's masters were: in Quarta, Johann Valentin Wagner; in Tertia, Johann Heinrich Arnold; in Secunda, Conrector Johann Jeremias Böttiger; and in Prima, Rector Johann Christoph Kiesewetter, an erudite scholar later promoted to Weimar, where Sebastian resumed acquaintance with him on another footing. Wagner and Böttiger are mere names among the characters that cross Sebastian's path. Arnold, who also functioned as Cantor, was unpopular with colleagues and pupils alike. During 1696–7 two boys in Prima were withdrawn from the school 'ob turbas a Domino Cantore Arnoldo excitatas'. Two others, one of them Sebastian's Arnstadt cousin Johann Ernst Bach, were removed from Tertia into Secunda to escape his 'intolerabilis disciplina'. His character, too, was bad: a note in the church books in 1697 records with satisfaction that 'in der Schule ist der Gotlosse Cantor Arnold (*pestis scholae, scandalum ecclesiae et carcinoma*

---

[1] B.-G. XXXVI, No. 41 ; P., Bk. 215, p. 34.
[2] Thomas, p. 19; see also p. 99 *infra*.   [3] Rudloff, p. 13.
[4] *Ibid.* The illustration, No. 13, indicates the former situation of the school on the left side facing the church. Later, the school shared the buildings now occupied by the Bürgerschule to the east of the church. In 1870, on the purchase of the Schloss by the Gotha government, the school was housed in the north wing of that building, where it remains. Formerly known as 'Gräflich Gleichensches Gymnasium', it has since 1906 been styled the 'Realschule zu Ohrdruf (Gräfl. Gleichensche Stiftung)' (Heiss, p. 71). For its Aula the school uses an apartment in the north-west angle, where Victor Mignot's picture of Bach hangs.
[5] On 20 July 1696 the school register contained 287 names. See Thomas (2) generally on the school and its curriculum.

civitatis) durch Urtheil und Recht removiret'.[1] In his place came
Elias Herda, with whom Sebastian associated more agreeably.

Sebastian's schooldays at Ohrdruf were spent under the influence of the only educational movement of consequence in
seventeenth-century Germany. Prompted by the eminent educa-
tionist Comenius, Duke Ernst of Sachsen-Gotha (*d.* 1679) had
instituted a remarkable reform of popular education in the duchy,
which reached Ohrdruf before Sebastian entered the school. At
the Duke's instruction, Andreas Reyher, Rector of the Gotha Gymnasium, prepared a memorandum on school method, with particular reference to Gymnasia and lower schools, and published his
conclusions in 1642 under the spacious title: 'A special and particular Report showing how, under the guidance of the Lord,
the boys and girls of villages, and of the lower class of the population in this Principality of Gotha, can and shall be plainly and
successfully instructed.' The curriculum comprised religion, reading, writing, arithmetic, singing, and elementary natural science
(including geography). As far as was possible, children were encouraged to handle or observe the objects about which they were
instructed. A detailed time-table was imposed on teachers, annual
examinations of the scholars were instituted, and school attendance
was made compulsory under penalty of fines. Model schools were
instituted, new text-books were prepared, and the status of teachers
was improved. This unique experiment in State-directed education came to an end on Duke Ernst's death. But, pursued for a
generation, it left a permanent mark upon the schools of the duchy,
inculcating in them a standard which justified the popular boast,
that Duke Ernst's peasants were better educated than noblemen
elsewhere.[2] In their good fortune Sebastian participated.

The Ohrdruf school register, a venerable volume between vellum
covers, records the years 1686 to 1708[3] but is silent for 1694–5.[4]
Sebastian's name first appears in it in July 1696 as 'novitius'.[5]
It would appear that, coming to Ohrdruf from Eisenach, probably
in February 1695, he worked his way out of Quarta in half a year.
He was barely ten when he entered the class, the average age of
whose pupils was twelve. Its curriculum comprised 'Teutsche
Materien' (Catechism, Gospels, Psalms), Comenius's *Vestibulum*,
Reyher's minor Dialogues, essays (*exercitia styli*), and Greek rudi-

---

[1] The school register records that he died 'miserrime' at Erfurt in 1698.
[2] Cf. William Boyd, *History of Western Education* (1921), p. 267.
[3] I express my thanks to Herr Studiendirektor Henkler for permitting me to
examine the register at Ohrdruf.
[4] Owing to an interregnum in the Rectorship.
[5] i.e. he entered the school in the course of the school year 1695–6.

ments. Promoted on the examinations held in August 1695, Sebastian passed up to Tertia and faced the unamiable Arnold, who taught more intensively the subjects already studied in Quarta, substituting Reyher's larger Dialogues for Comenius. Again Sebastian's precocity is evident: the youngest Tertian, he was in July 1696 first among the seven 'novitii'. By July 1697 he climbed to the top of the class and was promoted to Secunda. Here, besides studying Cicero's letters in Johannes Rivius's edition, he was introduced to that stout champion of Lutheran orthodoxy, Leonhard Hutter's (1563–1616) *Compendium locorum theologicorum* (1610), hard fare for a young mind. That it accorded with, perhaps founded, Sebastian's inclination to theological dialectic is evidenced by the library he amassed in later life.[1] At the end of his first year in Secunda (July 1698) he was fifth in the class, rose to the second place by July 1699, and after an abnormally short period in it was promoted to Prima, where Cicero's speeches and the Ποίημα νουθετικόν of Phocylides,[2] a favourite school text-book, instructed him.

Sebastian's stay in Prima was as brief as his earlier passage through Quarta. An entry in the register in Kiesewetter's hand records the untimely departure of his pupil, and the cause: 'Luneburgum ob defectum hospitiorum se contulit die 15 Martii 1700', while in the 'catalogus discipulorum finito examine d. xiv. Augusti MDCC completus', in which Sebastian is named fourth in a list of five, the statement is repeated: 'ob defect. hospit. Luneburg. concessit'.[3] It is a mark of his sons' ignorance of, or indifference to, the circumstances of their father's early career, that Sebastian's departure from Ohrdruf was attributed by them to his brother's death, which took place actually twenty years later. Forkel,[4] whose information was derived from them, supposed that the event made him 'once more destitute', and set him on a haphazard journey to Lüneburg in search of employment. The true facts are, that Johann Christoph, being no longer able conveniently to house him, availed himself of a fortunate opportunity to secure Sebastian's entertainment and education elsewhere. Since his brothers joined

---

[1] See p. 273, *infra*.
[2] The work in Prima is thus described in 1685: 'In Prima hat mann nicht wahrnehmen können, dass die discipuli zur elaboration der chrien und orationen angeführet werden.' The study of Greek dated from 1698, when a Sunday examination in the morning's sermon was also instituted. Of Phocylides' *Perceptive Poem* there is an English version by W. Hewett (1840).
[3] The later hand of some one who had followed his career has added a note in the register: 'factus primum musicus organicus Arnstadtensis in aede Sophiae, deinde Mulhusinus et paulo post aulicus Vinariae [Weimar]'.
[4] Forkel, p. 11.

his household two, perhaps three,[1] children had been born to him; another arrived eight months after Sebastian's departure. It was, in fact, exiguous accommodation rather than inadequate means that withdrew his hospitality; for in March 1700 Johann Christoph joined the school's staff with an augmented salary.[2] Moreover, it is improbable that Sebastian was a serious tax upon his finances. Like Eisenach, Ohrdruf had its 'chorus musicus', whose Currenden took place yearly in March, July, October, and the New Year. Its number did not exceed thirty, and the amount of 'Chorgeld' available for distribution was relatively large. Possessing a good treble voice,[3] Sebastian must certainly have been admitted to the choir, whose efforts in 1697, 1698, and 1699 earned respectively 240, 249, and 247 thalers. From those sums each Primaner drew about seventeen thalers, each Prefect twenty; more than eighty-nine thalers rewarded one boy in less than six years. If Sebastian received half as much while he was under his brother's roof it went far to balance the cost of his maintenance. But his departure from Ohrdruf needs no laboured explanation: at his confirmation in his fourteenth year (1699) he reached an age when the custom of his class called him into the world to seek a livelihood.[4] Johann Jakob, three years his elder, had already left school at that age [5] to be apprenticed to his father's successor at Eisenach.

The death of his father brought Sebastian to Ohrdruf. A happier accident took him out of it and decided the next stage in his career. The tyrannical Arnold was replaced in 1697 by Elias Herda, a young musician from whom each of the four upper classes received musical instruction for one hour weekly. Born at Leina, between Gotha and Waltershausen, and educated at Gotha, he had been admitted to the Klosterschule of the Michaeliskirche at Lüneburg, where Thuringian singers were in request for their musical proficiency. He remained there for six years, and, after a short period at Jena as a student of theology, came to Ohrdruf as Cantor and Tertius in Arnold's room, beginning his duties on 7 January 1698.[6] Ten days later (17 January) he enrolled in Tertia the sixteen-years-old Georg Erdmann, himself a native of Leina,[7] who probably lodged with him. Promoted at the end of that school year (July 1698), Erdmann passed up to Secunda, where his

---

[1] There is a gap of five years between the birth of the first and second of Johann Christoph's sons. In that interval certainly one and perhaps two daughters were born.   [2] Bi. i. 52; Thomas (2), p. 8.
[3] Forkel speaks of 'seine schöne Discantstimme'.   [4] Bi. i. 55.
[5] His name is among the Tertians who left in the course of the school year 1695–6 (Thomas (2), p. 13).   [6] Thomas (2), p. 16.
[7] Ibid., p. 15.

junior Sebastian was second in the class in July 1699 and was
promoted out of it into Prima. Erdmann, remaining behind in
Secunda, left the school on 19 January 1700. The register assigns
the same reason for his as for Sebastian's departure two months
later: 'ob defectum hospitiorum abiit Luneburgum.' The meaning
of the statement in his case can only be conjectured. Whatever the
cause of his departure from Ohrdruf, his presence in the select
'Mettenchor' of the Michaelisschule at Lüneburg at Easter (3 April)
1700 is clearly established, along with Sebastian's simultaneous
enrolment.[1] That the two owed their reception to Herda's recommendation is not doubtful, nor could so long a journey have been
adventured unless employment was assured beforehand. Herda
probably sent them as competent singers to fill vacancies of whose
existence his earlier association with Lüneburg made him aware.

Ohrdruf has its distinctive place in Sebastian's development.
His class record shows him exceptionally quick-witted and informed: he was barely fifteen when he passed out of Prima, a class
in which, while he was at school, the average age was never less
than seventeen.[2] Had his schooldays been prolonged to August
1702 he would have qualified to receive the University education
he afforded his sons.[3] Well grounded in the humanities, his
character absorbed the theological bias of the school, whose atmosphere was sternly orthodox and anti-Pietistic. At Ohrdruf, we
can feel sure, the simple faith which possessed him all his life took
root. In its pastoral atmosphere he came close to nature, to whose
sounds and manifestations his music declares him so sensitive.
At Ohrdruf, too, his natural genius began to reveal itself. His
brother's organ was at his service, and on it he developed sympathy
with the temperament and devotional intimacy of Pachelbel, his
brother's master. As a player he must already have discovered the
mastery that later made him famous to contemporaries otherwise
insensitive to his greatness. But one conclusion is definite: his life
and training at Ohrdruf decisively divorced him from the traditions of his immediate ancestry. Had his father lived, and had
Eisenach remained his home, it is not improbable that, like his
forebears, he would have entered their profession on its secular
side. As it was, he left Ohrdruf drawn, if not already dedicated,
to the service of the Sanctuary.

[1] Junghans, p. 4.   [2] Thomas (2), p. 7.   [3] Ibid., p. 13.

CHAPTER III

APPRENTICESHIP

FORKEL[1] remarks the limpet attachment of the Bachs to their Thuringian fatherland and their unreadiness to sever themselves from it. Yet, we may suppose, setting out from Ohrdruf on 15 March 1700, Sebastian turned his face with eager anticipation northward, for the North was a Land of Promise. Of the masters whose music fired his soul in his brother's moonlit attic Dietrich Buxtehude was at Lübeck, Georg Böhm awaited him in Lüneburg, Adam Reinken at Hamburg. Yet it needed courage in a lad of fifteen to adventure so far on an unknown road, and only the call to master his art, to explore its every form, afforded it. For two hundred miles lay before him, many to be tramped on foot, some on the seat of a jolting wagon, with the occasional luxury of a stage coach on the main highway. When Johann Jakob travelled to Poland four years later, Sebastian in a Capriccio[2] recalled his own experience, the lamentation of his friends (*Adagissimo*), their farewells, and the shrill notes of the *Cornetto di postiglione*:

as the straining horses rattled the rumbling coach over the pebbled street. His route we may conjecture: northward to Gotha, where Erdmann joined him; thence by stages to Langensalza and Mühlhausen, soon to be revisited; on over the Eichfeld, a climb past Göttingen to the Leine tumbling below among its woods, and thence to Northeim, with the Harz hazily distant to the east. So to Brunswick, Ülzen, and the Lüneburger Heide, through a landscape far different from his native Thuringia: heathery moorland, boggy lagoons, scattered plantations of larch and fir, green pastures watered by artificial channels in the sandy soil, infrequent streams in deep gullies. Even to-day the traveller scans a wide horizon where villages are absent and no habitation is apparent save an infrequent barn. At length, out of this unfamiliar landscape the coppered spire of the Johanniskirche at Lüneburg shot up a directing sign, and in the last days of Lent the travellers passed beyond

---

[1] Forkel, p. 6.   [2] B.-G. XXXVI, No. 40 ; P., Bk. 208, p. 62.

the great church to where the Michaeliskirche[1] raises its lofty bell-tower on the western wall. The long journey was over.

Lüneburg's history rolls back to Charles the Great and beyond, sometime the outpost of civilization against the heathen Wends, later a prosperous member of the Hansa, and for centuries a capital of the Guelphs sleeping in the vaults of the Michaeliskirche. Spacious and lofty houses on the Sand, Markt, and elsewhere, crowned with the characteristic 'Staffelgiebel', betoken a merchant community of culture, and on the Markt the magnificent Rathaus visibly asserts an opulent past. Topping every building in lavish altitude, three great churches, impressive monuments of ancient piety, declare the city's heirship of the Age of Faith—the noble Johanniskirche, the civic church since the fifteenth century, the Nikolaikirche's lofty buttressed nave, and the Michaeliskirche. Lüneburg owed allegiance since 1665 to Duke Georg Wilhelm, through his daughter's loveless marriage ancestor of the English House of Windsor, whose principal seat was at Celle, in the stately Schloss to which he had brought his French mistress, now his wife, Eléonore d'Olbreuse, for whom, too, he had built a dower house on the Marktplatz at Lüneburg. Sebastian owed to her his introduction to the music of her country.

The Michaeliskirche and its Particularschule, Sebastian's home for three years, stood just within the ancient wall overlooking the town on the west.[2] A church was there since the tenth century: the present building was already near three hundred years old when Sebastian's treble was heard within it, its squat red-brick tower with coppered cupola, green and picturesque, looming high above the warm red roof of the spacious nave and its tall windows. The conventual buildings of the Kloster exist no longer. With the northern wall of the church they formed a quadrangle, whose northern side housed the school; with the eastern wing it was demolished in 1918 in a dilapidated condition. Uffenbach, who visited 'die berühmte Academie' in 1710, found it mean in design, built of limestone from the neighbouring Kalkberg, and within it a large ill-lighted library containing two or three thousand volumes.[3] The Abbot's residence occupied the western wing; the present structure retains something of the cloistered peace that once pervaded the whole. The interior of the church Sebastian frequented is fortunately preserved for us in Joachim Burmester's

[1] Illus. No. 15.   [2] See the picture, No. 14.
The spire of the Nikolaikirche on the left did not exist in Bach's time.
[3] Zacharias Conrad von Uffenbach, *Reisen* (1753), p. 522. See the photograph, No. 17. It was taken in 1914.

painting.[1] It shows a lofty nave and apsed chancel lit by five windows uniform with those in the aisles. Its imposing altar-piece is somewhat hidden by the white-topped 'Lettneraltar', from which the Bible was read to the congregation in the nave.[2] Behind it, dividing nave from chancel, stands a wrought-iron screen, the two side-gates of which to-day are at Schnellenberg near Lüneburg.[3] Massive pillars rise to the vaulted roof, and, beyond the pulpit, galleries project into the nave. On the south wall, fronting the pulpit, pews support a narrow gallery. On the north wall opposite, the organ façade springs from between two side-chapels, rising in three tiers of pipes within a richly carved frame surmounted by a conventional 'Staffelgiebel' topped with three gilt crowns. The console is upon the lowest tier, concealed from the nave by the exterior pipes of the Rückpositiv, and, on the west, by a picture of St. Cecilia, shaped, it would appear, to afford the organist a view of the choir chamber beyond.[4] Under the organ, on the fifth northern pillar, the richly carved pulpit stands beneath a canopy, while the other pillars in its vicinity are decorated with flags, epitaphic monuments, and heraldic emblems. The font stands in the foreground on a circular platform raised above the tessellated floor, and over it, depending from the roof by a slender chain, hangs a seven-branched candelabrum. Beyond the font the plain rectangular monument of Duke Otto the Stern is visible,[5] and beside it a marble pedestal on which a tall taper burns, probably in his memory. Burmester exaggerates the length but accurately exposes the dignity of a fabric which Sebastian, fresh from Ohrdruf's plain 'Predigerkirche', must have found inspiring, a building whose chapels, altars, and exquisite Crypta perpetuated a tradition to which he, too, was heir.

---

[1] It is reproduced in No. 16. The original is in the Lüneburg Museum. Apart from its seating and interior decoration, the present church differs from Burmester's picture chiefly in the position of the organ, which was removed in 1707 to the west end (Junghans, p. 39), and in the fact that the galleries round the church are brought to the front of the pillars, whereas in 1700 the north and south aisles were partially open.

[2] The so-called 'little altar' stands on the same spot to-day.

[3] Reuter, p. 79. The rest of the screen no longer exists. The wrought-iron gates at Schnellenberg appear to be some seven or eight feet high, topped with ornamented spikes and fitted with a lock. The simple quatrefoil design is very finely executed. Uffenbach found them close locked in 1710, for a notorious robbery had denuded the altar of its treasures shortly before Sebastian's school-days at Lüneburg.   [4] It is not visible in Burmester's picture.

[5] Reuter, p. 79. Uffenbach describes the monument: 'In der Mitte dieser Kirche ist das Begräbnis Ottonis, das Schlöpken in seiner Bardevischen Chronik p. 269 ein Mausoleum nennet, so dass man sich ein Grosses davon einbilden sollte. Es ist aber nichts, als ein erhöheter, breiter steinerner Sarg, wie ein Tisch anzusehen' (*Reisen*, p. 521).

The Benedictine Kloster of St. Michael,[1] indeed, had shown stubborn fidelity to the ancient faith: the Johanniskirche and Nikolaikirche were already Lutheran when Abbot Baldwin sang the last Mass at its high altar on St. Michael's Day 1532. Ten weeks thereafter (9 December) Prior Herbord vom Holle and most of the brethren celebrated Holy Communion at a side-altar according to the Lutheran rite, at sight whereof the Abbot was stricken with paralysis and died, the last Catholic to hold that office. On 13 December 1532 Prior Herbord was elected his successor and ratified a capitulation establishing the Preacher, Schoolmaster, Sacristan, Organist, and 'Frühmettenschüler'[2] on the reformed foundation.[3] The wings of the high altar-piece were folded, the chancel was closed for sixty years, and the crypt and chapels, where Mass was wont to be said, were silent; only that of St. Benedict remained open for service on Fridays, while the Sunday offices were conducted in the nave.[4] Reformation, however, was not complete; the fraternity remained celibate as of old, dwelt in the cloister buildings, and met for meals in the common refectory. At length, in 1655, the conventual discipline was abandoned, celibacy was forsworn, and on 16 May 1656 the Kloster was transformed into a 'Ritteracademie', whose scholars replaced the Klosterherren in the eastern wing, adjoining the Particularschule, whose association with the church was not disturbed.[5]

The conversion of the Kloster to its new purpose accorded with its traditions and those of the Order. From its foundation a school was attached to the church, in which the local nobility, and even heathen Wends from the Mittelmark, Mecklenburg, and elsewhere, were baptized into the Christian faith.[6] Music, moreover, was prominent in its curriculum, though the office of Cantor was not created until 1555, when the first Lutheran Abbot instituted it.[7] But the reformed foundation inherited high traditions: Forkel, who followed Sebastian to the city more than half a century later, linked Lüneburg with Augsburg as the actual cradle of figural music in Germany.[8] Such music was sung in the Johanniskirche as early as 1516, and the Michaeliskirche probably was not less forward. Immediately after the establishment of the Ritter-

---

[1] Illus. Nos. 17, 18.   [2] i.e. the singing boys, 'Mettenchor'.
[3] Reuter, pp. 22–6.   [4] Reuter, p. 28.
[5] Ibid., pp. 33, 54. The Ritteracademien were a new product of the seventeenth century. Their object was to provide education for the sons of the nobility, with a view to the civil and military obligations of their caste. Such foundations became more numerous after the Thirty Years War, and Lüneburg was one of the earliest of them. Cf. Fr. Paulsen, German Education, Past and Present, tr. T. Lorenz (1908), p. 112.
[6] Reuter, p. 6.   [7] Ibid., p. 68.   [8] Junghans, p. 8.

academie, 'new style' music was enjoined (7 August 1656)[1] by
Pastor Hecht for performance on Sundays and festivals, a practice
which still held when Sebastian was a chorister, and for half a
century thereafter. Meanwhile, Hecht also instituted (1672) a school
'chorus symphoniacus' and arranged for the attendance of 'Bene-
fiziaten'—scholars who received remuneration and free board
(Freitisch; *beneficium coenobii*)—at Vespers on Saturdays and
festivals and at Matins daily.[2] Thus were constituted two choral
bodies, the general 'chorus symphoniacus', and the select 'Mettenchor', the latter restricted to 'poor children'.[3]

As with Schubert and Haydn, Sebastian's voice won him the first
step of his career. His name appears with Erdmann's in the list
of the Mettenchor for 3 April–1 May 1700, and again in that for
May 1–29; the select choir was thus constituted:[4]

	Soprano	Th.	Gr.
Koch *major*	. . . .	1	0
Schmidt	. . . .		12
Erdmann	. . . .		12
Bach	. . . .		12
Vogel	. . . .		8
2 Probationers, each	. . .		4
	Alto		
Schmersahl	. . . .		16
Platt	. . . .		8
Schön	. . . .		8
	Tenor		
Köhler, *adjunctus*	. . . .	1	0
Hochgesang *minor*	. . . .		16
Hochgesang *major*	. . . .		12
	Bass		
Franke, *praefectus*	. . . .	1	0
Mittag	. . . .		12

Besides these monthly payments, the Mettenchor shared with the
'chorus symphoniacus' the proceeds of the school Currenden and
fees for attendance at weddings and funerals (Chorgeld).[5] The
sum was considerable: in 1700 it amounted to 372 marks. The
Prefect's share was fifty-six marks, and that of Sebastian at least
fourteen. The value of these emoluments can be measured by the

---

[1] Reuter, p. 69.   [2] *Ibid.*
[3] An order of *c.* 1736 requires, 'Sie müssen armer Leute Kinder sein und gute
Discantstimmen haben.'
[4] Junghans, pp. 3–7. The earliest of these lists is dated 3 March 1694, the latest
29 May 1700. The 'chorus symphoniacus' numbered from 23 to 27 singers, the
Mettenchor from 13 to 18.   [5] Junghans, pp. 7, 12.

fact that the associate Pastor of the church on his appointment in
1694 received no more than one hundred thalers.[1]

The 'chorus symphoniacus', of which the Mettenchor was the
nucleus, contained probably four or five Basses, as many Tenors,
five or six Altos, and eight or ten Sopranos. It functioned regu-
larly on Sundays, with particular obligations on New Year's Day,
Epiphany, the Feast of the Purification, Quinquagesima, the
Annunciation, Easter Day, Jubilate (Third Sunday after Easter),
Ascension Day, Whit-Sunday, Trinity Sunday, the Feast of St.
John Baptist, the Visitation, the Tenth and Twelfth Sundays after
Trinity, the Feast of St. Michael the Archangel, the First Sunday
in Advent, and Christmas Day. On these occasions a 'Concerto',
'Dialogus', or 'Stück' was sung with orchestral accompaniment at
Hauptgottesdienst, the principal morning service, probably before
the sermon, as at Leipzig. On the high festivals, Christmas, Easter,
Whit-Sunday, a similar service was held on the following day. On
Sundays an *a cappella* motet for four or more voices was
substituted for 'die Music', and every three weeks or so a 'Stücklein' (a short movement for one or more voices with orchestral
accompaniment) was performed during Communion. Nachmittagsgottesdienst, or midday Vespers, on the three high festivals
began 'mit einer Figuralmusic', and the sermon was followed by
'ein fein Stücklein', for choir and orchestra in each case. On the
lesser festivals and on Sundays the post-Sermon 'Stücklein' was
sung with organ accompaniment, and the *Magnificat* also, probably
in simple form. On Saturdays and vigils of high festivals it was
customary at this service to perform one or two *a cappella* motets,
besides the German *Magnificat* sung to *tonus peregrinus*. Unlike
the Johanniskirche, the Michaeliskirche could not command the
service of the town's musicians, but it employed instrumentalists,
strings, flutes, oboes, bassoons, horns, trumpets, trombones, tuba,
and timpani. Nor were the services of the 'chorus symphoniacus'
and orchestra exclusively ecclesiastical. The birthday of the reigning duke received musical celebration. In 1663 the scholars of the
Ritteracademie performed a Masquerade, and in 1664 produced
a ballet entitled 'Die Riesen' (The Giants), in which fourteen boys
armed with clubs and stones were laid low by a clap of thunder,
the two singers being accompanied by five violins and two violas.[2]
Two compositions of similar character were in the Michaelisschule
library.[3]

The repertory of the 'chorus symphoniacus' was remarkably
comprehensive. Unfortunately, it was dispersed towards the end

[1] Reuter, p. 56.   [2] Fischer, p. 25.   [3] *Infra*, p. 43.

of the eighteenth century,[1] but catalogues of it reveal its eclectic range. The foundation of it was a collection of printed music gathered by Cantor Christian Praetorius immediately after the institution of the office in 1555. Added to by his successors, it passed to August Braun on his appointment to the Cantorship in 1696.[2] Included in it were the great collection of 5–8 part motets in the *Promptuarium musicum* of Abraham Schade (Schadaeus), published in four volumes 1611–17 and chiefly representative of the Italian school; Hieronymus Praetorius's *Cantiones sacrae* (1599), *Liber missarum* (1616), and *Magnificat* (1602); Erhard Boden-schatz's *Florilegium Portense* (1603 and 1621), a collection of motets of the German and Italian schools; Melchior Vulpius's *Cantiones sacrae* (1602 and 1604), a similar anthology; Michael Praetorius's *Musarum Sioniarum motetae et psalmi* (1607); Orlando di Lasso's *Selectissimae cantiones* (motets) (1604); the Netherlander Alexander Utendal's penitential Psalms (1570), and a collection of his motets (1570–7); the *Thesaurus musicus*, a collection of motets published at Nürnberg in 1564 by Montan (Johann von Berg) and Ulrich Neuber; two volumes of motets by various composers; and two of music in manuscript. This collection, comprising thirteen *volumina* and ninety-four *libri* bound in pigskin or parchment, formed the choir's repertory when the Kloster was constituted a Ritteracademie in 1656. Thus, from the moment of its institution the 'chorus sym-phoniacus' had at its disposal the finest examples of sixteenth- and early seventeenth-century polyphony.

The early Lutheran Cantors were alert to add to their store. Christian Gärtner acquired Samuel Scheidt's *Concerti sacri 2–12 voc. adjectis symphoniis et choris instrumentalibus* (1621 and 1622), prototypes of the Choral Cantata perfected by Bach, and his *Liebliche Kraftblümlein* for two voices with continuo accompani-ment (1625); Tobias Michael's *Musicalische Seelenlust*, a collection of sacred Concerti in from four to twelve parts published in 1634–7; Andreas Hammerschmidt's *Primitiae* for two voices and instrumental accompaniment, and his *Musicalische Andachten*, Parts I–III (1638–42), containing sacred Concerti, madrigals, and Sinfonien; Heinrich Grimm's *Vestibulum horti harmonici sacri* (1643), a series of 'Tricinia' with and without continuo; the Stral-sund organist Johann Vierdanck's *Geistliche Concerte mit 2, 3 und 4 Stimmen, neben einem gedoppelten Basso Continuo* (1642–3);

---

[1] Junghans, p. 28. The Director of Archives showed me in the Rathaus several volumes of MS. music which may have been part of the collection.
[2] Junghans, pp. 26–8, prints the 'Catalogus librorum cantionum' in its original much abbreviated form.

Johann Schop's *Cantiones*; 'Sachen' by Johann Jeep, probably his
Geistliche Psalmen und Kirchengesänge D. Martini Luthers (1607);
and some of Heinrich Schütz's sacred Concerti and 'Exequien'.

Thus enlarged, the library passed to Friedrich Emanuel Praetorius, who in the course of forty years added to it at an expenditure which proves the Cantors resolved to maintain the music of
the church at the highest standard. Among Praetorius's acquisi-
tions, Heinrich Schütz is represented by his *Psalmen Davids sampt
etlichen Motetten und Concerten* (1619) and other works; Michael
Praetorius, by his *Polyhymnia caduceatrix et panegyrica* (1619);
Johann Crüger, by his *Laudes Dei vespertinae* (1645); Thomas
Selle, of Hamburg, by his *Monophonia harmonica latina* (1633),
a collection of sacred pieces for two and three voices; Burchard
Grossmann, by his *Angst der Hölle und Frieden der Seele* (1619),
settings of Psalm cxvi by various composers, the only complete
copy of which appears to be in the Preussische Staatsbibliothek,
Berlin; Samuel Bockshorn (Capricornus), by his *Opus musicum*
(1655), *Geistliche Harmonien* (1659–60), and 'Lieder' (1660) from
his Passion music; Nikolaus à Kempis, by his *Symphoniae 1–5 in-
strumentorum adjunctae 4 instr. et 2 voc.* (1647–9); Wolfgang Carl
Briegel, by his *Evangelische Gespräche* (1660), *Geistlicher musicalischer Rosengarten* (1658), *Madrigalische Trostgesänge* (1670), *Musicalisches Tafelkonfekt* (1672), and *Musicalischer Lebensbaum über
die gewöhnlichen Fest- und Sonntage durchs Amtsjahr* (1680);
Andreas Hammerschmidt, by his *Gespräche über die Evangelia*
(1655–6), *Fest-, Buss- und Danklieder* (1658–9), *Kirchen- und Tafelmusic* (1662), and *Fest- und Zeitandachten* (1671); Johann Rodolph
Ahle, by his *Geistliche Chorstücke* (1664); Johann Stadlmayr, by
his *Hymni . . . totius anni* (1628); Johann Hermann Schein, by his
Diletti pastorali, Hirten-Lust (1624, 1650); Claudio Monteverdi, by
his *Selva morale e spirituale* (1640); Adam Krieger, by his *Arien*
(1657); Johann Caspar Horn, by his *Geistliche Harmonien durchs
ganze Jahr* (1680); and Johann Krieger, by his *Musicalische Ergetz-
lichkeit* (1684).

Such[1] was the store of printed music available for the choir's
use when August Braun became Cantor in May 1696. Eagerness
to acquire the most modern works is evidenced by the fact, that
in a large number of cases the year of acquisition was the year of
publication, or followed closely upon it. The selection, too, is
eclectic and catholic: Italy and Germany are represented, and the
masters of polyphony stand beside Schütz and the heralds of new

[1] I omit a few composers and works which I have not identified in the laconic
'Catalogus'.

forms. But there exists an even more remarkable indicator of the range of musical literature at the choir's disposal, in a Catalogue of MSS. left by Friedrich Emanuel Praetorius (1655–95) and taken over by August Braun in June 1696. It exhibits 1,100 items, attributed to no less than one hundred and seventy-five different composers and others grouped as 'Incerti'. The impressive list[1] includes works by the following:

Georg Ludwig Agricola, 1643–76, Gotha.
Johann Rodolph Ahle, 1625–73, Mühlhausen.
Vincenzo Albrici, 1631–96, Leipzig, Prague.
Georg Arnold, *fl.* 1651–72, Innsbruck, Bamberg.
Christian Heinrich Aschenbrenner, 1654–1732, Merseburg.
Heinrich Bach, 1614–92, Arnstadt.
Johann Christoph Bach, 1642–1703, Eisenach.
Lodovico Balbi, *d.* 1604, Venice, Padua.
Dietrich Becker, *d.* 1679, Hamburg.
Christoph Bernhard, 1627–92, Hamburg, Dresden.
Antonio Bertali, 1605–69, Vienna.
Nikolaus Bleyer, 1590–1658, Lübeck.
Erhard Bodenschatz, 1576–1636, Gross-Osterhausen.
Georg Böhm, 1661–1733, Lüneburg.
Giovanni Battista Bonani, *fl.* 1647.
Giovanni Andrea Bontempi, 1624–1705, Dresden.
August Braun, *d.* 1713, Lüneburg.
Wolfgang Carl Briegel, 1626–1712, Darmstadt.
Arato Buttner, *fl.* 1694–1709, Lüneburg.
Dietrich Buxtehude, 1637–1707, Lübeck.
Laurens Cappeller, *b.* 1634, Husum.
Samuel Capricornus (Bockshorn), 1629–65, Stuttgart.
Giacomo Carissimi, 1604–74, Rome.
Gasparo Casati, *d.* 1644, Novara.
Johann Anton Coberg, 1650–1708, Hanover.
Johann Georg Conradi, *fl.* 1690, Hamburg.
Daniel Danielis, *fl.* 1681, Güstrow.
Adam Drese, 1620–1701, Weimar, Arnstadt.
Daniel Eberlin, *d.* 1692, Eisenach, Cassel, Hamburg.
Balthasar Erben, *d.* 1686, Danzig.
Werner Fabricius, 1633–79, Leipzig.
Giovanni Pietro Finatti, *fl.* 1652.
Johann Georg Flixius, *fl.* 1650.
Christian Flor, 1626–97, Lüneburg.
Johann Wilhelm Forcheim, *d.* 1682, Dresden.
Caspar Förster, 1617–73, Copenhagen, Hamburg, Danzig.
Johann Philipp Förtsch, 1652–1732, Hamburg.
Nicolò (?) Fontei, *fl.* 1645, Verona.
Johann Wolfgang Franck, *b. c.* 1641, Ansbach, Hamburg, London.
Severus Gastorius, *fl.* 1675, Jena.
Joachim Gerstenbüttel, *d.* 1721, Hamburg.
Ignaz von Ghesel.

[1] Cf. Max Seiffert, I.M.G., Bd. ix, pp. 593-621.

Antonio Gianettini, 1649–1721, Modena.
Otto Gibel, 1612–82, Minden.
Johann Melchior Gletle, *d. c.* 1684, Augsburg.
Alessandro Grandi, *d. c.* 1637, Bergamo.
Bonifatio Gratiani, *d.* 1664, Rome.
Heinrich Grimm, *d.* 1637, Brunswick.
Michael Hahn, Lüneburg.
Andreas Hammerschmidt, 1612–75, Zittau.
Johann Nikolaus Hanff, 1630–1706, Schleswig.
Justus (? Jobst) Heider, *fl.* 1654, Hanover.
Ernst Dietrich Heindorff, *d.* 1724, Arnstadt.
Johann Andreas Herbst, 1588–1666, Frankfurt.
Johann Hildebrand, *fl.* 1645, Eilenburg.
Johann Caspar Horn, *fl.* 1678, Dresden.
Georg Hucke, *d. c.* 1653, Königsberg.
Daniel Jakobi.
Michael Jakobi, *fl.* 1656, Lüneburg.
Johann Jungknickel, *fl.* 1676.
Christoph Kaldenbach, 1613–98, Tübingen.
Johann Hieronymus Kapsberger, *d. c.* 1633, Rome.
Gottfried Keiser, *fl.* 1671–4, Teuchern.
Johann Caspar Kerll, 1627–93, Munich.
Johann Erasmus Kindermann, 1616–55, Nürnberg.
Johann Knüpfer, *fl.* 1633, Asch.
Sebastian Knüpfer, 1633–76, Leipzig.
Martin Koler (Köhler), *d. c.* 1703, Hamburg.
Jakob Kortkamp, *d. c.* 1677, Hamburg.
Adam Krieger, 1634–66, Dresden.
Johann Philipp Krieger, 1649–1725, Weissenfels.
Alberto Lazari, *fl.* 1637, Perugia.
Francesco Lilio, *fl.* 1673.
Vincent Lübeck, 1654–1740, Hamburg.
J. M. Mandl.
Tarquinio Merula, *fl.* 1620–80, Cremona.
Martin Mielezewski, 17th cent., Poland.
Claudio Monteverdi, 1567–1643, Venice.
Peter Morhardt, 1664–94, Lüneburg.
Johann Neubauer, *fl.* 1649, Hesse.
Georg Österreich, *fl.* 1678–1735, Brunswick.
Bartholomäus Pekiel, *fl.* 1650, Poland.
Marco Gioseffo Peranda, *d.* 1675, Dresden.
Joseph Petzel.
Augustin Pfleger, *fl.* 1681, Güstrow.
David Pohle, *fl.* 1677, Halle.
Francesco della Porta, *d.* 1666, Milan.
Paul Prevost, *fl.* 1650, Berlin.
Fra Sisto Reina, *fl.* 1664, Modena.
R. S. Roist.
Johann Rosenmüller, *d.* 1684, Wolfenbüttel.
Martin Roth.
Giovanni Rovetta, *d.* 1668, Venice.
Galeazzo Sabbatini, *fl.* 1625, Pesaro.
Erasmus Sartorius, 1577–1637, Hamburg.

Marco Scacchi, *d. c.* 1685, Warsaw.
Rayser (? Riniero) de Scarselli, *fl.* 1637, Venice.
Johann Hermann Schein, 1586–1630, Leipzig.
Johann Schelle, 1648–1701, Leipzig.
Melchior Schildt, 1592–1667, Hanover.
Johann Heinrich Schmelzer, *d.* 1680, Vienna.
Natan Schnittelbach, 1637–67, Lübeck.
Heinrich Schütz, 1585–1672, Dresden.
Christian Andreas Schulze, *fl.* 1680, Meissen.
H. (? Günther) Schweckenbacher, 1651–1714, Königsberg.
Heinrich Schwemmer, 1621–96, Nürnberg.
Johann Sebastiani, 1622–83, Königsberg.
Daniel Selich, *fl.* 1625, Wolfenbüttel.
Thomas Selle, 1599–1663, Hamburg.
Johann Stadlmayr, 1560–1648, Innsbruck.
Constantin Steingaden, *fl.* 1666, Constance.
Georg Christoph Strattner, *d.* 1704, Weimar.
Nikolaus Adam Strungk, 1640–1700, Dresden.
Thomas Strutius, *d.* 1678, Danzig.
Felician Suevus (Schwab), *b.* 1639, Constance.
Simplicio Todeschi, *fl.* 1637, Verona.
Pietro Torri, *d.* 1737, Munich.
Vincenzio Tozzi, *d. c.* 1675, Messina.
Franz Tunder, 1614–67, Lübeck.
Marco Ucellini, *fl.* 1630–60, Modena.
Giovanni Valentini, *fl.* 1620, Vienna.
Simon Vesi, *fl.* 1648, Padua.
Johann Vierdanck, *fl.* 1641, Stralsund.
Matthias Weckmann, 1621–74, Hamburg.
Johann Weichmann, 1620–52, Königsberg.
Johann Julius Weiland, *d.* 1663, Brunswick.
Andreas Werckmeister, 1645–1706, Halberstadt.
Christoph Werner, *fl.* 1650, Dresden.
Tobias Zeutschner, 1615–75, Breslau.
Johann Christoph Ziegler, *fl.* 1681, Wittenberg.

The inclusion of Heinrich and Johann Christoph Bach in this representative collection is interesting. The former was but recently dead, the latter still surviving, when their young relative entered the Michaelischule, bearer of a name whose distinction preceded him. Some latitude, it may be supposed, was allowed him on that account, whether to adventure the journeys to Hamburg and Celle he made from Lüneburg, or to explore the treasures of the library under the Cantor's eye. The Ohrdruf incident[1] is too characteristic for us to suppose it an isolated instance of his voracious curiosity. Spitta,[2] however, regards his inclination as so exclusively drawn to the organ at this period that vocal music interested him little, if at all; a conjecture apparently baseless.

[1] *Supra*, p. 25.   [2] Sp. i. 190.

The vocation he asserted a few years later already called him, while his earliest composition on a considerable scale, the Arnstadt Easter cantata (1704), reveals his study of the very forms to which Spitta supposes him indifferent. Hence, the Michaelisschule MSS., like its printed music, are highly significant in relation to the development of his genius, and must be counted among the influences which shaped his career. The traditions of his direct ancestry lay in the secular branch of his calling. But his father's death had placed him on another course, and at Ohrdruf, where his master was a church Cantor, organist, and pupil of Pachelbel, he definitely concluded to pursue it.[1] Yet, Ohrdruf was no better equipped than Eisenach to reveal to him the full resources of music in relation to church worship. For that instruction he was indebted to Lüneburg, a community whose musical apparatus exceeded any to which he was as yet accustomed, whose traditions encouraged its lavish use, and in whose library he could explore the whole range of relative literature. The manuscripts on its shelves were extraordinarily varied, rich in motets of the old school, arias of the new, madrigals, sacred and secular,[2] Quodlibets,[3] settings of the Psalms, *Kyrie*, *Magnificat*, *Sanctus*, and *Te Deum*, Introits, Responses, Latin hymns, 'Dialogi',[4] Choral melodies treated in many styles, and frequently with much elaboration.[5] Available also were early examples of the Choral Cantata and settings of the Passion story: *Passio Domini secundum Matthaeum, mit Instrument. à 26*, by Joachim Gerstenbüttel; another 'à 14 mit Instrumenten' by Justus Heider; a *Passio, sive Septem Verba Christi in cruce pendentis, à 7. 2 Viol. d'Brazzio. C.C.T.T.B. con Capell.* (C♭), by Augustin Pfleger; Heinrich Schütz's *Die Sieben Worte unsers Herrn Jesu Christi am Stamm des Creutzes gesprochen, à 10 ou 15* (E); Thomas Selle's *Passio Domini Nostri Jesu Christi secundum Matthaeum mit Instrumenten* (F♭); and Dietrich Becker's *Passio*

---

[1] Is it unlikely that divergence of view regarding his future career was at the root of Sebastian's disagreement with his brother over the MS. of organ music?
[2] *e.g.* Martin Roth's *Willkommen Jesu, du süsses Seelenbrodt*: Madrigal sub Communione à 7. C.T.B. con 4 violen (B.).
[3] *e.g. Die edle Musica kann meinen Geist entzücken*: à 4. 2 Violin. T.B. (G♭).
[4] *e.g. Cum esset David in plenitudine pacis*: Dialogus à 12. 2 Viol. e Clavic[embalo] è 9 Voc. C.C.C.A.A.T.T.B.B.(G♭); *So spricht der Herr, beschicke dein Hauss.* Esr. 38 u. 2 Kön. 20, 1 ff. 5 Viol. C.A.T.B. in Dialogo (C♭); *Unser Harffen ist eine Klage worden*: Dialogus Dom. 10 p. Trin. à 12 ou 18. C.A.T.B. 4 strom[enti]. 4 voc. in Cap. (B.); and *Was soll ich aus dir machen, Ephraim*: Dialogus à 5. 2 Violin. T.T.B. (A.). All of these are by unknown composers.
[5] *e.g. Nun dancket alle Gott*, à 19, 22 ou 25. 5 Viol. 2 Corn. 3 Tromb. 2 Clarin. 1 Tymp. C.A.T.B. 1mo Choro. C.A.T.B. 2do Choro. C.A.T.B. in Rip. (C♯), by an unknown Composer; and J. A. Coberg's *Nun dancket alle Gott*, à 12 ou 17. 2 Tromp. 2 Violin. 2 Viol. Fag. C.A.T.T.B. in Conc. C.A.T.T.B. in Rip. (C♮).

Domini secundum Johannem (E♯). Included also were two secular cantatas: *Nunc Giorgio Wilhelmo plaude Musa principi, à 10 ou 15.* 5 Strom. 5 voc. in Conc. C.C.A.T.B. 5 voc. in Rip. (G♮), in honour of Eléonore d'Olbreuse's husband; and Marco Gioseffo Peranda's *Sursum deorsum symbolum Sereniss. Elect. Saxon. J. G. II. à 6. 3 Violin. C.C.C.* (B.), in honour of Elector Johann Georg (*d.* 1680). Though not so named, the majority of the collection were 'Stücke', elaborate anthems, later classified as Cantatas, many of them concluding with a Choral. Excepting Jubilate Sunday and the Visitation of the B.V.M., all the occasions already named for special music were provided for, and pieces were also available for the first, fourth, and fifth Sundays after Epiphany, Septuagesima, Lent and Passiontide, the second and fifth Sundays after Easter, and the first, second, fifth, ninth, eleventh, fourteenth, twentieth, twenty-first, twenty-third, and twenty-seventh Sundays after Trinity, a fact which suggests that concerted music was not confined to the occasions for which it was originally prescribed. It would be difficult to imagine an environment more stimulating to the genius of the youthful Bach.

The officials of the church and school with whom Sebastian was chiefly associated can be named. From the foundation of the Ritteracademie the church was served by a Pastor primarius and Diakonus, who wore the black Lutheran 'Chorrock', and (until 1787) during the celebration of the Communion, the 'Chorhemd', a sleeveless surplice still in use at Leipzig and elsewhere, the 'Halskrause' or neck-ruff, and the biretta.[1] While Sebastian was at Lüneburg, Martin Georg Hülsemann was Pastor and Inspector of the school, in which he also taught.[2] Johann Jakob Boje, a young man of twenty-nine in 1700, was Diakonus and later succeeded to the Pastorate.[3] Of the Cantor August Braun's earlier career nothing is known. Twenty-three of his compositions were in the school repertory, including settings of the *Sanctus, Magnificat, Kyrie*, madrigals, and several 'Stücke'. The originals are lost, and with them the means to test their composer's ability. His office was conjoined with that of Sacristan (Oberküster), and on the school staff he ranked after the Rector and Conrector.[4] Christoph Morhardt, the organist, who succeeded his father Peter Morhardt in 1690, held the post until 1707, when he was pensioned, an event coincident with the reconstruction of the organ and its re-erection on the west wall.[5] His abilities perhaps were not deemed adequate to the enlarged instrument, which was formally

[1] Reuter, p. 43.   [2] *Ibid.*, pp. 44, 56.   [3] *Ibid.*, p. 57.
[4] *Ibid.*, p. 68.   [5] Junghans, p. 39.

opened on the Dedication Festival of St. Michael 1707. Part of the old organ was incorporated in the present instrument, some of whose pipes Sebastian himself may have sounded: a youth so precociously accomplished would hardly be denied access to it, though his Lüneburg compositions suggest that a clavier rather than a pedalled organ was then at his disposal.

A time-table [1] for 1695 reveals the curriculum to which Sebastian was subject. The school was divided into five classes under as many masters. Into which of them he was placed is not on record, but his Ohrdruf prowess makes it probable that he entered Prima at once, or after the briefest stay in Secunda. The latter class was taught by the Conrector, Eberhard Joachim Elefeld, a versatile pedagogue who imparted the rudiments of Hebrew, Greek and Latin grammar, Latin prosody, as well as 'ars gnomonica et optica mechanica'. The Cantor, besides expounding the subtleties of Leonhard Hutter's *Compendium*, whose 'quaestiones' Sebastian had pondered at Ohrdruf, extended the class's knowledge of Latin grammar to the terminus of supines and preterites, corrected its proses, expounded Terence's *Eunuchus* and Cicero's *Epistolae*, and gave instruction in 'arithmetica'. In Prima, the Rector, Johann Büsch, in a weekly lesson dived with his pupils deeper into Hutter's didactic orthodoxy, elucidating his views on election, good works, penitence, the Ministry, and the Church. Twice weekly he defined 'simple terms' in the first Book 'e logica Gothana',[2] and spent as many hours with the seniors on Cicero's *De inventione*, while the juniors studied tropes and syllogisms. In classics the Primaner read Cicero's *Catiline* and Virgil's fourth *Aeneid*. The Conrector and Cantor added further tasks: the former read with them Quintus Curtius, Cicero's *De officiis*, and selected Odes of Horace; also the Πίναξ or *Tabula* of Cebes of Thebes, perhaps in the Latin translation made by Salmasius in 1640, a work which develops the Platonic theory of pre-existence, demonstrating that character is the goal of true education, and the Ποίημα νουθετικόν of Phocylides, which buttressed the doctrine of immortality with philosophic argument. As in Secunda, the Cantor was responsible for 'arithmetica'. Besides their class exercises, the Primaner visited the Rector and Conrector individually for history, geography, genealogy, heraldry, German poetry, mathematics, and physics—a full diet![3]

[1] Junghans, p. 40.
[2] The book referred to is the *Systema logicum . . . ad usum Gymnasii Gothani* published anonymously at Gotha by Christoph Reyher in 1691. The first of its three Books is entitled 'Prolegomena logica de natura logicae'. A copy of the work is in the Gotha Herzogl. Bibliothek (Philos. 8°, 154).
[3] Junghans, pp. 40–1, quotes the concise Latin syllabus, but is at no pains to

Apart from his enrolment as a descantist in the Mettenchor, positive information upon Sebastian's circumstances at Lüneburg is lacking. Entering the choir at fifteen, he cannot long have retained a serviceable treble voice. It broke, says the Nekrolog, while he was singing in the choir, played him tricks for a week, falling irresponsibly to a sudden octave, and then left him altogether. Spitta [1] consequently infers that his abilities as an instrumentalist thereafter maintained him at the school. It is, at any rate, evident that he was accorded unusual liberty, a fact which may point to his promotion to a Prefectship, or to a post as accompanist. While not withdrawing him entirely from academic tasks, or releasing him completely from school discipline, such a situation would provide opportunities [2] to investigate neighbouring musical centres which, even before he left Ohrdruf, must have attracted his interest. To do so was the easier because, since 1661, the choir's activities were either suspended or curtailed during the summer months,[3] when Sebastian's visits to Celle and Hamburg were probably made. But, after all, the young organist who took a long French leave of Arnstadt in 1705 may be supposed as capable of mapping an independent course at Lüneburg.

Before journeying afield, two local musicians invited Sebastian's acquaintance. The elder, Johann Jakob Loewe, was since 1682 organist of the Nikolaikirche. Born in 1628, he had studied at Dresden under Heinrich Schütz, became Capellmeister at Brunswick in 1655, and on Schütz's recommendation passed to Zeitz in 1663, proceeding to Lüneburg (1683), where he died twenty years later. Famous as a composer—the Michaeliskirche used his *Geistliche Concerte*—it was as a pupil of Schütz that Sebastian probably sought him. He was one of the few men of his period to write Lieder for a solo voice, and was also known for his *Synfonien, Gagliarden, Arien, Ballette, Couranten, Sarabanden mit 3 oder 5 Stimmen* (1658), Suites in the French form with which Sebastian became simultaneously acquainted at Celle. He had also produced operas at Wolfenbüttel, *Amelinde* in 1657, *Orpheus* in 1659, and, as a man of independent outlook, was for that reason especially attractive to the younger musician. Junghans conjectures that

---

identify the works and authors, who are mentioned in contracted forms. I have failed to find the *Ars combinatoria et diatribe de veterum cruce et crucifixione*, which the Corrector expounded to the Primaner.
[1] Sp. i. 188.
[2] At Leipzig long absences from school, such as Sebastian took at Lüneburg, were sufficiently common to call for particular legislation.
[3] Reuter, p. 69.

Loewe, who styled himself 'von Eysenach', was actually responsible for Sebastian's presence at Lüneburg, and that their common associations with Eisenach brought them together there.[1] Spitta attributes to Loewe the Michaeliskirche's possession of Heinrich and Johann Christoph Bach's motets, whose composers he supposes to have been personally known to him.[2] In fact, Loewe was born at Vienna and had no personal connexion with Eisenach at all, other than the circumstance that his father, who represented the Saxon Elector at Vienna, was born there long before any Bachs were living in the town. Still, Sebastian may have been encouraged to make himself known to one who held Eisenach in evident regard.

Between Sebastian and Georg Böhm, organist of the Johanniskirche, many common associations existed. Böhm was a native of Hohenkirchen, a village not far from Ohrdruf, born there in 1661, nearly twenty-four years before Sebastian came into the world. His father, organist at Hohenkirchen, probably sent him to Ohrdruf Lyceum, whose Cantor, Johann Heinrich Hildebrand, had served his apprenticeship at Arnstadt under Heinrich and Christoph Bach, when Sebastian's father and uncle also were apprentices there. Removed from Hohenkirchen by his father's death in 1675, Böhm's fourteenth year found him at Goldbach under Pastor Wolfgang Heinrich Mahn, whose brother, Cantor at Goldbach, frequented Arnstadt school when Heinrich Bach's sons were active there. In the Gotha Gymnasium, too, which Böhm entered in 1678, the name Bach was quite recently familiar: Jakob Bach, ancestor of the Meiningen branch, left the school only four years before. And among the town's musicians of Gotha the Bachs were a household name: its organist[3] was a pupil of Johannes Bach of Erfurt, and Sebastian Nagel stood godfather to Sebastian himself seven years later. So, however withdrawn was the Michaeliskirche from the civic life of Lüneburg, however obstructive its encircling wall, the lad who walked to Hamburg to hear Reinken is little likely to have neglected Böhm at his door. Indeed, Böhm's influence upon him is evident where most we should expect to find it. Sebastian's essays in composition dated from his earliest years.[4] Pachelbel, so far, had chiefly guided his creative impulse, but to his Lüneburg years appear to belong a number of compositions which suggest another model,[5] notably a Prelude and Fugue in C minor:[6]

---

[1] Junghans, p. 12.   [2] Sp. i. 190, 191.   [3] Egidius Funck.
[4] Cf. p. 20, *supra*.   [5] Pirro (3), p. 29.
[6] B.-G., Jhrg. XXXVIII. 3; P. 243, No. 5; Aug. i. 124.

and another Fugue in C minor:[1]

also a Prelude in G:[2]

and a Prelude and Fugue in A minor:[3]

as well as the Variations 'O Gott, du frommer Gott', 'Christ, der du bist der helle Tag', and 'Sei gegrüsset, Jesu gütig'. All these pieces exhibit the young composer's timidity, inexperience, sensitive temperament, and sympathetic reaction to the inspiration of the North German school of Buxtehude and Reinken. No other than Böhm, himself a pupil of Reinken, can have set him upon this new path, and he may even have listened to Sebastian's youthful exercises in the loft of the Johanniskirche.[4]

From Böhm to Reinken was a natural step; Böhm himself would urge his pupil to drink at the fount from whence he had drawn

[1] B.-G. XXXVIII. 101; P. 243, No. 9; Aug. ii. 428.
[2] B.-G. XXXVIII. 85; P. 247, No. 11; Aug. iii. 664.
[3] B.-G. XXXVIII. 17; P. 242, No. 9; Aug. iii. 612.　　　[4] Illus. No. 19.

nourishment, though a thirst so insatiable as Sebastian's wanted little prompting to satisfy its need. So, a summer vacation, probably of 1701, found him on the road to Hamburg, thirty English miles distant, a full day's journey on foot over the Heide. Just turned sixteen and still under school discipline, a prolonged absence can neither have been granted nor afforded. But Hamburg had attractions which more than a single visit was needed to reveal. The Opera was at its zenith and Reinhard Keiser's name reverberated through Germany as the most accomplished, as he was the most prolific, composer for the stage. But Reinken was the compelling magnet. The old man, now entering his eightieth year, had for half his life been organist of the Catharinenkirche,[1] patriarch of the brilliant North German school, exuberant, diffuse, and skilled in the art of improvisation, in which, reversing their relations, Sebastian twenty years later demonstrated his equality with the veteran. For the moment he was a listener somewhere in the dim spaces of the great church, on a Sunday morning or at afternoon Vespers, when a Prelude on such a melody as 'An Wasserflüssen Babylon' rumbled round the aisles, a lengthy and brilliant exercise of virtuosity, but lacking the note of emotion which the young listener knew how to add to its finished technique. How close a study he made of the older master is evident in the Clavier Sonatas in A minor and C major written at Cöthen nearly twenty years later, once regarded as his own; they are arrangements[2] of the first and eleventh instrumental Suites of Reinken's *Hortus musicus* (1687), Sebastian's possession of which may date from this or a subsequent visit. For the long road to Hamburg was covered more than once. Friedrich Wilhelm Marpurg published in 1786[3] a story which Bach himself found it pleasant to repeat: returning with empty pockets from Hamburg at a late afternoon hour along an inhospitable road, he sat down outside a tavern and hungrily sniffed the savours from the kitchen. Above him a window opened and at his feet fell the heads of two herrings, sea-fish much prized in inland Thuringia. Picking them up eagerly, he found in each a Danish ducat, which satisfied his present hunger and aided a future visit to Reinken.

Pirro[4] observes a parallel between the youthful Bach and his contemporary Leibniz. Guided by chance along the path of knowledge, each obeyed the imperative rein of curiosity, the impulse to master the completest knowledge of the subjects that engaged their interest. The recollections of Sebastian which sur-

---

[1] Illus. No. 20.   [2] B.-G. XLII, Nos. 4, 5; P. 213, Nos. 1, 2.
[3] In his *Legende einiger Musikheiligen.*   [4] Pirro (2), p. 391.

vived among his sons—the coveted manuscript at Ohrdruf, the long pilgrimage to Reinken, the greater adventure to Lübeck—all focus on his fundamental characteristics—an indomitable purpose, consuming curiosity, amazing sureness in plotting his course, and an independent habit which mocked impeding authority. To such a one it was a stroke of fortune that brought him to Lüneburg, so conveniently neighboured by Hamburg's high traditions on one side, and on the other by Celle, seat of another school. The vogue of France was predominant over Germany in the last generation of the seventeenth century. Her princes affected the polished manners of Versailles. French clothes, French food, French furniture, French words, and French music were hall-marks of refinement. Paris was a magnet that drew her nobles and afforded teachers who 'donnaient volontiers des leçons de musique et de table à MM. les étrangers, et surtout aux Allemands'.[1] The persecuted Huguenots carried their language and the music of their country with them into exile, and French players were welcomed in German courts long before Louis Marchand was routed by Bach at Dresden, a contest of international significance.[2] Especially at the Court of Celle French music was preferred. A memorandum by the Court organist Wolfgang Wessnitzer in 1663 instructs his master Duke Christian Ludwig upon the personnel of a well-appointed Capelle:[3]

1. A Director Musices.
2. An Alto ⎫
3. A Tenor ⎬ capable of playing the viol in French music.
4. A Bass ⎭
5. Two violists competent in the French and other styles of music. These we have here already.
6. A viola da gamba player, whom also we have here.
7. An organist, already available here.
8. A trombone or fagotto player competent to take a vocal part and play the violin in French and ordinary music.
9. A cornetto player, able to take the violin part in French music.
10. Two choirboys.
11. An organ-blower.
    In all thirteen persons.

The vogue of French music in Celle was encouraged by Duke Georg Wilhelm's accession in 1665. A jovial, travelled soldier who had known the splendours of Versailles, his reign of forty years gave his capital a brilliance it had never yet displayed. He enlarged the comely Schloss,[4] laid out pleasure gardens with fountains and statues to grace its avenues, commanded ballets, operas, and concerts to enliven its household, and invited players, singers, and

[1] Pirro (2), p. 437.   [2] *Infra*, p. 111.   [3] Wolffheim, p. 425.   [4] Illus. No. 21.

actors to exhibit their skill. A musician was as welcome at Celle as a sportsman or soldier, observed a contemporary.[1] The queen of this gay Court, Eléonore Desmier d'Olbreuse, a beautiful and lively Poitevine, had met Georg Wilhelm in Paris and married him *à la main gauche*: for the Duke was pledged to celibacy by his younger brother, now (1665) of Hanover, with intent to the eventual union of their duchies. But desire to improve the status of his mistress and their only daughter, perhaps the importunity of Eléonore herself, prevailed against his word. The alcoved room in the Schloss is shown in which Sophia Dorothea was born in 1666, before the new apartments were ready in the opposite wing. She was ten when her mother became Duchess of Lüneburg-Celle and her own birth was legitimated. A Huguenot herself, Duchess Eléonore befriended the victims of Louis XIV's dragonnades. Celle consequently sheltered a French colony, whose neighbourhood, and Georg Wilhelm's disposition to copy Paris fashions, gave his Court a French tone and atmosphere.[2] The ducal archives[3] show the preponderance of Frenchmen in his Capelle until his death broke it up in 1705, when Eléonore retired to her dower house at Lüneburg. In 1684–5 the establishment numbered fourteen persons, all but two of whom were Frenchmen:

Wolfgang Wessnitzer, Court organist (*d.* 1697).
Johann Lorenz Hickethier, Court Cantor (*d.* 1704).
Claude Pécour (also dancing-master to the Court pages).
Thomas de la Selle (? violinist).[4]
Guillaume Joffe.
Denis de la Tourneur (*d.* 1698).
François Robeau (Robbeau) (*d.* 1692 or 1693).
Louis (? Charles) Gaudon (succeeded Wessnitzer as organist 1698).
— Saint-Amour.
Étienne Forlot.
Philippe de Courbesar (Courbasature) (*d.* 1704).
— de la Garenne (Garrene).
Pierre Maréchal.[5]
—— Mignier.

The Capelle grew somewhat in later years, during which the following additions or replacements were made:

1690. Pierre de Vivier (Vivierre).
1692 or 1693. Henri de Hays (? de la Haye).
1697. Bernhard Graep (a recruit from France).

---

[1] In 1687. See Pirro (2), p. 423.
[2] See Horric de Beaucaire's *Une mésalliance dans la maison de Brunswick* (Paris, 1884), and Grégoire Léti's *Abrégé de l'histoire de la maison sérénissime et électorale de Brandebourg* (Amsterdam, 1687).   [3] Wolffheim, pp. 427–9.
[4] Cf. Pirro (1), p. 26.   [5] He was the teacher of J. E. Galliard, who entered the Capelle in 1698 (Fischer, p. 25).

1698. Johann Ernst Galliard (son of a Celle wigmaker of French origin; from about 1706 in Court service in London).
„   Ernst Heinrich Grimm (d. 1704).
„   Hans Jürgen Voigt (oboist).
„   Pietro Agustino Bonadei (left at New Year 1705).
1704. Franz Nagel, Court Cantor.
1705. Johann Franciscus Graep.

Philippe la Vigne was Capellmeister, at a salary of 512 thalers, and the establishment included ten trumpeters.[1]

Eléonore's Schloss at Celle stands picturesquely within pleasances less spacious than of old, shorn of its French grace within, but externally as Georg Wilhelm's builders left it when they carved 'Georgius Wilhelmus anno 1670' upon the inner western wing, a yellow-stuccoed quadrangular pile under red-tiled roofs, showing warm rents of brick on weathered walls. The Guelph Lion and Unicorn look down from the main portals of the eastern wing, and at the top of the main staircase to-day stand sentinel over the offices of the Prussian administration. The buttressed south-east angle holds a priceless miniature, the superb fifteenth-century chapel,[2] an unsurpassable epitome of the Dutch Renaissance, its winged altar, pulpit, organ, galleries, and *loges* a blaze of pictorial decoration set in a golden frame. The ducal pew behind a golden grille faces the exquisite pulpit, and beyond, set at an angle, such an organ is visible as St. Cecilia may have played, a small eight-stopped instrument with rich 'Flügel' front. Wessnitzer and his successor Gaudon can have accommodated only the two choirboys in their little loft; the instrumentalists, if they attended, must have been seated below.

In the north wing across the courtyard Georg Wilhelm and his duchess had their private apartments, accessible from below by a wide and winding stairway. The bare walls to-day still look down upon a floor of such glossiness that intruders muffle their shoes in a covering of felt before treading its polished surface. On the same landing is the theatre,[3] a miniature galleried auditorium with a serviceable stage. The ducal Capelle performed here, and until 1681 plays were acted by a troupe which alternated between Hanover and Celle. Thereafter till 1700 the Duke maintained his own company of twelve to sixteen players, who performed 'Comoedien und andere Lustspiele', the musicians of the Capelle receiving extra remuneration when the former were given.[4] Like his brother Ernst August at Hanover, Georg Wilhelm was an enthusiastic devotee of Italian Opera and attracted expensive artists from Italy

[1] Fischer, p. 25.
[2] Illus. No. 22.
[3] Illus. No. 23.
[4] Wolffheim, p. 427.

as well as players of French comedy. In 1692 his operatic company numbered twelve Italians, three of them *prime donne*, of whom Diana Constantini drew five hundred thalers, and the rest three hundred and fifty thalers each. Occasionally the company performed at Hanover, dispersing in summer to its native Italy, when the Constantini received 200 thalers as journey money. Ballets also were provided, as in 1674, when 'Les amours de Mars et de Venus, ou le Vulcan jaloux' was produced. Altogether the Capelle cost 2,565, the opera and comedies 8,883 thalers annually.[1]

To this minor Versailles, its sparkling folk and French music, Sebastian was imperatively drawn. The Nekrolog and Forkel both declare that more than once [2] he plodded the sixty miles separating it from Lüneburg, halting for the night, we suppose, at Ülzen, along a road on which the pedestrian progressed more rapidly and agreeably than the traveller on wheels. Uffenbach, who made the journey a few years later, execrated the district's wild inhospitality, its 'inconceivably horrible roads' obstructed by roots and rank foliage, its infrequent villages, and a coach-way so rude that to traverse it was torture. In a post-chaise from Ülzen to Lüneburg, half the distance to Celle, his journey took from half-past seven in the morning till four o'clock in the afternoon over 'the notoriously forbidding Heide'.[3] The rigours of the highway were not the only obstacles between Sebastian and the accomplishment of his purpose. The ducal orchestra performed in the Schloss, and it is not clear how he obtained admission to it. Pirro [4] discovers an apothecary named Scott, a member of Celle's Huguenot community and son-in-law of Lüneburg's Bürgermeister Reinbecke, who may have introduced the eager stranger. Spitta [5] supposes an acquaintance among the ducal players who conveniently opened the door. Again, trumpeter Johann Pach is proposed [6] as a relative and sponsor. Sebastian may have entered by one or another of these doors; but it seems more natural to look for him in the orchestra than in the audience. The possibility that he found temporary employment in it is not excluded by the absence of his name from the official lists, and is supported by the fact that almost immediately he obtained a similar engagement elsewhere.

---

[1] Fischer, p. 25.
[2] 'bisweilen' (Forkel) ; 'durch öftere Anhörung einer damals berühmten Capelle' (Nekrolog).
[3] *Merkwürdige Reisen* (1753), i. 460. Uffenbach travelled in January 1710.
[4] Pirro (2), p. 423.   [5] Sp. i. 198.
[6] Wolffheim, p. 430. As his name is also written Jean Pack, it seems probable that he was a Frenchman named Pâque rather than a German named Bach.

These speculations are unimportant beside the fact that Celle introduced Sebastian to French music and French instrumental technique—finished elegance, with meticulous indication of and regard for embellishments (Manieren), whose shorthand he transliterated in later life for the education of his son.[1] In 1703 French *manières* had not found their way into general German use: the clavier player Johann Caspar Ferdinand Fischer seems to have been the first, in 1699, to use ornaments in the French manner. Hence, when the authors of the Nekrolog declare that 'französische Geschmäcke' were a novelty in North Germany *circa* 1700, they probably refer as much to technique as to repertory.[2] Sebastian was attracted by both. From the Lüneburg period probably dates a copy made by him of a Suite in A major by Nicolas de Grigny (1671–1703), organist at Reims, and of a similar composition in F minor by Charles Dieupart, afterwards cembalist and violinist in London. Appended to it is a table of twenty-nine French *manières* with directions for playing them.[3] He also copied out, apparently at this period, de Grigny's *Livre d'Orgue*, which he cited in after years to support his own method.[4] The sixth counterpoint in his *Kunst der Fuge* is marked 'in Stile francese', while his clavier and instrumental scores show his familiarity with the works of Louis Marchand, André Raison (from whom the subject of the organ Passacaglia is borrowed), Gaspard le Roux, and others.[5] He appreciated and recommended to his pupils the compositions of Couperin, a Rondeau by whom he copied into his wife's 'Notenbuch' in 1725; in large measure, too, he adopted his *manières*. It was to a player thoroughly equipped in the elegancies and idiom of his own school that the Frenchman Louis Marchand succumbed at Dresden in 1717.[6]

Sebastian was not yet eighteen when he bade farewell to Lüneburg after three[7] fruitful years and turned homewards to Thuringia, precociously equipped at every point for the career awaiting him. Circumstances had denied him Handel's benefit of a University education. But fortune otherwise had favoured him: at no stage of his adolescence was he distant from stimulating models in the craft in which he was pre-eminent. Johann Christoph Bach at Eisenach, his own brother (Pachelbel's pupil) at

---

[1] In the 'Clavier-Büchlein vor Wilhelm Friedemann Bach' (1720). Bach's 'Explication' will be found on p. 14 of Hermann Keller's edition (1927).
[2] See Pirro (2), p. 422. [3] Sp. i. 199.
[4] The MS. is in the possession of Herr Hans Prieger, Bonn.
[5] Pirro (2), p. 425.
[6] For examples of Bach's borrowing from French models see Pirro (2), p. 429, and B.-J. 1910, p. 33. [7] April 1700–? August 1702.

Ohrdruf, and at Lüneburg those giants, Böhm and Reinken, assisted his development. That Dietrich Buxtehude had not been added to his experiences was due to causes the next chapter will explore. Meanwhile, he had acquired a technique which carried him into instant employment and won him the increasing admiration of his contemporaries. He had also discovered a genius for composition, not derived from his immediate parentage, but nurtured on fare at once rich and various. In the Michaelisschule the great masters of polyphony, German, Dutch, Italian, had shown him their treasures, while the music of the critical century that intervened between the birth of Heinrich Schütz and his own was not less familiar to him. Himself the link between past and future, he had schooled himself with indomitable pertinacity to explore the foundations on which he builded. 'I worked hard,' he replied to one who asked the secret of his mastership in later days; 'if you are as industrious as I was, you will be no less successful.' [1] We must challenge the deduction, but not the statement: it is a concise epitome of Sebastian's years of apprenticeship.

[1] Forkel, p. 106.

A HEYDUC UNIFORM.

CHAPTER IV

THE YOUNG ORGANIST

'THE biographical notice of my father in Mizler, dearest friend,' writes Carl Philipp Emanuel Bach to Forkel in January 1775, 'was put together by the late [Johann Friedrich] Agricola[1] and myself. Mizler added the paragraph at the end regarding his Society.[2] The article is not of great value; for, like all true musicians, my father was no lover of dull and prosaic detail.' To Forkel's closer questioning he replied, 'I have no information regarding the circumstances which took my father from Lüneburg to Weimar.'[3] They can, however, be reconstructed. Bach had not reached an age when withdrawal from the school was imperative, and one simple fact permits the conclusion that he left it prematurely: he returned to Thuringia without visiting Buxtehude at Lübeck, an intention so urgent that he retrod his steps almost immediately, and inconveniently, to realize it. We must therefore suppose a sudden summons, and circumstances indicate whence it came.

In the latter part of 1702 an attractive organ was nearing completion in the Bonifaciuskirche at Arnstadt, a town in which the tradition of his family was so strongly established, that Bach would seize an apparently providential opportunity to begin his professional career there. At Arnstadt, moreover, his candidature would be less prejudiced by the only defect that could be alleged against him: he was barely eighteen and without experience. On the other hand, his opportunities at Lüneburg had conclusively revealed his abnormal skill on the instrument with which his fame as an executant is most closely associated. Circumstances compelled him to rely on his violin or viola for his earliest income, but he left Lüneburg conspicuous for his promise as an organist. And if he, on his part, watched the situation in Arnstadt with close interest from the remote north, the prospect of securing him for its new organ was probably as hopefully entertained there. As the instrument was not completed until the summer of 1703, Bach meanwhile sought

---

[1] Bach's pupil; *d.* 1774.
[2] The 'Societät der musicalischen Wissenschaften', to which Bach was admitted in June 1747. See *infra*, p. 254.
[3] The letter is printed as an appendix to Max Schneider's *Bach-Urkunden* (N.B.G. XVII (3)).

employment of a similar nature elsewhere. At no other period of his career than this can he have competed for the organistship of the Jakobi- or Marktkirche at Sangerhausen, a circumstance he recalled more than thirty years later (1736), when recommending his son Johann Gottfried Bernhard for the organ of that very church.[1] The earlier vacancy was caused by the death (3 July 1702) of 'Stadt-richter und Figuralorganist' Gräfenhayn.[2] Bach came forward as a candidate and, despite his youth, so impressed the electors that he was voted the appointment. Higher authority, however, intervened: the Dukes of Sachsen-Weissenfels were lords of the town, and Duke Johann Georg indicated his preference for Johannes Augustin Kobelius, a man eleven years Bach's senior, who was further recommended by the fact that his maternal great-grandfather, Nikolaus Brause, had been Hoforganist at Weissenfels.[3] Ducal influence prevailed and Bach turned elsewhere for a livelihood.

Between the Courts of Weissenfels and Weimar existed a relationship Bach's subsequent career illustrates. Not improbably it was now invoked to mitigate his disappointment at Sangerhausen. Certainly on Easter Day (8 April) 1703 [4] he was enrolled in the household of Duke Johann Ernst, younger brother of the reigning Duke Wilhelm Ernst of Weimar, whose more exalted service he entered in 1708. Meanwhile, he served the younger, music-loving prince, who maintained a small chamber orchestra, to which Bach's violin or viola gained him admission. The young Duke was completing the Gelbes Schloss, a picturesque building near the imposing Schloss Wilhelmsburg of the reigning Duke. Built for Johann Ernst's wife Dorothea Sophie of Hessen-Homburg, the northern wing bears along its face her initials: C[harlotte] D[orothea] S[ophie] D[ux] S[axoniae] L[andgravia] H]essen] H[om-burg]; while in the twined monograms above the window[5] they are repeated. The western wing, along the Kollegiengasse, contains the main gateway, facing the Stadthaus, and, surmounted by the coats of arms of the builder and his wife, the date 1704 extends along its front.[6] Within, upon the first floor of the north wing, looking out above the monogrammed window, a chamber may be visited whose heraldic ceiling exhibits the arms of Sachsen and Hessen surrounded by portraits of the Duchess's relatives, while on either hand are apartments allegorically decorated. Bach

---

[1] *Infra*, p. 233. Bach speaks of his candidature as having occurred 'nahe 30 Jahren' earlier. Excepting 1702, however, no vacancy occurred at that period. See Fr. Schmidt's paper in 'Zeitschrift I.M.G.' Jhrg. 3, 1901–2.
[2] Werner, p. 78.   [3] Kobelius was elected in Nov. 1702.   [4] Bojanowski, p. 1.
[5] The window originally was a door, as in a drawing in Paul Kühn's *Weimar* (1921), p. 40.   [6] See the illustrations, Nos. 37–39.

often made music here after Johann Ernst's death in 1707; for Dorothea Sophie and her children resided in the Schloss when he returned to Weimar in 1708. Meanwhile, in 1703 Johann Ernst occupied the adjoining Rotes Schloss, a sixteenth-century building originally the dower-house of Duke Johann Wilhelm's (*d.* 1573) widow, connected with Schloss Wilhelmsburg by the so-called 'Roter Gang' that bridged the castle moat.

Duke Johann Ernst, himself a cultured amateur, had sons who inherited his musical taste. For the elder Bach in later life made one of the many adaptations of his secular cantata 'Was mir behagt'. The younger, Johann Ernst, who died when barely nineteen in 1715, exceptionally talented, a violinist, clavier player,[1] composer, owed his violin technique to Eilenstein, his gentleman-in-waiting, though not improbably he took lessons from Bach. Johann Gottfried Walther, organist of the Stadtkirche, was his instructor in composition, and found him an apt pupil. Nineteen instrumental works are attributed to him,[2] of which six violin concertos in the Italian style, published by Philipp Telemann in 1718, won the applause of so critical a pen as Mattheson's of Hamburg. Three of the so-called 'Vivaldi' violin concertos adapted by Bach for the clavier actually are the young prince's compositions,[3] and to his interest Bach's activity in transcribing other examples of the Italian school may be attributed. Until the duke's untimely death Bach's relations with his household were close and cordial. Among its frequenters was Johann Paul von Westhoff, a violinist of distinction who published at Dresden in 1694 six violin sonatas with continuo accompaniment, with which Bach and his master no doubt were familiar.[4] Duke Wilhelm Ernst in 1704 received the dedication of another[5] from Westhoff, a travelled *virtuoso* who twenty years before had toured Italy, Holland, France, as a concert-giver and entertained the Court of St. James's.[6] To Johann Effler, Hof-organist, Bach cannot fail to have been known, for Effler followed Johannes Bach at Erfurt and preceded Michael Bach at Gehren. An old man, burdened with secretarial duties in the ducal chancery,[7] he probably admitted Bach to his organ-loft; indeed the Arnstadt Consistorial minute of 13 July 1703 specifically names Bach 'fürstl. Sächs. Hof-Organist zu Weimar',[8] a statement which, though in-

[1] Bojanowski, p. 11.   [2] Sp. i. 408.
[3] Schweitzer i. 193. Telemann's edition was found at Weimar in 1903. Johann Ernst's compositions are Nos. 11, 13, 16 in B.-G. XLII. Cf. B.-G. XXXVIII, p. 196 for No. 13. Nos. 11 and 16 are in Telemann's edition.
[4] Riemann, p. 1415.   [5] Bojanowski, p. 15.
[6] Pirro (2), p. 433. He died in 1705.
[7] Bojanowski, p. 15.   [8] Weissgerber, p. 12, note 3.

accurate, is significant. It suggests that his activities at Weimar were not restricted to the Rotes Schloss, but that he found opportunity to demonstrate his skill upon his peculiar instrument. It implies a relationship of some sort with Schloss Wilhelmsburg, and permits the conjecture that his promotion to Effler's place in 1708 was consequent upon a reputation established five years earlier. Meanwhile Weimar only briefly detained him. His keenest desire was for an organ of his own, and Arnstadt at length satisfied it.

Arnstadt, capital of the Counts of Schwarzburg-Arnstadt, lies some eleven miles southward of Erfurt, agreeably situated on the slopes of the Alteburg, at whose base the Weisse and Gera send their channels round and through the town. Fountains bubble on every hand, plashing the cobbled streets, whose medieval walls and towers here and there remain to define the ancient boundaries: the Riedthurm and Jakobsthurm on the higher ground of the south, and, to the west, the Neuthorthurm, below the Gartenhaus where Wilhelm Friedemann Bach in later years sojourned among the memories of his ancestors. The Count's seat, Schloss Neideck, of which a tower and crumbling masonry alone survive,[1] lay eastward amid watered pleasances. From it and other points in the town's oval circumference irregular streets push inwards to the spacious Marktplatz, a fair prospect of ancient buildings: the gaily coloured Rathaus at the north-eastern corner, with its Bier-Glöckchen, at whose evening signal each tavern discharged its guests; the 'Galerie' or Colonnade, a row of timbered houses sheltering a promenade bounding it on the east; and, opposite the Rathaus, an ancient hostelry, now the 'Schwarzburger Hof', whose liquor in Bach's time tempted truants from the Sunday sermon. Just within the western wall, beyond the Untermarkt, stands the glory of Arnstadt, the Liebfrauenkirche, an ancient fane served by other Bachs.[2] Adjoining it on the north is the Gymnasium, whose scholars provided the churches with their choirs. Southward from the Marktplatz and opposite the Rathaus, the Oberkirche, or Barfüsserkirche, a Franciscan foundation, still exhibits traces of its former cloister.[3]

Yet a third church ministered to Arnstadt's not considerable community. Near the Rathaus, where the Alteburg makes its last dip to the level, and farmers penned their pigs round the Hopfen-

[1] The present Schloss was built 1728–32.
[2] Its present clock-tower has not the appearance it presented in 1703. The smaller spired towers also have been renovated.
[3] The present Pfarrhaus forms the west side of the quadrangle, whose opposite walls reveal the arches of the ancient cloister.

brunnen on market days, there stood on the Ledermarkt for centuries before the Reformation a church dedicated to St. Boniface.[1]
On 7 August 1581, Bürgermeister Hans Nebel, dwelling near by
on the north side of the Marktplatz beside the 'Green Lion', was
foolishly minded to tar his roof on a day of broiling heat. A neighbour hinted the risk of fire and was brusquely commended to the
devil. At the ominous word the pitch burst into flame, which leapt
from roof to roof along the Marktplatz, fanned by a westerly
breeze, till the Rathaus was soon ablaze. Scurrying sparks fired the
Bonifaciuskirche, and by nightfall, along with nearly four hundred
houses round it, the church was a smouldering ruin.[2] For a century
its blackened shell reproached a heedless community, and a terrific
thunderbolt on 8 July 1617 wrought further havoc to its crumbling masonry The earlier catastrophe was annually recalled in
a service of commemoration, at which, in 1661, Archidiakonus
Augustin Fasch reproached the town for its neglect.[3] Indeed
restoration was urgent; for the Oberkirche could not accommodate the population at Hauptgottesdienst, while the Liebfrauenkirche was used only for the earlier Frühgottesdienst.[4] But
fifteen years passed before, in 1676, the work of reconstruction was
begun; seven years later, on 24 April 1683, the Bonifaciuskirche,
henceforward known as the Neukirche, was reopened for public
worship.[5]

Outwardly the Bonifaciuskirche[6] presents itself with sombre and
somewhat dingy dignity. Within, it is cold, undecorated, a typical
'Predigerkirche', with barrelled roof, lancet windows, and rude
galleries. Its bare walls support two or three undistinguished
monuments, while at its eastern end stands an unimpressive altar
beneath a cloth-hung pulpit. In 1683 the church was without an
organ, and so remained for eighteen years while the community
leisurely collected funds. By 1699 over one thousand gulden were
available, and the generosity of Johann Wilhelm Magen provided
eight hundred more.[7] In 1701 the Mühlhausen organ-builder
Johann Friedrich Wender was commissioned to begin the work,
and completed so much of the instrument between Whitsuntide
and the winter of that year as made it available for use.[8] An
organist was found in Andreas Börner, son-in-law of Christoph

---

[1] It was also known as the Sophienkirche (Bi. i. 61). See p. 28 *supra*, note 3.
[2] Richard Hertel, *Arnstadt und seine Umgebung* (Arnstadt, 1924), p. 72.
[3] Bi. i. 62.   [4] Weissgerber, p. 5.   [5] Bi. i. 62.   [6] Illus. Nos. 24, 25.
[7] Magen (*b.* 1655), a native of Grenssen, was a merchant and member of the
Arnstadt Rath. His benefaction gained him a vault in the church.
[8] Sp. i. 218 is in error in stating that the organ was completed by the winter
of 1701.

Herthum, himself old Heinrich Bach's son-in-law and successor at the Liebfrauenkirche and Oberkirche. Börner's abilities apparently were mediocre, though he also functioned as organist in the Count's private chapel.[1] However, after an interval, Wender was instructed to complete the organ, and by 3 July 1703 finished the work.[2] Though Bach never had at his disposal an instrument of his own worthy of his skill, Wender's, if moderately planned, was good and adequate to the building it served. It comprised a Pedal Organ of five speaking stops, three of sixteen-foot tone, with a coupler to the manuals; a Great Organ (Oberwerk: upper manual) of twelve stops, strong in diapason tone; and a brilliant Brustwerk [3] of nine stops, with a coupler to the Great. Set high on the western wall under the roof, the unornate case filled the top gallery, whose front of wooden balusters curved inwards towards the console over two tiers of box-pews, flush with the galleries surrounding the church.[4] The manuals, pedals, and stop-handles of this historic instrument are preserved in the Arnstadt Museum in their original frame, and exhibit the specification shown on the opposite page.[5]

'It may easily be imagined,' remarks Spitta, 'that, being at Weimar, Bach would not delay to visit Arnstadt, the traditional assembling-place of his family, in order to see his relatives there. He went, played the organ, and convinced the Consistorium that he was the man they required.'[6] The actual circumstances were more formal and more flattering. On 3 July 1703, on the report of the experts who examined his instrument, Wender received his certificate.[7] Ten days later (13 July) the expenses of Herr Johann

---

[1] Spitta's implication that Börner was not trusted, because he had to deliver up the key of the organ gallery to Bürgermeister Feldhaus, who was in charge of the building operations, is groundless. Börner gave up the key on Sundays because the builders were at work during the week.

[2] A protocol of this date in the Arnstadt archives testifies that the work had been completed in accordance with the contract (Weissgerber, p. 12, note 3).

[3] See note 4, p. 79, *infra*.

[4] See the picture of it, No. 27. It shows the existing instrument, built in 1863. The choir gallery has been enlarged by dropping its front to the level of the middle gallery in the picture. A large picture of Bach now hangs above the console.

[5] I copied the names of the stops from the old stop-handles. They were exceedingly dirty and ill-tended, and some of their lettering is almost undecipherable. The numerals prefixed to the names of the stops indicate the position of the stop-handles on either side of the manuals. Reading from the left the topmost stop-handle of each of the four rows may be identified as 9, 1, 15, 23 respectively. From each of them the numeration is downwards: 9–14, 1–8, 15–22, and 23–28.

[6] Sp. i. 219.

[7] 'von denjenigen, die es beschlagen und probieret haben' (Weissgerber, p. 12, note 3).

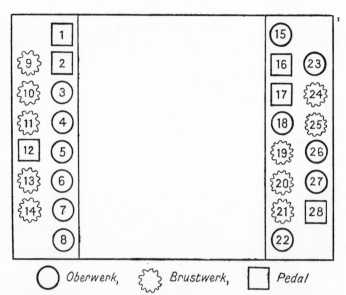

○ *Oberwerk,* ⚙ *Brustwerk,* ▢ *Pedal*

Oberwerk.	*Brustwerk.*	*Pedal.*
*8. Principal, 8 ft.	*13. Principal, 4 ft.	*1. Principal Bass, 8 ft.
*7. Viola da gamba, 8.	¶21. Gedackt, 8.	†2. Sub-Bass, 16.
*26. Quintaton, 8.²	25. Spitz-Floete, 4.⁶	†16. Posaun-Bass, 16.
27. Gedackt, 8.	20. Quinte, 3.³	17. Violon-Bass, 16.⁸
¶ 6. Quinte, 6.³	24. Sesquialt.	12. Hohl-Floete, 8, von
*5. Octave, 4.⁴	11. Nachthorn, 4.	g–d.⁹
¶ 3. Mixtur, 4 ranks.	10. Mixtur, 4 ranks.	28. Pedal-Copp.
¶22. Gemshorn, 8 ft.	19. Octave, 2 ft.⁷	
¶18. Cembal, 3 ranks.⁵	9. Glocken-Accord.	
4. Trompete, 8 ft.	14. Manual-Copp.	
15. Tremulant.		
23. Glocken-Accord.		

* The pipes of these stops, according to Bi. i. 63, were of 'Zinn'.
¶ The pipes of these stops, according to Bi. i. 63, were of 'Metall'.
† The pipes of these stops, according to Bi. i. 63, were of 'Holz'.
Six stops of Bach's organ are incorporated into the present organ:

No. 22 on the first manual;

Nos. 7, 26, 27 on the second;

Nos. 21, 11 on the third.

The organist, Herr L. Rittermann, demonstrated to me their soft and mellow tone.

¹ Illus. No. 28.   ² Bi. i. 63 and Sp. i. 221 give 16 ft. I read 8, and Williams (p. 26), who copied the lettering of the stop-handles in 1899, confirms me.   ³ I could not decipher this figure.   ⁴ Very illegible.
⁵ Sp. i. 221, Bi. i. 63, and Pirro (3), p. 84, give two ranks. I read '3 fach.' and Williams confirms me.   ⁶ I read this as 2.
⁷ Very illegible. The script is in two lines: 'Oc .... a T .... 2 F.'
⁸ Sp. i. 221 omits this stop.
⁹ This is the correct reading. Williams has 'Octava, 2'; Spitta has 'Flötenbass 4' and 'Cornetbass 2'.

Sebastian Bach, prophetically styled 'fürstl. Sächs. Hof-Organist zu Weimar', who had shared that task, were submitted and paid. They amounted to 2 thalers 16 groschen. An extra florin met the cost of his entertainment, and four thalers were disbursed to Georg Christoph Weller for the hire of a horse and attendant for his journey; '*Summa* 8 fl. 13 gr.'[1] It was Bach's first commission of this nature, and his selection for so responsible and technical a task discloses the high reputation he had already acquired. As was customary, the examination of the organ was completed by a public inauguration of it on a following Sunday. Bach played, was forthwith offered the post of organist, and on 9 August 1703 received from the Consistorium the minute of his appointment:[2]

Whereas our right honourable and gracious Count and Lord, Anton Günther, one of the 'Vier Grafen des Reichs',[3] Count of Schwarzburg, &c., hath been pleased to appoint you, Johann Sebastian Bach, to be organist of the New Church, you shall in particular be faithful, loyal, and service-able to his lordship, and in general show yourself apt and habile in your calling, eschewing other tasks and occupations, and on Sundays, feast days, and other seasons appointed for public worship in the said New Church, shall attend at the organ committed to you and perform thereon as shall be required of you. You shall moreover use all care and diligence, that if any part thereof fall into disrepair, the fault be notified and amended forthwith, though none may be admitted thereto save with the consent of the Herr Superintendent [Olearius]; and at all times you shall take heed that it suffer no hurt and be maintained in good order. In your conduct and behaviour you shall be God-fearing, temperate, well-dis-posed to all folk, eschewing ill company, and in all ways show yourself an honourable servant and organist before God and your worshipful masters. In return you shall, against your receipt, receive for yearly pay and enter-tainment 50 florins, and for board and lodging 30 thalers,[4] drawn as

[1] Weissgerber, p. 12, note 3, prints the document in full: 'Uf des hochgräffl. Consistorii Befehl allhier ist Hr. Johann Sebastian Bach, fürstl. Sächs. Hof-Organiste zu Weimar, das neue Orgel Werck in der neuen Kirche zu besichtigen anhero erfordert worden, undt belaufen sich die Kosten uf folgende masse, alss 2 Thlr. 16 gr. Georg Christoph Wellern pferde miethe Kost und bothen lohn, 4 Thlr. Hrn Bachen zum recompens und 1 fl. währender Zeit dass er hier gewesen, vor Kost und Quartier, ist in der Summa 8 fl. 13 gr. Sign. Arnstadt, den 13 Juli 1703. Martin Feldthaus.' Endorsed: '8 fl. 13 gr. H. Bachen die neue Orgel probieren und zum ersten Mal schlagen müssen 13 July 1703.'
[2] Akten of the Consistorium, preserved at Sondershausen. The original texts of this and other documents are in the German edition of this work.
[3] The Counts of Schwarzburg were one of the select four of their numerous order who sat in the Reichstag, in which collectively they cast a single vote. Hence the title 'der Vier Grafen des Reichs' expressed a dignity above that of the local lordship.
[4] 50 florins+30 thalers = 84 gulden, 6 groschen =73 thalers, 18 gr. (Weiss-gerber, p. 6). Thus, 1 florin = 21 groschen; 1 gulden = (roughly) 12½ groschen. D.J.F.L. (p. 47) gives the equation '3 th. = 3 fl. 9 gr.', or, 1 florin = 21 groschen. So, the florin was slightly less than the thaler (24 gr.), while the gulden was about half their value. Bach's successor only received 40 gulden, and the organist of the other two churches in 1728 only 77 (Sp. i. 220).

follows: from the Beer money [1] 25 florins, from church funds 25 florins, and the residue (30 thalers) from the Hospital.[2]
Given under the seal of his lordship's Chancery and signed as is customary, 9 August 1703.

Charged with these obligations, Bach was formally inducted 'durch Handschlag'[3] five days later (14 August). He was more than half a year short of nineteen, yet none of his name at Arnstadt had been so well provided. Old Heinrich Bach, his great-uncle, had long passed to his rest; Christoph Herthum occupied the house on the Kohlenmarkt whence Andreas Börner, whom Bach superseded, had taken his wife. Uncle Johann Christoph, too, was dead, but his widow and her daughter Barbara Catharina, just turned twenty-three, probably still lived in the Kohlgasse.[4] Bach's step-mother may have returned to Arnstadt with her daughter and step-daughter when the Eisenach home was broken up eight years before. But the young organist found another lodging at the Golden Crown,[5] a comfortable three-storied house at the foot of the Ledermarkt, looking on the roomy Holzmarkt. To-day the legend 'Benj. Kiesewetter Nachfolger' is above the antique doorway through which he passed in and out.

For the first time Bach had an organ at his own disposal. To obtain one had long been his chief desire, and having achieved it, he made the fullest use of his opportunity to perfect himself. He began 'assiduously to study the works of the celebrated organists of his period', declares Forkel,[6] repeating the Nekrolog. The

---

[1] *i.e.* the tax on Beer-houses. The salary was considerable and the church lacked funds. Hence the use of other resources.
[2] The Hospital St. Georg und St. Jakob in the Erfurterstrasse maintained a number of old people and contained a small chapel, equipped with an organ, in which services were held. Bach drew his 30 thalers for playing it.
[3] Weissgerber, p. 7.
[4] Sp. i. 169, on what authority I do not know, declares the widow to have been in bad circumstances. Her son Johann Ernst succeeded Bach at the Boni-faciuskirche in 1707.
[5] See the picture of it, No. 26. To-day the house is disfigured by shop windows. The arguments supporting the claim of the Golden Crown to have been Bach's Arnstadt lodging are set forth by Herr P. Thalmann of Arnstadt in the Erfurt 'Mitteldeutsche Zeitung' of 29 July 1925. He quotes documents that establish the payment of money to Bürgermeister Martin Feldhaus 'vor [Joh. Seb. Bach's] jährliche Kost, Bette und Stuben von anno 1706/1707'. Feldhaus owned the Golden Crown, and also the Stone House near by on the Ledermarkt. He was related to Bach by marriage, active in the building of the new organ, doubly interested therefore in Bach, who, as a bachelor, was not in a position to take a house of his own. Whether Bach lived with Feldhaus from his first arrival in Arnstadt cannot be stated, nor can it be declared positively that the Golden Crown and not the Stone House was his residence. Tradition favours the former; it replaced a house burnt down on 12 April 1693 and was not ready for occupation until 1704. Till 1704 Bach may have lived with Feldhaus elsewhere, or with his aunt in the Kohlgasse.

tones of his organ swelling out from an empty church must have
been a daily greeting to the householders on the Ledermarkt,
and his official duties left him ample leisure for his absorbing
occupation. Attendance at church was required of him at Hauptgottesdienst on Sundays from 8 to 10 a.m.; on Mondays at an
intercessory service (Betstunde), which, on the analogy of Leipzig
use,[1] included a few hymns, prayers, Bible reading and exposition;
and on Thursdays at Frühpredigt (7 to 9 a.m.), at which hymns were
sung. As the church lacked a Cantor, Bach was disagreeably
saddled with the training of his choristers,[2] an unruly company
drawn from the Gymnasium. 'They have no respect for their
masters,' the civic Council complained in 1706, 'fight in their
presence, behave in a scandalous manner, come to school wearing
swords, play at ball games in their classrooms, even in the House
of God, and resort to places of ill repute. Out of school they play
games of hazard, drink, and do other things we shrink from
naming. At night they disturb the town with their mischievous
pranks, promenading, and shouting.'[3] Responsibility for their in-
discipline rested with the Rector, Johann Friedrich Treiber, a
scholar of parts, whose son, Johann Philipp, at this time living
with him, was a competent musician.[4] On the staff of the school
Bach had no place, and Stadtcantor Heindorff probably took the
best singers for the Oberkirche.

Outside his official duties Bach found interest and employment
in the musical inclinations of Count Anton Günther at Schloss
Neideck, whose chimneys and tower were visible from his lodging
across the Holzmarkt. Countess Augusta Dorothea, a daughter of
Brunswick, emulating her cousins at Celle and Hanover, had built
the Augustenburg[5] for theatricals and music, after the pattern of
her father's theatre, inaugurating it on 23 August 1700 with the
performance of a secular cantata written by Salomo Franck,[6]
Bach's collaborator in future years. As was customary, the Count's
household provided him with musicians: a list for the year 1690
gives a total of 21 players, who included five trumpeters, a fagottist,
and two oboists. The Gymnasium furnished singers and also
players, the services of Heinrich and Johann Christoph Bach were
occasionally requisitioned, and even Michael Bach was summoned
from Gehren.[7] Immediately arrived from ducal Weimar, Bach is
not likely to have been overlooked; he is indeed the alleged composer of the Opera 'Die Klugheit der Obrigkeit in Anordnung des

[1] B.C.T., p. 30.
[2] His commission (9 Aug.) does not mention this duty, and Bach was unwilling
to fulfil it.   [3] Weissgerber, p. 5.   [4] Ibid.
[5] It no longer exists.   [6] Sp. i. 225.   [7] Ibid. i. 167.

Bierbrauens' (The sagacity of our magistrates in the regulation of brewing) performed in the Augustenburg, May 1705. In four Acts and a Prologue,[1] it employed thirty singing characters fantastically named—Pachpechpichpochius, Bynemetrius, Hyginius, Barbonius, Vernaculanus, Doliopulsantius, Vehivasius, Bibisempria, Corrasia, and others, some of whom spoke the broad Thuringian dialect. The Prologue unfolds the thesis: as the civil state needs laws, so the brewing of beer needs regulation, an undramatic theme turgidly developed in four Acts, concluding with a paean to Arnstadt's 'fettes Bier' and the wisdom of her 'Brauer-Ordnung':

> Deine Brauer-Ordnung zeiget
> Deiner klugen Obern Last,
> Die dem Unheyl vorgebeuget,
> Das der Brauer Wohlstand hasst.
>
> . . . . . .
>
> So kanst du in stiller Ruh
> Dich mit fetten Träncken pflegen,
> Und lobsingen Gott dazu.

This humourless work probably was the production of Rector Treiber, whose classical knowledge is apparent in the names of the characters, the barmaid Bibisempria, the cooper's apprentice Doliopulsantius, and others. The music, which is lost, perhaps was written by Treiber's son, resident in Arnstadt during the years 1704–6,[2] when he published *Der accurate Organist im General Basse*, in which task the young organist of the Bonifaciuskirche may have been serviceable to him. Bach's collaboration in the Rector's Opera is improbable. But his association with its performance is perhaps revealed in a disagreeable incident. A few weeks later Bach was returning from the Schloss accompanied by his cousin Barbara Catharina. Passing up the Ledermarkt to the Marktplatz, he was proceeding along the Gallery,[3] presumably towards the Kohlgasse, when a senior pupil at the Gymnasium, a bassoon player named Geyersbach, accompanied by five other lads, came up with threatening cane and demanded apology for an alleged reflection on his ability as a performer. Bach repudiated the allegation, and Geyersbach, shouting 'Hundsfott' (cowardly rascal), fell to with his stick. Bach made such play with his sword, however, that the testy fagottist was in some jeopardy till his companions intervened. The scuffle stirred the community: on 5 August 1705 Bach, summoned before the Consistorium within the Schloss precincts, admitted that he had called Geyersbach a 'Zippel-

---

[1] The libretto is printed in Bi. iv. 52.   [2] Sp. i. 223.
[3] See *supra*, p. 58. The incident took place near the 'Lang Stein', which stood in front of the Rathaus and was removed in 1825. See *infra*, p. 72 note 4.

F

fagottist'.[1] Neither now nor later did he suffer the incompetent gladly.

Bach's first year at Arnstadt witnessed a family reunion and parting to which he gave musical commemoration. Since their school days at Ohrdruf he and his brothers had followed diverging paths. Johann Jakob had returned to Eisenach to learn his father's craft, and now, lured by the magic of a name and the prospect of good pay, proposed as an oboist to enter the service of Charles XII of Sweden, then campaigning victoriously in Poland. Before starting, he visited Ohrdruf and Arnstadt to take leave of his brothers, and Sebastian marked the occasion by presenting both with mementos of his affection and skill. The first, 'Capriccio sopra la lontananza del suo fratello dilettissimo,' has already been referred to [2] as an effective piece of programme music. We listen first to the traveller's friends, who, in an almost wheedling subject, seek to dissuade him from a hazardous adventure. The second movement, humorous in treatment, is fugal in form: first one, then a second, a third, a fourth voice declares the dangers ahead in a hub-bub that dies and swells to concluding chords in which all speak at once. In the third movement (*Adagissimo*), over a pathetic *basso ostinato* anticipatory of the 'Crucifixus' of the Mass in B minor, the company lament their friend's decision in chromatic phrases, sobbing sequences that die down to the pathetic groan of a solitary bass. The moment of departure arrives, and the friends gather round in a mood of resignation, disturbed by the postilion's horn (*Aria di postiglione*). Off goes the coach to an entertaining fugue on the postilion's air, a movement of bustling vitality that brings the composition to an end.[3]

To the year 1704, probably, also belongs the earliest example of Bach's genius in the cantata form, eloquent of the northern influences to which Lüneburg had exposed him. Though it may date earlier than 1704, it hardly can belong to a later year, and probability points to its production on the first Easter Sunday after his appointment. Entitled 'Denn du wirst meine Seele nicht in der

---

[1] Weissgerber, p. 13. Johann Heinrich Geyersbach (*b.* 1682) left the school in 1706.

[2] *Supra*, p. 31. We cannot be sure that the Italian title was given by Bach himself, but it is probable.

[3] Sp. i. 232 demonstrates conclusively that Bach's model was Johann Kuhnau, whose Clavier Sonatas on Bible subjects (*Musicalische Vorstellung einiger Biblischer Historien*) were published at Leipzig in 1700. Bach's Sonata in D (P. 216, p. 14), containing a macaronically entitled 'Thema all' Imitatione della Gallina Cucca', was similarly inspired. Kuhnau's work was not in the Lüneburg library. Bach's 'Capriccio in honorem Joh. Christoph Bachii, Ohrdruf ' is in P. 216, p. 4. For a general indication of his other clavier compositions of this period see Forkel, p. 153. The Sonata and Capriccio are in B.-G. XXXVI, p. 19 and No. 41.

Hölle lassen' (No. 15), its libretto consists of Psalm xvi. 10, followed by a seven-stanza Easter song, probably by a local poet, which unfolds the Easter story in a spirit of almost pagan jubilation: [1]

> A truce to thy bluster, thou minion of hell!
> Who is it thy throat hath close clutched, hound of ill?
> Thou Serpent, who hath to dust crushed thy foul head
> And stripped from thy crest the bays bloody and red?
> Speak, Satan! how is it thy vaunted might's fled?

Pompously scored for three trumpets, drums, and strings, accompanying a quartet of solo voices, with a concluding Choral, it must have taxed the resources its composer commanded : with difficulty one pictures its performance in the inconveniently small gallery of the New Church: Bach himself at the organ, the four singers behind him, drums and trumpets cramped under the roof on one side, his choir on the other, the strings (violins, violas, violone) along the balustrade in front. Doubtless the display gratified the congregation. But Bach did not repeat the experiment, and for a reason he imparted to the Consistorium on 29 August 1705, when the fracas with Geyersbach was again under consideration. He declared himself willing to perform 'Stücke', provided he was assisted by a 'Director Musices' to train and conduct the choir, a condition which drew the reproof, that ' Man lebe mit *imperfectis* ', and that he would obtain more satisfactory results if he cultivated better terms with his singers.[2] The admonition reveals a characteristic which Bach exhibited throughout his life: he was a bad disciplinarian, easily provoked to temper, and prone to outbreaks which diminished his authority, even lowered his dignity, in the eyes of those under him.

Hardly had gossip over the Geyersbach affair subsided before Bach applied for leave of absence. With money saved in his frugal pocket, and obeying an imperative call, he proposed to visit Dietrich Buxtehude at Lübeck, whose brilliant technique, instrumental style, and mastery as organist and composer urgently attracted him. The convenient presence of his cousin Johann Ernst eased his application by providing an efficient substitute, and leave of absence for one month was accorded in October 1705.[3] Bach again took the long road to the north, a journey of 300 [4] miles which the Nekrolog and Forkel declare him to have covered on foot, an improbable achievement in view of the time at his disposal. Two years earlier (Aug. 1703) Handel, a young man of eighteen, made the shorter journey from Hamburg in company with Johann

---

[1] B.C.T., p. 213.   [2] Weissgerber, p. 13, prints the minute of 29 Aug. 1705.
[3] Weissgerber, p. 8.   [4] Spitta's English translators have 'fifty miles'.

Mattheson, whose reputation gained for them agreeable courtesies. In view of Buxtehude's age (he was nearly seventy), Mattheson came as his potential successor, and Handel was ready to weigh the situation should his friend decline it.[1] Bach, too, was not indifferent to the reversion of a post distinguished, remunerative, and influential. But the appointment was conditioned by an obligation none of the three was willing to accept. It was customary for an organist to accomplish his retirement by marrying a daughter to his successor, at whose charge, and often in whose house, he passed his declining years. Thus, at Arnstadt, Christoph Herthum married Heinrich Bach's daughter to secure his office, and Andreas Börner had taken Herthum's daughter, anticipating a similar reversion. Buxtehude himself was the son-in-law of his predecessor Franz Tunder (d. 1667), and desired to ease his last years by the normal mode of retirement. But his daughter's attractions did not assist his design. Mattheson, twenty-two years old in 1703, abandoned a situation which involved matrimony with a woman of twenty-eight.[2] Handel was similarly repelled. In 1705 Anna Margreta Buxtehude was thirty, Bach was twenty, already carrying tender thoughts of the Gehren cousin he married soon after. He, too, surrendered hopes of a situation burdened with Anna Margreta, who eventually found a husband in Johann Christian Schiefferdecker, a widower ten years her junior, who succeeded her father in 1707, survived her death in 1717, and married again.[3]

Bach timed his departure from Arnstadt (October 1705) to permit attendance at the famous 'Abendmusicen' conducted by Buxtehude in the Marienkirche at Lübeck, which, though altered in character, had been in existence for at least a generation. Under Buxtehude and his successors, till the nineteenth century, the five performances took place at the close of Nachmittagsgottesdienst (Vespers), about four o'clock, on the last two Sundays after Trinity and the second, third, and fourth in Advent.[4] The omission of the first Sunday in Advent was due to its recognition as a fast-day, a reversal of Leipzig custom. The programme of the series held in 1700[5] reveals their character. The first (Trinity XXV) opened with a 'Sonata ariosa', followed by a Halleluja 'cum tubis et timpanis', Psalms 96 and 98, and four stanzas of the hymn 'Allein Gott in der Höh' sei Ehr' '. On the second (Trinity XXVI) a 'Dancklied' was rendered by soli and chorus, followed by an Aria and the hymn 'Erhalt mir Leib und Leben'. On the third

---

[1] Mattheson, p. 94, describes the visit.
[2] She was born in 1675, the fourth of seven daughters (Stahl, p. 38).
[3] David, p. 57.   [4] Stahl, p. 58.   [5] Stiehl, p. 173.

(Advent II) Psalm 124 was followed by a cantata and the hymn 'Es wolle Gott uns gnädig sein'. On the fourth (Advent III) a hymn opened the service, which also included a 'Winterlied' and the hymn 'O Vater aller Frommen'. On the fifth (Advent IV) a 'Jubiläum oder Hundertjähriges Gedicht' was rendered. The music was performed upon a scale and amid popular interest to which Bach and his native Thuringia were not accustomed. Some forty instrumentalists besides the choir participated, and were accommodated in the side galleries whose balustraded fronts are visible high on the north and south walls of the nave.[1] The singers, provided by the Catharinenschule, were the regular choir of the church.[2] The programme for 1705 has not survived, but on Wednesday, December 2, an 'extraordinaire Abend-Music' was held in memory of the Emperor Leopold I, when Buxtehude's 'Castrum doloris' was sung, and on the following day the newly elected Kaiser Joseph I was acclaimed in that composer's 'Templum honoris'. On the first occasion the church was hung with funeral trappings, and the trombones, trumpets, and strings were decorously muted. So large an attendance was expected to view the funeral pomp, that two corporals and eighteen privates controlled the two doors that admitted the congregation.[3] Undoubtedly Bach was present on both occasions.

The Lübeck visit is of high importance in the development of Bach's genius. It confirmed impressions formed at Lüneburg, and gave him a conception of music's relation to public worship which never left him, an ideal tardily realized at Leipzig. In frequent contact with Buxtehude[4] he found a powerful stimulus and great example. His brother had taught him Pachelbel's idiom, Böhm had added his own technique, and Buxtehude furnished a third ingredient to the crucible whence Bach's originality emerged. Not infrequently, we may be sure, he played where Handel and Mattheson had played before him, at the console behind the organ façade splendidly poised above the western arch of the Marienkirche, receiving the commendation and advice of one whose genius was touched by the poetic fire that lit his own. In this stimulating intercourse the weeks sped unheeded. November turned to December, December to January, before Bach set his face reluctantly homewards. Halting at Hamburg, where Reinken was still in harness, and at Lüneburg, where Böhm awaited him with a welcome,

---

[1] Stahl, pp. 17, 59. See the picture, No. 29. [2] *Ibid.*, p. 61. [3] *Ibid.*, p. 69.
[4] Forkel's (p. 15) incredible statement, that Bach did not make himself known to Buxtehude, was founded on the word *behorchen* in the Nekrolog, meaning 'to listen secretly'.

he was in Arnstadt by the end of January 1706, with less pride and anticipation, it may be, than at his first coming three years before.[1]

The congregation found instant opportunity to judge that their young organist, remote on his lofty seat, had returned with new virtuosity of disturbing power. Bach now accompanied the Chorals with an exaggerated freedom that closed the mouths of the congregation, groping blindly for the melody among his coruscations, or stupefied by the audacity of his improvisation between the verses. Remonstrance proving futile, authority was invoked, and on 21 February 1706 Bach again visited Schloss Neideck to confront the Consistorium. The minute of the meeting is among the Consistorial archives at Sondershausen; its endorsement tersely declares the grounds of summons:

'Joh. Sebastian Bach, organist of the New Church, summoned to explain his prolonged absence and discontinuance of figural music. 1706.'

Superintendent Johann Christoph Olearius presided and conducted the examination:

Olearius: The Consistorium desires to know where you have been for so long, and who gave you leave of absence.

Bach: I have been to Lübeck to study my profession, and before I went, Herr Superintendent, I asked your permission.

Olearius: That is so; but you said you would be away four weeks and have been absent four months. What explanation do you offer?

Bach: I thought my deputy would satisfactorily fill my place, and consequently that no complaint would be made.

Olearius: Complaints have been made to the Consistorium that you now accompany the hymns with surprising variations and irrelevant ornaments, which obliterate the melody [2] and confuse the congregation. If you desire to introduce a theme against the melody[3], you must go on with it and not immediately fly off to another. And in no circumstances must you introduce a *tonus contrarius*.[4]

There is another matter: we are surprised that you have given up performing figural music, and conclude that the omission is due to your bad relations with the pupils of the Gymnasium. We must therefore ask you to tell us explicitly that you are prepared to practise them in figural music

---

[1] On 24 Feb. 1706 he signed at Arnstadt a receipt for 6 gulden, 3 groschen, 3 pfennige due to him from the church funds 'zum Quartahl Reminiscere' (2nd Sunday in Lent). The amount is less only by a few groschen than the sums he acknowledged on 26 March, 15 Sept., and 15 Dec. 1706. It may therefore be assumed that he had earned a full month's pay on 24 Feb. 1706. These four documents have recently been found in the Arnstadt Rathsarchiv. Through the kindness of Pastor Hoppe I was able to inspect them. Bi. i. 82 prints another receipt dated 28 June 1707. An unpublished receipt (in the Sondershausen Staatsarchiv), dated 15 June 1707, acknowledges 18 gulden, 15 gr., 9 pfg. due from the previous 16 Sept. 1706 (Loses Blatt, No. 18).

[2] 'in dem Choral viele wunderliche Variationes gemachet, viele fremde Thöne mit eingemischet'.

[3] 'tonus peregrinus'.   [4] *i.e.* conflicting with the melody.

as well as in the hymns. We cannot provide a Cantor, and you must tell us categorically, yes or no, whether you will do what we require. If you will not, we must find an organist who will.

Bach had been posed with the same question six months earlier,[1] before he left for Lübeck, and repeated the answer he gave then: he would do what was asked of him, provided a 'Director Musices' was appointed. His contumacy was not due solely to obstinacy. His career shows him meticulously careful to insist that the conditions of his employment were observed by those he served. In the present case he could point to the minute of his appointment to support his refusal to train his choir in concerted music. Moreover, he had no official connexion with the Gymnasium, whence his singers were drawn, and could reasonably contend, in accordance with custom elsewhere, that since both the Oberkirche and Neukirche drew their choirs from the same fund of singers, the musician who trained for the former church should now train for both. The Consistorium was evidently disinclined to take extreme measures against its brilliant but provoking organist. After a consultation with his colleagues, Olearius gave their decision: Bach might take a week to reflect on the matter.

Bach's place at the table of correction was taken by Johann Andreas Rambach,[2] Chorpräfect under him at the New Church and tale-bearer against him to the Consistorium. Invited to explain the uncordial relations of Bach and his singers, Rambach either could not or dared not say more than that Bach preludized at too great length before the hymns, and, after being reprimanded by Olearius, had gone to the other extreme. He was reminded that Bach had complained about his conducting, that he had slipped out of the organ gallery to visit the 'Schwarzburger Hof', or another beer-house, during the preceding Sunday's sermon, and was admonished to behave better in future under penalty of forfeiting his emolument as Prefect. If he had complaints to prefer against his organist he was ordered to do so in a constitutional manner. Meanwhile, he was condemned to 'carcer' for two hours on four successive days, and the Rector received instruction to execute the sentence. Rambach probably was an offensive bully, but his relations with Bach, along with the Geyersbach incident, unmistakably indicate that Bach's association with those with whom he worked was uncordial.

For more than half a year Bach's life at Arnstadt passes without

---

[1] In connexion with the Geyersbach inquiry.
[2] Sp. i. 314 finds Johann Andreas Rambach employed in the Neukirche in 1705 'wegen Choral-singens'.

recorded incident. He neither made the submission demanded by
the Consistorium nor obeyed their instructions to rehearse his
choir. With the inexorable concentration of purpose that distinguished him he devoted himself absorbingly to the organ. Fired
by Buxtehude, his pen, too, was busy.[1] His uncommon abilities
were noised abroad, and from more than one quarter invitations to
leave his present employment were received.[2] He had, in fact,
already exhausted the opportunities Arnstadt afforded him. Meanwhile, the Consistorium reminded him of its recent orders, and on
11 November 1706[3] summoned him to another interview. He was
reproved for his persistent neglect to rehearse his choir, and received an imperative order to do so or take the consequences. As
before, he neither promised nor would discuss the matter; he
undertook to reflect upon it and give his answer in writing. He
was, indeed, contemplating the resignation of his office, and the
Consistorium's interference in another matter clinched his resolution—he was asked to explain the presence in his organ-gallery
of 'die fremde Jungfer', whose voice had been heard in the empty
church as he practised. The offending singer was his cousin Maria
Barbara Bach, granddaughter of old Heinrich and daughter of his
gifted son Michael of Gehren (d. 1694). Her mother, an Arnstadt
woman, Catharina Wedemann, was daughter of a former town
clerk; her death in 1704 probably brought back Maria Barbara to
her maternal relatives, if indeed her mother had not returned to
Arnstadt after her husband's death ten years earlier.[4] The cousins
met before Bach visited Lübeck, and on his return acquaintance
warmed to affection, a mutual inclination notable because, notwithstanding Bach clannishness, theirs is the only established instance of intermarriage between two of their stock; noteworthy,
too, because it united Bach with the only Bach sept boasting
musicians whose genius could be set beside his own. The grand-
daughter of Heinrich and daughter of Michael cannot have been
without talent beyond the ordinary; we can measure its dimensions
in the fact that she bore her husband the most gifted of his sons.[5]

Though gossiping interest in his private relationships determined
Bach to seek an appointment elsewhere, more fundamental reasons

---

[1] For a list of his compositions at this period see Forkel, p. 154. Cf. Sp. i. 315;
Grace, p. 14; Pirro (3), p. 28.
[2] Forkel, p. 15.   [3] Weissgerber, p. 10.
[4] The cousin who accompanied Bach at the time of the Geyersbach fracas may
have been Maria Barbara herself.
[5] Before the Consistorium raised the matter, Bach had spoken to the Prediger
of the Neukirche, Justus Christian Uthe, regarding his cousin's visits to the
church while he was practising.

weighed with him. He had been drawn to Arnstadt by the imperative desire to obtain an organ of his own, to secure the opportunity to perfect himself. With rare exceptions he had composed organ music only. He had taken a long leave of his duties to put himself under Buxtehude at Lübeck, and in face of authority had refused to function except as an organist. But the letter in which he resigned his position at Mühlhausen in 1708 is eloquent of his conviction of a call to dedicate his whole art to the service and glory of God. He returned from Lübeck with that conviction fortified, and conveniently an opportunity presented itself to find his 'vocation' elsewhere, with resources more considerable and in an atmosphere apparently removed from the annoyances which of late had disturbed him.

The death of Johann Georg Ahle, on 2 December 1706, deprived the Kirche Divi Blasii [1] of Mühlhausen of a distinguished musician and organist. The appointment of his successor rested with the 'conventus parochianorum', a committee of resident parishioners, Ratsherren (members of the civic Council), who for the selection of candidates nominated a quota of their number, the confirmation of their choice lying with the Council itself. Whether Bach was invited to compete, or came forward spontaneously, cannot be decided. Johann Ernst, applying for the vacant post in the Neukirche, stated that the Mühlhausen organ had been 'offered' to his cousin,[2] and the fact that Bach fulfilled his 'Probe' so late as Easter Day (24 April) 1707 supports him; for the delay and the prominence of the occasion indicate that he was called after other candidates had been rejected. A month later (24 May), when the 'conventus parochianorum' met in the church to make the appointment, Bürgermeister (*dominus senior consul*) Dr. Conrad Meckbach at once proposed Bach's name;[3] none other was suggested, and Herr Bellstedt was instructed to communicate with him. Six days later (30 May) a catastrophic fire almost involved the church in ruin. Besides stables, outhouses, and other minor buildings, nearly four hundred dwellings were laid in ashes; even two weeks later some of the signatories to Bach's appointment declared that they lacked pen and ink wherewith to append their signatures, and had been too shocked by the event to focus their minds on other topics.[4]

---

[1] St. Blaise or Blasius, bishop of Sebaste or Sivas, martyred under Diocletian in 316, was especially venerated in Roman Catholic Germany, where his Festival was observed on 3 February.
[2] 'My cousin has had the vacant post of organist in the famous Kirche Divi Blasii offered to him and [nach erhaltener Vocation] has accepted it' (Sp. i. 332).
[3] The minute describes him as 'N. Pachen von Arnstadt'.
[4] Thiele, p. 64.

In such depressing conditions Bach came to Mühlhausen on 14 June 1707 and was invited by Herren Gottfried Stüler, A. E. Reiss, and Johann Georg Stephan to state the terms on which he would accept the appointment. He asked for the sum he was receiving at Arnstadt and begged a wagon for the conveyance of his goods and chattels therefrom. That he demanded no more was due to the fact that his salary largely exceeded that of his predecessor Ahle,[1] an old and honoured member of the Rath. His terms were accepted with an alacrity that testifies to the negotiators' eagerness to secure him, and on the following day (15 June 1707) his commission was signed and sealed:[2]

We, the assembled parishioners, burgomasters, and councillors of the Parish of St. Blaise in the Free Imperial City of Mühlhausen, herewith make known: Whereas the office of organist in the said church is vacant through the demise of our late colleague Herr Johann Georg Ahle, and so falls to be filled, we have appointed Herr Joh. Sebastian Bach, presently of the Bonifaciuskirche, Arnstadt, to hold the said office in the said church of St. Blaise, requiring him to be faithful and courteous to those in authority therein, to have at heart the welfare of our city and contribute thereto, show himself willing in the fulfilment of his duties, and in especial conscientious and regular in their execution on Sundays, feast-days, and other appointed occasions, maintaining the organ committed to him in good repair, reporting to the Overseer[3] such blemishes as may appear therein, and aiding him in their correction. He shall, moreover, conduct himself discreetly, eschewing ill company and persons of bad repute. Now, seeing that the said Herr Bach has pledged himself by the shaking of hands to observe the conditions above written, we do hereby agree to pay him a yearly revenue of 85 gulden in money, with the following allowances:
    3 measures of corn,
    2 trusses of wood, one of beech, one of oak or aspen,
    6 trusses of faggots, delivered at his door, in lieu of arable.
In witness whereof these presents are executed under the affixed seal of the Chancery.
    Given this 15th day of June 1707.
L.S. Eingepfarrte bey der Keyserlich freien und des heiligen Reiches Stadt Mühlhausen.

Returning to Arnstadt, Bach visited the Rathaus a fortnight later (29 June 1707) to announce his appointment, acknowledged the Council's generous provision for him, and begged permission to surrender the key of his organ. His resignation, formally

---

[1] Ahle received 66 gulden, 14 groschen (Sp. i. 333).
[2] Mühlhausen Stadtarchiv: Akten betr. Organistenstelle D. Blasii 1604–1764. The minutes of 24 May, 14 June, and 15 June are in Thiele, p. 63; Bi. iv. 88; Sp. i. 851; Jordan, p. 30.
[3] On the analogy of Leipzig use the Vorsteher was a Ratsherr specially charged with the concerns of the church.

accepted in July, took effect at Crucis (14 September).[1] On a day in early autumn the promised wagon from Mühlhausen stood at his door in the Holzmarkt, received his clavicembalo, moderate store of books and furniture, and carried them and their owner northward. The lofty roof of the Bonifaciuskirche and the pointing spear of the Schlossthurm sank slowly out of view, while Love and Hope beckoned confidently ahead.

At the age of twenty-two Bach became the subject of a Free Imperial City,[2] whose dignity the turmoil of the seventeenth century had somewhat impaired. It stood picturesque within its cincture of turreted walls, ancient flanking towers, and deep-sunk moat, a city of narrow tortuous streets, of houses with timbered fronts and gaudy corniced gables, high above whose roofs three great churches[3] dominate the prospect. Most northerly, upon the ancient Steinweg that pierces the city east and west, stands the noble Marienkirche, where once was set a Romanesque Basilica. We thread a narrow alley to the south of it, cross the Jewry, and on the Kornmarkt face a huge brick fabric, the Franciscan Barfüsserkirche or Kornmarktkirche. Southward of it, at a short distance, on the Untermarkt, stands the Kirche Divi Blasii,[4] with which Bach was now associated, dignified and comely under its twin spires. Its interior offers substantially the picture Bach saw from his organ-loft, approached, as now, by a circular stairway in the northern tower under groined and grimy vaulting. The organ is on the western wall, within a gallery of moderate accommodation supported by the two westernmost pillars of the nave.[5] Eastward the chancel is visible through the sturdy pillars of the nave, which rise to the roof unencumbered with galleries.[6] Beyond the wrought-iron screen, more than half a century old when Bach viewed it, a massive gilt reredos over the altar-piece displays the coronation of Our Lady. Carved stalls of medieval workmanship decorate the chancel on either hand, and ancient glass diffuses a reverent light, fills the windows of the nave, and from a rose-window floods the transept with a ruby glow. A splendid fane, whose beauty appealed

---

[1] The minute of 29 June 1707 is in Bi. i. 82. The formal acceptance of Bach's resignation is not recorded, but an undated subsequent minute (*ibid.*, p. 83) proves that it was tendered in July and that he sacrificed a portion of his salary for the period 29 June–14 September (Quartal Crucis) to his cousin Johann Ernst, his successor. It may be assumed that he took office at Mühlhausen as from 15 Sept. 1707.   [2] Illus. No. 30.
[3] The following churches also existed in 1707: St. Jakobi, St. Kiliani, St. Nikolai, St. Petri, St. Georgii, and St. Martini.   [4] Illus. No. 31.
[5] The front of the gallery to-day exhibits heraldic panels, on one of which Bach's name and seal are emblazoned. See a representation of the latter in the illustration, No. 76.   [6] Illus. No. 32.

vividly to its young organist after the barren Bonifaciuskirche, a
fitting temple in which to dedicate his new resolve!

Mühlhausen boasted high musical traditions, from which it
had somewhat degenerated before Bach's arrival. Joachim Müller
(à Burgk), eminent among the early Protestant composers, was
organist of Divi Blasii and the Marienkirche during the second half
of the sixteenth century, and died here in 1610. Ludwig Helmbold,
the admired hymn-writer, his contemporary, was Pastor of Divi
Blasii (*d.* 1598). Johannes Eccard (*d.* 1611), a prolific composer,
was a native of the city, and Georg Neumark (*d.* 1681), author of
hymns beloved by the German people, spent his youth here. For
more than fifty years before Bach's coming the organ-loft of Divi
Blasii was occupied by two native-born musicians, Johann Rodolph
Ahle, and his son Johann Georg Ahle, Bach's immediate predecessor, whose art preferred the sacred Aria with instrumental *ritor-
nelli* to the Cantata form the North German musicians were
bringing to maturity. Aware of the backwardness of his new public
in their recognition of the seemly association of music and worship,
Bach, as the letter declares in which he sought his demission, made
its instruction his major purpose. Though the church was equipped
with a Cantor to select and provide 'music', and in marked
contrast with his behaviour at Arnstadt, Bach was indefatigable
in copying manuscripts to replace the Ahles' less adventurous
repertory, aided by Johann Martin Schubart, the earliest of his
many distinguished pupils, and Johann Sebastian Koch, his Choir
Prefect.[1]

Meanwhile, domestic events delayed his high purpose. On
10 August 1707, shortly before he began his duties at Mühlhausen, his maternal uncle Tobias Lämmerhirt died at Erfurt.[2]
Probably he was not intimately known to his dead sister's scattered
family; but they were his most immediate kin, and his will devised
to each of them fifty gulden, a sum considerably more than half
Bach's annual stipend. Gratitude and respect for his mother's only
close relative commanded his presence at the funeral, and it has
been suggested[3] that Cantata 106, 'Gottes Zeit ist die allerbeste
Zeit', was composed for and sung at his uncle's Gedächtnispredigt.
The libretto, austere, Biblical, and similar in character to others
of the Mühlhausen period, supports the hypothesis, though the
music exhibits a maturity that separates it by an immense interval

[1] J. G. Walther, *Musicalisches Lexikon* (1732), *sub voc.* 'J. M. Schubart', 'J. S.
Koch'. Walther perhaps received his information from Bach at Weimar.
[2] The will, made on 1 Aug. 1707, was read on 18 Sept. 1707. It is printed in full
in B.-J. 1925, p. 122.　　　　　　　　　　[3] Pirro (1), p. 87.

from the Arnstadt anthem. Substantial and convenient, the legacy aided Bach to give his household the mistress for whom it waited. Accordingly, the Seventeenth Sunday after Trinity found him once again in Arnstadt. On the morrow (17 October 1707), with his bride and a few friends, he took the old Marktweg that rises steeply from the town, and, traversing the yellow stubble fields, reached the little village of Dornheim, whose Pastor, Johann Lorenz Stauber, married Maria Barbara's aunt Regina Wedemann a few months later. Bach had known him as a theological student in Arnstadt, and presumably it was as the bridegroom's friend that Stauber tied the knot in his own church.[1] Bach's recent relations with the Arnstadt clergy made his services the more agreeable.

Dornheim church,[2] quaint and irregular without, shows itself within an unpretentious, white-walled village Predigerkirche, its galleries supported by rough-hewn wooden pillars, with here and there a glass-fronted *loge* for those in authority. The effigy of a sixteenth-century knight, incongruous with its bare surroundings, faced Bach as he stood before the altar, made his vow 'in the presence of this Christian congregation', and heard the timid 'Ja' of his bride. Rings were exchanged, and the solemn injunction was given, 'Was Gott zusammen füget, soll kein Mensch scheiden'.[3] The registers of Dornheim and Arnstadt record the event:

On 17 October 1707 the worthy Johann Sebastian Bach, bachelor, organist of the church of Divi Blasii, Mühlhausen, lawfully begotten son of the deceased honourable and distinguished Ambrosius Bach, town's organist and musician of Eisenach, to the virtuous Maria Barbara, spinster, youngest surviving daughter of the late right worthy and distinguished Michael Bach, organist at Gehren, here in the house of God, by permission of his lordship the Count, and after banns duly called at Arnstadt.[4]

Evening found the young couple returned to Arnstadt, where, we suppose, Regina Wedemann entertained them. Erfurt and the cousins there were visited on the short honeymoon, and before another Sunday came round they were in their own home.[5] Research has failed to determine its location. Tradition places it in the northern suburb of Margaretan, behind the Haarwand,[6] outside the medieval walls and remote from the Unterstadt, where Bach's duty lay. So much of that part of the town had been laid in ruins by the recent fire, that the inconveniently distant lodging is not improbable.

[1] Bi. i. 84.   [2] Illus. Nos. 34 and 35.   [3] B.C.T., p. 531.
[4] See the facsimile in No. 36. The two registers differ slightly.
[5] A wedding 'Quodlibet' for S.A.T.B. and continuo, arranged by Bach for the occasion, was probably sung at Arnstadt or Erfurt. See *Music and Letters*, Jan. 1933.   [6] Jordan, p. 33.

Marriage, consecrating the high resolve with which Bach faced
his new office, launched him on a year of great activity. Looming
immediately ahead was a civic function which afforded opportunity
to prove his powers and demonstrate his purpose. A sovereign
member of the German Reich, Mühlhausen was governed by a
Council of six Burgomasters and forty-two Ratsherren, a total of
forty-eight, divided into three bodies of sixteen (two Burgomasters
and fourteen Ratsherren), each of which, holding office for a year,
inaugurated its period with a service in the Marienkirche, the seat
of the Ratstuhl, where a sermon was preached and special music
was performed. For the ceremony in 1708 Georg Christian Eilmar,
Archidiakonus in Mühlhausen and Pastor of the Marienkirche,
provided a libretto which Bach set to music in a style that exhibits
Buxtehude's influence[1], embellished by his own audacious mastery.
The manuscript of the score[2] attests the care he devoted to a work
given with resources and pomp till now unfamiliar in his experience. The invariable petition 'Jesu Juva' heads the title 'Gott ist
mein König', whose capitals are emphasized with elaborate flour-
ishes, while a tail-piece of intricate design stands below the indication 'de l'anno 1708. da Gio: Bast: Bach Org: Molhusino'. On
4 February 1708 the work was performed with civic circumstance
within the Marienkirche[3] in the presence of Herren Adolph Strecker
and Georg Adam Steinbach, the two Burgomasters, and their
fourteen colleagues. Aloft in the gallery above the western porch,
so much more spacious than that of St. Blaise's, Bach directed his
forces, while the organist of the Marienkirche, for whom the composer provided a figured continuo, was at his instrument.[4] The
brilliant and glittering trumpets acclaiming 'das neue Regiment'
and Kaiser Joseph would have the greater effect upon an audience
whom the Ahles had accustomed to music of another style. The
publication of its parts was voted, and was accomplished in pri-
mitive type[5] which declares the ravages of the recent fire. It is
the only one of Bach's cantatas that got itself into print in his
lifetime.

[1] It is visible in the florid treatment of the Choral melody in the second movement, in the division of the orchestra into four 'choirs', in the choice of the word
'Motetto' to describe the work, and of 'capella' to indicate the full chorus.
[2] Now in the Preuss. Staatsbibliothek, Berlin.   [3] Illus. No. 33.
[4] The movements in which a figured continuo alone supports the voices are
absent from the organ part, a fact which suggests that Bach himself accompanied
them on a clavier.
[5] Jordan, p. 35. The Mühlhausen Stadtbibliothek possesses the libretti of other
'Rathswechselcantaten' so distinguished, but not the music, from which it may
be inferred that Bach's work received particular consideration. He again conducted the 'Ratskantate' on 5 February 1709, and received his travelling expenses

Encouraged by the goodwill surrounding him, Bach approached his masters regarding his organ, in which he discovered defects whose remedy he desired. A fortnight after the inauguration of the new Council, the 'conventus parochianorum' met (21 February 1708) in the Rathaus under the presidency of Bürgermeister Conrad Meckbach, who had proposed Bach's election in the previous summer.[1] He now presented on his behalf a report on the organ prepared by him, a document[2] of interest, since, though the proposed specification was largely based upon that of the St. Georgenkirche organ at Eisenach,[3] with which his earliest memories were associated, it indicates Bach's preferences regarding his especial instrument, and his minute knowledge of the organ-builder's craft:

Specification of work to be done on the organ of St. Blaise's Church.

1. The present deficiency of wind-power needs to be corrected by the provision of three new and adequate bellows to feed the Oberwerk, Rückpositiv, and Brustwerk.[4]

2. The pressure on the four existing bellows must be increased, so as to allow the new 32 ft. Sub-Bass [Untersatz] and the lower pipes of the other stops to speak.

3. The existing soundboards of all the Bass stops will have to be removed and new ones introduced, of such capacity that, no matter whether one or more stops are sounding, there shall be no unsteadiness in the tone, an important quality which the existing system does not provide.

4. To give a foundation of tone, a 32 ft. Sub-Bass [Untersatz] must be put in, with a sound-board of its own.

5. The Bass Posaune requires new and larger *corpora*, and the embouchures of the pipes must be reshaped so as to produce more sonorous volume.

6. A new carillon of twenty-six bells of 4 ft. tone on the Pedals, desired by the parishioners and to be provided at their cost, must be introduced by the organ-builder.[5]

7. The Tromba on the upper manual must be replaced by a 16 ft. Fagotto, whose introduction will permit many new combinations of tone and the more delicate accompaniment of figural music.

from Weimar. Probably the cantata of the previous year was repeated. There is no trace of a new composition at Mühlhausen, Dr. Brinkmann informs me.
[1] The minutes are in Bi. i. 86; iv. 91; Sp. i. 853; Thiele, p. 65.
[2] Mühlhausen Stadtarchiv: Akten betr. Organistenstelle D. Blasii 1604–1764.
[3] Herr Hans Löffler is responsible for this statement. Cf. B.-J., 1925, p. 100.
[4] Oberwerk means literally the upper keyboard, or Great Organ. The Rückpositiv, or Choir Organ, was so called because its pipes were at the organist's back (Rücken). The Brustwerk took its name from the fact that its pipes faced the player. It may be regarded as equivalent to the Swell Organ, though its pipes were not in Bach's time enclosed in a box.
[5] It was never put in. Cf. Bi. i. 87.

8. The Gemshorn on the upper manual needs to be replaced by an 8 ft. Viola da Gamba, which will blend admirably with the 4 ft. Salicional on the Rückpositiv.

9. *Item*: the 3 ft. Quint should be replaced by a 3 ft. Nasard. All the other stops on the upper manual can be retained, as also those of the Rückpositiv, if they are revoiced during the repairs.

10. The Brustwerk, which is to be added, must have the following stops:

> 3 Principals placed on the front, namely, a 3 ft. Quint, a 2 ft. Octave, and an 8 ft. Schalmei, all of good tin of 14 loth.[1]
>
> A Mixture, 3 ranks.
>
> A Tertia, which in combination with other stops gives a fine Sesquialtera tone.
>
> A soft 4 ft. Flute, and lastly,
>
> An 8 ft. Stillgedackt, to fill in the continuo when accompanying figural music. If made of wood it will be more resonant than a metal Gedackt.

11. A coupler is needed between the Brustwerk and Oberwerk. Finally, the whole instrument must be revoiced and the Tremulant made to vibrate properly.

The parochial 'conventus' accepted Bach's report without amendment, and committed the work of reconstruction to J. F. Wender, already known to him as the builder of the Bonifaciuskirche organ at Arnstadt. Twenty years earlier Wender had repaired the St. Blaise organ, and now agreed to receive in part payment a small organ the enlarged instrument made unnecessary.[2] The work was put in hand at once, but before it was completed Bach had gone elsewhere. The fact is strange and noteworthy, that, holding the position of organist, he never had a three-manual instrument at his disposal. Meanwhile, his specification illustrates a characteristic of him which impressed his contemporaries. Forkel, who received the statement from Bach's sons,[3] remarks that his unconventional registration astonished organists and organ-builders alike, and was in large measure founded on intuitive recognition of the acoustics of the building in which he happened to be playing. He was therefore exacting in his requirements, severe and thorough in his tests, demanding from others the observation that distinguished himself. He was, moreover, so competent in the technique of the builder's craft that no defect escaped him. In testing an organ he first of all drew out all the stops, to discover, as he put it, whether the instrument had good lungs,[4] a quality in which many were deficient. Lack of wind-power was the principal defect he found in St. Blaise's organ. But his report on the instru-

---

[1] Of 14 parts pure to 2 alloy.
[2] This appears from the minute of 26 June 1708 recording Bach's resignation.
[3] Forkel, p. 64.
[4] *Ibid.*, p. 68.

ment is otherwise illuminating. He suggests a 16 ft. Fagotto in place of the Tromba on the Great, and the introduction of a Stillgedackt, a species of Bourdon, on the Brustwerk, advocating the first on the ground that the proposed stop 'in die Music sehr delicat klinget', and the second because the Stillgedackt 'volkommen zur Music accordieret'. Clearly, he desired to make his instrument efficient in the figural or concerted music his predecessors had neglected. The Contra-Fagotto's soft and 'delicate' tone would agreeably blend with the violone and other continuo instruments and be especially valuable when the organ filled in the harmonies above a figured Bass. The Stillgedackt promised to be similarly useful, providing an accompaniment of soft *sostenuto* tone for the flutes and oboes.[1]

Bach's attention to these details, and the terms of his valedictory letter, make it the more strange that, excepting 'Gott ist mein König', we cannot point to a single cantata of his as having been performed in the Mühlhausen churches. His pen was not inactive: the lost score of Cantata No. 131, 'Aus der Tiefe rufe ich, Herr', bore the statement in his autograph that it was composed at the request of Pastor Eilmar, who probably provided the libretto. Its occasion is not specified, but the words associate it with a service of public humiliation, perhaps the commemoration, on or near 30 May 1708, of the disastrous fire of the previous year.[2] A week later, on Tuesday, 5 June 1708, Bach and his wife probably visited Arnstadt for the wedding of Johann Lorenz Stauber, who had tied their own knot eight months earlier, to Regina Wedemann, from whose house Bach took his bride. A setting of Psalm cxv. 12–15, 'Der Herr denket an uns' (Cantata 196), scored for strings, organ, and continuo, suggests itself as having been composed for the occasion. If the conjecture is well founded, Bach himself took part in its performance.[3]

Notwithstanding the friendship of Eilmar and the confidence of the 'conventus parochianorum', Mühlhausen presented stubborn obstacles to the course upon which Bach's young enthusiasm was set. In the past generation there had arisen within the Lutheran body a reaction against dogmatic formularies which usurped the authority Luther conceded to the Bible alone, against

[1] Cf. Pirro (3), p. 78.
[2] This seems to me a more probable date than Wustmann's choice of August 1707, which I adopted in B.C.T., p. 551.
[3] Stauber's first wife, Anna Sophie Hoffmann, died at Dornheim on 8 June 1707; he married her on 28 Feb. 1688 when Pfarrer of Rudisleben near Arnstadt. His father, Justin Stauber, or Staubert, was a glover in Arnstadt. Regina Wedemann (*b.* 19 Sept. 1660) was the daughter of Johannes Wedemann, sometime town clerk of Arnstadt.

a Church which had become creed-bound and sacramentarian. The dissidents received the name Pietist, whose direct originator, Philipp Jakob Spener (d. 1705), preached a moral and religious reformation and achieved a spiritual revival which surged over northern and central Germany, but encountered stalwart opposition from orthodox Lutherans who set greater store on authoritative doctrine than the Christian life. In Mühlhausen these divisions were accentuated by the public and acrimonious contentions of its clergy, and perhaps by an inherited disposition to indulge in religious controversy: during the Reformation the town was notorious as a stronghold of Anabaptism, whose leader, Thomas Münzer, indeed, was executed within its walls. Johann Adolph Frohne, Pastor of St. Blaise's and Superintendent in Mühlhausen since 1691, had long been working under Spener's influence to wean his people from the excessive formalism of the orthodox Confession.

With the coming of Georg Christian Eilmar to the Marienkirche in 1699 [1] opposition to Pietism, whipped into action, engaged the pulpits of the two churches in so acrimonious a warfare that the Council imposed a veto upon their fulminations. But while Bach was in office the wordy duel broke out afresh, and involved him in its consequences. Brought up at Ohrdruf and Lüneburg on the purest milk of Lutheran orthodoxy, he was naturally drawn to Eilmar, who, notwithstanding an austerity his libretti reveal, was no opponent of music's place in public worship. A younger man than Frohne by thirteen years, he attracted Bach on that ground also, and retained his friendship when they ceased to be associates. Yet Bach's genius, as his music reveals it, was closer to Frohne, his own Pastor, and his simple piety had much in common with a school of religion which put faith before formalism, though he deplored the Puritan severity which ruled out art from the adornments of the Sanctuary. For Art was the lode-star of his young life, and, as the conviction grew that Mühlhausen denied it the avenue he demanded, he accepted with characteristic decision an opportune invitation to Weimar. On 25 June 1708, almost exactly a year since he penned a similar missive at Arnstadt, he indited a letter of resignation to his Mühlhausen employers: [2]

Your Magnificence,[3] noble and learned gentlemen, my gracious patrons and masters,

With dutiful gratitude I acknowledge my obligation to your Magnificence, and my other honoured patrons, for the office of organist in the

---

[1] Sp. i. 354 elucidates the relations of the two men.
[2] Mühlhausen Stadtarchiv: Akten betr. Organistenstelle D. Blasii 1604–1764.
[3] Bürgermeister Conrad Meckbach.

church of St. Blaise that became vacant a year ago, and for the enlarged emolument attached thereto. It has been my constant aim to accord with your desire that church music should be so performed as to exalt God's glory, and, as far as my humble ability has allowed, I have assisted that purpose also in the villages, where the taste for music is growing, and in whose churches its performance not infrequently excels our own.[1] Moreover, without regard to the cost, I have got together from various sources far and near a select collection of sacred Stücke, have dutifully submitted a report on the deficiencies in the organ which call for repair, and in all manners and times have cheerfully fulfilled the tasks incidental to my office. But I have not been allowed to do my work without opposition, and there does not seem to be the least *apparence*[2] that it will abate, though, in time, perhaps some of our church's congregation may be brought to approve. Moreover, if I may say so respectfully, frugal as is my household, I have not enough to live on, having regard to my rental and needful *consumption*.

God has been pleased, however, to open to me an unexpected situation, a more adequate *subsistence*, and the opportunity to pursue the object which concerns me most, the betterment of church music, free from the opposition and vexations encountered here: His Serene Highness the Duke of Sachsen-Weimar has been graciously pleased to give me the *entrée* to his Capelle as one of his chamber musicians.

I convey this information to you, most gracious patrons, with humble and profound respect, begging your generous permission to retire, and that you will *respect* indulgently the services I have rendered. If in the future I can be further useful to your church, I can promise, so long as life is granted me, to show my willingness in deeds no less than words.

Most honoured sir, most gracious patrons and gentlemen,

Your most obedient servant,

Joh. Seb. Bach.

Mühlhausen, 25 June *an.* 1708.

A submissive memorial to the honourable and distinguished parochial councillors of St. Blaise's.

Courteous and temperate in its reference to past difficulties and controversies, Bach's letter closed the door upon any reconsideration of his resolve; his employers could not alter the conditions which impeded his work, nor did he invite it. On the following day (26 June 1708) Bürgermeister Meckbach communicated his letter to the 'conventus parochianorum', in whose formal minute[3] lurks an evident note of regret: 'Since his mind is made up, consent to his departure is necessarily accorded.' In offering his future services Bach had in mind the unfinished organ, whose enlargement had been undertaken at his desire. His resignation was therefore

---

[1] Spitta (Sp. i. 340) found the incomplete copy of one of Bach's cantatas among the Cantor's music at Langula, near Mühlhausen.

[2] As was customary in his period, Bach's letters are full of words of foreign derivation, technical import, or uncolloquial usage, which he distinguishes by the Latin script. To reproduce him minutely in this habit would be irritating: *e.g.* to italicize *organist*. But definitely non-German words employed by him are so distinguished. [3] Bi. i. 93.

conditioned by the stipulation that he should continue to superintend the work, a task which the neighbourhood of Weimar rendered easy and convenient. The renovated instrument was ready
in 1709, when Bach came over from Weimar for the annual Ratswahl service to display its powers in a Prelude on the appropriate
melody 'Ein' feste Burg', in which he registered the new Fagotto
stop for the left hand, on the upper manual, and Sesquialtera tone
(produced by the new Tertia) for the right.[1]

The friction which attended Bach's departure from Arnstadt
a year before was not repeated at Mühlhausen, and there are
evident proofs that he and his wife took with them to Weimar the
regard of those from whom they parted. Friedemann Meckbach[2]
and Frau Anna Dorothea Hagedorn stood godparents to their
eldest boy at Weimar.[3] And a quarter of a century later, when his
son Johann Gottfried Bernhard was a candidate for the organistship of the Marienkirche, Bach recalled and acknowledged the
favours he had himself received. Meanwhile, the modest household behind the Haarwand was dismantled, and Bach, his wife,
and apprentice, J. M. Schubart[4], took the road to Weimar. As at
Arnstadt, the post he vacated was filled by a cousin: on 4 July 1708
Johann Friedrich Bach, son of Johann Christoph Bach of Eisenach,
was appointed to the Divi Blasiikirche in his room, but not at his
stipend; it reverted significantly to the Ahle standard.[5]

[1] The Prelude is in B.-G. XL. 57; P. Bk, 245, 58; Aug. iv. 926; Novello ed.
xviii. 30. Its use on the occasion is conjectural but probable.
[2] Sp. i. 354 names him Meckbach; Bojanowski, p. 33, Weckbach. The
Weimar Taufregister confirms the latter, as I am informed by Pfarrer Otto
Michaelis. But the Taufregister is in error. Friedemann Meckbach was the
son of Bürgermeister Conrad Meckbach and died unmarried at Meiningen as
Cammerrat in 1731. He bequeathed his valuable library to Mühlhausen, where
it is still preserved. I am indebted to Dr. Ernst Brinkmann, Archivar and
Bibliothekar, Mühlhausen, for the information.
[3] Sp. i. 354 mentions a book once in Bach's possession which was a gift from
one of the Oehme family at Mühlhausen.
[4] According to Walther's *Musicalisches Lexikon*, Schubart (b. 1690) was with
Bach for the ten years 1707-17.
[5] Bi. iv. 92.

CHAPTER V

WEIMAR

WEIMAR displays no worthy memorial of one whose association powerfully supports her claim to be a 'Kulturstadt'.
Goethe and Schiller stand conspicuous on their common pedestal;
their dwellings, and Wieland's too, are maintained with honourable
care, Meccas for the pious. Liszt names a street; Moltke and Bismarck also are remembered in the local nomenclature. Bach is
disregarded, obliterated by more recent memories. His dwelling-
house, in which his eldest son was born, still stands.[1] But the
palace in which he functioned is rubble beneath the Schloss Goethe
raised upon its charred ruins. Not even a street perpetuates his
memory, and visitors explore the town with guide-books that omit
his name. Yet, even had his career stopped at 1717, the work of
his Weimar years places him among the immortals. They announced him to his contemporaries as the foremost organist of his
period; they inspired his greatest compositions for the instrument
on which he excelled; they contributed some of the finest examples
of the Cantata form he developed to its zenith at Leipzig, and no
small amount of chamber music. Weimar received from him a
reputation for culture which Goethe, Schiller, and Liszt prolonged
but did not originate. Her insensitiveness to his association with
her casts a deep reproach on her community.

Bach came to Weimar to serve a prince of unusual seriousness
and high purpose. Wilhelm Ernst, Duke of Sachsen-Weimar,[2] was
conspicuous among the sovereigns of a period remarkable neither
for virtue, religion, nor philanthropic industry. Born in 1662, he
was under fifty when Bach returned to Weimar, a lonely, childless
man, separated from an uncongenial wife, looking out on his people
from the windows of the Schloss with a benevolent regard that
anticipated the enlightened despots of a later generation. The friction of circumstances estranged him from his nearest relative, his
brother Johann Ernst[3] (d. 1707); for an agreement compacted by
an earlier generation (19 March 1629), while it vested the executive
authority in the eldest brother or cousin, associated the younger
with him as co-ruler, with a consultative voice and representation
in the 'Gesammtcammer'. The arrangement worked uneasily, and

---

[1] See note 7, p. 115 *infra*.   [2] Illus. No. 44.   [3] Illus. No. 45.

withdrew Wilhelm Ernst more than ever to the solace of his individual tastes. Naturally pious, religion was his absorbing consola-
tion, his motto, 'Alles mit Gott'. As a boy of seven he had
exchanged his ducal seat for the pyramidal pulpit above the altar
in the Schloss chapel to preach (Ash Wednesday 1670) before
respectful courtiers a sermon[1] precociously prepared beneath the
eye of Hofprediger Conrad von der Lage, and subsequently printed
under the title *Der durchlauchtigste Prediger*. All his life the Schloss
chapel was the centre of the court's ceremonial. He performed his
devotions in it assiduously and required his suite to be as regular.
When he attended the Sunday Abendmahl he emerged from a
period of seclusion, and closely prescribed the order in which his
courtiers should communicate. Men of sober and serious habit
had his favour, and he delighted above others in the company of
his clergy, whom in 1710 he convened at a General Synod, in whose
deliberations he took part with zest. A general Visitation five years
later was conducted under his immediate direction. Holding a
middle course between orthodox zealotry and fanatic Pietism, he
curbed the acerbities of ecclesiastical controversy and ruled his
churchmen with Erastian firmness. He restored (1699) the rite of
Confirmation, which had fallen into desuetude for more than a
century, and imposed upon juveniles a thorough grounding in the
Catechism. Little interested in the larger politics of Germany, he
was as active in promoting the cultural well-being of his subjects
as his contemporary Friedrich Wilhelm I of Prussia. He rebuilt
the St. Jakobskirche in Weimar, founded a Home for Orphans, set
up a Seminar for probationers of the teaching and clerical pro-
fessions, converted the old Weimar school into the present Gymnasium, housed it in new buildings, and staffed it with masters of
distinction. Interested in old manuscripts and books, he founded
the fine ducal library, assembled and housed the public archives,
formed a collection of coins, in whose expansion he took lively
interest, and generally established a tradition of culture which
developed to the Augustan age of Goethe and Schiller. His birthday, 30 October, is still commemorated as 'Gross Wilhelmstag'.

The Puritan austerity of a court whose lights were extinguished
at eight in winter and nine in summer was relieved by occasional
and decorous relaxation. The exercises of the chase were not dis-
dained, and in his younger days Wilhelm Ernst maintained a company of comedians, whose dispersal synchronized with Bach's
arrival. On his accession to the duchy in 1683 he continued, though

[1] His text was Acts xvi. 31: 'Believe on the Lord Jesus Christ, and thou shalt
be saved, and thy house.' Cf. Marconnay, p. 13.

briefly, the traditions of his predecessor. On 28 December 1684 his wife's birthday was celebrated by the performance of an opera, 'Erlösete Treue und Unschuld', in the Garden House.[1] In 1696 a Schauplatz was contrived in the Schloss itself, where in 1697 Salomo Franck produced a dialogue play, 'Himmelaufflammende Wunschopfer'. Similar performances were given in the succeeding years, and, as the musical establishment for 1700 shows,[2] the Capelle was equipped accordingly. But, long before Bach came to Weimar, these performances had ceased, though occasions of special public interest, such as Prince Eugène's liberation of Temesvar in 1716, and the earlier battle of Blenheim in 1704, received musical celebration.[3] In 1706 the Duke built Lustschloss Ettersburg, where, in after years, Schiller finished his *Maria Stuart* and Goethe played 'Orestes' in his own *Iphigenie*. Wilhelm Ernst's entertainments were as 'classic' as their successors, but music rather than drama attracted him. While other princes beggared their treasuries to secure exorbitant *prime donne*, he latterly was content to support a court orchestra, uniformed in the hussar habit,[4] which discoursed Italian and other music in the ducal apartments and took part on Sundays and festival occasions in the services within the Schloss Chapel. Bach shared his master's lack of interest in stage music, and looked forward to receiving from him the warmest support in the great purpose which had carried him so hopefully into Mühlhausen and so despondingly out of it.[5]

An atmosphere of artistic culture was round the neighbouring Gelbes Schloss,[6] where, since Duke Johann Ernst's death in 1707, his widow Dorothea Sophie lived with her two sons, Ernst August and Johann Ernst. The latter, talented as a player and composer, died prematurely in 1715.[7] The elder, Ernst August, born in 1688, came of age in April 1709, assumed his father's place as 'Mitregent', and consequently entered upon a relationship with his uncle so uncordial, that in 1724 the Family Law of 1629, cause of so

---

[1] The present Bibliothek, close to the Schloss.
[2] *Infra*, p. 91.   [3] Bojanowski, p. 19.
[4] 'in Heyduken-Habit gekleidete wohlabgerichtete Musicanten' (Sp. i. 377). The Heyducs, who occupied a particular district in Hungary, were famous as soldiers and were recruited as guards and servants by the higher officers and nobility. They wore the uniform of the Hungarian hussar, a busby or high cylindrical cloth cap, a jacket with heavy braiding, and a dolman or pelisse hanging from the left shoulder, with tight breeches and high boots. The name, character, and costume were widely copied by other countries. We must imagine Bach himself thus clothed. See the picture at p. 54 for such a livery as he probably wore. I am indebted for it to the kindness of Ministerial Councillor Dr. Norbert Kovács, of Budapest.
[5] For Ernst Wilhelm cf. *Allgem. deutsche Biographie*, vol. xliii, p. 195.
[6] Illus. Nos. 37–9.   [7] See *supra*, p. 57.

much bickering,[1] was abrogated. The closeness of Bach's relations with the younger brother has already been remarked.[2] With the elder, also, he stood in the relation of master to pupil,[3] and years later revisited Weimar from Leipzig to offer the homage of his music.[4] Not improbably he was involved in the discords which embroiled uncle and nephew, and his failure to secure the coveted post of Capellmeister in 1717 may in part be attributed to that fact.[5]

Round these august personages revolved a society cultured in art and letters, indifferent to the theological controversies which had withered Bach's ardent hopes at Mühlhausen. Eminent among the courtiers was Salomo Franck, since 1702 secretary of the Consistorium, Custodian of the ducal library, and Keeper of the collection of coins and medals. A man of deep piety, and a prolific hymn-writer, he was also the author of two volumes of Cantata libretti of superlative ability. Their mysticism, sincerity, and feeling for nature attracted Bach powerfully and probably drew him into close association with their author; after his appointment as Concertmeister in 1714 he made frequent use of them. Their earliest collaboration was in Cantata 31 for Easter Day 1715. Thenceforward till Bach's Weimar service ended, with a single exception, his extant Cantatas show him to have employed no other librettist.[6] The Duke possessed another poet in Hofadvocat Johann Christoph Lorber, whose merits had won him the laureate's crown from the Kaiser. Salomo Franck esteemed him highly, and his writings, notably his *Lob der edlen Music*, discover so true an appreciation of music that, despite a difference of forty years in their ages, it is impossible to doubt that he and Bach were acquainted; like Franck, he outlived Bach's residence in Weimar.[7] The reconstituted Gymnasium attracted scholars with whom, also, Bach associated agreeably. Johann Christoph Kiesewetter, his former master at Ohrdruf, was installed as its first Rector in 1712;[8]

[1] For the whole period of his brother's illness in 1707 Wilhelm Ernst never once visited or inquired regarding him. The two men were antipathetic in character. Dorothea Sophie writes to her elder son in 1705: 'Ew. Liebden papa in 4 Dagen nicht auss dem Bette kommen ist, der apetit ist auch gar schlecht, welches alles der starcke Sect und tabac verursachen'; and again in 1706: 'Seine Durchlaucht mein Herr sich auch wider incommodiret befunden weil er etwas mehres getrunken wie es wohl wehre nötig gewest' (Marconnay, pp. 11, 12, 25).
[2] *Supra*, p. 57.
[3] The ducal accounts for 1711–12 (Bi. iv. 96) contain the entry: '2 fl. 6 gr. an 1 Claffter Flossholtz [1 cord of floated timber] dem Organist Bachen pro Informatione desselben [Duke Ernst August] auf dem Clavier, 28 Juli 1711.'
[4] A reconstruction of his 'Was mir behagt'. See *infra*, p. 108.
[5] Spitta, Pirro, and other writers ignore Ernst August.
[6] B.C.T., p. 8.　　　　　　　　　　　　　[7] Bojanowski, p. 40.
[8] He succeeded Philipp Grossgebauer, for whose funeral in 1711 the 'Actus Tragicus' (Cantata 106) may have been composed. But see p. 76 *supra*.

he brought with him memories Bach would not be backward to recall. Three years later (1715) there came to the Gymnasium as Conrector[1] another scholar, with whom Bach renewed acquaintance heartily at Leipzig seventeen years later, Johann Matthias Gesner, a sincere lover of music and admirer of Bach's transcendent skill. In his own art also Bach found society agreeable and stimulating. In particular, Johann Gottfried Walther, since 1707 organist of the Stadtkirche, six months his senior in age and doubly linked with him by associations: his mother was a Lämmerhirt,[2] his first music teacher, Johann Bernhard Bach, organist of the Kaufmannskirche at Erfurt, his native town. Walther was a good player, sound teacher, and second only to Bach himself as a composer in the organ Choralvorspiel form, an example of which, on the melody 'Gott der Vater wohn uns bei', is printed as Bach's in the Peters and Bachgesellschaft editions.[3] Walther's name is chiefly remembered as the compiler of the earliest German dictionary of music, published under the title *Musicalisches Lexikon* at Leipzig in 1732, a work of great industry and peculiar interest as containing the earliest biographical notices of Bach and Handel. Observing the brevity of the paragraph relating to Bach, Spitta[4] drew the inconsequent inference that the two men were not then on friendly terms. The Handel paragraph, however, is even shorter than the Bach article, which not only fully states all the steps in Bach's career, but in its final sentence implies that the two men were still in touch.[5] Their cordiality at Weimar is not doubtful: Bach stood godfather to Walther's eldest son on 26 September 1712.[6] The two men exchanged mementoes of their skill in canon form, in which both excelled. Walther's

Canone infinito gradato à 4 voci, sopra

A solis ortus cardine.[7]

[1] Bojanowski, p. 41.
[2] Johann Stephan Walther, his father, married Martha Dorothea Lämmerhirt in the Kaufmannskirche, Erfurt, on 26 Oct. 1678. She was a near relative of Bach's mother. Cf. B.-J. 1925, pp. 109, 128.
[3] B.-G. XL. 177; P. 245, No. 24.   [4] Sp. i. 388.
[5] 'welches vielleicht daher kommt, dass sogar die Buchstaben bach in ihrer Ordnung melodisch sind (diese Remarque hat den Leipziger Hrn. Bach zum Erfinder)'.   [6] Sp. i. 386.
[7] The exercise is a canon at the fifth on the ancient melody. It was written,

drew from Bach the rejoinder:[1]

Canon â 4 voc: perpetuus.

Dieses Wenige wolte dem Herrn
Besizer zu geneigtem Angedencken
hier einzeichnen

Weimar, d. 2 Aug. 1713.

Joh. Sebast. Bach.
Fürstl. Sächs. Hofforg. u.
Camer Musicus.

Walther is also concerned in an incident recorded by Forkel.
Bach's ability to play music at sight was amazing. Aware of his
powers, he boasted to Walther that he would perform without
error any piece put before him. Walther elaborately plotted his
undoing. Arriving a day or two later, while awaiting his apparently
absent host, Bach sat down before the clavier, on which a piece of
music was displayed. He began to play it, but soon was arrested
by an intricate passage. Beginning again, he stumbled at the same
obstacle, while laughter from an adjoining room revealed the plot
and declared his discomfiture.[2] Bach read full scores with equal
facility, and, like Mozart, was as fluent if the separate parts were
arranged round him. He preferred to read a new trio or quartet
in that way, and, however incompletely it might be figured, could
improvise an additional part from the continuo.[3]

along with a 'Resolutio', on the fly-leaf of an album now in the Berlin Preuss.
Staatsbibliothek. It cannot positively be stated that the MS. was in Bach's
possession. I owe to Prof. Johannes Wolf, of the Preuss. Staatsbibliothek, a copy
of the canon and resolution.   The parts ascend a tone at each repetition.
[1] Sp. i. 386 copied this canon from the autograph, at that time owned by
Herr Generalconsul Clauss of Leipzig. That it was intended for Walther is
conjectural, but probable. The Alto, Tenor, Bass enter at the places indicated
on the MS.   Herr Clauss's collection was sold, but his descendants are unable
to name the purchaser; his granddaughter, Fräulein Redlich, supposes that it
went to America in Sept. 1871. I have failed to trace it. See B.-G. XLV(I) for
Bach's canons.   [2] Forkel, p. 57.   [3] Ibid.

Among the godparents of a short-lived daughter born to Bach in February 1713, Georg Theodor Reineccius, Cantor and Quartus of the Weimar Gymnasium, is named.[1] Bach therefore was on terms of friendship with him, though much junior to him in age.[2] He was a skilful composer for whom Gesner had a high regard.[3] Bach was not officially connected with the Gymnasium, but after his appointment as Concertmeister in 1714, when it became his duty to produce cantatas in the Schloss chapel, Reineccius probably was helpful in augmenting his choir on special occasions. The ducal choir was directed by Hofcapellmeister Johann Samuel Drese, a man over sixty (b. 1644) when Bach returned to Weimar, and so enfeebled by illness that during the whole of Bach's service his duties were performed by a deputy.[4] Until his death in April 1704, Georg Christoph Strattner, a man of Drese's age but of greater ability, acted in that capacity. His melodies, current in the hymn-books of the period, e.g. Freylinghausen's (1704), are often distinguished by their aria form, a fact which suggests his influence on Bach, who probably made his acquaintance during his earlier service in Weimar.[5] Drese's son Johann Wilhelm succeeded Strattner as Vice-Capellmeister in 1704, and his subsequent elevation to his father's office was the immediate cause of Bach's departure from Weimar.

Weimar's ducal Capelle, of which Bach was a member, varied in its composition according to the tastes of its master. A 'Beamtenstaat' for 1700, when opera was still performed, shows the following establishment:[6]

Capellmeister: Johann Samuel Drese.
Vice-Capellmeister: Georg Christoph Strattner.
Prime donne: Magdalene Elisabeth Döbrichtin.
Christine Elisabeth Döbrichtin.
Justina Elisabeth Döbrichtin.
Falsettist: Adam Emanuel Weldige.[7]
Altists: Joh. Friedrich Ganz.[8]
Joh. Peter Martini.
Tenorist: Johann Döberniz.[9]
Bassists: Gottfried Ephraim Thiele.
Christoph Alt.

[1] Bojanowski, p. 33.   [2] He was born in 1660.
[3] 'Vir bonus cui fidem habere poteram', wrote Gesner of him. Cf. Sp. i. 390.
[4] Cf. Walther's *Lexikon.*
[5] Zahn publishes many of them. See his vol. v. 438. Riemann's *Lexikon* calls Strattner 'eins der bedeutendsten Mittelglieder zwischen Heinrich Schütz und Bach'.
[6] Bojanowski, p. 18.   [7] Also functioned as Master of the Pages.
[8] Instructor of the Duke's nephews.
[9] He also played the bassoon. See the list for 1714, *infra.*

Organist: Johann Effler.
Violinists: Johann Paul von Westhoff.[1]
Johann Georg Hoffmann.
Violonist: Johann Andreas Ehrbach.[2]
Fagottist: Christian Gustav Fischer.[3]
Capellist: Johann Andreas Westphal.[4]
Groom of the Palace: Martin Buchspiess.
Groom of the Apartments: Johann Christoph Heininger.[5]
Trumpeters: Johann Martin Fase.
Johann Georg Beumelburg.
Johann Wendelin Eichenberg.
Johann Martin Fichtel.
Dietrich Dekker.
Timpanist: Andreas Nikol.

Excluding the ceremonial trumpeters, the establishment numbered twenty, of whom nine were singers. Other than the organist,
trumpeters, and timpanist, only four instrumentalists are named:
three string players and a fagottist. It may be inferred that those
to whom no instrument is assigned were competent to play one,
and that the trumpeters were not restricted to their own. The
establishment for 1714 shows many changes, but reveals the
Duke's conservative preference for old servants, a trait illustrated
by the case of Capellmeister Drese, and in part accounted for by
the fact that singers and players usually fulfilled other duties in
the ducal household:[6]

Capellmeister: Johann Samuel Drese.
Vice-Capellmeister: Johann Wilhelm Drese.
Concertmeister: Johann Sebastian Bach.
Altists: Johann Jakob Graf.
Gottfried Blühnitz.
Tenorists: Andreas Ablinger.[7]
Johann Döberniz.
Bassists: Gottfried Eph. Thiele(?)
Christoph Alt.
Violinists: August Gottfried Denstedt.
Johann Georg Hoffmann.
Andreas Christoph Ecke.
Violinist: Johann Andreas Ehrbach.[8]
Fagottist: Bernhard Georg Ulrich.

[1] Cammersecretarius. See *supra*, p. 57.
[2] Bojanowski, here and elsewhere, wrongly calls him a 'Violiniste'. In the
original document the word is distinctly written 'Violoniste'.
[3] Also 'Kromsdorfl Gerichtsinspector'.
[4] Probably his office was equivalent to that of sacristan.
[5] In the list for 1714 he is named among the trumpeters.
[6] Bojanowski, p. 18.
[7] 'Secretarius'. The Christian names of some in the lists have been supplied by
the Weimar Staatsarchiv.   [8] Kunstcämmerer'.

Trumpeters: Johann Christoph Heininger.[1]
　　　Johann Christian Biedermann.[2]
　　　Johann Georg Beumelburg.
　　　Johann Wendelin Eichenberg.
　　　Johann Martin Fichtel.
　　　Dietrich Dekker.
　　　Conrad Landgraf.
　Timpanist: Andreas Nikol.

A third list represents the establishment at the end of Bach's service and before the death of Drese, which occurred on 1 December 1716. It distinguishes those who were boarded in the Schloss from those who were housed outside it; Bach was in the latter category:[3]

Court Secretary, Master of the Pages, and Bassist: Gottfried Ephraim Thiele (boarded in the Schloss).
Fagottist: Bernhard Georg Ulrich.
Groom of the Apartments and Trumpeter: Johann Christoph Heininger (draws table allowance).
Palace Steward and Trumpeter: Johann Christian Biedermann (draws table allowance).
Trumpeters: Johann Martin Fichtel (draws table allowance).
　　　Johann Wendelin Eichenberg (draws table allowance).
　　　Johann Georg Beumelburg (draws table allowance).
　　　Conrad Landgraf.
Timpanist: Andreas Nikol (draws table allowance).
Capellmeister: Johann Samuel Drese (draws daily rations and one stoup of beer from the cellar).
Vice-Capellmeister: Johann Wilhelm Drese.
Concertmeister and Organist: Johann Sebastian Bach.
Secretary and Tenorist: Andreas Aiblinger.
Cantor and Tenorist: Johann Döberniz.
Cantor and Bassist: 'Coll. Quint.'[4] Christoph Alt.
Altist: Christian Gerhard Bernhardi.
Falsettists: Johann Philipp Weichard (draws free rations).
　　　—— Germann.
Chamber Musician: Johann Andreas Ehrbach.
Musician and Violinist: Andreas Christoph Ecke.
　　　Johann Georg Hoffmann (lives at Jena, but is boarded in the Schloss when here).
Secretary, Musician, and Violinist: August Gottfried Denstedt.
　　　Six singing boys.

The relationship of the two Courts explains the fact that several of Wilhelm Ernst's musicians came from Weissenfels. The three sisters Döbrichtin, or Döbricht, probably were daughters of Daniel Döbricht, falsettist in the Weissenfels Capelle in 1677, who died in 1694; 'die Jungfer Döbricht' was an opera singer at that Court

---

[1] Groom of the Apartments.　　　[2] Palace Steward.　　　[3] Sp. i. 854.
[4] *i.e.* fifth master (Quintus) in the Gymnasium.

in 1698.[1] Adam Emanuel Weldige, or Weldig, an alumnus of the Leipzig Thomasschule, falsettist and Master of the Pages, may be added to the number of Bach's close friends. In 1713 he received similar appointments at Weissenfels, where on 22 March 1714 Bach, 'loco H. E. Secretär Eylenberg', stood godfather to his son. A fortnight earlier Weldig had undertaken similar responsibility at the baptism of Bach's son Carl Philipp Emanuel.[2] Johann Georg Hoffmann perhaps is identical with Johann Hoffmann, violinist in the Weissenfels Capelle in 1677 and skilful on other instruments.[3] Johann Christoph Heininger, or Heiniger, was a trumpeter at that Court in 1690.[4] Johann Christian Biedermann held a similar post there in 1707, and, as one who advocated the employment of 'gelernte Musicanten' in civic establishments,[5] may be supposed an agreeable recruit to Weimar's artistic circle.

The lists reveal the materials at Bach's disposal for the performance of the cantatas which his office of Concertmeister required him to compose and perform from March 1714 onwards. His choir numbered six boys and, apparently, two singers in each of the under parts, twelve persons in all. The number is small, but the male voices were mature and experienced, qualities lacking in the larger body Bach controlled at Leipzig. The incompleteness of his instrumental resources is evident in the scores of his Weimar cantatas. Instruments other than those in the lists probably could be supplied by the trumpeters, whose disproportionate strength is accounted for by their duties in the chase. More than one of the singers also could readily be changed from 'musicus vocalis' to 'musicus instrumentalis', and that the town's musicians were available is the more probable, seeing that the Bürgermeister himself served the Duke in the menial office once filled by Bach's grandfather.[6] The establishment of 1716 makes it clear that the 'Cammermusici' represented an inner body of the full Capelle. As Concertmeister, Bach was responsible for their direction, leading them with his violin; they numbered four string players.

Bach's actual situation at Weimar on his arrival from Mühlhausen is not clearly defined. His letter of resignation speaks of his appointment to the 'Hof Capelle und Cammer Music', that is, to the Duke's general musical establishment and the select body of string players who performed in his private apartments. The 'canon perpetuus' which he autographed on 2 August 1713,[7] however, announces him as 'Hofforg. u. Camer Musicus', while in the

[1] Werner, pp. 58, 67, 72, 109.   [2] Ibid., p. 85. Joh. Christoph.
Eulenberg was master of the pages (m. 27 Nov. 1719).   [3] Ibid., pp. 57, 76.
[4] Ibid., p. 92.   [5] Ibid., p. 91.   [6] Bojanowski, p. 19.   [7] Supra, p. 90.

Genealogy he describes himself as 'Cammer und Hoforganist in Weimar, An. 1708'. That he held the position of Court Organist from the moment of his arrival is probable: the letter resigning his Mühlhausen post declares that he was drawn to Weimar by the prospect of dedicating his art to the service of God, unhampered by the impediments that confronted him at Mühlhausen. The Nekrolog states that he was appointed organist after demonstrating his powers to the Duke. It must therefore be inferred that Johann Effler was dead or had resigned, though there is no record of his burial at Weimar, and the ducal archives are silent regarding him.[1] Unquestionably Bach held his office for the year Michaelmas 1710 to Michaelmas 1711, when he drew 150 florins, with an allowance of 6 fl. 15 gr. for firewood and 12 gr. for charcoal to warm the chilly organ chamber in the Schloss chapel. His salary for 1711–12 was increased to 200 florins, with 8 fl. 12 gr. for wood, and an honorarium of two florins on the Duke's birthday (Wilhelmstag).[2] For the year 1712–13 he received 203 fl. 15 gr. 9 pf., with eight florins for wood, 12 gr. for charcoal, and two florins on Wilhelmstag. His promotion to be Concertmeister increased his salary to 232 fl. 10 gr. 6 pf. in 1713–14, to 250 fl. in 1715 and thereafter, with augmented allowances for wood, but no increase of the Wilhelmstag honorarium.[3] Thus, during his nine years at Weimar his income nearly doubled, and at its lowest was almost twice as large as the amount he found inadequate at Mühlhausen. Judged by its purchasing power his income throughout his life was comfortable, though not generous.

The Weimar of Bach's period did not greatly differ in appearance from the town of which Goethe wrote:

> O Weimar, dir fiel ein besonderes Los:
> Wie Bethlehem in Juda, klein und gross !

Its population of 5,000 souls dwelt within their ancient walls, came and went through the four turreted Ports, and traversed ill-paved streets between mean houses.[4] Its public buildings were neither numerous nor distinguished. The Stadthaus and ancient Rathaus embellished the Marktplatz, and the Stadtkirche, not yet corrupted by 'classical' taste, exhibited the triptych of the Crucifixion by Lucas Cranach, himself an example of his native city's early

---

[1] I am indebted to Pfarrer Otto Michaelis for a fruitless search of the Register of Burials of the Stadtkirche for the years 1706, 1707, 1708. Herr Archivdirektor Dr. Pischel informs me that the Staatsarchiv throws no light on Effler.
[2] Weimar adopted the New Style in Wilhelm Ernst's lifetime. He celebrated his birthday therefore on 30 October instead of 19 October, the actual date.
[3] The Gesammt-Cammerrechnungen for 1710–17 are printed in Bi. iv. 93–6. See *supra*, p. 62, note 4.   [4] Cf. Marconnay, p. 18.

reaction to culture. 'Something between a capital and a village,' Herder defined Weimar, though Madame de Staël, in a more penetrating phrase, called it 'a large palace'. To this day palaces of a ducal dispensation not yet remote stand detached but contiguous amid green parks along the western bank of the Ilm. Dominating them all, within its moat rises the Schloss Goethe planned, the last of three upon that site, the first that fire has spared. A relic of the first, destroyed in 1618, is still visible in the Schlossthurm that overlooks the Bastille,[1] throwing a tapering shadow on the Gelbes Schloss hard by, as when Bach came and went beneath it. But of the palace in which he made music not a stone stands; fire consumed it in 1774. The present Schloss began to rise on its foundations under Goethe's superintendence after an interval of fifteen years and was completed in 1803.

The Schloss in which Bach functioned was built by Wilhelm Ernst's grandfather, Duke Wilhelm IV (d. 1662), between 1650 and 1654 and bore his name, Wilhelmsburg. A view[2] of its northeast angle from across the Ilm reveals a well-proportioned three-storied pile, somewhat French in design, whose dormer roof was broken on its northern front by a clock tower, while the dome of the older Schlossthurm topped the southern face. A bridged moat surrounded the palace, whose waters discharged into the Ilm above a weir. A stone bridge, as now, but guarded then with drawbridge and portcullis, spanned the river and carried the Wilhelms-Allée over the moat into a recessed quadrangle of the palace. Beyond it the Roter Gang connected Wilhelmsburg with the Rotes Schloss, about which gardens spread. The southern (distant) end of the east front housed the Chapel, externally symmetrical with the rest of the building and contiguous to the Duke's private apartments. Originally dedicated to St. Martin, it was reopened on 28 May 1658, Wilhelm IV's birthday, and thereafter was known as 'Der Weg zur Himmelsburg' or, shortly, Himmelsburg.[3] The chapel, whose garish walls first re-echoed Bach's majestic themes, perished in the fire of 1774. Happily we can rebuild an interior not otherwise distinguished.

Not one of the sanctuaries Bach served matched so ill with his art as Duke Wilhelm's Himmelsburg. The chapel, incongruously baroque and bizarre,[4] filled the south corner of the east front of the Schloss. Its interior, a parallelogram of confused colour, rose in

---

[1] Illus. No. 40.   [2] See Richter's picture, No. 41.   [3] Bojanowski, p. 20.
[4] See the picture of it, No. 46. The original, saved from the fire of 1774, is in the Schlossmuseum, to whose Director, Prof. Dr. Köhler, I am greatly indebted for friendly assistance on the occasion of my visit.

three stories from a slabbed floor of reddish brown, its walls and roof blue-grey or mauve in tone. The arches on the bottom floor were decorated with dark red mouldings and brown marble inlay. The pillars of the middle story were jade-green, and, prominent beneath the roof, twenty Hermae stone-grey in colour projected. Set upon a black and white tessellated floor behind a balustrade, the altar stood under a pyramidal canopy rising to the roof. The base of the pyramid served as the pulpit, a design in red-brown relieved with white marble cornices, a balustrade, and little cherubs climbing the 'Weg zum Himmel'.[1] Upon the floor on either side of it yellow-framed doors admitted to six *loges* or pews. Similar doors in the middle and upper galleries gave access on each level to as many more. The ducal *loge* probably faced the pulpit and opened directly from the private apartments on the first floor,[2] a situation which permitted a view of the organ in the balustraded gallery in the roof. It was set against the south wall, on which, amid a background of blue sky and white clouds, cherubs made music on either side of the projecting organ-case, whose gilded pipes, graded and festooned, were disposed in the heavy frame to expose an oval window in the outer wall. Accommodation for singers and players can have been found with difficulty, and Bach's consumption of winter charcoal was imperative.

His migration from Mühlhausen brought Bach to an organ inferior to the one he surrendered. Gottfried Albin Wette, however, praised it as 'unvergleichlich' and gives the following specification of it in 1737:[3]

Oberwerk.	Brustwerk.	Pedal.
1. Principal, 8 ft.	1. Principal, 8 ft.	1. Gross Untersatz, 32 ft.
2. Quintaton, 16.	2. Viol da Gamba, 8.	2. Sub-Bass, 16.
3. Gemshorn, 8.	3. Gedackt, 8.	3. Posaune, 16.
4. Gedackt, 8.	4. Trompette, 8.	4. Violon, 16.
5. Quintaton, 4.	5. Kleingedackt, 4.	5. Principal, 8.
6. Octave, 4.	6. Octave, 4.	6. Trompette, 8.
7. Mixture, 6 ranks.	7. Waldflöte, 2.	7. Cornett, 4.
8. Cymbel, 3 „	8. Sesquialtera.	
9. Tremulant.[4]		
10. Cymbelstern.		

[1] The pyramid appears to have been removed by Duke Ernst August, who succeeded his uncle in 1728 (Bojanowski, p. 21).
[2] Dr. Köhler showed me the design of the moulded doorway through which the Duke passed to the chapel.
[3] *Historische Nachrichten von der berühmten Residenz-Stadt Weimar* (Weimar, 1737), p. 174.
[4] Neither Sp. i. 380 nor Pirro (3), p. 84, mentions the Tremulant. Wette names it in another paragraph along with the Cymbelstern. He does not attach them specifically to the Oberwerk.

H

In view of Bach's specification of a Glockenspiel for the Mühl-hausen organ, it is interesting to observe that the stop was added to the Weimar instrument towards the end of his residence there.[1] In May 1716 the organ-front was decorated with a carved wooden shield bearing the Duke's name and coronet within palm-leaves,[2] and four years earlier (1712) Heinrich Nikolaus Tröbs[3] received payment for 'eine Positiv Bank in fürstl. Schlosscapelle'.[4] A com-parison of the specifications of the Weimar and Arnstadt organs shows the former superior in the range and sonority of its Pedal; but in regard to the manuals the advantage was with Arnstadt, whose Oberwerk had twelve as against Weimar's ten speaking stops; its Brustwerk nine against eight; while the Weimar Brust-werk provided only a 2 ft. against a 4 ft. Flute, no Nachthorn, Mixture, or Glocken-Accord. But the player was greater than his instrument, and seated aloft among the cherubs poured out music as worthy as theirs to take the road to heaven.

From the day she stood beside him before the altar at Dornheim until at Cöthen, thirteen years later, he came home to find her dead, Maria Barbara stands in the background of her husband's story. She was his helpmeet in years when most he needed a wife's faith and encouragement, controlled a busy household of pupils and apprentices, and with submissive regularity added to it children of her own. The eldest, Catharina Dorothea, was carried to the Stadtkirche for her christening on 29 December 1708, a few months after the young parents set up their Weimar home. Georg Christian Eilmar of Mühlhausen stood godfather to his friend's firstborn, who received her names from her kinswomen and god-mothers, Martha Catharina Lämmerhirt, widow of Uncle Tobias, the opportune testator, and Aunt Johanna Dorothea, wife of Bach's Ohrdruf brother Johann Christoph.[5] Two years later (22 Novem-ber 1710) was born Wilhelm Friedemann, that unstable son who most inherited his father's genius. Again Mühlhausen friends were summoned as godparents to the christening: Anna Dorothea

---

[1] '28 fl. 1 gr. 3 pf. vor zu Nürnberg gefertigte Glocken zum Glockenspiel in die Schloss-Orgel' (Ducal accounts for 1715–16 in Bi. iv. 95).

[2] *Ibid.*, p. 96. It is not visible in the picture.

[3] For Bach's relations with Tröbs see B.-J. 1926, p. 156. In 1742–3 they col-laborated in building the organ at Bad Berka, near Weimar. Cf. *Musik und Kunst*, Heft 3 (1931).

[4] Bi. iv. 93, under date 17 March 1712. Ten days earlier occurs the entry: '16 gr. dieselbe zu beschlagen.' Again, on 18 June 1712: '2 fl. zwei Zimmer-leuten und 2 Taglöhnern so die Orgelbalgcammer zernommen und die Blase-bälge abgehoben.' Evidently Bach remarked the deficiency of wind-power of which he had complained at Mühlhausen.

[5] Catharina Dorothea died a spinster on 14 Jan. 1774. Bojanowski, p. 33, names her godparents.

Hagedorn, wife of a Mühlhausen lawyer, Friedemann Meckbach of the same profession, along with Wilhelm Ferdinand Baron von Lyncker, 'Cammerjunker' to Duke Wilhelm Ernst in Wilhelmsburg. A little more than two years later shortlived twins named Maria Sophia and Johann Christoph were added (23 February 1713) to the nursery. For the daughter Bach found godmothers at Suhl, whence two of his great-uncles had taken their wives, and a godfather in Cantor Reineccius of the Gymnasium.[1] We observe the range of his friendships in his recurring choice of godparents. Meanwhile, his rising reputation widened the circle and increased his household. His earliest apprentice, Johann Martin Schubart, accompanied him from Mühlhausen and succeeded him at Weimar in 1717. Another pupil, Johann Caspar Vogler, who perhaps had received instruction from him at Arnstadt,[2] eventually succeeded Schubart at Weimar. Johann Tobias Krebs, organist and Cantor at Buttelstedt near Weimar in 1710, placed himself under Bach's tuition and later entrusted his sons to him at Leipzig. About the year 1715 Bach received his nephew Johann Bernhard from Ohrdruf, whose Lyceum he too had attended, and to whose organist-ship he eventually succeeded. Last of the Weimar pupils, Johann Gotthilf Ziegler, afterwards organist at Halle, has recorded a detail of his master's teaching: 'Herr Capellmeister Bach, who is still [1746] living, instructed me when playing hymns not to treat the melody as if it alone were important, but to interpret the words through the melody,'[3] a confirmation in Bach's own mouth of his peculiar sensitiveness to verbal suggestion.[4]

Informed by Bach's sons, his most distinguished pupils, Forkel devotes a few pages[5] to his characteristics as a teacher. He truly observes that the successful master must have submitted himself to the discipline of self-instruction before he can hope to meet and overcome the difficulties of others. Bach pre-eminently possessed that advantage; as a teacher consequently he was clear, instructive, definite, and successful. He accustomed his clavier pupils first of all to hold their hands poised above the keys with the three middle fingers curved inwards, and so able instantly to execute their every command. The movement of his own fingers was so slight as to be barely perceptible; only their extremities seemed to move, and his hands preserved their rounded shape in the most intricate passages.[6] For months he pinned his pupils to finger exercises, or to

---

[1] Bojanowski, p. 33.   [2] Forkel, p. 100.   [3] Sp. i. 519.
[4] Bach's method is illustrated by the treatises of Carl Philipp Emanuel and Kirnberger, both of whom were his pupils.
[5] Forkel, p. 92.   [6] *Ibid.*, p. 50.

little pieces of his own composition incorporating a particular discipline. Then he passed on to 'Manieren' and eventually to more advanced tests, which it was his habit to play over to them, remarking, 'That's how it ought to go.' Heinrich Nikolaus Gerber, his pupil at Leipzig, recalled these early exercises, 'Inventions' Bach termed them, which, when they could be played to his satisfaction, were followed by his French and English Suites and 'Well-tempered Clavier'. Bach played the latter through to Gerber three times, with such charm that the hours passed as minutes.[1]

Bach's method of teaching composition was no less practical and thorough.[2] Omitting theoretical counterpoint, he started his pupils forthwith on four-part harmony, providing a figured Bass for their transliteration. He required them to write each part on a separate stave, in order that each should receive a definite melodic form, and also be clearly followed in relation to the parts above and below it. He next gave them the unfigured Bass of a hymn-tune, inviting them to add an Alto and Tenor, and eventually to supply all three under parts to a given melody. The qualities he emphasized are patent in his unapproachable Chorals, some of which were written as models for his pupils.[3] Until they completely apprehended those essentials he did not permit them to pen compositions of their own. He insisted upon his pupils composing *mentally*, and discouraged them from putting pen to paper until they had something original to say. He ridiculed as 'Clavier Horsemen' those who found inspiration in their fingers, careering wildly over the keyboard in search of an idea. He was as severe to those who showed him clumsy part-writing, reminding them that each part must be regarded as an individual conversing with his fellows, who, when he speaks, must speak grammatically and complete his sentences, and if he has nothing to say, had better remain silent. When his pupils' study of harmony had progressed sufficiently, he introduced them to counterpoint, and within limitations allowed them unusual liberty. Consistency of expression, variety of style, rhythm, and melody were the qualities he called for.

It was from Weimar that Bach at length announced himself to his countrymen as a player of unrivalled technique, a master of the most inventive genius, faithful to the traditions of German polyphony, yet able to endow it with new life, building a new fabric on the ancient traditions, and expanding their uses in every

---

[1] Dahms, p. 87.
[2] Cf. his rules and instructions (1738) in Sp. ii. 913 and at the end of Anna Magdalena Bach's 'Notenbuch' (1725).
[3] Cf. the Introduction to my 'Bach's Four-part Chorals' (Oxford Univ. Press).

direction; gifted, moreover, with a power of melodic utterance which
no one before him had approached, and of astonishing boldness
in harmonic invention and resource. The 'Great' Preludes and
Fugues in A minor and C minor, the C major and F major Toccatas
and Fugues, and other masterpieces, which reach us in imagination
from some vast and vaulted Gothic fane, were first conceived and
heard in Duke Wilhelm's incongruous chapel. As early as 1716,
before Bach had reached his thirtieth year, Johann Mattheson of
Hamburg, whom Bach was at no pains to impress, called him 'der
berühmte Organist', 'der berühmte Bach'.[1] His services were
increasingly in demand to test organs, or to examine candidates
for vacant organ-lofts, and in 1713 a hearty call invited him to
forsake Weimar for Halle, whose Liebfrauenkirche lacked an
organist since the death of Handel's master, Friedrich Wilhelm
Zachau, in August 1712. A new organ was in course of erection
there by Christoph Cuntius of Halberstadt, a large instrument of
63 speaking stops, costing 6,300 Reichsthalers, whose inauguration
was proposed for Easter Day 1714.

On 6 November 1713 Bach attended the opening of the rebuilt
Jakobskirche at Weimar, third in a procession of seven musicians
in ducal employ who walked from the Schloss to the church.[2]
Shortly after, he visited Halle and was so attracted by the new
instrument that he declared his willingness to undergo the customary Probe, being warmly urged to do so by Dr. Heineccius,
Pastor primarius of the church. Bach accordingly prepared a
'Stück' which he rehearsed and conducted. It can be identified as ' Ich hatte viel Bekümmernis ' (No. 21), which was also
performed at Weimar on the Third Sunday after Trinity in the
following year (17 June 1714). But its introductory Sinfonia, its
proportions (it is in two Parts), its rich treatment of the text, and
the fact that Bach inscribed the cover of the Parts with the additional direction 'Per ogni tempo', all point to the conclusion that
it was written for another occasion. If in fact it was performed at
Halle, Bach found pleasure in associating Zachau's memory with
it by its references to Zachau's greatest pupil: the cantata contains positive indications of his familiarity with Handel's 'Almira',[3]
produced at Hamburg in 1705 and in 1713 famous throughout
Germany. Bach's music so greatly impressed the Halle electors that
on 14 December 1713 they dispatched to Weimar a 'Vocation' in

[1] Dahms, p. 109.   [2] Bojanowski, p. 26.
[3] Robinson, p. 196. In 'Wachet, betet' (No. 70) Bach's borrowings from Handel
are still more obvious. If No. 21 was not performed at Halle, Bach may have
come upon Handel's score during his visit. But it would most probably be
known to him already.

duplicate, declaring the conditions of the appointment, and inviting Bach to sign one of the copies in token of his acceptance of it. Their communication was in the following terms:[1]

Wewhose names are underwritten, the Elders and Eight[2] of the Church of Our Lady, on behalf of ourselves and our successors in the Collegium, hereby make known that we have by these presents appointed the right worthy and competent Herr Johann Sebastian Bach to be organist within the Church of Our Lady, to which and to ourselves he shall show himself faithful and serviceable, exemplary and virtuous in his living, constant to the Augsburg Confession, adding to or subtracting naught therefrom, as also to the *Formula Concordiae*[3] and other formulas of belief. He shall present himself regularly at the altar and be an attentive hearer of the Word, in such wise that his Christian deportment and belief may be visible to the congregation.

Regarding his general duties, he is required:

1. To play the large organ with his best skill and ability on high days and festivals and their vigils, on Sundays, Saturday afternoons, at the customary Catechism sermons,[4] and at public weddings. On high festivals particularly he shall also accompany the hymns and figural music[5] on the small organ and Regal.[6]

2. On high days and festivals, and on the third Sunday in each month, he shall produce and perform an agreeable and harmonious cantata[7] in association with the Cantor, choir, and town's musicians, and on the second and third days of high festivals[8] shall perform a short piece of figural music with the Cantor and choristers, occasionally accompanied by violins and other instruments, in such manner that the congregation may be moved more reverently to receive God's Word.

3. He shall betimes submit the texts to be set to music to the Oberpastor of the church, Herr Consistorial-Rath Dr. Heineccius, for his approbation, should he have his instructions to that effect.

4. The hymns in general, as well as those selected by the ministers for use before and after the sermon, on Sundays, feast-days, at Vespers, and on Vigils, he shall accompany quietly on four or five stops with the Principal, so as not to distract the congregation, altering the registration for each verse, but eschewing the use of Quintatons, reeds, syncopations, and suspensions, allowing the organ to support and harmonize with the congregation's singing, and stirring them with devotional desire to praise and thank Almighty God.

5. In regard to the large and small organs, the Regal, and all other instruments whatsoever belonging to the church and scheduled in the inventory herewith, he shall take heed that the bellows, stops, registers, and all that pertains to them, are maintained in good order and tune. If any defect or damage appear, he shall forthwith notify the Vorsteher,[9] or,

[1] Halle: Akten der Marienkirche.   [2] 'Väter und Achtmanne.'
[3] Issued on 25 June 1580, the jubilee of the Augsburg Confession, as an attempt to heal Lutheran divisions, the *Formula Concordiae* had a very limited acceptance. Saxony, however, adopted it, and at Leipzig Bach was again required to declare his fidelity to it.   [4] Cf. B.C.T., p. 28.
[5] *i.e.* a Cantata.   [6] A small portable organ.   [7] 'Musique'.
[8] At Christmas, Easter, and Whitsun the festival was prolonged into the two days following Christmas Day, Easter Day, and Whit-Sunday.
[9] Augustus Becker.

if the defect is trivial, the Collegium of the church, in order that it be repaired and greater hurt avoided. Having been purchased out of church funds, the Regal and all the other musical instruments are for use at divine service in our church and none other, much less at secular concerts, unless permission is expressly granted. Should any be lost or suffer damage through neglect, the responsibility rests on him alone.

In payment he shall receive yearly from the church's revenues 140 thalers stipend, 24 thalers for lodging allowance, and 7 th. 12 gr. for firewood. For every piece of Catechism music composed by him he shall receive 1 thaler, and a like amount for attendance at weddings in church. So long as he draws these emoluments he is pledged to devote himself solely to the service of the church. Notwithstanding, provided his duty thereto be not impeded, he may receive pupils and accept fees for services occasionally rendered elsewhere.

The conditions of this appointment we have set out in duplicate under the seal of the church for the Herr Organist's signature, one copy of which he shall preserve, returning the other for preservation among the church's archives.

Given at Halle the 14 Dec. 1713.

Signed: Andreas Ockel.   A. Matthesius, Dm.
         Augustus Becker.   Friedrich Arnold Reichhelm.
                          Christoph Semler.
                          Christianus Knaut.
                          Ct. W. Möschel.
                          Johann Gotthilf Kost.

Bach gave deliberate consideration to this unanimous and flattering call; for the Christmas festival laid extra duties upon him in the Schloss, and the birthday of the Duke's nephew Johann Ernst, celebrated on 26 December, increased them. However agreeable the opportunity to secure an instrument worthy of his powers, the much larger stipend he was receiving at Weimar could not be lightly sacrificed, especially at a time when his family was increasing with periodical regularity. But, whatever his inclination, the chief obstacle to acceptance was Wilhelm Ernst. Without his consent Bach could not move, and, as circumstances showed in 1717, the Duke disliked the migration of his servants, especially when their departure robbed him of men of talent and character. So, when the Christmas and New Year festivities were over, Bach, before approaching his master, penned a belated reply to Halle, which left the door open for further negotiation: [1]

Distinguished and learned Sir,[2]

I duly received the *vocation* in duplicate with which you favoured me and am flattered by the invitation it contains. I find great satisfaction in the knowledge that your honourable Collegium has sent a unanimous

---

[1] Halle: Acta betr. Orgelbau 1712, I, No. 21.
[2] The letter, though unendorsed, was doubtless addressed to Augustus Becker, a lawyer, as was that of 19 March.

call to my unworthy self; and I am the more inclined to follow the direction of Providence indicated therein. But, distinguished Sir, you will not take it ill that I cannot forthwith declare a positive *resolution*: for (1) I have not yet received my *dimission* here, and (2) there are one or two matters relating to the *salarium* and duties of the post which do not satisfy me, upon which I propose to communicate again with you this week. In the meantime I return one of the duplicate copies, begging your honour not to take it ill that I cannot attach my signature to it, and thereby *engage* myself to you, until I am definitely released from my service here. If we can arrive at an agreement regarding the conditions of the appointment, I propose to come in person and sign the document in token of my acceptance. Meanwhile, honoured Sir, commend me, I pray you, to your colleagues on the Collegium and beg them to *excuse* my inability at once to declare a *categoric resolution*. Preparations for my Prince's birthday and my duties in the ducal chapel have denied me leisure. But you shall without fail know my decision this week. I received your agreeable communication with all *respect*, and I am hoping that your honourable Collegium will agree to remove certain of the conditions named therein which impede my acceptance.

Desiring a speedy and agreeable conclusion of the matter, I am, honourable and distinguished Sir,

Your humble servant,

Joh. Sebast. Bach.

Weimar, the 14 Jan. 1714.

The promised letter was dispatched, but, as Halle would not vary the conditions of the appointment, Bach sent a formal withdrawal, which drew the ungracious taunt, that he had entertained the invitation only to better his position at Weimar.[1] That, in fact, was the outcome. Threatened with his organist's resignation, Wilhelm Ernst reshaped his Capelle. Drese's duties as Capellmeister were still fulfilled by his son, and included the obligation[2] to perform pieces of his own composition in the Schloss chapel. There is reason to suppose young Drese's talents mediocre, and not improbably Bach occasionally had relieved him of the task, though only one of his cantatas can be attributed to the period preceding March 1714, 'Gleich wie der Regen und Schnee' (No. 18),[3] produced at Sexagesima (4 February) 1714, that is, at the moment when Bach's continuance at Weimar hung in the balance. On 2 March 1714 he received the 'Predicat'[4] of his appointment as Concertmeister, with seniority after the younger Drese, and the instruction to produce 'monatlich neue Stücke' in the Schloss chapel. His stipend was forthwith increased to 250 florins.[5] A year later (20 March

---

[1] None of this correspondence has survived.
[2] Strattner certainly had to comply with this condition. Cf. Sp. i. 391 for Strattner's commission.
[3] B.C.T., p. 180. Spitta proposes a less probable date, Sexagesima 1713.
[4] Quoted in Dahms, p. 31, from the *Nachrichten* of Hofsecretär Bormann.
[5] Bi. iv. 95.

1715) the Dreses' *accidentia* and casual *honoraria* were transferred to him, and his own as Cammermusicus passed to Biedermann,[1] who, no doubt, succeeded to his desk as a member of that body.

The betterment of his circumstances at Weimar gave ground for the insinuation, from which the Elders and Eight of the Lieb-frauenkirche did not refrain, that Bach had used their invitation as a lever to extract promotion and a larger salary at Weimar, an unworthy and unwarranted charge, to which on 19 March 1714 he penned a reproving but temperate answer:[2]

Most distinguished, learned, and honourable Sir,
    It does not surprise me that the worshipful Collegium of your church should wonder at my refusal of the appointment; for they appear to imagine I was anxious to obtain it, and so, completely misapprehend the actual situation.
    Whereas it is suggested that I eagerly sought the appointment, nothing is further from the facts. I declared myself a candidate and the Collegium offered me the position. Having had an interview on the spot my mind was made up to return to Weimar forthwith. But Dr. Heineccius strongly urged me there and then to compose and perform the required cantata. Nor is it usual for a person to accept a post poorer than the one he abandons, or to come to a decision in two or three weeks' time regarding a financial situation in which *accidentia* form part of the income: he cannot estimate in a fortnight the value of an asset it may take him years to find out. And so you have the reason why I accepted your invitation to an interview and presented myself for that purpose. To insinuate that I played a trick upon your worshipful Collegium in order to compel my gracious master to increase my stipend here is unwarranted; he has always been so well-disposed to me and my art that, certes, I have no need to use Halle's persuasion to influence him. I am distressed that our negotiations have not reached a satisfactory conclusion, but I would ask whether, even if Halle offered me an emolument equivalent to my stipend here, I could be expected to leave my present situation for the new one. You, as a lawyer, can answer that question. Begging you to convey this defence of my conduct to your worshipful Collegium, I remain your Honour's obedient
                                                    Joh. Seb. Bach,
                                        Concertmeister and Hoforganist.
Weimar, the 19th of March 1714.
Endorsed: A Monsieur
        Monsieur A. Becker, Licentié en Droit,
        Mon très honoré Ami à Halle.
        p. couvert.

---

[1] Dahms, p. 31. Dahms omits the interesting addendum (Thüringer Staats-archiv, Weimar, Bl. 45ᵃ): 'N.B. Das Probieren der Musical. Stücke im Hause oder eigenen Logiament ist d. 23 Mart. 1714 geändert, und dass es jedesmal uf der Kirchen-Capelle geschehen soll, expresse befohlen worden.' In other words, the rehearsals of the cantatas, which so far had been held in Drese's house, were henceforth to take place in the Schloss chapel. Strattner's commission, already referred to, directed him to rehearse in Drese's house. Bach's, we must assume, was either inconveniently equipped, or he was temporarily houseless. See note 7, p. 115 *infra*.
[2] Halle: Acta betr. Orgelbau 1712, I. No. 21.

In the midst of these preoccupations Bach's most famous son, Carl Philipp Emanuel, was born at Weimar on 14 March 1714. Again the list of godparents declares Bach's ability to make new friends and retain old ones. Weldig, lately of the Weimar Capelle and now at Weissenfels, gave the infant his third name; Georg Philipp Telemann, Capellmeister at Frankfurt, added his second; and Frau Catharina Dorothea Altmann, wife of the Court Chamberlain at Arnstadt, stood godmother.[1] Bach's acquaintance with Telemann, his most distinguished contemporary in Germany, perhaps was made through their common association with the gifted young prince Johann Ernst,[2] whose relations with Telemann probably dated from the latter's employment at the Eisenach Court during Bach's first residence at Weimar. In 1721 he settled in Hamburg, where he held the post of Capellmeister which passed at his death in 1767 to his godson.

His new office tardily fulfilled the purpose which had attracted Bach from Mühlhausen: from Easter 1714 until the end of 1716 he produced in the Schloss chapel a series of cantatas, for the most part to texts by Salomo Franck, on paper, a costly item, provided by the ducal treasury.[3] With inveterate diligence he was at the same time copying the Italian masters: a MS. of Frescobaldi's 'Fiori musicali' (1635), 104 pages entirely in his hand and dated 1714, is preserved in the Staatliche Akademie für Kirchen- und Schulmusik, Berlin. The lengthy task may have been undertaken during enforced inactivity; for at some period in the financial year 1714–15 Bach received twelve florins from the ducal treasury in respect to an accident which had befallen him.[4] At the end of 1714, however, he was well enough to pay a visit to Cassel, which brought him a rare mark of princely favour and inspired a eulogy of his astonishing dexterity as a player.

The date of Bach's visit to Cassel is decided largely by the Peace between France and the Empire signed at Baden on 7 September 1714; for it brought home from the wars the Hereditary Prince Friedrich, who had held a command, and in January 1715 left Germany to find a bride and a crown in Sweden.[5] It must have been towards the end of 1714, therefore, that Bach visited Cassel for a purpose not precisely ascertained. Spitta concluded that he was summoned to examine a new organ.[6] There is no record of

[1] Bojanowski, p. 34. [2] *Supra*, p. 57.
[3] '2 fl. 6 gr. dem Handelsmann Johann Christian Hindorffen vor 2 Stück Saiten, so der Concertmeister Bach verschreiben lassen, den 21 Juni 1715'; '13 fl. 15 gr. vor 6 Ries Schreib- und 12 Ries Druckpapier zu den Kirchen-Cantaten, 9 Juli 1715' (Bi. iv. 95). [4] Bi. iv. 95.
[5] Cf. *Allgem. deutsche Biographie*, vii. 522. [6] Sp. i. 508.

such a commission in the archives of the Hofkirche or elsewhere, and it is more probable that Bach accompanied his master on a ceremonial visit, perhaps not unconnected with the matrimonial prospects of the Duke's heir. The Landgraf and Hereditary Prince, who nineteen years earlier had visited Weimar (1695), were distinguished for their musical tastes, in particular, for their support of Italian Opera[1] in a capital where Louis Spohr subsequently conducted. It was therefore natural for Wilhelm Ernst to bring with him his accomplished organist, whose performance on the organ of the Hofkirche filled the future King of Sweden with admiration and amazement. Thirty years later, Constantin Bellermann, Rector of Minden Lyceum, penned a vivid impression of Bach's artistry:[2] 'His feet, flying over the pedals as though they were winged, made the notes reverberate like thunder in a storm,' till the Prince, 'cum stupore admiratus', pulled a ring from his finger and presented it to the player. 'Now bethink you,' commented Bellermann, 'if Bach's skilful feet deserved such a bounty, what gift must the Prince have offered to reward his hands as well?'[3] Johann Matthias Gesner, a frequent listener to Bach at Weimar, and his colleague later in Leipzig, penned a still more vivid eulogy.[4] Commenting, in his edition of Quintilian's *Institutiones Oratoriae*, on that author's illustration of the lyre-player, who simultaneously plays his instrument, beats time with his foot, and sings, he remarked:

You would think very little of these accomplishments, Fabius, my friend, could you rise from your tomb and see our Bach, whom I introduce to your notice because he was once my colleague in the Leipzig Thomasschule. You would observe that he uses two hands, and every finger of them, upon a keyboard which is the equivalent of many lyres, a king of instruments, we may call it, whose innumerable pipes emit sounds by the agency of bellows. You would remark his hands moving in one direction and his feet going with incredible agility in another, producing a complex of sounds blended into one harmonious whole. He accomplishes by himself what any number of your lyre-players and a thousand of your flautists could never do: for, whereas your lyrist sings and plays a single tune, Bach is thirty or forty players rolled into one, controls this one with a nod, another with the pulse of the measure, a third with a directing finger.

[1] Sp. i. 508.
[2] *Programma in quo Parnassus Musarum*, etc. (1743). Jakob Adlung quotes Bellermann in his *Anleitung* (1758), p. 690. Bellermann seemingly is not correct in his statement that Bach had been summoned to inspect an organ on this occasion. Probably he confused this earlier with the later visit Bach paid to Cassel in 1732, when the Crown Prince was not in residence. See *infra*, p. 211,
[3] Prof. Dr. Luthner, who most kindly examined the Landgraviate archives for me, found nothing whatever in them relative to Bach's visit in 1714. Cf. Dr. Carl Scherer's article on the Cassel visit in Monats. f. M.G. Jhrg. 25, p. 129.
[4] Dahms, p. 122.

One of them sounds at the top of the scale, another deep at the bottom, and a third midway. Yet, seated solitary amid these clashing sounds—stupendous task!—he can compel each voice to pause to silence, keep them all going together, brisk up the backward, and give confidence to the timid. Rhythm is in every limb of him, all the harmonies are gathered up in his sensitive ear, and the several parts speak with the unanimity of one. I'm an honest admirer of your ancient world, but I tell you this Bach of mine, or another, if you can find one like him, is worth any number of Orpheuses, and twenty singers like Arion.

Early in 1716 the Weimar Court was occupied with the marriage of Duke Ernst August to the widowed Duchess Eleonore Wilhelmine of Sachsen-Merseburg, sister of the reigning Prince Leopold of Anhalt-Cöthen, a union destined to influence Bach's future. The wedding took place at Schloss Nienburg on 24 January 1716,[1] and a month later Wilhelm Ernst paid a visit to Duke Christian of Sachsen-Weissenfels, who on 23 February 1716 celebrated his birthday. As was customary, his Capelle, conducted by Capellmeister Augustin Kobelius, inaugurated the festival with a morning Serenade, 'Irrgarten der Liebe, oder Livia und Cleander'.[2] To crown the day's hunting and conclude the evening feast Wilhelm Ernst provided a 'Tafelmusic' within the great hall of the barrack-like Schloss[3] above the town, where the guests sat down to a banquet at tables set amid exotic shrubs, cypress, orange, almond, and myrtle, whose fragrance turned a winter's evening to summer.[4] In such an auditorium Bach produced his earliest secular cantata, 'Was mir behagt', whose libretto Salomo Franck had written in the classical vein tradition demanded to laud the prowess of the host. Bach suited his score to the personnel of the Weissenfels Capelle, which perhaps lacked an Altist. His friend Weldig may have sung the music of Pales. Bach thought highly of the composition and revived it on at least two occasions.[5]

Bach had barely returned from Weissenfels when he received a communication which assured him that an earlier controversy was no longer remembered with bitterness. The organ in the Halle Liebfrauenkirche had at length been completed, and on 20 April 1716 he was invited to examine and report on it. Andreas Noack, who brought the invitation, carried back Bach's reply:[6]

Most honourable and distinguished Sir,
     I am greatly honoured by the *confidence* your Honour and the members of your worshipful Collegium express in me. As it has always been my *plaisir* to serve your Honour, so it will be particularly agreeable to attend

---

[1] Marconnay, p. 48.   [2] Werner, p. 119.   [3] Illus. No. 74.
[4] Werner, p. 124.   [5] B.C.T., p. 632.
[6] Halle: Acta betr. Orgelbau 1712, I. No. 21. Cf. Max Seiffert's article, 'Joh. Seb. Bach 1716 in Halle', in I.M.G. July–Sept. 1905, p. 595.

and do my utmost to give *satisfaction* in the examination you invite me
to undertake.

I beg you therefore to communicate to the Collegium my instant *resolution* to accept their commission, along with my bounden *respects* and
gratitude for the confidence they express in me.

I beg to give thanks to your Honour for your kindly interest on my
behalf on this as on former occasions, and to assure you that, as long as
life lasts, it will be my pleasure to subscribe myself, most honourable and
distinguished Sir,

Your devoted servant,

Joh. Seb. Bach,

Concertmeister.

Weimar, the 22 April 1716.

To Herr Augustus Becker, the distinguished Licentiate in law and
Vorsteher of the Liebfrauenkirche, Halle, my most distinguished patron.

A week later (28 April) Bach arrived at Halle and met his colleagues in the quarters arranged for their accommodation. Associated with him were Christian Friedrich Rolle, of Quedlinburg,
and Johann Kuhnau, whom he succeeded at Leipzig seven years
later. The civic accounts reveal elaborate care for their comfort
and appetite. A staff of servants and coachmen was at their service
from 28 April to 3 May; guests were invited to join them at
Abendessen, and shared a generous fare of eggs boiled in brine,
cold meats, ox tongues, and saveloys, washed down with Rhenish
and Franconian wine and beer. Wednesday and Thursday (29 and
30 April) were devoted to an exhaustive examination of the organ.
Friday and Saturday were employed in drafting and presenting
their report, flattering to the builder and eloquent of their close
attention and technical knowledge.[1] On Sunday, 3 May, Hauptgottesdienst was conducted with unusual brilliance, and the new
instrument was formally opened and dedicated. Thereafter the
Collegium entertained the visitors at a banquet, whose bounteous
dimensions matched those of the organ itself. The Speisekarte is
preserved:[2]

*Vor Speisung des hochlöbl. Collegii der Kirchen bei der
Investitur der neuen Orgel.*

1 Stück Bäffallemote (Bœuf à la mode).

Hechte mit einer Sartelle beu (Pike with anchovy butter sauce).

1 gereuchert Schinken (smoked ham).

1 Aschette mit Erbsissen (dish of peas).

1 Aschette mit Erteffen (dish of potatoes).

2 Aschetten mit Spenadt und Zerzigen (sausages and spinach?).

1 gebraten Schöpseviertel (quarter of roast mutton).

Gesodtner Kerbisse (boiled pumpkin).

Sprützkuchen (fritters).

[1] The document, dated 1 May 1716, is printed in Bi. iv. 96.

[2] Max Seiffert, *loc. cit.*

Eingemachte Zitronschalle (candied lemon peel).
Eingemachte Kirschen (preserved cherries).
Warmer Spargel Saladt (asparagus).
Kopf Saladt (lettuce).
Rettisgen (radishes).
Frische Butter (fresh butter).
Kellberbraten (roast veal).

Little wonder that a big blot fell on the 'Bach' as the writer signed a receipt for six thalers, his fee! By 11 May he was at home again for the first birthday of the last child born to him by Maria Barbara that survived infancy—Johann Gottfried Bernhard, who gave him much anxiety in after years. Johann Andreas Rheuert, Court Registrar at Ohrdruf, and Johann Bernhard Bach, of Eisenach, stood godfathers at the christening, and as godmother, Frau Sophia Dorothea Emmerling, wife of the head cook at Schloss Neideck, Arnstadt.[1] Three weeks later, on Whit-Sunday (31 May 1716), Bach produced 'Wer mich liebet' (No. 59) in the Schloss chapel, his first cantata to a libretto by Erdmann Neumeister, Pastor of the Jakobikirche at Hamburg, whose texts were decisive in fashioning the Cantata form, and who a few years later vainly hoped to secure Bach as his organist. Spitta supposes[2] that at this period Bach visited his relatives at Meiningen. He was familiar with, admired, and copied the compositions of his cousin Johann Ludwig Bach, Hofcantor there. But there is no indication of a visit in the Meiningen archives,[3] and a copy of Nikolaus Bach's Mass in E minor, dated 'Meiningen, d. 16 7br 1716', which has been relied on to support it, cannot be accepted in evidence: the manuscript is now in the archives of Breitkopf and Härtel at Leipzig, and, though attributed to Bach in their printed catalogue, may not be regarded as his.[4]

The year 1717 blazed Bach's name throughout Germany and also ironically recorded his disgrace. In or about September[5] he visited Dresden, where the Opera flourished under the sceptre of Augustus II; in 1717 Antonio Lotti was directing an Italian season there which lasted till 1719. Bach, however, was not drawn from Weimar to attend it. Even from Leipzig's closer neighbourhood in later years it was with the air of an elder bending to the ignorance of youth that he would say to his eldest son, 'Well, Friedemann, shall we go over to Dresden to hear the pretty tunes [Lieder-

---

[1] Bojanowski, p. 34.   [2] Sp. 1. 565.
[3] So I am informed by the Director of the Meiningen Herzogl. Öff. Bibliothek.
[4] I am indebted to Herr Dr. Archivar Wilhelm Hitzig for the opinion.
[5] Sp. i. 815 establishes the month from an entry in the Saxon archives relating to Marchand. See his elaborate article on the affair.

chen]?'[1] Unlike Handel, he was little attracted by the Italian tradition of the seventeenth century. Moreover, his situation at the moment was anomalous. A few weeks earlier, for reasons which will be explored, he had received appointment as Capellmeister to the Prince of Anhalt-Cöthen, but was unable to take up his duties there owing to his Duke's obstinate refusal to release him. That he should visit Cöthen was in the circumstances natural, while his inveterate inclination to listen to other masters of his instrument carried him on to Dresden, where the distinguished French organist and clavier player, Louis Marchand, was winning the plaudits of its Court and public.

Marchand, who since 1708 held the position of Court Organist, had recently fallen into disgrace at Versailles. A man sixteen years (b. 1669) Bach's senior, he was one of the eminent players of his generation and a composer whom Bach held in regard. His pupil Krebs, no doubt at Bach's bidding, copied one of Marchand's Suites in 1714. Andreas Bach had another in his repertory, and Friedrich Wilhelm Marpurg received from Bach's own lips an acknowledgement of his admiration of their composer.[2] If the occasion presented itself, he was therefore fully competent to meet the Frenchman on his own ground. Highly gifted and flattered by Paris society, Marchand was conceited, improvident, arrogant. If the story is credible, he dared to show temper before his royal master, who, for the support of Marchand's neglected wife, had assigned to her half the organist's salary. Marchand made a daring rejoinder: in the middle of the service at Versailles he closed the organ, remarking, 'If my wife receives half my stipend, let her play half the service.' Dismissed in 1717, he found his way to Dresden, played with applause before the Court, and was rewarded with two medals valued at one hundred ducats.[3] F. W. Marpurg asserts[4] that at one of these recitals Bach was present by royal permission, and, after listening to Marchand, took his seat at the clavier and improvised variations on the theme the Frenchman had used. The Nekrolog unfolds in a more dramatic scene the tradition that survived in Bach's family. According to this version, Jean-Baptiste Volumier, Concertmeister and Tanzmeister at the Dresden Court, whose sympathy, as a Latin, we should expect to have been with Marchand, summoned Bach from Weimar to confound the invader, and secreted him in a position whence he could judge Marchand's abilities. That Bach had an opportunity to hear his rival before challenging him is probable; that he was sum-

[1] Forkel, p. 111.   [2] Pirro (1), p. 52.   [3] Sp. i. 817.
[4] In his *Legende einiger Musikheiligen* (1786).

moned from Weimar to undo him is the gloss of legend. Probably
the simultaneous appearance in Dresden of two distinguished
players suggested a contest between them. Adlung, indeed, who
professed to have the story from Bach, declares [1] that the competition was devised to determine whether France or Germany
could boast the better clavier player. Burney, whose narrative
otherwise is full of errors, concludes impartially, 'It was an honour
to Pompey that he was conquered by Caesar, and to Marchand to
be only vanquished by Bach.' [2]

The contest is detailed in substantial agreement by Johann
Abraham Birnbaum,[3] writing with Bach's authority, and by
Forkel,[4] upon information supplied by Bach's sons. Hitherto
chiefly famous as an organist, Bach was incited to send a challenge
to the Frenchman, proposing to play at sight any music put before
him, provided his opponent submitted to the same test. Marchand
accepted the wager, and a day and hour were arranged in the house
of Count von Flemming, Bach's patron in later years, who may
be regarded as the contriver of the spectacular contest to which
Dresden society was forthwith invited. Bach arrived at the appointed hour, and with the umpires and a large company awaited
his opponent. Marchand did not appear, and a messenger dispatched to his lodging returned with the news that he could not
be found. He had, in fact, left Dresden that morning in order, it
was assumed, to avoid a contest in which he anticipated defeat.
Bach thereupon performed alone and excited the admiration of his
audience, who applauded his personal triumph, and, with less
reason, concluded the inferiority of French to German art. Marchand's defeat did not lessen the estimation of his countrymen,
among whom he lived prosperous till his death at Paris in 1732.[5]
The substantial accuracy of the German narratives of the contest,
made public after his death, does not appear to have been challenged in France, where, however, Marpurg's version[6] is preferred, according to which Bach challenged Marchand to a contest
on the organ, after a public concert at which the two masters had
already matched their powers on the clavier.

A sharp reverse in his fortunes followed Bach's triumph in a field

---

[1] In his *Anleitung* (1758), quoted in Dahms, p. 40.
[2] *Present State of Music in Germany* (ed. 1775), ii. 82. Burney represents Marchand as the challenger and Bach as prevailing after Dresden's native champions
had shirked the French Goliath's challenge.
[3] Cf. his reply to Joh. Adolph Scheibe, in Dahms, p. 39.   [4] Forkel, p. 17.
[5] The statement made by the Nekrolog and Forkel, that Bach was deprived of
a substantial honorarium by the dishonesty of a Court official, is probably
apocryphal.
[6] In his *Legende einiger Musikheiligen* (1786).

in which his country's eminence till now was not admitted. The
circumstances of his disgrace and departure from Weimar are
inferential, but not obscure.[1] The death of the elder Drese on
1 December 1716 excited in him hopes which were not realized:
for nearly three years Bach had fulfilled one of his chief duties, and
had reasonable grounds to expect a 'Predicat' as his successor. In
fact, the Duke promoted Drese's son, whom already in March 1714
Bach had superseded as composer of the cantatas performed in the
Schloss chapel. The abnormal title of Concertmeister then conferred on Bach, however, was not withdrawn, though the lack of
any cantatas from his pen after November 1716 suggests that
the new Capellmeister resumed the full obligations of the post.
Bach's chagrin is intelligible and invited him to look elsewhere for
employment. Moreover, he was involved in the feud between the
Duke and his nephew Ernst August.[2] Embittered correspondence,
appeals to the Kaiser and relatives, arrests of officials, and other
forcible acts, punctuated their unseemly bickering, while members
of the ducal Capelle were categorically inhibited from attendance
at the Rotes Schloss under penalty of ten thalers,[3] an order extended to the 'dames' and 'cavaliers' of the Court.[4] Bach's relations with the Red Schloss were so intimate that the Duchess
Eleonore Wilhelmine stood godmother to the last of his first wife's
children,[5] who bore the princely names Leopold Augustus for a life
of less than a year. Bach consequently drew on himself the Duke's
suspicion, and, being torn between two allegiances, seized a way out
of his dilemma which further incensed the martinet of Wilhelmsburg. Duchess Eleonore's brother, Prince Leopold of Anhalt-
Cöthen, a musical amateur of high ability, whom Bach probably
met at the Rotes Schloss, offered him the office of Capellmeister
at his Court. Bach declared his willingness to accept it, and on
5 August 1717, a few weeks before his routing of Marchand, it was
conferred.[6]

The evident hand of his nephew in what he regarded as an
intrigue, a constitutional disinclination to part with his servants,
and genuine appreciation of Bach's character and musical ability,
combined to fortify Wilhelm Ernst's refusal to grant the release
he craved. To accept the Duke's masterful refusal was alien to
Bach's independent nature, and the *réclame* of his meeting with
Marchand buttressed his determination to force a 'dimission'.

[1] Neither the Nekrolog nor Forkel throws any light upon the event.
[2] Marconnay, pp. 52 ff., displays their acrid relations.
[3] Bojanowski, p. 46.   [4] Marconnay, p. 61.
[5] Sp. i. 620. The child was born at Cöthen in 1718.   [6] Cf. *infra*, p. 119.

I

Returning to Weimar from Dresden, he found preparations in progress for celebrating the second centenary of the Reformation in
'das Weimarsche Zion' on 31 October 1717 and the two following
days.[1] Salomo Franck had prepared a series of cantata texts, whose
performance followed Wilhelm Ernst's birthday (30 October), an
occasion marked by the Duke's foundation of a fund to endow the
members of his Capelle.[2] As organist Bach took his share in the
ceremonies, but either was not invited, or declined to put music to
Franck's texts.[3] Immediately after the festival he renewed his
application for release from ducal service, with an insistence to
which Wilhelm Ernst was not accustomed. Hofsecretär Theodor
Benedikt Bormann laconically notes the consequences:[4] 'On
6 November [1717] Bach, till now Concertmeister and Hof-
organist, was put under arrest in the justice room for obstinately
demanding his instant demission. He was released on December 2
with a grudging permission to retire from the Duke's service.' His
month of detention was not unprofitable if, as has been suggested,[5]
he employed it in planning the 'Orgelbüchlein' and partially completing its design.

   With the termination of his Weimar service Bach for ever
abandoned the official functions of an organist, and at the moment
when his pre-eminence as a player was acknowledged. As a composer his greatness was not yet revealed, but the routing of Marchand had given him national fame. Johann Mattheson, who heard
them both and was the friend of Handel, declared that if any one
could surpass the latter 'es müsste Bach in Leipzig seyn'.[6] Johann
Joachim Quantz, Frederick the Great's Cammermusicus and
Court Composer, pointed to him as the player who had developed
organ technique to its highest perfection.[7] Georg Andreas Sorge,
Hoforganist at Lobenstein, styled him 'the prince of organists',[8]
and the Nekrolog concisely recorded the judgement of his generation: 'Bach was the finest player that has ever been known.'
Legends grew round him, as round Handel, apocryphal, yet
indicative of the awe in which he was held. It was told of him, that
he liked to visit village churches to play the organ, in order to
enjoy the amazement excited by his skill, or to hear the organist
declare: 'This must be Bach or the Devil!' Bach ridiculed such
stories, having too much respect for his art to subject it to his
vanity. Necessarily he realized his superiority and found the

[1] Bi. i. 121.   [2] Bojanowski, p. 46.
[3] Sp. i. 577 is certainly wrong in supposing that Bach set some or all of these
libretti.   [4] Thüringer Staatsarchiv, Weimar, Blatt 66ᵇ anno 1717.
[5] T.B.C. iii. 18   [6] Dahms, p. 109.   [7] Forkel, p. 67.
[6] Ibid., p. 69.

deference shown him not disagreeable. But his modesty was invincible: if asked the secret of his mastership, he would reply, 'There is nothing wonderful about it. You merely strike the right note and the organ does the rest.'[1] He was fond of listening to other players, and, if he heard a fugue played in church, would indicate to his companion how its subject should be treated, nudging him with gratification if his anticipation was realized.[2] Throughout his life his unique powers were recognized by constant invitations to test new organs and examine candidates for vacant organistships. If the instrument pleased him he would, when he had finished his official task, display his splendid talent on it for his own pleasure and that of his audience. On such an occasion he would choose a theme for extemporization, treating it first in the Prelude and Fugue form, then on solo stops, interweaving it next with a familiar hymn melody, and ending with a fugue to show off the full resources of the instrument.[3] It was observed of him that, before he began to extemporize, he preferred to play something already familiar, as though his inventiveness needed stimulus.[4] Such displays never failed to excite wonder and, among connoisseurs like Reinken of Hamburg, the conviction that in Bach the gift of extemporization reached its highest perfection.[5] But officially he ceased to be an organist on 2 December 1717, and for the remaining thirty-three years of his life diverted his genius to activities in which his sublimity was not realized by the communities within which he dwelt, still less by the wider world outside, until long after he passed to the immortals. Meanwhile, in Advent his pupil Schubart received his posts as Hoforganist and Cammermusicus at Weimar,[6] and before the New Year of 1718, with his nursery of young children, the eldest of them nine, Bach opened a new chapter of his career at Cöthen.[7]

[1] Sp. ii. 744. [2] Forkel, p. 108. [3] *Ibid.*, p. 67.
[4] Sp. ii. 744 quotes the testimony of a contemporary of Bach to this effect.
[5] Forkel, p. 21. [6] Bojanowski, p. 49.
[7] Herr Karl Bechstein has recently (1929) brought to light the fact that, prior to 1713, Bach, his wife, and her sister lodged in the house of his friend, Adam Emanuel Weldig, a building which, early in the nineteenth century, was attached to the Hotel Erbprinz, which bounded it on the west. A tablet placed on its north front in 1930 states: 'Hier wohnte Johann Sebastian Bach 1708–1717.' But Weldig sold the house on 22 August 1713, on his removal to Weissenfels, and Bach's continued residence in it is merely conjectural. See Illustration No. 42.

CHAPTER VI
CÖTHEN

BACH'S migration to Cöthen offers a problem to his biographer. That he coveted the title Capellmeister is very evident from his later disinclination to surrender it.[1] Financial considerations may have influenced him: his children were growing in years and number, and provision for their education needed to be made. Prince Leopold's generous increase of his salary cannot have been unwelcome on that account, though his necessity was not yet compelling. At a time when intimacy between princes and musicians was unusual, Bach would be flattered by the admiring friendship of his young master, who, until he tardily submitted to the yoke of matrimony, lavished upon his Capellmeister and his art the affection of an ardent nature. But these considerations, though weighty, hardly drove Bach from Weimar. Probably he was beginning to find the martinet rule of his Duke irksome, the family jars of the Court disagreeable and distracting. Clearly he had set his heart on Drese's post, and though his master cannot be blamed for preferring an older, though less competent, servant, Bach held his action a slight on himself, on his art. There was, too, in his nature a disposition to irritability which swelled easily to pugnacity under provocation. The circumstances of his retirement from Arnstadt exhibit the combativeness that nearly twenty years later opposed every authority in Leipzig until his alleged wrongs were righted. In such a mood he now shook the dust of Weimar from his feet, surrendered the declared object of his life, and divorced his art from the exalted purpose to which he had dedicated it. For the Cöthen Court was 'reformed', its chapel an unlovely vault in which only stern Calvinist psalm tunes were heard, an atmosphere which stifled the fullest expression of Bach's art and challenged his most rooted convictions. At Ohrdruf, Eisenach, and Lüneburg he had been fed on the milk of Lutheran orthodoxy. Luther's *Works* was the most costly book in his library at his death. Franz Klinge's *Treuhertzige Warnung vor Abfall von der Lutherischen Lehre* kept it company, along with fiery Dr. August Pfeiffer's *Anticalvinismus, Evangelische Christenschule*, and *Antimelancholicus*. Bach fortified his faith amid the theological

[1] See his letter to Erdmann, *infra*, p. 204.

pits that surrounded him at Cöthen by studying them; for their
titles are noted on the cover of the 'Clavierbüchlein' he prepared
for his second wife in 1722.[1] The deprivation of an adequate
organ at the zenith of his renown as a player was another disadvantage.[2] Hence, if his career at Cöthen was placid and happy,
and though he retained his situation for more than five years,
he was ready, if opportunity arose, as in 1720, to return to the
pastures whence he had strayed.

Situated some eighty miles north-east of Weimar, Cöthen[3] since
1603 was the capital of a principality within the once undivided
Duchy of Anhalt, a country of sandy plains, pine forests, and rich
pasture. To-day it is a quiet ancient town of white house-fronts
and winding streets ringed by modern suburbs. The Wallstrasse,
where Bach's bust looks from its pedestal upon the 'reformed'
St. Jakobskirche, had newly been laid out when he came from
Weimar;[4] the town still sheltered within its medieval walls, whose
Magdeburger, Schalaunischer, and Hallischer towers to-day raise
their hoary heads.[5] Isolated within its moat and pleasure grounds,
the Schloss[6] presents an agreeably irregular pile of gabled roofs,
with three tall towers[7] standing sentinel above its northern and
southern wings. When Bach knew it, it filled three sides of an
inner quadrangle, whose eastern face opened on a vista of terraces
and gardens,[8] while the main bridge and portal across the moat
pierced its western front. The Prince's apartments lay in the
southern wing,[9] the Ludwigsbau, which to-day houses the Lud-
wigs-Gymnasium. Less pretentious and imposing than Weimar's

[1] Cf. a facsimile in B.-G. xliv. Bl. 17, and Reimann, p. 22.
[2] The St. Jakobskirche possessed a fairly large organ some forty years old, and
a small one was installed in the St. Agnuskirche (Bunge, p. 28). It is improbable
that Bach denied himself access to the former because it stood in a 'reformed'
building. The St. Agnus organ had a pedal of unusual range, two and a half
octaves up to F♯. Pirro (3), p. 50, associates it with the Prelude (Toccata) in
F major (B.-G. XV. 154):

The pedal in *In dulci jubilo* (Orgelbüchlein) touches F♯.   [3] Illus. No. 47.
[4] Schulze, p. 50.   [5] Between 1700 and 1720 Cöthen doubled
its population, and by 1750 was the largest town in Anhalt (*ibid.*, p. 60).
[6] Illus. Nos. 48–50, 55.   [7] They are known locally as 'the Artichokes'.
[8] To-day a hideous brick prison completes the quadrangle on the east and ruins
its picturesqueness.   [9] *i.e.* to the left of the picture, No. 55.

Wilhelmsburg, the Schloss afforded a more intimate setting for the
chamber music, now immortal, whose notes were first borne across
its stagnant moat from Leopold's hall in the southern wing, an
apartment which, modernized and mirrored, now serves the Gymnasium as Aula. Below it, to the left of the main staircase, looking
out through recessed windows upon the quadrangle,[1] may be seen
a dingy, groined, and whitewashed chamber, the Schloss chapel,
whose mean proportions and barren walls must have chilled Bach's
soul.[2] The 'Fürstenstuhl' stood on the western wall near the door,
a small organ of two manuals with ten stops and a pedal of three[3]
at the other end. Bach's duty did not require him to play it, and
its insignificance can rarely have invited him to do so.

   Prince Leopold,[4] the youthful master of Cöthen and its people,
was the son of his father's romantic union with the accomplished
Gisela Agnes von Rath, a *mésalliance* of birth and religion: she was
a Lutheran, her husband a Calvinist. They were married in 1692
and in 1694 Leopold was born. The town church (St. Jakobskirche) being Calvinist, she moved her husband to build the
St. Agnuskirche, on whose chancel walls to-day hang her portrait
and Lucas Cranach's 'Last Supper'. Her fellow-Lutherans owed
to her also a school for their children, whose classrooms the young
Bachs attended, and a Home for their needy women of gentle
birth. As her husband died in 1704, when Leopold was ten, the
regency passed to herself. Residing with her children in the modest
house opposite the St. Agnuskirche, she ruled with wisdom; her
memory to this day is green in Cöthen.[5] Late in 1710 Leopold
set out on the conventional grand tour, visited England and Holland, enjoyed the Opera at Venice, and at Rome took lessons from
Johann David Heinichen, an alumnus of the Leipzig Thomasschule then in vogue as a composer of Opera. The Prince returned
home in 1713 an accomplished amateur on the violin, viola da
gamba, clavier, and a competent singer, of whom Bach declared[6]
that he not only loved music, but was proficient and understanding
in the art. His romantic temperament is revealed in his portrait,
the high brow, long, waving, undressed chevelure, the large clear
eyes, beneath exaggerated eyebrows inherited from his mother, and
a countenance open, fresh, and friendly.

---

[1] Illus. No. 51.   [2] The present floor is raised about 2·30 metres
above the original level (Bethge, p. 17).
[3] *Ibid.* Leopold's Capelle did not include an organist. Perhaps Johann Jakob
Müller, organist of the St. Jakosskirche, functioned. The organ no longer exists.
The chapel (Schlosskirche) is now the Singesaal of the Gymnasium. The other
wings of the Schloss are occupied as public administrative offices.
[4] Illus. No. 53.   [5] Cf. Schulze, p. 46; Bethge, p. 16.
[6] In his letter to Erdmann, *infra*, p. 204.

Leopold came of age in December 1715 [1] and reigned alone in his bachelor palace, while Gisela Agnes retired to the Schloss on the Saale which gave her the title Gräfin von Nienburg, conferred by the Kaiser after her marriage.[2] Under her husband's puritanic rule the Cöthen Court maintained no Capelle, and a revenue of 7,600 thalers [3] was inadequate to support Opera. Thriftily administering her resources during her son's minority, Gisela Agnes so far yielded to his insistence as to set up (October 1707) a modest establishment of three musicians: Johann Jakob Müller, later organist of the St. Jakobskirche and, probably, Quintus on the school staff, Wilhelm Andreas Harbordt, and Johann Freytag, all of whom served under Bach.[4] Returned from his continental tour, Leopold expanded his Capelle to a size more commensurate with his tastes. In July 1714 he had created a Capellmeister, Augustinus Reinhard Stricker, whom as a student at the Ritteracademie he had known at Berlin in 1708, appointing at the same time Frau Catharina Stricker as sopranist and lutanist.[5] The Capelle in 1716 numbered eighteen players,[6] who, with some omissions and additions, constituted its membership under Bach. Stricker and his wife retired in August 1717: probably the Prince's partiality for instrumental music denied the singer adequate opportunity to display her talent. Their withdrawal enabled Leopold to offer the post of Capellmeister to Bach, who was known to him since his sister's wedding at Nienburg in the previous year. Bach received the appointment on 5 August 1717;[7] his name consequently appears in the

Protocolle der Fürstlichen Capelle und Trompetergagen
von Johannis [24 June] 1717 bis dahin 1718.[8]

Th. Gr.

Joh. Sebastian Bach, the newly appointed Capellmeister, at a
monthly salary of 33 th. 8 gr., from 1 August 1717 to June
1718 . . . . 366 16

---

[1] Bunge, p. 22. His birthday was 29 November 1694.
[2] Bethge, p. 16; Schulze, p. 46. [3] Wäschke, p. 32.
[4] The rescript of 15 Oct. 1707, and the petition of 28 Sept. 1707 on which it was founded, are printed in Bunge, pp. 17, 18.
[5] Bunge, pp. 21, 25. [6] Wäschke, p. 31.
[7] The Protocol of 1717–18 dates his pay from 1 August. A document in the Cammerrechnung for 1717–18 in the Anhalt. Staatsarchiv at Zerbst (fol. 24) states that Bach 'vom 1 Aug. seine Gage empfangen'. His *dimission* in 1723 gives the date as 5 August (Bunge, p. 30). I am informed by the Herr Archivrat at Zerbst that Bach's appointment was dated 5 Aug., but that his pay, as was usual, was drawn from the first of the month.
[8] Zerbst: Anhaltisches Staatsarchiv, Abteilung Cöthen, A 12, No. 66. Prince Leopold's desire to establish a Capelle was aided by the dissolution of the Hofcapelle at Berlin on the death of Friedrich I in February 1713. Besides

Th. Gr.

*Josephus Spiess, first Cammermusicus [at 16 th. 16 gr.], from
August 1717 to July 1718 .   .   .   .   . 200[1]
*Johann Ludwig Rose,[2] Cammermusicus [at 12 th. 12 gr.],
from August 1717 to June 1718 .   .   .   . 137 12
*Martin Friedrich Markus, Cammermusicus[3] [at 10 th. 20 gr.],
from July 1717 to June 1718 130
*Johann Christoph Torlee, Cammermusicus [at 10 th. 20 gr.],
from July 1717 to June 1718 122
*Johann Heinrich Freytag, Cammermusicus [at 7 th. 20 gr.],
from July 1717 to June 1718[4] 94
*Christian Ferdinand Abel,[5] Chamber violinist and gambist,
[at 12 th.], from July 1717 to June 1718 .   .   . 144
*Johann Gottlieb Würdig, Cammermusicus [at 7 th.], from
July 1717 to June 1718 84
*Christian Bernhard Linigke,[6] Cammermusicus [at 12 th.
12 gr.], from July 1717 to June 1718 .   .   . 150
*Johann Kräuser,[7] Copyist, from July 1717 to November 1717 88 12
*Johann Freytag, sen., Musicus [at 2 th. 16 gr.], from 17 July 1717
to 16 July 1718 .   .   .   .   .   . 34 16
*Wilhelm Harbordt, Musicus [at 4 th.], from 17 July 1717 to June
1718 .   .   .   . 38 16
*Adam Weber, Musicus [at 4 th.], from July 1717 to June 1718 48
Johann Bernhard Göbel, Copyist [at 2 th.], appointed 1 Dec. 1717,
to June 1718 14
*Emanuel Heinrich Gottlieb Freytag, Musicus, 5 thalers due
quarterly, unpaid.[8]
*Johann Ludwig Schreiber, trumpeter [at 9 th.], from July 1717
to June 1718 108
*Johann Christoph Krahl, trumpeter [at 9 th.], from July 1717 to
June 1718 108
*Anton Unger, drummer[9] [at 6 th.], from July 1717 to June 1718 72

* Members of the Capelle in 1716-17 (Wäschke, p. 31).

Stricker and his wife (Catharina Elisabeth Müller), the following players came
to Cöthen from Berlin: Christian Bernhard Linigke, violoncellist; Joseph Spiess,
violinist; Johann Ludwig Rose, oboist; Christoph Torley (Turley, Torbey,
Torlee), fagottist; Martin Friedrich Marx or Marcks (Markus), violinist; and
Bach's copyist Johann Kräuser (Kreyser). See 'Personalien der Hofkapelle unter
Friedrich III (I)' in Curt Sachs's Musik und Oper am kurbrandenburgischen Hof
(Berlin, 1910).
[1] In Oct. 1719 Harbordt's pay was added to this sum (Wäschke, p. 36).
[2] Rose was an all-round man, could play the oboe, and taught the pages fencing
(Wäschke, p. 39).
[3] Left the Capelle in June 1722 (Wäschke, p. 39).
[4] He died in 1720-1 (ibid., p. 37).
[5] Father of Carl Friedrich Abel, later associated with Bach's son Johann
Christian in England.   [6] Bunge has 'Linike'.
[7] Bunge has 'Kreyser'.
[8] In the establishment for 1719-20 he received 8 th. 12 gr. a month, or 102
thalers a year (Wäschke, p. 36). This was increased in 1720-1, after Joh. H.
Freytag's death, when he went to Berlin to study (ibid., p. 37).
[9] He also kept an inn, at which visiting musicians were entertained (Bethge,
p. 25).

The Protocol records the names of those who first heard and
performed the chamber music Bach produced at Cöthen, the
Sonatas, Concertos, and orchestral Suites. Imagination does not
wander from the path of probability in supposing that Josephus
Spiess and Johann Ludwig Rose gave the first performance of the
Concerto for two violins, on some evening when the candles were
lit in the great room between the high towers; that Schreiber and
his colleague Krahl first sent their trumpets' rollicking notes to
the rafters in the closing Gigue of the Suite in D; that the Prince
himself was active in the Sonatas for clavier and viol da gamba;
and that reinforced, as will be shown, by visiting players, the
Capelle played the Brandenburg music before it was offered elsewhere. For its composition suffered little change as long as Bach
controlled it. Wilhelm Harbordt, a survivor of the original three,
fell early out of the list.[1] In 1718–19 the copyist J. B. Göbel gave
place to Bach's Ohrdruf nephew and pupil, Johann Bernhard,
who in turn was replaced by one of the Schloss lackeys, Emanuel
Leberecht Gottschalk.[2] Carl Friedrich Vetter is named as copyist
in 1719–20.[3] Christian Rolle, organist of the St. Jakobskirche,
entered the Capelle at Midsummer 1722,[4] the last recorded
change in its composition before Bach migrated to Leipzig. Otherwise[5] this band of musicians were his colleagues in a period which
Bach's genius and activity made fruitful in the development of
secular instrumental music. The rehearsals of the Collegium
Musicum, as the Capelle was styled, are stated to have been held
in the house of a shopkeeper named Lautsch.[6] But the accounts
preserved at Zerbst show that for the year December 1718–
December 1719, and thereafter, Bach received twelve thalers
annually for conducting them 'in seinem Hause'. His pay otherwise was at the high rate of 400 thalers a year, as against the 250
florins he received at Weimar, a stipend which exceeded by over
120 thalers the joint income of his predecessor and his wife,[7] and
put him on a financial equality with the Hofmarschall, the second
highest functionary of the princely Court.[8]

The Capelle accounts reveal not infrequent visits of musicians,
singers, and players, upon particular occasions whose character is

[1] Wäschke, p. 35. Their pay was on a lower standard than that of the others.
[2] Ibid., p. 35. I find his Christian names in the document at Zerbst. He was
named after Leopold's father.
[3] As he received money on 11 Jan. 1720 to attend his mother's funeral at
Leipzig (Wäschke, p. 37), he was perhaps a son of Daniel Vetter, organist of
the Nikolaikirche there.
[4] Wäschke, p. 39.
[5] Johann Valentin Fischer is named in the establishment for 1719–20.
[6] Bethge, p. 25.   [7] Bunge, p. 21.   [8] Bethge, p. 18.

not stated. In 1717–18 Nikolaus Jungk was entertained at Unger's inn and received a fee of twenty thalers for an unrecorded service.[1] In 1719 a singer from Weissenfels was paid fifteen thalers on 24 July; a week later a performer entertained the Court on a 'Bandoloisches Instrument'; on 17 August a Düsseldorf lutanist was engaged, and on 20 October 1718 a descantist from Rudolstadt. Ginacini, a male descantist, received twenty thalers on 21 March 1719, and thirty-six thalers remunerated two Berlin musicians on 19 September 1721. On 6 June 1722 a fee of fifteen thalers was paid to 'die beyden Waldhornisten',[2] whose engagement indicates a performance of the first Brandenburg Concerto in F major. The Master of the Pages, a Frenchman named Jean François Monjo,[3] was the father of two daughters whose services as singers Bach occasionally employed;[4] their abilities invited them sometimes to a more august audience at the Prussian Court.[5] Occasionally the Collegium Musicum participated in theatrical performances. A 'Comödien-Theatrum' was erected in July 1718 in the Orangery beyond the Schloss garden,[6] whose situation gave the present Theaterstrasse its name. Here, for a season that lasted till March 1719, Johann Ferdinand Becker performed comedies in a theatre furnished with carpets and chairs from the Schloss.

When Bach went to Cöthen secular instrumental music was only on the threshold of an independent existence. Most German princes had their private orchestra, or Capelle, but instrumental music had for long been under the ban of the Church, the construction and technique of available instruments were little understood, and the possibilities of their combination were hardly explored. Monteverdi (d. 1643) in Italy, Purcell (d. 1695) in England, Lully (d. 1687) in France, had begun to set the orchestra on a course of its own; but Corelli's concerti had been only recently (1712) given to the world when Bach was invited to make music for a composite instrument which had little literature and few recognized conventions of its own. An inventory of the Cöthen Capelle library, taken in 1768,[7] discloses a considerable collection of violin concertos, trios, and quartets, suites, Divertimenti, Sinfonien, and occasional vocal works, few of whose composers bear a distinguished name. At Bach's disposal were the Sinfonien of Johann Adolph Hasse, Baldassare Galuppi, and Johann Fischer, an

[1] Wäschke, p. 35.
[2] These details are extracted from the Cammerrechnungen in the Anhalt. Staatsarchiv at Zerbst.
[3] A 'Monjo, aus Paris' was among the teachers of French at Leipzig in 1736 Cf. D.J.F.L., p. 59.   [4] Wäschke, p. 37.
[5] Bunge, p. 27.   [6] Wäschke, p. 36.   [7] It is printed in Bunge, p. 44.

unsatisfactorily meagre repertory. Francesco Manfredini, among the Italians, was serviceable in other forms. Corelli and Vivaldi were not represented at all, and examples of Couperin and the French school were entirely absent. On the other hand, the Prince owned excellent instruments for the use of his Capelle: a viola by Stainer dated 1650, a violoncello piccolo by the same maker of the same date, three others by Hoffmann, a contraviolon by Hoffmann dated 1714, three flutes, two oboes d'amore, a bassoon, tromba marina, lute, theorbo,[1] zither, two pairs of timpani, a 'Bogen-flügel', one or two 'Flügel', and a 'Reiseflügel'.[2] Bach himself tuned and quilled the claviers,[3] an art in which he was particular and proficient. 'No one could adjust the quill plectrums of his clavier to his satisfaction but himself,' writes Forkel. 'He was so skilful in the operation that it never took him more than a quarter of an hour.'[4]

Released from Weimar on 2 December 1717, Bach hastened to Cöthen, where, since receiving his appointment in August, he had settled his household.[5] The locality of his lodging is not precisely known. Pohlmann's bust of him[6] in the Wallstrasse perpetuates a tradition that he lived there, a locality outside the ancient wall on which houses were beginning to spring up. Another site has been proposed in the Marktstrasse, near the St. Jakobskirche and Rathaus,[7] where Kühn's premises stand to-day. A tradition that Bach was disturbed by the clatter of a water-mill has suggested that he lived beyond the Schloss garden, near the Orangery. The Schloss gardens, however, extended in the opposite direction as well, to another mill whose existence is indicated by the present Mühlenstrasse. Near by, in the Schalaunische Strasse,[8] two houses stand just within the Schalaunisches Thor, to-day numbered 29 and 30, occupied by an optician (A. Heidenreich) and saddler (Franz Berger). The supposition that Bach lived in one or other of them is strengthened by the knowledge that the Prince lodged some of his retainers immediately opposite, in a house behind

---

[1] A large double-necked lute. [2] Bunge, p. 41.
[3] The Capelle accounts at Zerbst contain the following entries: '12 Sept. 1722. Dem Capellmeister Bachen vor Reparatur des Fürstl. Cimbalo, ohne die Saiten, 1 th.'; '30 Dec. 1722. Denselben vor eine Befederung des grossen Clavecins, einsch. der Saiten, 1 th. 8 gr.'; '20 Mar. 1723. Dem Capellmeister Bachen, der dieses Clavecin zu befedern, 1 th.' [4] Forkel, p. 59.
[5] That he was settled in his house by 10 Dec. 1717 is clear from an entry in the Capelle accounts for 1 Oct. 1718 (Seite 35): 'Dem Capellmeister Bachen einjährigen Hausszinss vor das Collegium Musicum von d. 10 Dec. 1717 biss dahin 1718, 12 Rth.' He also received on 7 Aug. 1717 the sum of 50 thalers 'zum gnädigsten Recompens', probably to facilitate his removal from Weimar.
[6] Erected on the bicentenary of his birth (21 March 1885).
[7] Illus. No. 52. [8] Illus. No. 56.

which an insignificant stream may still be traced. Moreover, a former occupant of No. 30, one Schrader, a wood-turner, found in its attic during his tenancy a quantity of manuscripts, including a fragment of Bach's music.[1] There is, however, an alternative and preferable domicile. The higher dignitaries of the Prince's bachelor Court were accommodated in the Schloss itself, and Bach's generous stipend indicates that he ranked among them. The probability that quarters were assigned him in it must therefore not be excluded, and is supported by authoritative evidence. His son Leopold Augustus was baptized in the Schloss chapel on 17 November 1718, a fact which can be attributed to the presence of the Prince as godfather.[2] But, three years later, Bach's second marriage is also recorded in the Schlosskirche register, where it is stated to have taken place within his lodging.[3] The inference is, that the event was registered within the jurisdiction in which it occurred, and the fact that the burials of Bach's first wife and her children are recorded in the St. Agnuskirche register does not weaken the implication; for the Schloss had no burial-ground of its own.[4] Probability therefore points to Bach's lodging having been in the north or west wing of the Schloss, the more so because his name is absent from the contemporary civic register of house-holders. It is, at any rate, agreeable to associate him with a fabric that preserves the features with which he was familiar, to picture him making music with his Collegium Musicum in its candle-lit apartments, or taking his walks abroad across the bridged moat between the sentries into the exercise ground, where sleek horses stood in comfortable stables, and the princely carriages were visible within the great doors. A happy playground for the young Bachs this sometime tilting-ground must have been.

Bach had hardly arrived in his new surroundings, in December 1717, before he was invited to Leipzig to examine the organ lately erected in the University Church (Paulinerkirche) there. Probably he owed the invitation to Johann Kuhnau, his associate at Halle in the previous year. The compliment was the greater because the examination was entrusted entirely to himself by the University authorities, who as long ago as September 1710 had commissioned the builder, Johann Scheibe, to rebuild the organ in the west gallery of their lofty church upon the Augustusplatz. Scheibe having completed the work on 4 November 1716, the Rector, Dr. Recken-berg, and a small committee were tardily empowered to invite

---

[1] A clairvoyant, Herr Max Moecke, has recently (1930) professed to identify Wallstrasse 26 as Bach's dwelling-house.
[2] Cf. *infra*, p. 127.　　　　　[3] Cf. *infra*, p. 137.　　　　　[4] Bethge, p. 23.

a competent authority to examine it. Bach was proposed, accepted the commission, and in the last weeks of 1717 arrived to fulfil it. The organ [1] was a large one of three manuals, in whose examination Bach was attended by Lorenz Liebenroth, the Mansfeld organ-builder, and Michael Steiner, organist of the Leipzig Johanniskirche, representing Scheibe.[2] On 17 December he presented his report: [3]

Having received instructions from the worshipful Dr. Reckenberg, Rector Magnificus of the illustrious Academy of Leipzig, to examine the organ which has been renovated and enlarged in the Paulinerkirche, I have completed my task to the best of my ability, noted certain *defecta* in the work, and now present my report on the whole structure.

1. First of all, I would observe that the instrument has been set up in a very contracted space, and consequently it will not be easy to get at parts needing repair. It is fair to Herr Scheibe to point out, however, that the case was not built by him; he had to use it as he found it and adapt his plans to suit it. Moreover, he asked for more space and was denied it.

2. The usual principal parts of the instrument, wind-trunks, bellows, pipes, roller-boards, and so forth, have been carefully executed. The wind pressure, however, would be bettered by being more *equal*; it is somewhat variable at present. The roller-boards also should have been set up in frames to prevent them creaking in bad weather. On the other hand, Herr Scheibe has put in panels of his own design, and assures me that the effect will be the same as if he had introduced frames. I therefore do not press the matter.

3. The materials used are in conformity with the specification and contract *qualitate* and *quantitate*, excepting that two reed stops, the 4 ft. Schalmei and 2 ft. Cornet, have been left out, no doubt on the instructions of the distinguished Collegium. Instead, a 2 ft. Octave has been introduced on the Brustwerk and a 2 ft. Hohlflöte on the Hinterwerk.

4. Certain minor *defecta* will be put right by the builder: the bottom pipes of the Trombone and Bass Trumpet are inclined to speak roughly instead of with steady pure tone. The other pipes also are *inaequal* and need adjustment when the instrument is tuned again, a simple task in better weather than we have had lately.

5. The trackers might be lighter, and the manuals might with advantage have been set higher. This, however, is due to the contracted space at the builder's disposal and cannot be remedied. There is, however, no danger of the notes sticking in action.

6. Though it was not contracted for, the builder has made a new wind-trunk to the Brustwerk, replacing the old one and its unsatisfactory 'Fundament Brete'.[4] Further, its old manual had the old-fashioned short

---

[1] Its specification is in Sp. ii. 117; Pirro (3), p. 85. Cf. Schering, p. 317; Flade, p. 49.   [2] Bi. iv. 100, quoting Sicul's Jahrbuch for 1718.
[3] Leipzig: Universitäts-Acta, Repert. II/III, No. 5. Litt. B. Sect. II. Fol. 63.
[4] Regarding the Fundamentbrett, which carried the wind pressure to the soundboards, see Flade, p. 115: 'Silbermann pflegte zwischen die Kanzellen [wind apertures] nicht Leisten einzuleimen und sie dadurch "zuzuspünden", wie das fast alle Orgelbauer seiner Zeit taten, sondern er bedeckt durch ein darübergeleimtes Brett das sogenannte "Fundamentbrett".'

octave. Hence, since it was not possible to add new *claves* to make the three manuals uniform, and as a *déformité* would have resulted had it been retained, the builder was obliged to put in a new one, to avoid *defecta* and secure *conformité*. I am of opinion that he should be paid for this additional work, in regard to which he ought not to be allowed to be out of pocket.

The builder has asked me also to represent to the illustrious Academy, that inasmuch as certain details of the work were not committed to him, *item* the carving, gilding, and ornamentation, which was given to Herr Vetter *pro inspectione*, at a cost still to be reckoned, he may not be held accountable for them, as indeed is not usual; had it been so he would have made terms accordingly. He therefore begs that he may not be charged for these details.

In conclusion, I make the following representations: (1) As much of the window as lies immediately behind the organ should be built up or covered with a strong metal plate on the inside, to prevent damage to the instrument through bad weather. (2) It is customary, and in every case advisable, for the builder to give a year's guarantee to make good any defects that may arise, an undertaking he is usually very willing to offer, provided he receives speedy and complete *satisfaction* for work done outside his actual contract.

I have nothing further to report in regard to my inspection of the organ, save to place myself entirely at the disposal of the right worshipful Rector Magnificus Dr. Reckenberg, and the illustrious Collegium, subscribing myself

Their most obedient servant,
Joh. Seb. Bach,
Capellmeister to the excellent
Prince of Anhalt-Cöthen.

Leipzig, 17 December 1717.[1]

If Bach owed his Leipzig visit to Kuhnau's representation, probably he also received an invitation to function in one of the two churches with which, as Kuhnau's successor, he later was so intimately connected. Upon the manuscript of his Advent cantata 'Nun komm, der Heiden Heiland' (No. 61) is a note in his handwriting outlining the order of the Leipzig morning service (Hauptgottesdienst).[2] It indicates his unfamiliarity with the Leipzig ritual, and also a performance of the cantata on the occasion under

---

[1] Spitta omits the following report by Daniel Vetter to the University; it is found on ff. 73–6 of the docket containing Bach's report. Vetter writes on 28 Jan. 1718: '. . . und endlich der gantze Bau durch Gottes Gnade, den 4 Nov. anno 1716 vollführet, auch das Werck von dem Cötischen Capell Meister Herrn N. Bach, welcher dasselbe auf e. löbl. Universität Begehren, am 16 Decembr. 1717 examinieren müssen, ohne eintzigen Haupt-defect, und dergestalt befunden worden, dass er solches nicht genugsam rühmen und loben können, sonderlich derer Ramen Register, welche neu verfertiget, und in sehr vielen Orgeln nicht zu finden, wie auch ein jeder Verständiger, der dieses Werck höret, nicht genugsam loben und rühmen kann.' The docket has no further reference to Bach, nor is there any record of his fee. I am obliged to Dr. Reinhard Fink for a transcript of Vetter's letter. For 'N. Bach', cf. p. 73 *supra*, note 3.

[2] A facsimile of Bach's note is in B.C.T., p. 32, ascribed, however, to 1722.

his own direction. The cantata had received its first performance in the Schloss chapel at Weimar in 1714. Spitta's supposition [1] that it was produced in one of the Leipzig churches in that year is untenable: there are no circumstances known to us to make such an association probable. Another writer,[2] observing the inconsistencies of Spitta's hypothesis, has advanced the suggestion that Bach performed the cantata at Leipzig on Advent Sunday 1722, during the interregnum between Kuhnau's death and his own appointment to succeed him. This conjecture encounters the objection, that at the period of the alleged performance Bach's name was not before the Leipzig authorities as a candidate.[3] On the other hand, he was certainly in Leipzig during Advent 1717, and it is eminently probable that, before beginning his task in the Paulinerkirche, he was invited to direct his cantata at Hauptgottesdienst on Advent Sunday, either in the Thomaskirche or the Nikolaikirche.

In May 1718 Prince Leopold set out to drink the waters at Carlsbad, travelling southward through Leipzig to cross the Erzgebirge from Zwickau. The ancient watering-place was the fashionable rendezvous of the German aristocracy, and a few years before (1711) had erected its first Kurhaus near the Mühlbrunnen. Desiring to exhibit himself as a patron of music, or merely to relieve the tedium of his 'cure', the Prince took with him a sextet from his Capelle—Bach, Rose, Marx, Torley, Abel, and Linigke;[4] his clavicembalo also made the journey in charge of three servants.[5] Details of the visit are not recorded, but it is not doubtful that the Prince entertained his guests with the music of his accomplished Capellmeister. In June Leopold was again in Cöthen, and a few months later gave a signal proof of his friendliness by standing godfather to the last of Bach's children by his first wife. The infant was carried to the Schloss chapel on 17 November 1718 to receive the names Leopold Augustus from his godfathers, the Prince and his younger brother Augustus Ludwig. Their sister Eleonore Wilhelmine stood godmother, while Councillor Jost von Zanthir and Frau Juliana Magdalena von Nostiz, wife of the Prince's Hofminister, shared with their sovereign obligations which endured but briefly.[6] More aristocratically sponsored than

---

[1] Sp. i. 513.   [2] Prof. Bernhard Fr. Richter, in B.-J. 1905, p. 57.
[3] Cf. *infra*, p. 143.
[4] The Protocol for 1717–18 (Seite 4) names them and shows that each of the six received on 6 May his salary for June in advance.
[5] Wäschke, p. 34.
[6] The infant was born on 15 November (Sp. i. 619). Bi. i. 131 wrongly declares the child to have been born on 15 June.

any of Bach's other children, the infant died within the year,[1] a loss followed too soon by another which inflicted a more grievous wound.

The preoccupation of his contest with Duke Wilhelm Ernst at Weimar, and the consequent delay in taking up his appointment at Cöthen, had put it out of Bach's power to celebrate Leopold's birthday in 1717 by a composition of his own. His inclination to do so, spurred by the Prince's condescension to his infant son, was fulfilled ten days [2] after the baby's christening, when Bach entertained his master with a Serenade. The libretto of 'Durchlaucht'ster Leopold', though conventional in character, has qualities of simplicity, sincerity, and metrical facility which point to Bach as its author: [3]

> Golden season, happy moment,
> Heaven-sent for our contentment,
> Smiling look on our enjoyment!
> Ring out, sing out, strings attune ye!
> Tell our prince's fame and glory!
> Leopold's most courtly graces
> Every tongue must loud acclaim.
> Sight and seeing, breath and singing,
> One and all together joining,
> Loud exalt his splendid name.
>
> .   .   .   .   .   .
> Take, then, mighty prince, our praise,
> Every gift we have to offer!
> Faithful service here we proffer.
> May thy days be glorious!
> May thy people reap the blessing
> They in thee are now confessing!

These sonorous aspirations Bach wedded to a score which reveals the slender materials at his command. Scored for strings, cembalo, and two flutes, the eight numbers engage only two singers, a Soprano and a Bass. The Bass singer is not known; but we can be sure that the composer had in mind his Prince's voice, a Baritone rather than a Bass. Leopold doubtless was captivated by the exquisite duet in minuet form.

[1] The Schlosskirche register records: '1719 den 28. September ist Herrn Johann Sebastian Bachens, Hochfürstl. Capellmeisters, Söhnlein beigesetzet' (Bi. i. 133).
[2] Leopold was born on 29 November. His birthday in 1722 was celebrated on 28 November, the next day being the First Sunday in Advent.
[3] B.C.T., p. 587, where I have erroneously suggested 1717 as the year of the Cantata's production. Since a cantata can be assigned to 1722, there remain the four years 1718–21, in one of which 'Durchlaucht'ster Leopold' may have been produced. The year 1720 is excluded by Bach's circumstances, and in 1721 Leopold's birthday is overshadowed by his wedding. Of the remaining dates, 1718 is preferable, since Bach naturally would seize the earlier opportunity to associate his art with the anniversary.

The Capelle accounts for 1719 reveal Bach's activity. On 8 July, and thereafter frequently, the bookbinder Günther received payment 'vor Musicalia zu binden'.[1] That the volumes contained Bach's own compositions is evident from the inventory of the library made in 1768, wherein he is indexed among the composers of Sinfonien in two bound volumes.[2] But the chief event of the year was clumsily marred by chance. In February, Handel descended magnificently upon the Continent out of England in search of singers for his Academy. At Düsseldorf he engaged Benedetto Baldassarri, and proceeding to Dresden, where Antonio Lotti and his company were stars in a firmament of peculiar brilliance, secured other artists, played before the Court, and earned Marchand's fee of one hundred ducats. The circumstances of that famous encounter doubtless were detailed to him, and Count von Flemming, who had staged it, perhaps was eager to arrange another. 'I tried to get a word with Mr. Händel,' the Count wrote to one of the master's pupils, 'and to pay him some civility for your sake, but I could accomplish nothing. I used your name in my invitation to him to come and see me, but he was always out or else ill. *Il est un peu fou là, ce qu'il me semble.*'[3] The letter throws Handel's situation into vivid contrast with Bach's: the one the idol of a wealthy public, released from the obligation of deference to men in high places; the other still functioning in the feudal atmosphere in which his ancestors had lived. On his way to Dresden, Handel would visit the quiet home of his ageing mother at Halle. He returned thither before proceeding to London, where the Royal Academy of Music opened its doors on 2 April 1720.[4] Flemming's letter was written on 6 October 1719, while Handel, probably, was still in Halle. Cöthen was only twenty miles distant, but neither now nor later was Handel interested to meet his only rival. Bach, on the other hand, reacted instantly to the impulse which had set him in his youth on the road to Hamburg and Lübeck: Handel was a master of his craft, who awoke his curiosity and invited the courtesy of a ceremonious call. Perhaps in 1713 and 1716 Bach had visited Frau Händel and talked of her famous son. He now seized the opportunity to meet the son himself. Mounted on one of the Prince's pads, he took the road to Halle, perhaps with a command from Leopold to bring back the distinguished exile with him. Forkel declares [5] that Bach set out immediately on hearing of Handel's presence in Halle. On his

[1] The entries run from 8 July 1719 to 25 May 1720 (Cammerrechnungen 1719–20, Seite 42).   [2] Bunge, p. 45.
[3] Streatfield, *Handel*, p. 87; Hugo Leichtentritt, *Händel* (1924), p. 114.
[4] Streatfield, p. 88.   [5] Forkel, p. 110.

K

arrival, however, Handel had left for England, and ten years passed before the two men were again within calling distance.

In May 1720 Prince Leopold, accompanied by members of his Capelle, again sought the waters of Carlsbad, and prolonged his visit into July. It ended tragically for Bach. He left his wife hale and hearty, but returned to find her dead and already buried.[1] His only daughter, Catharina Dorothea, barely twelve years old, was too young to take her mother's place in the household; his sons, Wilhelm Friedemann, Carl Philipp, and Johann Gottfried Bernhard, now ten, six, and five respectively, were at an age when a mother's care was most needed; and Bach himself mourned the helpmeet of thirteen years. His sorrow bred the desire to remove from the scene of his loss, and perhaps stirred again the ambitions Maria Barbara shared with him when he brought her home to Mühlhausen, and laid his art on the altar of God.

Two months after his bereavement, opportunity came to remove himself from Cöthen to the paths from whence he had strayed.[2] On 12 September 1720 Heinrich Friese, organist and clerk of the Jakobikirche, died at Hamburg.[3] Two months passed before Erdmann Neumeister, Pastor of the church, the two 'Kirchspiel-Herren' (churchwardens), and four 'Herren in der Beede', meeting in the church hall on 21 November, approved the motion of Herr Bernhard Crop to invite eight candidates to compete: Matthias Christoph Wideburg, formerly Hofcapellmeister at Gera; Heinrich Zinck, organist at Itzehoe; Vincent Lübeck, son of the distinguished Hamburg organist; Herr Frenkel, organist at Ratzeburg; Johann Joachim Heitmann, Hans Heinrich Lüders, Johann Sebas-

---

[1] The Nekrolog states that Maria Barbara was 'gesund und frisch' when Bach left for Carlsbad at the end of May, and adds the almost incredible detail, that he was unaware of her death until he re-entered the house on his return. The register of burials has the entry: '1720 den 7. Juli ist Herrn Sebastian Bachens, Hochfürstl. Capellmeisters, Eheliebste beigesetzet.'

[2] My narrative of Bach's Hamburg visit discards Spitta's hypothesis. He assumes that Bach planned it before his wife's death, postponed it in consequence of that event till November, and visited Hamburg in ignorance of the Jakobikirche vacancy. This structure of supposition rests upon the argument, that in 1720 he wrote a cantata on unusual paper and therefore, it is assumed, at Carlsbad, in preparation for an impending engagement. The text of the Cantata (No. 47) connects it with the Seventeenth Sunday after Trinity, that is, for a date at the end of September, whereas Bach did not visit Hamburg until later. It is an extravagant supposition that he made the long journey to Hamburg merely to play to Reinken, and with a Cantata in his portfolio for a Sunday long past. In my view Bach went to Hamburg definitely to examine the situation created by Friese's death, was unable to remain for the much-delayed Probe, but, before he left, gave Reinken, who was one of the assessors for the vacancy, an exhibition of his powers on the Catharinenkirche organ.

[3] I follow the Acta of the church, now in the Hamburg Staatsarchiv, printed by Max Seiffert in the Bückeburg Archiv. f. M.W. 1921, Heft 2, pp. 123-7.

tian Bach, and Johann Georg Hertzog, of Hamburg. Of the eight, Bach and Wideburg alone were distinguished, while the pre-eminence of the former was so patent that the vacancy might well have been offered to him outright. Apparently that course was proposed and rejected; it was resolved to hear all the candidates. The veteran Reinken, Andreas Kniller, and Georg Preuss, organists of other Hamburg churches, were named adjudicators, and the procedure adopted after the death of the distinguished organist Matthias Weckmann in 1674 was agreed upon. Spitta supposes[1] that the appointment was not made on the merits of the competitors, but upon their willingness, if elected, to contribute to the church's funds. In fact, it was notorious, in regard to the Jakobikirche and other positions under the Hamburg Rath, that persons appointed to them were expected to make a money payment on taking office. The rule was recognized and Bach and his fellow-competitors cannot have been ignorant of it. Moreover, the committee in charge of the election announced, that the candidates' ability, rather than their capacity to pay, would determine it, though the person appointed was free to make a contribution or financial acknowledgement. The hearing of the candidates was fixed for Thursday, 28 November, 'nach der Betstunde'.

The date appointed by the committee put it out of Bach's power or inclination to compete. Arrived probably towards the end of October, he sought out Reinken to revive memories of his earlier discipleship, and to pay his respects to the musical Nestor of his generation, who, twenty years old when Monteverdi died in 1643, lived till within ten years of Haydn's birth in 1732, and in the interval witnessed the Renaissance of which Bach and Handel were portents. According to the Nekrolog, Bach demonstrated his powers in the Catharinenkirche,[2] 'vor dem Magistrate und vielen andern Vornehmen der Stadt'. An official ceremonial is improbable, and the event is more impressive if we picture the two masters alone in the roomy loft behind the gilded Rückpositiv, after climbing the staircase whose precipitous ascent must sorely have tried the veteran. The scene and the organ to-day are substantially as then. Electrical devices which assist the modern player are absent now, as in 1720. On either side of the four manuals, and on a frame flush with them, five rows of stops project on either hand, heavy wooden rods with cumbrous knobs like those of the old Arnstadt organ; to reach the extreme handles is an effort, to pull them out a strain.[3] Here, beneath the plump cherubs,

---

[1] Sp. i. 631.   [2] Illus. No. 57.
[3] So I found, with the connivance of a lenient custodian.

and with Reinken at his side, Bach demonstrated his mastery of
an art in which the older man had once been pre-eminent. He
chose the plaintive sixteenth-century melody 'An Wasserflüssen
Babylon', which Reinken also had illustrated, extemporizing upon
it in variation after variation, till Reinken in amaze declared, 'I
thought this art was dead, but I see it still lives in you.'[1]

Another of Bach's familiar works first echoed[2] round the stalwart pillars of the Catharinenkirche, beneath its vaulted roof
remote and impenetrable. Pirro[3] connects the Fantasia and Fugue
in G minor with Bach's Hamburg journey in 1720. The supporting evidence is interesting. In 1731 Mattheson printed in
his *Grosse Generalbass-Schule* the following subject and countersubject for extemporization, as having been given to a candidate
for an organistship, observing that the subject was familiar, and
the player who first used it with success well known:

SUBJECT.

COUNTERSUBJECT.

With minor differences, we have here the subject and counterpoint
of Bach's G minor Fugue, and, since Mattheson's text was put
before a Hamburg candidate already familiar with it, we must
conclude that Bach's Fugue is referred to. His reason for playing
it to Reinken is perhaps revealed by the fact that its subject is a
Dutch folk-song:[4]

[1] Forkel, p. 21. A revision of Bach's extemporization is probably identified in
B.-G. XL. 49 (P. 245, No. 12ᵃ). Cf. B.C. iii. 104.
[2] In fact, as I noticed, there is little echo in the church.
[3] Pirro (3), p. 53. Cf. Sp. ii. 23.   [4] Cf. Z. f. M. Sept. 1924.

As Reinken had close ties with Holland and lived there as a young man, Bach's G minor, like his 'An Wasserflüssen Babylon', can be regarded as an act of homage to the veteran master. Both demonstrated that their composer could surpass as well as imitate his model.

Shortly before the date appointed for the hearing of the candidates, Bach left Hamburg, clearly obeying the commands of his Prince to prepare his birthday celebrations at the end of the month. Lübeck withdrew on 25 November, Hertzog on 27 November, while Wideburg did not trouble to answer the committee's communication. Hence, on the appointed date only four candidates were present at the Jakobikirche, along with the judges, Reinken and Kniller, who at first declined to attend, Johann Kortkamp, Georg Schlingmann, local organists summoned in their place, with Georg Preuss; five in all. The candidates, assembled in the organ chamber,[1] drew lots to appear in the following order—Heitmann, Frenkel, Zinck, Lüders—and in turn accomplished the prescribed tests: (1) to treat the melody 'O lux beata Trinitas'; (2) accompany the hymn 'Helft mir Gott's Güte preisen'; and (3) extemporize a fugue on the subject

The assessors retired to the church hall, made their report, and were dismissed with thanks. Not one of the candidates having satisfied them as competent, further consideration of the situation was postponed till 12 December. It was then suggested that the rejected four should be heard again, a proposal which was vetoed at once as 'gantz inconvenabel'. In fact, the committee was hopeful that Bach would accept the situation were it offered him, and already, after the unsatisfactory trial on 28 November, Herr Johann Luttas, one of the four 'Herren in der Beede', was authorized to approach him. Bach, however, definitely refused, and on 19 December Luttas communicated his answer to the committee, who thereupon resolved 'in Gottes Nahmen zur Wahl zu schreiten', and by a majority of *viva voce* votes gave Heitmann the post. On 22 December the church's Collegium confirmed his appointment, and a fortnight later (6 January 1721) he paid the sum of 4,000 marks in token of his 'Erkäntlichkeit'. Neumeister's disappointment at losing Bach as a colleague was sincere, and his comments on the election were so caustic that his relations with Heitmann

<hr />

[1] 'auff der Orgel'.

cannot have been agreeable. As Christmas followed hard upon the appointment, Neumeister employed the Gospel story to insinuate in a sermon, that even had one of the angelic throng descended on Hamburg to compete for the organ of the Jakobikirche, he would have been rejected unless he brought money with him.[1] What considerations guided Bach's refusal are not known; his letter has not survived. Probably he discovered on the spot disadvantages not apparent from a distance, and was little drawn to a situation obtainable only at some years' purchase of its income. Leopold's wishes certainly guided his decision.

On 22 February 1721 Bach lost his Ohrdruf brother, Johann Christoph, to whom in youth he was indebted, and with whom he had since maintained close relations. His death reduced their generation to three survivors—Bach himself, his brother Johann Jakob in Sweden, and their sister Maria Salome Wiegand, whom common interest as heirs of the Lämmerhirt estate brought together a year later, in circumstances to be noticed in their place. Meanwhile, Bach completed the most perfect example of the music which the conditions of his service required him to produce, his first essay in the realm of absolute symphonic instrumental music, easily surpassing anything that had gone before it of its kind. The six Brandenburg Concertos, according to the dedication attached to their score, were composed in obedience to a command from Markgraf Christian Ludwig of Brandenburg in the year 1718 or 1719. Perhaps the Markgraf was at Carlsbad during the earlier of Bach's visits, and, being an eager amateur, attended Leopold's musical assemblies. Bach leisurely fulfilled the commission, and on 24 March 1721 added a dedicatory note in French, interesting as one of only three examples of his composition in this style.

> *A son altesse royale, Monseigneur Crétien Louis,*
> *Marggraf de Brandenbourg, &c., &c., &c.*

Monseigneur,

Two years ago, when I had the honour of playing before your Royal Highness, I experienced your condescending interest in the insignificant musical talents with which heaven has gifted me, and understood your Royal Highness's gracious willingness to accept some pieces of my composition. In accordance with that condescending command, I take the liberty to present my most humble duty to your Royal Highness in these Concerti for various instruments, begging your Highness not to judge them by the standards of your own refined and delicate taste, but to seek in them rather the expression of my profound respect and obedience. In

---

[1] Mattheson tells the story in his *Der musicalische Patriot* (Hamburg, 1728), p. 316. The present organ in the Jakobikirche was renovated in 1836 and again in 1862. The stop-handles are of the same heavy kind as those in the Catharinenkirche; portraits of Bach and Handel are displayed on either side of the console.

conclusion, Monseigneur, I most respectfully beg your Royal Highness to continue your gracious favour toward me, and to be assured that there is nothing I so much desire as to employ myself more worthily in your service.

With the utmost fervour, Monseigneur, I subscribe myself
Your Royal Highness's most humble and most
obedient servant,
Jean Sebastien Bach.

Coethen, 24 March 1721.[1]

The gift was planned to arrive for the Markgraf's impending birthday.[2] There is no record of any acknowledgement to the composer, and the condition of the autograph suggests that, like the parts of the *Kyrie* and *Gloria* of the B minor Mass at Dresden, it was never performed by its recipient. In the catalogue of his library, which contained many things of value, Bach's score was not deemed worthy of mention, and, after the Markgraf's death in 1734, was assembled with other manuscripts for sale in a job lot.[3] Ultimately it came into the possession of Princess Amalia of Prussia, and so to its present locality in Berlin.[4] Bach, however, retained a copy of the score and performed the music at Cöthen. The first Concerto is scored for two horns, an instrument just coming into vogue, of which Bach made no other use at Cöthen. His Capelle contained no horn-player, and an entry in the accounts, under the date 6 June 1722, 'an die beyden Waldhornisten, so sich alhier hören lassen, 15 thaler', indicates with considerable certainty a performance of the Concerto, and not improbably the first one.

Meanwhile, domestic obligations drew Bach to compositions of another kind. Much occupied as he was, he was not willing to surrender the musical education of his children to other hands. Friedemann, his eldest boy, was nine years old, the age at which, if the Nekrolog is reliable, Bach himself began his systematic instruction on the clavier under his brother's tuition at Ohrdruf. Friedemann's commenced on 22 January 1720, when Bach wrote his son's first lesson in an exercise-book which, with characteristic particularity, he inscribed: 'Clavier-Büchlein vor Wilhelm Friedemann Bach. Angefangen in Cöthen den 22 Januar Ao. 1720.'[5] We can follow the lad's progress in it, and his father's method. On the first page, written with meticulous care, are the various clefs. Transliterations of the Manieren follow, after which, under

[1] Rust, in the Vorwort to B.-G. XIX, queries the month as March or May. The date actually is March. Prof. Johannes Wolf was so good as to verify it for me.   [2] He was born on 14 May 1677.
[3] Sp. i. 737.   [4] It is No. 78 in the Amalienbibliothek.
[5] It has recently (1927) been published by the Bärenreiter-Verlag (Cassel); ed. Hermann Keller. The autograph belongs to Herr Siegfried Krug, Pasing, bei München.

the invocation 'I[n] N[omine] I[esu]', there comes an 'Applicatio'
(exercise in fingering) which reveals Bach's system. Hitherto no
uniform rule for the beginner's guidance existed. The conventional position of the hands was flat, and, being too remote from
the keys, the thumbs never came into action; the middle finger,
acting as the bridge, crossed above its neighbours as required. It
has been observed already,[1] that Bach made his pupils hold their
hands as he held his own, with the tips of their fingers immediately
over the notes, a position which brought the thumbs into use by
a method of fingering Friedemann's 'Applicatio' illustrates:

Right hand

3 4 3   4 3 4 3 1   3 4 3 4 5   5 4 3 2 3 2 1 5

Left hand

3 2 1 2 1 2 1 2

There follow a number of pieces, of which a Suite (No. 25) by
Johann Christoph Richter, afterwards Hoforganist at Dresden,
another (No. 48) by Gottfried Heinrich Stölzel (1690–1749) of
Gotha, and a third (No. 47) by Telemann, are the only exceptions
to Bach's habit of exercising his pupils in his own music, a preference which exposes the secret of his successful teaching: from
first to last it was founded on his own experience. It is the
privilege of genius to take short cuts to perfection, while the
ordinary man follows a course charted by authority. Bach is
the rare example of a genius who deliberately disciplined himself.
The sons of his second marriage, as well as Carl Philipp and
Gottfried Bernhard, were all brought up on Friedemann's paper-
bound exercise-book of 71 leaves, and in their proficiency declare
its sound system.

To instruct his children in the technique of his art was, for Bach,
a lesser obligation than to bring them up in the traditions of recti-
tude he had himself inherited. The man whose children were
taught to invoke the name of Jesus before playing a five-finger
exercise would not be less exacting in the deportment of their daily
lives. For that reason, above others, he deplored the void in his
motherless house. Its domestic management since Maria Barbara's

[1] *Supra*, p. 99.

death may have been undertaken by a housekeeper, a convenient neighbour, or one of his Thuringian relatives. But his children had come to years when a more authoritative voice was needed, and the growing calls on him from outside increased the urgency of the demand. He was no longer of the impressionable age, when youth is attracted by superficial graces, and the character of his second wife reveals the more abiding qualities he preferred. She was Anna Magdalena Wilcken,[1] youngest daughter of Johann Caspar Wilcken, formerly Hoftrompeter at Zeitz, and since 1719 in similar employ at Weissenfels. Their marriage on 3 December 1721 took place, by the Prince's express permission, in Bach's own lodging.[2] Like her bridegroom, the bride was of Thuringian origin: Anna Magdalena's paternal grandfather, Stephan Wilcken, had been Stadtmusicus at Schwerstedt. On her maternal side, too, she came of musical stock: her mother was the daughter of Herr Liebe, organist at Friessnich near Weida in the principality of Reuss. Born at Zeitz on 22 September 1701,[3] she had barely completed her twentieth year when marriage made her the step-mother of a daughter only seven years younger than herself. Possessing a soprano voice of singular charm, she probably owed her training to a member of the Zeitz Capelle, which broke up when the Duchy of Sachsen-Zeitz fell to the Elector in 1718. Her father found fresh employment at Weissenfels,[4] while Anna Magdalena secured an engagement at the little Court of Anhalt-Zerbst,[5] whose relationship to that of Cöthen accounts for her appearance there in the autumn of 1720 in a similar capacity. A few weeks before her marriage she stood godmother, on 29 September, to the daughter of one of the Schloss lackeys, and is described in the register as 'Jungfer Magdalene Wülckens, Fürstliche Sängerin allhier'.[6] She retained that situation after her marriage, and her income, exactly half her husband's, perceptibly augmented the

---

[1] The name is also spelt Wülcken, Wölckner, Wülken, Wülckens.
[2] The Schlosskirche register has the entry: 'Den 3. December 1721 ist Hr. Johann Sebastian Bach Hochfürstl. Capellmeister allhier, Wittwer, und mit ihm Jungfer Anna Magdalena, Hrn. Johann Caspar Wülkens Hochfürstl. Sächs. Weissenfelsischen Musicalischen Hof- und Feld-Trompeters ehl. jüngste Tochter, auf fürstl. Befehl im Hause copuliret worden' (Bi. i. 139).
[3] She was baptized on 23 Sept. 1701. Her godparents were the wives of the Court organist Joh. Siegmund Liebe and the Court cook Brühl, and Herr Lobeck, master of works and inn proprietor.
[4] Later he became Hoftrompeter at Zerbst, where he had a son to whom Bach stood godfather on 3 March 1729. He married as his second wife on 10 April 1731 the widow of Christian Gottfried Biesenbruch, Pastor of Nutha, near Zerbst, 1719–27. [5] For the Wilcken family cf. Werner, p. 93.
[6] B.-J. 1907, p. 178. Anna Magdalena appears to have first visited the Cöthen Court in 1716, 'gastweise' with her father.

revenue of his establishment.[1] She proved herself a true help-meet in his work, and gave him a family patriarchal in multitude. How fond was the love she kindled in him may be read in the green-covered music-book he made for her four years after their marriage. A husband of forty, he wrote in it the lines:

> Ihr Diener, werthe Jungfer Braut,
> Viel Glücks zur heutgen Freude.
> Wer so in ihrem Cräntzchen schaut
> Und schönen Hochzeit-Kleide,
> Dem lacht das Herz vor lauter Lust
> Bei ihrem Wohlergehen,
> Was Wunder, wenn mir Mund und Brust
> Vor Freuden übergehen.[2]

Coincidently with Bach's marriage, Prince Leopold, till now a conspicuous bachelor, himself succumbed to Cupid, and, a week after his Capellmeister's, celebrated (11 December 1721) his nuptials with his cousin Friederica Henrietta,[3] daughter of Prince Carl Friedrich of Anhalt-Bernburg. Not for a generation had Cöthen welcomed a bride to the princely Schloss, and a round of masquerades, balls, illuminations, prolonged for five weeks, followed the ceremonial entry of the sovereign pair. Stadtmusicus Würdig, with his band of players, and the Prince's Capelle, made their contributions, while Bach produced a congratulatory Ode which has not survived.[4] It was not yet apparent that the installation of a mistress in the hitherto Eve-less Ludwigsbau would, and not distantly, drive him from Cöthen. Meanwhile, his last year in Leopold's service saw the completion of the first Part of the 'Well-tempered Clavier', his conclusive contribution to the controversy raging round the tuning of the clavichord, which this collection of preludes and fugues in every key, major and minor, settled in favour of equal temperament, against the traditional preference to tune a few keys perfectly and neglect the others in which accurate

---

[1] The Capelle accounts for 1721–2 (Seite 39): 'Für Bach wieder 400 Rth. Ausser-dem: Dessen Ehefrau soll monatlich haben 26 Rth. 16 gr.' And for 1722–3 (Seite 44): 'Dessen Ehefrauen dergl. von 10 Monat biss den 1 May, laut Bach sub pag. 2., 166 th. 16 gr.'

[2] Your slave am I, sweet maiden bride,
> God give you joy this morning!
> The wedding flowers your tresses hide,
> The dress your form's adorning,
> O how with joy my heart is filled
> To see your beauty blooming,
> Till all my soul with music's thrilled,
> My heart's with joy o'erflowing.

[3] Illus. No. 54.
[4] Wäschke, p. 38. In regard to the Ode, see note 2, *infra*, p. 168.

intonation could not be obtained.[1] Strange that a technical controversy should have been resolved by a volume of gems so alien in feeling from the academic debate which invited them! To the same year belongs the 'Clavierbüchlein vor Anna Magdalena', an intimate anthology for his young wife's instruction, with the warning against Calvinismus to which reference has already been made.[2] Three years later he and she compiled a second 'Notenbuch' (1725), which shows their relation of master and pupil persisting in pleasant comradeship.[3]

A legacy from Tobias Lämmerhirt, his maternal uncle, facilitated Bach's first marriage. By a curious coincidence, Tobias's widow died a few weeks before Bach's second marriage [4] and brought him another windfall from that source. He had maintained friendly relations with her: she stood godmother to his eldest child at Weimar. By the terms of her husband's will, after paying the legacies which Bach and his brothers and sister had received in 1708, Frau Catharina was left residuary legatee, with the stipulation that upon her death half of Tobias's estate should pass to his 'nächste Freunde', namely, his niece Anna Christina Lämmerhirt and his sister's four children, while the remainder was left at his widow's disposal for distribution 'auf ihre Freunde'.[5] On 8 October 1720 the widow executed her own will, which became operative a year later: it was read on 26 September 1721, two weeks after her funeral. After making a number of benefactions, it devised the residue in ten equal parts to her husband's 'nächste Freunde' and her own relatives. It appears from Bach's letter [6] that he and his coheirs received the quota to which they were entitled under Tobias's will, i.e. one-fifth of the half estate. But the testatrix acted as though her husband's effects were wholly at her disposal, and thereby invited suspicion that Tobias's 'nächste Freunde' were receiving less than they would have obtained had the half of his fortune been paid to them forthwith. The suspicion seized Anna Christina Zimmermann (née Lämmerhirt), who lodged a claim, on her own behalf and that of her four cousins, to receive their legal half of the estate, along with so much of Frau Catharina's portion as might not have been exhausted by her personal benefactions, the latter fund to be divided equally between

---

[1] Part II did not appear till 1744. The influence of Johann Caspar Ferdinand Fischer, Hofcapellmeister at Baden (1650–1746), is suggested. Cf. B.-J. 1910, p. 63.　　　　[2] *Supra*, p. 117.
[3] Johannes Schreyer (B.-J. 1906, p. 134) questions its preparation for Anna Magdalena's use.
[4] She was buried on 12 Sept. 1721 (B.-J. 1925, p. 113).
[5] Cf. par. 3 of the will in B.-J. 1925, p. 123.　　　　[6] *Infra*, p. 140.

Tobias's and his widow's 'Freunde'. With her action Bach's sister
Maria Salome Wiegand associated herself. She lived at Erfurt,
where her husband, Johann Andreas Wiegand, was in business as
a furrier.[1] Without consulting their coheritors, Frau Zimmermann
and Frau Wiegand lodged a *caveat* at Erfurt on 24 January 1722,
challenging the action of the executors of Frau Catharina's will.
The parties to the motion were named as Anna Christina Zimmermann, Maria Salome Wiegand, Johann Sebastian Bach, his brother
Johann Jakob, and also Johann Christoph, of Ohrdruf.[2] In fact,
none of the males was a consenting party to the motion, and, as
soon as it came to his notice, Bach intimated his refusal to be
involved in it:[3]

Most honourable and learned gentlemen and *Patroni*,
  Your Worships are aware that my brother Johann Jakob (now in
Swedish service) and I are coheirs of the Lämmerhirt estate. It has come to
my knowledge indirectly that the other coheirs intend to institute a *process*
to contest the *testament*, an act which will do no service to me or my
absent brother. Far from desiring to raise an action, we are quite satisfied
with our share of the estate. This letter therefore gives notice on my own,
and, *sub cautione rati nomine*, my brother's behalf, that we are not parties
to the said *process* and oppose it by a formal *protestation*. I deem it necessary to inform your Worships to this effect, respectfully inviting you to
receive my *renunciation* and *protestation*, and to deliver to my brother and
myself our *quotas* of the estate now lying *in deposito*, as also any sums
which may accrue hereafter. Thanking you right heartily for your *faveur*
in the matter, I subscribe myself
                          Your Worships' most obedient servant,
                                   Joh. Seb. Bach,
                          Capellmeister to the Princely Court of
                                                 Anhalt-Cöthen.
Cöthen, the 15th of March ao: 1722.
  To the worshipful and learned gentlemen, the Magistrates, Burgomasters, Syndic, and members of the Council, my most honoured
patroni, at Erfurt.

Bach's action apparently stayed the threatened lawsuit, and
brought him the tenth part of an estate valued at 5,507 th. 6 gr.,
roughly 500 thalers, a sum exceeding his annual stipend, and, in
view of his imminent migration from Cöthen, not unwelcome.
The birth of Prince Leopold's daughter, a second Gisela Agnes,
on 21 September 1722,[4] no doubt invited celebrations and gave

[1] Their marriage took place on 24 Jan. 1700 in the Kaufmannskirche, Erfurt
(B.-J. 1925, p. 126).
[2] Johann Christoph died in Feb. 1721. It must be assumed that his death was
unknown to his sister.
[3] Erfurt. Stadtarchiv. A facsimile in Reimann, p. 16. On the whole matter
cf. Hugo Lämmerhirt's article in B.-J. 1925, p. 101, and Sp. i. 761.
[4] Wäschke, p. 39.

additional brilliance to the Prince's birthday a month later. The Capelle accounts for 28 November 1722 record the payment to Bach of two thalers 'zur Cantate wegen des Hochfürstl. Gebuhrts-Tages',[1] a composition that may probably be identified with the incomplete 'Mit Gnaden bekröne', whose references to the Princess assign it to this year.[2] But the skies over Cöthen had clouded since Leopold's marriage twelve months before. He was no longer free to follow bachelor paths. His wife exacted his punctilious attention, disliked his musical tastes and companions, and pouted vexation at Herr Capellmeister's serious strains. She was, Bach styled her illuminatingly, an 'amusa',[3] feather-headed and young, a little jealous of her husband's attachment to his older friend, and disposed to make her disfavour visible. She died, it is true, while Bach was in her service, but too late to divert him from his resolution to retire. Practical motives were not absent. Cöthen provided inadequate facilities for his children's education: his stubborn Lutheranism would not allow them to attend the more efficient Stadtschule. Probably his desire to give his elder sons the University training denied to himself also disposed him to remove them elsewhere.

The chain of events that brought Bach from Cöthen to Leipzig in the spring of 1723 is traced from the death of Johann Kuhnau on 5 June 1722, six months after Bach's second marriage. Kuhnau had held the Cantorship of the Leipzig Thomasschule since 1701, and though, in Bach's judgement at least, the office ranked below a Capellmeistership, the vacancy attracted more than one distinguished candidate. Six weeks (14 July)[4] after Kuhnau's death the civic Rath, in whose gift the appointment lay, entertained the names and discussed the merits of six applicants: Johann Friedrich Fasch, Hofcapellmeister at Zerbst, Kuhnau's pupil; Georg Balthasar Schott, organist of the Neukirche, Leipzig; Christian Friedrich Rolle,[5] Bach's colleague at Halle in 1716; Georg Lembke,[6] Cantor of Taucha, near Leipzig; Johann Martin Steindorff, Cantor of Zwickau, a man sixty years of age; and Georg Philipp Telemann. By far the most notable of the six, Telemann had recently (1721) settled at Hamburg, where he held the post

[1] 1722–3, Seite 45.
[2] The possibility that it was written for the wedding celebrations in 1721 cannot be excluded.   [3] Cf. his letter to Erdmann, infra, p. 204.
[4] The Council minutes relative to the appointment are printed in Bi. iv. 102–9. Cf. Prof. B. Fr. Richter's article in B.-J. 1905, p. 48, and also Kroker.
[5] The minute of 14 July 1722 (Bi. iv. 102) names him 'Johann Christian Keller'. As 'Johann Christian Rolle' is found in the minute of 23 Nov. 1722, the error is clear.   [6] Bi. iv. 102 calls him Lincke.

to which Carl Philipp Emanuel Bach succeeded in 1767. He was well known and admired in Leipzig as the sometime organist of the Neukirche, conductor of the University Collegium Musicum, and composer of operas performed at the then flourishing theatre. In coming forward, however, he expressly declined to undertake the pedagogic duties of the Cantorship, which required its holder to teach other subjects than music in the school. Anxious to secure a musician so distinguished and popular, the Council yielded to his objections, and on 14 July invited him to fulfil the customary Probe. Telemann did so on 9 August[1] and was unanimously appointed, the presiding Bürgermeister mooting the question whether German or Latin was the appropriate language of congratulation. Upon Telemann's petition, the University also conferred on him the directorship of the University church, and on 13 August he attended the civic Council to receive official intimation of his election, 'weil er nun wegen seiner Music in der Welt bekannt wäre'. As representing the Consistorium, Superintendent Deyling was informed of the Council's choice, and on the following day (14 August) Rector Ernesti of the Thomasschule received a similar intimation, with instruction to arrange the hours of the new Cantor's duties.

But Telemann was not serious in his candidature, willing to sacrifice Leipzig if his Hamburg employers increased his stipend. So far from arranging his duties with Ernesti, he returned to Hamburg (14 August), again drawing 22 gulden 18 groschen for the expenses of his journey. A month passed before, on 25 September, he was again in Leipzig and spent a fortnight with the actuary Johann Christoph Götz. The negotiations with him are not recorded in the Council's minutes, but their nature is not doubtful. Returning again to Hamburg about the middle of October,[2] Telemann threatened resignation there unless his stipend was augmented. Regretting to lose a distinguished musician so lately appointed, the Hamburg authorities yielded. The Leipzig Cantorate again was vacant,[3] and the Council took up its task anew. On 23 November 1722, besides Fasch, Schott, Lembke, and Steindorff, it entertained for consideration the names of Georg Friedrich Kaufmann, Capellmeister at Merseburg, and Andreas Christoph

---

[1] For his expenses he received 22 gulden 18 gr. The libretto of the cantata he performed was printed at the Council's expense and 600 copies were bound for the congregation's use, at a cost of 5 gulden 15 gr. Neither Bach nor Graupner was thus favoured in similar circumstances. Cf. Kroker.

[2] Kroker's researches have filled the gap August–November 1722 in the history of the Leipzig election.

[3] Telemann candidly admitted his motives. Cf. Mattheson, p. 366.

Tufen, of Brunswick. Regret was expressed at Telemann's withdrawal. Councillor Platz observed, however, that the Cantor was required to teach in the school as well as to direct the music, and that, as Telemann had refused to undertake the former obligation, they were free to appoint a Cantor who would be more amenable. He named the veteran Fasch, author of a German edition of Weller's *Grammatica Graeca*,[1] Rolle, and Tufen, as the three candidates most worthy of consideration. Bürgermeister Adrian Steger agreed, and voted for hearing all three, 'sowohl in musiciren als auch in informiren', allowing each a gratuity of twenty thalers for travelling expenses. Councillor Dr. Born also gave his vote for that course, but declared a preference for Kaufmann, who, however, like Telemann, refused to undertake pedagogic duties. The rest concurred.

Bach would not be ignorant of events at Leipzig, and his circumstances at Cöthen invited him to consider the propriety of his own candidature. Telemann's appearance in the field, however, deterred him from declaring himself, and even after his friend's withdrawal he made no sign. At the Council's meeting on 23 November his name was not mentioned.[2] It is evident, however, that he followed the situation closely, and was aware that the Leipzig authorities were not satisfied with the candidates to whom their choice was restricted. Indeed, after their meeting on 23 November, it is probable that the Council took unofficial steps to widen the field of choice, by enlisting candidates of stronger calibre than those it had already resolved to hear. They were successful: on 21 December 1722, moving deliberately towards a decision, the Council minuted that Fasch had withdrawn, alarmed at the prospect of pedagogic duty, but that Capellmeisters Graupner of Darmstadt and Bach of Cöthen had come forward. They were forthwith joined with Kaufmann, Schott, and Rolle for consideration, the Council at the same time intimating its refusal to divorce from the Cantorship the obligation of school teaching, that bugbear of musicians whose humanities were rusty with disuse. Of the selected five, Graupner was preferred. Two years older than Bach, and an alumnus of the Thomasschule, he was strongly supported by the Dresden Capellmeister David Heinichen. Since 1712 he had held the post of Capellmeister to the

---

[1] In the Council minute of 23 November 1722 he is named as 'ein geschickter Mensch'.

[2] Prof. B. Fr. Richter (B.-J. 1905, p. 57) suggests that Bach performed his Cantata 61 at Leipzig on Advent Sunday (29 Nov.) 1722. A more probable date is 28 November 1717, before he examined the Paulinerkirche organ. See *supra*, p. 126.

Landgraf Ernst Ludwig of Hessen at Darmstadt, whose Capelle he had raised to high excellence; he was also known as a clavier player of merit.[1] He came to Leipzig to direct the music for the Christmas festival, on the first day of which it was customary at Vespers to perform a Latin *Magnificat*, produced a setting of his own,[2] and three weeks later (17 January 1723), on the Second Sunday after Epiphany, performed his Probe, conducting his cantata 'Lobet den Herrn, alle Heiden'.[3] Thereafter he returned to Darmstadt, with forty thalers in his purse and a letter to his master in his pocket.[4] Already on 15 January, before he fulfilled his Probe, members of the Council had questioned his freedom to accept the post. Telemann's conduct made them suspicious, and though the three Burgomasters spoke strongly in his favour, and reported weighty recommendation of him from Dresden and elsewhere, all desired to know how he stood at Darmstadt before offering him the post. Only one man mentioned Bach, to suggest that he should at least be heard. His name was Wagner![5]

Graupner carried back to Darmstadt a complimentary letter to the Landgraf, dwelling on his Capellmeister's Leipzig upbringing, and intimating the Council's wish to appoint him Cantor 'nach vorhergehender gnädigster Erlassung seiner bisherigen Dienste'.[6] Graupner announced from Darmstadt on 7 February 1723 that the letter had been delivered. But, as a month passed without further news, on 12 March Bürgermeister Dr. Lange wrote to beg a decisive reply. Ten days later (23 March) it was dispatched, with a letter from Graupner announcing the Landgraf's refusal to surrender him;[7] he had, in fact, raised his Capellmeister's already generous stipend, made him a present of 3,100 florins, and undertook to watch the interests of his wife when widowed, and of his children when they reached an age to earn their livelihood.[8] Graupner accordingly brought the business to a conclusion on 4 May 1723, in a letter to Leipzig which expressed his thanks for the honour he could not receive, and made a handsome recommendation of Bach, 'ein Musicus ebenso starck auf der Orgel wie erfahren in Kirchensachen und Capell-Stücken', who could be relied on to 'honeste und gebührlich die zugeeignete Function ver-

---

[1] Kroker.
[2] For Graupner's *Magnificat* see B.-J. 1913, p. 147. Graupner was the guest of Daniel Petermann, Protonotarius of the Consistorium.
[3] And also 'Aus der Tiefe rufen wir'. [4] Kroker.
[5] One is glad to identify this councillor as Baumeister Gottfried Wagner, residing 'am Marckt im Bürgermeister Wincklerischen Hause' in 1723, according to D.J.F.L. for that year.
[6] The letter is in the Darmstadt archives and is printed in B.-J. 1905, p. 54.
[7] Kroker prints the letter. [8] B.-J. 1905, p. 55.

sehen'.[1] Schott, meanwhile, had fulfilled his Probe on the Feast of the Purification (2 February 1723),[2] and on the following Sunday, Quinquagesima (7 February), Bach took his place,[3] performed his cantata (No. 22) 'Jesus nahm zu sich die Zwölfe', appropriate to the Gospel for the Day,[4] and on the following day returned to Cöthen, with twenty thalers 'vor Reise- und Zehrungs-Kosten',[5] to await the issue of the Council's negotiations with Graupner. At the Old-Style New Year he greeted Leopold and his Princess with a 'Poesie'.[6] It was his last tribute to the 'amusa', who died at midday on 4 April 1723,[7] ten days before her husband reluctantly accorded his *dimission* to one whose art she had belittled, and whom events were now calling loudly to Leipzig.

Throughout March, Graupner's decision being unknown, Bach frequented Leipzig, where on Good Friday (26 March) he directed in the Thomaskirche a work which demonstrated his fitness for the position he sought. When he entered the field in November 1722, the Leipzig Council, in view of the continuing vacancy, had arranged for the composition of the large works whose performance was imminent, a Latin *Magnificat* on Christmas Day, a Passion on Good Friday. Graupner was invited to provide the first, Bach to compose the second. Though it yields only to the 'Matthäuspassion' in sublimity, the 'Johannespassion' exhibits, both in libretto and music, evident signs of the distractions amid which the Council's commission was fulfilled. Bach appears to have arranged his own libretto, for whose lyrical movements he drew upon the popular text by Barthold Heinrich Brockes. The arrangement of his material betrays inexperience, while frequent, and sometimes incongruous, repetitions in the music indicate the haste and stress under which he composed a work which

---

[1] B.-J. 1905, p. 55.
[2] Kaufmann, too, had fulfilled his Probe. Rolle is not mentioned in the proceedings on 9 April.
[3] 'Den 7 Feb. Dom. Esto Mihi legte Herr Joh. Seb. Bach, als damahliger Capellmeister zu Cöthen, seine Probe ab zu dem von Herrn Kuhnaus seel. Tode vacirenden Stadt-Cantorat. Vor ihm hatten auch andere ihre Proben gethan, als der Capellmeister von Altenburg [Merseburg], ferner Herr Graupner, Capellmeister von Darmstadt, und den 2 Febr. Festo Purif. Mariae Herr Georg Balt. Schott, Director Musices in der Neuen Kirche allhier' (Sicul, *Annalium Lipsiensium* (Leipzig, 1726), p. 445). Bach's Probe is also recorded in Joh. Sal. Riemer's *Leipzigisches Jahrbuch*, 1714–71. Cf. Dahms, p. 45.
[4] B.C.T., p. 187.   [5] Kroker.
[6] The Zerbst archives 1722–3, fol. 45, have the entry: '3 April. Denselben vor die Neujahrs Poesie fertigen zu lassen und dieselbe zu binden, 2 th.' The dedication page of the libretto was found in the Cantor's quarters at Leipzig when the school was demolished in 1902–3. It is now in the Bach Museum at Eisenach. Bach had offered a similar tribute in 1719. Cf. B.-G. XXIX, p. xxix.
[7] Wäschke, p. 39.

surpassed all its predecessors and set a new standard in its form.[1] He appears already to have received private intimation, probably from Bürgermeister Lange, that the Cantorship was his if Graupner declined it, and if he declared his readiness to fulfil its pedagogic duties. Graupner's decision was before the Council on 9 April. Bach at once applied for his 'dimission' from Leopold's service, and on 13 April received it in the following form:[2]

We Leopold, by God's grace Prince of Anhalt, &c. &c., to all whom it may concern.

Whereas on 5 August 1717 we appointed the right worthy and accomplished Johann Sebastian Bach to the office of Our Capellmeister and Director of chamber music, We hereby declare ourselves at all times satisfied with his conduct therein. And now, seeing he is minded to seek employment elsewhere, and thereto hath sought our gracious permission to retire, We do by these presents accord him the same, commending him heartily to others.

In witness whereof We have signed this discharge with Our own hand and sealed it with Our princely seal. Given at Cöthen this 13th day of April 1723.

A week later, armed with his official release, which, in view of their experience at the hands of Telemann and Graupner, the Leipzig Councillors would particularly require, Bach executed a document ('Revers')[3] which gave the assurances demanded of him:[4]

Whereas I the underwritten have offered myself as a candidate for the post of Cantor of the Thomasschule now vacant in this town of Leipzig, and whereas the right worshipful Council has my appointment under its consideration, I do positively declare that, should the office be conferred on me, I am already free, having for some three or four weeks past[5] been released from my situation at the princely Court of Anhalt-Cöthen, as my certificate of discharge doth declare. Furthermore, should I be appointed to the office of Cantor, I am prepared to conform to the arrangements now in force within the school, or as they may hereafter be appointed. In particular, I undertake not only to give instruction to the classes in the ordinary way, but also to give private lessons in singing to the students without extra recompense, and to discharge dutifully whatsoever else may be required of me. Notwithstanding, I beg the worshipful Council to entertain favourably my request to be allowed to delegate to another, at my own charges and without expense to the worshipful Council, the duty of giving lessons in Latin. In witness whereof I herewith put my hand and seal.

Done at Leipzig this 19th day of April 1723.

[1] Cf. the present writer's *Bach: The Passions*, Bk. I (O.U.P., 1926).
[2] Zerbst: Anhaltisches Staatsarchiv, Abt. Cöthen, St. A 10. No. 16³, fol. 64. Bunge, p. 31, incorrectly dates the document 17 April.
[3] Wäschke, p. 39, supposes that Bach removed his household from Cöthen on 13 April. It is hardly probable that he did so before his appointment was confirmed at Leipzig. Moreover, considerable repairs were being made to the Cantor's quarters in the Thomasschule.
[4] Leipzig. Rathsarchiv, Urkundenkasten, 79, No. 42.
[5] Though his *dimission* is dated 13 April, it took effect financially from 1 April.

The way at length was clear. On Thursday, 22 April 1723,[1] the three sections of the Council met in joint session in the Rathaus under the presidency of Dr. Gottfried Lange, Bürgermeister of the year. He reminded the members of his hopes to secure Telemann for the vacant Cantorship. But as he, and Graupner after him, had declined the appointment, it had been necessary to weigh the merits of Bach, Kaufmann, and Schott. Of Kaufmann and Schott he said nothing. But he assured them they would have no cause to regret Telemann if they appointed Bach, who excelled as a player and was able and willing to teach grammar and the *Colloquia* of Corderius.[2] Bürgermeister Platz emphasized the urgent need to make an appointment after so long an interval, and dwelt on the fact that Bach had pledged himself to share in the general teaching of the school, for which reason he had his vote. Bürgermeister Steger supported his colleagues' recommendation; he regarded Bach as not less distinguished than Graupner, but hoped he would avoid theatricality[3] in his music. The others expressed a similar preference, and Lange closed the meeting with an appeal to support a musician whose distinction could be expected to attract round him University students to support his activities. No dissentient voice was raised, and the 'Consultation' ended with an assurance that Bach's 'Dimissions-Schein'[4] from Cöthen would be forthcoming.

Bach parted from his Prince at Cöthen on terms of friendship never broken until at his obsequies, six years later, he performed a 'Trauer-Music' familiar in another setting.[5] Meanwhile, on 5 May 1723 he attended at the Council chamber in the Leipzig Rathaus, and from behind the Councillors' desks received from Bürgermeister Lange intimation of his unanimous appointment, as being the most 'capable' of those who had sought the office. In a sentence Bach expressed his gratitude and promised to fulfil his duties faithfully and with diligence.[6] The Bürgermeister intimated that the appointment would be notified at once to Superintendent Deyling, in order that the confirmation of the Consistorium might be forthcoming, and to Pastor Christian Weiss, of the Thomaskirche. Bach again expressed his thanks, and withdrew to sign in duplicate the following bond:[7]

Whereas the worshipful Council of this town of Leipzig has appointed

---

[1] Sp. ii. 847.   [2] Mathurin Cordier (d. 1564).   [3] 'nicht theatralisch'.
[4] Bach uses this phrase in his bond (*infra*).
[5] Cf. *infra*, p. 195.
[6] 'Ille. Dankte gehorsamst, dass man auf ihn Reflexion machen wollen, und verspräche alle Treu und Fleiss' (Sp. ii. 848).
[7] Leipzig. Rathsarchiv, Urkundenkasten, 79, No. 42.

me to be Cantor of the Thomasschule, and requires me to observe the conditions hereunder set out, to wit:

1. To show good example to the scholars by my seemly life and conduct, perform my school duties diligently, and conscientiously instruct my pupils.

2. To maintain the music in both churches [1] in good repute, to the best of my ability.

3. To show due respect and deference to the worshipful Council and maintain its reputation and credit in all seasons; and if a Councillor requires the scholars to provide music on occasion, to offer no impediment. Notwithstanding, I may not permit them to attend funerals or weddings outside the town, without the express permission of the Bürgermeister of the year and the Vorsteher [2] of the school.

4. To show proper respect to the Inspector [3] and governing authorities of the school, and fulfil such orders as they may give in the name of the worshipful Council.

5. To admit to the school no one insufficiently grounded in music, or such as are inapt for training therein, without permission from the Inspector and Vorsteher.

6. To instruct the scholars diligently in instrumental and vocal music, to the end that the church services be not unduly costly.

7. To see that the music provided is neither too lengthy nor operatic in style, but such as shall encourage the congregation to true devotion and reverence in church.

8. To supply the Neukirche with competent singers. [4]

9. To treat the scholars in a considerate and friendly spirit, punishing with moderation such as offend and reporting them to the proper authority.

10. To perform my lessons in school and my duties elsewhere diligently.

11. In such subjects as I am not prepared to teach myself, to provide a competent substitute at my own charges, and without expense to the worshipful Council or the school purse.

12. Not to leave the town without the consent of the Bürgermeister of the year.

13. To walk alongside the scholars in funeral processions as often as possible, in accordance with custom. [5]

14. To accept no office in the University without the consent of the worshipful Council. [6]

I do hereby pledge myself well and faithfully to perform the above conditions, under pain of forfeiture of my situation. In witness whereof I have signed and sealed these presents at Leipzig, this fifth day of May 1723.

[1] St. Thomas's and St. Nicholas's.
[2] The Vorsteher (Overseer) was the member of Council charged with the affairs of the school. At this period he was Baumeister Gottfried Conrad Lehmann. Each school and church was similarly provided.
[3] Pastor Weiss, of the Thomaskirche.
[4] On this and Bach's duties generally see *infra*, p. 159.
[5] *i.e.* such funerals as the Cantor was expected to attend in person, as opposed to those at which he was represented by a Prefect. The obligation was determined by the proportion of the school that attended, and the proportion was regulated by the amount of the fee paid.
[6] The Council imposed a similar condition upon the Rectorship. Cf. *infra*, p. 207.

Three days after his visit to the Rathaus, Bach appeared before the Consistorium [1] at its quarters in the Thomaskirchhof. He was presented to the members by Superintendent Deyling, who exhibited a certificate from his colleague, Dr. Johann Schmid, attesting the candidate's theological fitness, as revealed by an oral examination conducted by him: [2]

Dn. Jo. Sebastianus Bach ad quaestiones a me propositas ita respondit ut eundem ad officium Cantoratus in schola Thomana admitti posse censeam.

D. Jo. Schmidius
Consentit D. Salomon Deyling.

Bach appeared again before the Consistorium on the following Thursday (13 May), subscribed the *Formula Concordiae*,[3] and was thereafter confirmed in his office and sworn. A fortnight passed while he installed himself in the Cantor's official quarters, and rehearsed the Cantata with which he proposed to inaugurate his office. On 30 May, the First Sunday after Trinity, in the lofty and inconvenient gallery of the Nikolaikirche, he conducted at Hauptgottesdienst the first of the mighty anthems that distinguished his Cantorate, 'Die Elenden sollen essen' (No. 75).[4] It is in two Parts, an innovation in Leipzig use, and its second Part, performed after the sermon, opens with the only orchestral movement Bach ever wrote upon a hymn-tune, a fitting inauguration of the new dispensation. Two days later, at half-past eight on the morning of Tuesday 1 June,[5] he was formally introduced to the

---

[1] This body, in 1736, consisted of ten Assessors, lay and clerical, a protonotary, actuary, registrar, and messenger. It represented the ecclesiastical authority of the town and district, whose approval was necessary in respect of persons appointed by the civic Council to office in the churches and schools.
[2] Sp. ii. 9.   [3] Cf. *supra*, p. 102.
[4] Bi. i. 189 quotes a contemporary (1723) record, which states that Bach 'mit gutem Applause in Leipzig seine erste Music aufgeführt'.
[5] That Bach was inducted on Tuesday 1 June, and not (as Sp. ii. 9) Monday 31 May, is proved by the following minute in the Leipzig archives, which both Spitta and Bitter overlooked: 'Den 30 Maij 1723 wurde von E. H. Rath allhier zu dem Herrn Superintendenten Dr. Deylingen, wie auch dem Herrn Pastor an der Thomaskirche Lic. Weissen, ich endesbenanter zu gehen befehligt, und nebst Abstattung dienstlichen Grusses denenselben zu hinterbringen, wasmassen E. H. Rath den neuen H. Cantorem Bach auf künfftigen Dienstag zu Gott zu introduciren beschlossen, daher sie ersuchet würden ob sie sich wollten gefallen lassen besagten Tages früh nach ½ 9 Uhr auf der Schule zu S. Thomæ darbey mit einzufinden u. solchem actui mit beyzuwohnen; Worauff dieselben nach dessen Hinterbringung nebst Gegen Compliment an E. H. Rath sich vernehmen lassen, wie sie vor geschehene Notification danckten und würden nicht ermangeln angeregten Tages zu bestimter Zeit alda zugegen zu seyn. Paul Otto Lösner, Registr. jnr.' (Rathsakten, VII. B. 117, Bd. 2, fol. 235). The minute addressed to the Council describing the induction was written on the date of the event and is dated 1 June. So also is an unpublished letter of Pastor Weiss to the Council, defending the part he had taken in the proceedings. It begins:

school. At that hour Gottfried Conrad Lehmann, the Vorsteher, and Town Clerk Carl Friedrich Menser, representing the Council, presented themselves at the school door in the Thomaskirchhof and were admitted to the Aula.[1] Here Christian Weiss, Pastor of the Thomaskirche, representing the Consistorium,[2] and the masters of the school joined them, and all being seated, the scholars, conducted by a Prefect, sang a piece of music at the door before entering. The Town Clerk then rose to say that, God having been pleased to call to his rest Herr Johann Kuhnau, late Cantor, the worshipful Council had appointed in his room Herr Johann Sebastian Bach, lately Capellmeister to the princely Court of Anhalt-Cöthen, being assured that he would show respect to his patrons, cultivate agreeable relations with his colleagues, and bring up his scholars in the fear and wisdom of God. Pastor Weiss interposed a word in the name of the Consistorium, after which the Vorsteher 'presented' the new Cantor to his colleagues and the school. Bach declared his obligation to their worships his patrons, assured them of his resolve to perform his duty diligently and loyally, to show deference to those above him in authority, and to conduct himself in such a manner that nothing less should appear to be his aim. His new colleagues offered words of welcome, more music was sung, and the company dispersed.[3] None, least of all Bach's assertive 'patrons' and 'superiors', realized that Clio, turning a page, had dipped her pen to narrate such a chapter in the history of music as had not yet been written.

'Heute, den 1 Jun. 1723 bin ich gegen 9 Uhr in die Thomas-Schule gegangen, nicht allein vor mich als Inspector, der Introduction des Herrn Cantoris auf invitation E. E. Hochw. Raths beyzuwohnen, sondern auch auf des Herrn Superintend. H. D. Sal. Deylings Commission, denselben im Nahmen des Consistorii und H. Superintend. zugleich in das Cantorat-Amt bey der Schule zu S. Thomae, dem Herkommen gemäs, an- und einzuweisen.' Finally, a letter written by Deyling himself late on the afternoon of 1 June speaks of 'der heutigen introduction des Cantoris zu S. Thomae'. Both Weiss's and Deyling's letters are among the 'Acta die Besetzung des Cantoramts bei der Schule zu St. Thomä zu Leipzig betr.' The correspondence grew out of the jealousy with which the Council regarded Weiss's interference in the ceremony as representing the Consistorium.

[1] 'das obere Auditorium'.
[2] See Deyling's letter in Chap. viii, *infra* p. 176.   [3] Sp. ii. 850.

CHAPTER VII

DAS JETZT FLORIRENDE LEIPZIG

LEIPZIG lies above the junction of three small rivers, Pleisse, Elster, Parthe, the first of which her poets delighted especially to associate with their city of the Muses. Matthew Seutter's[1] plan unfolds 'eine florisante auch befestigte Handels-Stadt und weitberühmte Universitäts-Stadt', already a prominent commercial centre, and conspicuous in the printing and publishing trade, with which the name of Breitkopf, since 1719, was connected. Its University was ancient and famous, numbering among its professors Johann Christoph Gottsched, author and critic, with whom Bach twice collaborated, and others with whom his pen is associated. Fortified walls, flanking bastions and escarpments still enclosed the 'befestigte Stadt', outside which spread pleasant promenades, leafy suburbs, and gardens umbrageous with lime-trees. On every side fields and farms were in view, especially on the west,[2] where the Pleisse meandered sluggishly and mill-wheels clattered noisily behind the Thomaskirche. Entering the town from this approach through the Ranstädter Thor, the visitor found an agreeable avenue: the mellow walls of the ancient fortifications, the broad Brühl exhibiting enticing hostelries, 'The Black Bear', 'The Wild Man', 'The Three Swans', 'The Ostrich', 'The Red Oxen', 'The Black Wheel', and many another, rising massively four or five stories high under steeply angled roofs, their yellow fronts brilliant with gaudy frescoes. No less attractive were the private houses of the well-to-do, embellished with gilded decoration and carved timbers, window-sashes bright with rosemary, myrtle, gilliflowers, and violets, and musical with the notes of nightingales and other caged singing-birds. The streets, broad and pebbled, were none so narrow but an ox-drawn wagon, and even two, could pass along them, some named after the churches and buildings to which they admitted, some from the trades that frequented them, others from historical associations that clung to them, and all cleansed with running conduits and gushing fountains. In the midst, the square-towered Rathaus stood conspicuous on the ample Marktplatz, where thrice weekly, on Tuesdays, Thursdays, and Saturdays, meat, bread, vegetables, and other victuals were sold at the booths. In the Naschmarkt fish and cheese were exposed, and at Fair times the horse-market added another busy centre. Close

[1] Illus. No. 58.　　　　　　　　　　[2] Illus. No. 59.

to the Rathaus, on the Marktplatz, stood Apel's House, the residence of the sovereign on his not infrequent visits, from whose windows he looked down on a torch-lit square and heard Bach's Collegium Musicum make music in his honour. At nightfall the streets were lit with seven hundred oil lamps exposed on oak standards, while, in each of the four Wards, night-watchmen, armed with rattles, told the hours and warded the sleeping town against thieves and vagabonds.[1]

Leipzig contained a population of about 30,000 when Bach came to the town,[2] grouped in four Wards: the 'Grimmaisches Viertel' on the east, through whose port the citizens made their last journey to God's acre round the Johanniskirche outside the walls; 'Peters Viertel' on the south, leading to the Windmühlgasse and the windmill amid gardens, where Bach in summer-time rehearsed his Collegium Musicum; the 'Ransches Viertel' on the north-west, whose Ranstädter Thor led out to Lindenau; and the 'Hallisches Viertel', whose port led to the Parthe through the Gerbergasse, where the tanners plied their trade. The government of this community was vested in a Rath of thirty Assessors and three Burgomasters (or Consuls), forming three bodies, which took office annually in rotation on St. Bartholomew's Day (24 August). An Electoral diploma of 1711 accorded the Burgomaster of the year the style and precedence of a *Comes palatinus Caesareus*.[3] Two deputy Burgomasters (*proconsules*) and one-third (10) of the Assessors completed the ruling Council for the year, with a staff that comprised a principal clerk, clerk, actuary, three registrars, two 'Copisten', a door-keeper, and three messengers.[4] The Elector's military authority was represented in the Pleissenburg, a fortified building in the south-west angle of the wall, whose establishment consisted of the 'Gouverneur der Stadt Leipzig und Vestung Pleissenburg',[5] a Lieutenant and Adjutant, Commandant, and other officers.[6] Subject to the Governor was the Town Guard, to which each Viertel contributed a captain, lieutenant, ensign, 'Muster-Schreiber', and its quota of rank and file.[7]

With a population at once leisured, cultured, industrial, and professional, Leipzig was the seat of a High Court of Justice (Ober-Hof-Gericht), served by a presiding judge, thirteen Assessors

[1] My description is based on contemporary documents in Beier, ii, pp. 1 ff.
[2] The population was 32,384 in 1753. Between 1721 and 1750 the number of births recorded was 26,387 (*Statistisches Bureau: Leipziger Bevölkerung*, Heft 6).
[3] Count palatine of the Empire.
[4] I take the facts regarding Leipzig's civic government from D.J.F.L., p. 61.
[5] In 1736 the Governor was Count von Flemming, whose brother witnessed Marchand's discomfiture at Dresden.
[6] D.J.F.L., p. 21.   [7] *Ibid.*, p. 138.

of noble rank, fifteen others, and a large array of advocates ordinary and extraordinary, actuaries, attorneys, messengers, and minor officials. The Court sat quarterly in March, June, September, and December, beginning its sessions on the fifteenth of the month, or on the Monday preceding that date.[1] Ecclesiastical authority was vested in the Consistorium, a court whose jurisdiction perpetuated episcopal authority, and whose procedure was judicial in form. It consisted of ten Assessors, chiefly laymen, and had its chambers in the Thomaskirchhof, hard by the Thomasschule. Its executive staff consisted of a protonotary, whose lodgings were in the official building, an actuary, registrar, and messenger. Four advocates in ordinary and a larger number of *advocati extraordinarii* practised before it, among the latter, Dr. August Florens Rivinus,[2] to whose father (?), Johann Florens Rivinus, Bach dedicated his 'Die Freude reget sich'. As the capital of an administrative Circle (Kreis) Leipzig was the head-quarters of an exchequer and excise jurisdiction, quartered in the Amt-Haus. At its head was Herr Cammer-Junker und Kreis-Hauptmann Carl Heinrich von Dieskau,[3] who commissioned Bach to compose the Peasant Cantata in 1742. A large postal service also radiated from the town, among whose officials was Herr Ober-Post Commissarius Christian Friedrich Henrici, residing in Frau Maye's house in the Burgstrasse,[4] who, under the pen-name 'Picander', was Bach's most regular literary collaborator. Post coaches plied from their stables near the Grimma Gate to Dresden, Berlin, Jena, Coburg, Brunswick, Hanover, and Hamburg, while pillar post-boxes of sandstone, decorated with the royal arms and monogram, stood at the town gates for the public convenience,[5] where also the Excise took toll from incomers.[6]

At the eastern extremity of the town, near the Grimma Gate, stood the plain and unimposing buildings of the University, within the shadow of the Paulinerkirche, the University chapel.[7] Nearly 40 of the 148 pages of the Leipzig Directory for 1736 are devoted to the officials, faculties, councils, and graduates of an institution which had its origin in the secession of the German 'nation' from the University of Prague in 1409, an exodus which incidentally enriched the Paulinerkirche with some of its choicest treasures. The University's executive head was the Rector Magnificus, elected twice a year, on St. George's Day (23 April) and St. Gall's Day (16 October). He, with four Assessors representing the four Nations (Saxony, Meissen, Bavaria, Poland), elected on the

---

[1] D.J.F.L., p. 1.   [2] *Ibid.*, p. 6.   [3] *Ibid.*, p. 10.   [4] *Ibid.*, p. 14.
[5] Beier, ii, pp. 23, 24.   [6] D.J.F.L., p. 19.   [7] Illus. No. 70.

Wednesdays after Trinity and Advent Sundays, and others, constituted the 'Concilium perpetuum'. Discipline was controlled by a Delegation (Deputation), which sat weekly on Tuesdays and consisted of the Rector and Syndicus *ex officio*, one member of the Law Faculty, and two representatives of the Nations, the last three being elected yearly. The General Council (Concilium nationale) comprised doctors, licentiates, and masters, who had graduated by examination or disputation. The professors (Professores ordinarii) numbered twenty-nine, five in the Faculty of Divinity, eight in Law, five in Medicine, and, in Philosophy, eleven Chairs devoted to Physics, Classics, Mathematics, Poetics, Hebrew, Rhetoric, Aristotle (August Fr. Müller), History, Philosophy (Joh. Christoph Gottsched), Morals and Politics.[1] Outside its classrooms the University was active in many Societies (Collegia), anthological, philobiblical, exegetic, and poetic, a 'Teutsch-übende Gesellschaft', a 'vertraute Redner-Gesellschaft', and two musical Collegia. One of the latter, of which Bach became conductor in 1729, met at Gottfried Zimmermann's garden in the Windmühlgasse in summer-time on Wednesdays from 4 to 6 p.m., and, in winter, at his coffee-house in the Catharinenstrasse on Fridays from 8 to 10 p.m. The other, directed by Johann Gottlieb Görner, met on Thursdays from 8 to 10 p.m. in the Klostergasse in summer, and, in winter, at Enoch Richter's coffee-house on the Marktplatz.[2] His University association was highly valuable to Bach: it augmented his orchestra on festival occasions, and provided him with material for the performance of his secular music, vocal and instrumental, permitting him to voice the community's mood on occasions of public ceremonial.

For its recreation Leipzig chiefly sought the gardens and coffee-houses without the walls. They were available on every hand, but especially on the west, where the Pleisse and Elster, spanned by many bridges, meandered in tortuous channels. Here lay Apel's garden, thus belauded thirty years after Bach's death:[3]

> Das unscheinbare Thor, das dort halb offen steht,
> Ist das, durch welches man in Apels Garten geht . . .
> Längst an der Wasserkunst, und weiter noch hinaus
> Glänzt noch manch Lustrevier, strahlt noch manch Gartenhaus . . .
> Was stehn Sie so erstaunt vor diesem Hause da?
> 'Das ist ja ein Pallast, ein prächtig Lustschloss!' Ja!

Beyond the Hallisches Thor, Johann Christoph Richter's garden

---

[1] D.J.F.L., pp. 23–8.
[2] *Ibid.*, p. 58. Görner's Collegium was founded by Johann Fr. Fasch in 1708 (Schering, p. 344).   [3] Beier, ii. 6.

also was much frequented, and drew the praises of the same pen in 1781:

Weil dieses Gartens Reiz die Sinne so entzückt,
Und Flora keinen hier mit schönern Blumen schmückt,
Weil durch der Bäume Laub, das freundlich sich umschlinget,
Der Sonne heisser Stral, des Mittags selbst, nicht dringet,
Und kurz, weil da die Kunst, die, was sie baut, auch ziert,
Japanisch von Geschmack ein Lusthaus aufgeführt;
So gieng ich jüngst hinein.

Thirty years before Bach's arrival, the Opera had been introduced to a town frequented by foreigners at the annual Fairs, and among whose citizens French and Italians abounded.[1] In 1693 Nikolaus Adam Strungk performed his 'Alceste' in the newly-built Opera-house on the Brühl, inaugurating a venture which concluded in 1729[2] and was intermittently in vigour in Bach's early years as a citizen. Its influence upon the Thomasschule was baneful: Kuhnau more than once complained that his best singers were enticed from him by the prospect of good pay and agreeable publicity as 'Operisten'.[3] On the Ritterstrasse another company presented comedies of excellence; a visitor declared in 1725 that their like was not found elsewhere; eighteen years later they drew the encomium of J. Chr. Müller.[4] For its secular music the community depended chiefly upon the University Collegia, until, in 1743, enthusiasts founded a civic society whose concerts proved so agreeable and popular that, in 1747, it held meetings at fortnightly intervals, from 1 June onwards, on Thursdays at 5 p.m., in the 'Concert-Saal' of the 'Three Swans' on the Brühl, and weekly from Michaelmas to Easter. Its device was a maiden playing the lyre,[5] and its motto *vetat tristari*.[6] Bach's life was then nearing its close; he cannot be counted among the founders of a movement whence developed the famous Gewandhaus Concerts of the next century.

Leipzig's lavish provision of spiritual sustenance to her population was notorious. 'Hier,' said a writer in 1732, 'giebt der Herr das Wort mit grossen Schaaren Evangelisten.'[7] Besides the Paulinerkirche, five churches were available for parochial use, all of them within the walls except the Johanniskirche. Senior in age, and in Bach's time in standing, was the Nikolaikirche,[8] a massively irregular building in the Ritterstrasse, whose present loftier middle tower was raised under Bach's eyes in 1730–1. Much altered externally since his days, it still presents features with which he was

---

[1] Cf. D.J.F.L., p. 96. [2] Schering, p. 446; Sp. ii. 27.
[3] Sp. ii. 854, 858. [4] Beier, p. 47. [5] See the cover of this volume.
[6] The advertisement and a reproduction of the ticket are in Riemer's *Chronik*, 1747. [7] Gerber, p. 398. [8] Illus. Nos. 67, 69.

familiar: the lofty pillars springing high beneath the roof, the large quadrangular nave with recessed chancel, and the small western organ and choir gallery inconveniently adapted to the performance of concerted music. Throughout Bach's career in Leipzig Superintendent Salomo Deyling was Pastor of the church, whose other clergy were the Archidiakonus, who preached the Monday sermon, the Diakonus, who preached on Friday, the Sunday Vespers Preacher, and the preacher on Saturday afternoon.[1] The organist till 1730 was Johann Gottlieb Görner, on whose transference to the Thomaskirche Johann Schneider received the post, and held it till 1787. He was Bach's pupil at Cöthen, a player for whom he had much respect, and to whom, not improbably, he entrusted the clavier instruction of his youngest sons.

Between the Thomaskirche and the Ranstädter Thor, looking out upon its mill on the Pleisse, stood the Neukirche, now the parish church of St. Matthew. A fifteenth-century foundation, this Barfüsserkirche had fallen into disuse until it was restored and reopened for public worship on 24 September 1699. By 1703 it received outward embellishments which were not materially altered till 1879, and in 1704 it had Georg Philipp Telemann briefly as its organist. Georg Balthasar Schott, its organist in 1723, a candidate for the Cantorship in that year, succeeded Telemann in the conductorship of the Collegium Musicum, which Bach took over from him in 1729. The organist in 1736 was Carl Gotthelf Gerlach, Bach's pupil, who directed a simple and conventional service in which figural music had no place. The clergy consisted of an Oberdiakonus and the Vespers (Sunday) Preacher.[2]

Thirteen years after the Neukirche reopened its doors, another ancient building was recovered to the service of religion. The Peterskirche, hard by the southern Port, had fallen into disuse by 1543, and served as a lime-shed until services were resumed in it in 1712. Hemmed in by tenements, it presented no external features of architectural interest, and internally remained inadequately furnished till the end of the century (1799). It possessed neither organ nor choir gallery, simple congregational music was sung in it, and its choir was provided by the least efficient of Bach's singers. Its staff consisted of a morning Preacher, who did occasional duty in St. Thomas's and St. Nicholas's, and an evening Preacher, who also conducted Catechism on Mondays and Thursdays at 2 p.m.[3]

---

[1] D.J.F.L., p. 80.   [2] Ibid., p. 83.
[3] Ibid., p. 84. The foundation of the modern Gothic church was laid on 17 Sept. 1882.

In another quarter of the town, the 'Johannis- und Hospital-Kirche'[1] faced the Grimmaisches Thor outside the walls; its name declares its origin. The Hospice buildings still survive in part, but, excepting the tower, the present church is modern. In Bach's period its services (for which he was not responsible) were held on Sundays, Tuesdays, and Thursdays, and its staff consisted of a single Preacher. Its organist in 1736 was Johann Gottlieb Reinicke.[2]

The Paulinerkirche,[3] being the University church, was controlled and staffed by the Faculty of Theology. Its clergy consisted of six morning and six afternoon Preachers, but there had recently been instituted the so-called 'neu Gottesdienst' on Sundays at 9 a.m. and 3 p.m., the provision of whose music was an inherited topic of controversy between the University and the Thomascantor in Bach's early years. These Sunday services were an addition to those which had long been conducted in the church on the three high festivals, the Reformation Festival, and the quarterly University 'Orationes' and 'Promotiones doctorales', which together constituted the so-called 'alt Gottesdienst', at which the music director, Johann Gottlieb Görner, performed 'solemn music', assisted by students 'and other musicians'.[4] The music staff consisted of the 'Chori Musici Director', a 'Cantor choralis', and an organist.

In the Neukirche and Peterskirche Bach had no personal duties. In the Paulinerkirche he functioned rarely. With the Nikolaikirche his official relations were identical with those that bound him to the Thomaskirche. But it is round the latter that his memory clings most tenaciously, for of its ancient school he was Cantor, and as Thomascantor exercised general musical control over the four urban civic churches. The Thomaskirche[5] stands on the western fringe of the ancient town, just inside the enclosing fortifications, raising its huge bulk to-day externally little changed over four centuries: the lofty nave with dormered roof, the great buttressed windows of the north and south aisles, the disproportionately planned chancel, and, dividing nave from chancel, the clumsily inserted tower rising to its lofty cupola. The original church, an Augustinian foundation, was built about 1212 upon the site of the present building, overlooking the Thomaskirchhof, the town's burial-ground until the sixteenth century, a source of constant bickering between the monastery and the town, until interment was forbidden in 1536 and St. John's distant churchyard beyond the wall took its place. Fifty years earlier, Markgraf Dietrich's original church had been taken down (in 1482); at Quasi-

---

[1] Illlus. Nos. 73. [2] D.J.F.L., p. 85. [3] Illus. No. 71, 72. [4] 'von Studiosis und andern Musicis' (D.J.F.L., p. 32). Cf. Schering, p. 308. [5] Illus. Nos. 60, 63.

modogeniti[1] 1496 the present building was dedicated by Bishop Thilo von Trotha of Merseburg, and assumed its familiar external design by 1553.[2] It had already been reformed (16 August 1539), its side-altars and pictures were removed in 1540, and in 1543 it was constituted a parochial church under the control of the civic Rath. Besides the customary services on Sundays and festivals, Vespers was then instituted on Fridays for the exposition of the Lutheran Catechism, and a pious benefaction in 1569 enabled the Saturday sermon to be established also. Viewed from the western gallery, the interior of the church in Bach's time differed from the present building chiefly in the number of disfiguring galleries which choked the aisles and walls of the tower. The altar was new, a recent gift from the Elector dedicated on Christmas Day 1721, an occasion which Kuhnau marked by one of his latest compositions. The pulpit had been in use since 1575, and was furnished with a carved snuff-box, a more recent benefaction (1640).[3] The western gallery, though large enough to accommodate two organs,[4] was less spacious than the present one and trespassed less upon the nave. Below it stood a massive stone font, dating from 1615, and the floor of the nave was filled with pews facing the altar, the midmost reserved for women, their male folk on either side.[5]

The ministerial staff of the Thomaskirche consisted of the Pastor, Archidiakonus, Diakonus (Sunday Vespers Preacher), Subdiakonus, and Saturday Preacher. The staff's official residence was in the Burgstrasse, the Pastor having his lodging in the Thomaskirchhof.[6] During Bach's quarter of a century of service no more than fifteen persons held the regular ministerial charges: normally each was promoted as a vacancy occurred above him. The following is a complete table of Bach's clerical colleagues: [7]

Pastor.

Christian Weiss,[8] 1714–36.
Fr. Wilhelm Schütz, 1737–9.
Urban Gottfried Sieber, 1739–41.
Gottlieb Gaudlitz, 1741–5.
Romanus Teller, 1745–50.

Archidiakonus.

Johann Gottlieb Carpzov, 1714–30.
Urban Gottfried Sieber, 1731–9.
Gottlieb Gaudlitz, 1739–41.
Christoph Wolle, 1741–61.

---

[1] Low Sunday.   [2] See the picture in Sachse, plate 1, and Kemmerling, p. 6.
[3] Cf. *Führer durch die Thomas-Kirche in Leipzig* (Leipzig: n.d.).
[4] Cf. Schering, pp. 108, 109, for their specifications.
[5] See the picture of the interior in 1710 in B.C.T., p. 180.
[6] D.J.F.L., p. 82.   [7] *Führer*, pp. 86–7.   [8] or Weise.

Diakonus.

Urban Gottfried Sieber, 1714–31.
Justus Gotthard Rabener, 1731.
Gottlieb Gaudlitz, 1731–9.
Romanus Teller, 1739–40.
Christoph Wolle, 1740–1.
Carl Friedrich Petzold, 1741–6.
Christoph Sanke, 1746–52.

Subdiakonus.

Justus Gotthard Rabener, 1721–31.
Gottlieb Gaudlitz, 1731.
Christian Weiss,[1] jun., 1731–7.
Romanus Teller, 1737–9.
Christoph Wolle, 1739–40.
Joh. Paul Ramm, 1740–1.
Carl Friedrich Petzold, 1741.
Christian Gottlob Eichler, 1741–3.
Christoph Sanke, 1743.
Christian Gottfried Huhn, 1743–6.
Friedrich Wilhelm Schleusser, 1746–52.

Bach's relations with Pastor Weiss were cordial; there are grounds for believing that he was Bach's frequent librettist. The younger Weiss perhaps aided him in a similar manner. Among the officials of the church, the Custos, Johann Christoph Rost, is noteworthy. He served for the greater part of Bach's Cantorship, and has left illuminating notes on the ritual observed in the Thomaskirche; his lodging was in the Thomaskirchhof, next to the Consistorium's offices. Till 1729 the organist was Christian Gräbner, who was succeeded in 1730 by Johann Gottlieb Görner, a musician of mediocre ability but unbounded self-esteem.

Besides the parochial churches, services were conducted on Sundays and week-days in the House of Correction, and also in the ancient Hospital of St. George near the Ranstädter Thor.[2]

Into this generous programme of devotion 'Music', as Bach's generation understood the term, hardly entered at all. The week-day services included a few hymns sung by a reduced choir.[3] In the Peterskirche and Neukirche the Sunday services had the same simplicity; their choirs were furnished by Bach's least competent singers, led by Choir Prefects. St. John's and St. Paul's were not dependent on the Thomasschule for singers. Hence Bach functioned personally only in the two Hauptkirchen, St. Thomas's and St.

---

[1] or Weise.   [2] D.J.F.L., pp. 85, 86. Cf. Sachse, p. 110.
[3] For the week-day services a choir of nine singers was provided, according to a roster which gave each scholar a turn once in six weeks. An example of the roster for 1744–5 is in B.-J. 1907, p. 77.

Nicholas's, though his choirs, as has been shown, fulfilled a wider duty. Four Sunday services were held in both churches: *Früh-gottesdienst*, preceded by *Mette*, did not call for the choir's atten-dance; it included hymns and a sermon, and was intended for servants and others whom circumstances prevented from attending the principal service at a later hour. A similar purpose was served by the *Mittagspredigt*, which was held alternately in the two churches, commencing at 11.30 a.m. and concluding about 1.15 p.m. Here also only hymns were sung. Another sermon (*Vesper-predigt*) after the midday meal concluded the day's religious cere-monial. On normal occasions only hymns were included in it, but at the three high festivals a Latin *Magnificat* was performed by choir and orchestra. Thus, at the normal Sunday services 'Music' was performed only at the principal office of the day, the so-called Hauptgottesdienst, which began at seven in the morning and lasted till about midday. Its order was as follows: [1]

1. Organ voluntary.
2. Motet, from the collections of Bodenschatz or Vulpius.
3. Missa (*Kyrie* and *Gloria in excelsis*).
4. Collect (Latin).
5. Epistle.
6. Hymn *de tempore*.
7. Gospel (Latin).
8. Creed (Latin).
9. Cantata.
10. Luther's metrical version of the Creed, as a hymn.
11. Sermon.
12. Church notices.
13. Prayers and Intercessions.
14. Hymn, or Part II of the Cantata.
15. The Lord's Prayer and *Verba Institutionis*.
16. Administration of the Sacrament, during which hymns or (and) a Motet were sung.
17. Collects.
18. Blessing.

While the liturgy followed was the same in both Hauptkirchen, the treatment of its musical portions differed accordingly as the *chorus primus* or *chorus secundus* was present. The former attended the church whose turn it was to hear the Cantata, a privilege exercised by each on alternate Sundays, and performed it to the accompaniment of organ and orchestra. Other changes than the

---

[1] Cf. B.C.T., pp. 32 ff. where the liturgy is set out in full.

substitution of a hymn for the Cantata resulted from the presence of the *chorus secundus*: the settings of the *Missa* were simpler, and the versicles and responses throughout were less ornate. To rehearse the Sunday Cantata was the principal task of Bach's scholars during the week, to provide it was his regular duty, and to compose it was an obligation he fulfilled on the average once every four weeks. Excepting Lent and the second and following Sundays in Advent, a cantata was required on every Sunday, as well as on the three festivals of the Virgin Mary, those of St. Michael and St. John Baptist, New Year's Day, Ascension Day, the Epiphany, and the Reformation Festival. The annual inauguration of the civic Council was similarly observed. The three high festivals, Christmas, Easter, and Whitsun, were each continued for three days; on the first and third, a cantata was sung at Hauptgottesdienst in the Nikolaikirche,[1] repeated at Vespers in the Thomaskirche on the first; on the second, a cantata was sung at Hauptgottesdienst in the Thomaskirche. Thus Bach was called on to provide fifty-nine cantatas annually. His duty also required him to compose, or provide, the annual Passion music, performed with orchestral accompaniment at Vespers on Good Friday alternately in the two Hauptkirchen, as well as the festival *Magnificat*. Funeral music was occasionally called for to commemorate the passing of prominent citizens, and Bach's motets[2] represent his response to the demand. Prosperous citizens also distinguished their weddings by a musical service, in which Bach's *chorus primus* and the town's musicians participated. But these were irregular responsibilities. Excepting Thursdays, when the Sacrament was administered,[3] the normal choir did not attend church on week-days; its obligations were discharged on Sundays, when, divided into four *chori* (Cantoreien), it served the four churches the Council controlled, Bach himself, with his *chorus primus*, attending that one of the two Hauptkirchen whose turn it was to hear 'die Music'.

Lavishly provided with churches, Leipzig was inadequately equipped with schools. More than fifty years after Bach's death complaint was made that the only alternatives to the Thomasschule and Nikolaischule were the Winkelschulen (private schools) and private tutors.[4] As restricted a choice faced the Leipzig parent of Bach's generation. The Privatschulen, or Winkelschulen, gave instruction 'im Christenthum und andern benöthigten Stücken' under the inspection of the four junior clergy of the town churches,

---

[1] This was the rule in Bach's period; Salomo Deyling's connexion with the church gave the Nikolaikirche precedence.
[2] 'Lobet den Herrn, alle Heiden' is of a different character from the other five.
[3] Only hymns were sung.　　　　[4] Beier, ii. p. 87.

without whose *testimonium habilitatis* none might function. Private
teachers of French were plentiful, of Italian less numerous, while
Theodore Arnold, living in the Hallisches Viertel, was teaching
English in 1736. Writing and mathematical masters were numerous.[1] Of the two Stadtschulen, the younger, the Nikolaischule,[2]
stood on the Nikolaikirchhof; its buildings serve to-day as a police
station. It owed its foundation by Pope Boniface IX in 1395 [3] to
disputes between the town and the older Thomasschule, and
throughout Bach's Cantorship its foundationers provided a choir
of ten singers at the week-day services held in its own church.[4]
Otherwise it was open to the children of the burgesses, and was
staffed by a Rector, Conrector, Tertius, and three junior masters.
Its obligation to provide the simple music required at the week-day
services demanded a Cantor, who in 1736 was Johann Hieronymus
Homilius,[5] a relative, perhaps, of Bach's pupil Gottfried August
Homilius, the Dresden Cantor.

The Thomasschule,[6] which celebrated its seventh centenary in
September 1912, was founded in 1212, in association with the
Augustinian monastery, to uphold and expand Christianity and
German culture on a pagan frontier, though the school also admitted a responsibility to educate its own community. From the
earliest period its foundationers, ancestors of the green-capped
Thomaner of to-day, received their education, and in return provided the music in the church, followed the citizens to their
graves, and supported themselves, as elsewhere, by periodical Currenden.[7] The Reformation extended these obligations: 'Our ancestors', observed Gesner in 1733, 'intended the school to be a
seminary of music, whereby the singing in all our churches might
be provided.' [8] The Alumneum consequently grew as the calls
upon it increased, and as pious benefactions augmented its pre-
carious income; under Bach it numbered 55 foundationers. The
civic Council assumed its control on 1 May 1543, and ten years
later erected more adequate buildings for its accommodation;
begun on the Fourth Sunday after Easter 1553, they were completed on the following 13 December.[9] The earlier fabric lay
immediately in front of the west porch of the church,[10] but the
solid walls of the new erection were extended to the southward

---

[1] D.J.F.L.,pp. 60, 88, 114.   [2] Illus. No. 68.   [3] *Führer durch die Thomas-Kirche*,
p. 57.   [4] B. C.T., p. 28. Cf. Schering, p. 103.   [5] D.J.F.L., p. 87.
[6] Illus. Nos. 60–2.   [7] Those of the Thomasschule date from between 1516
and 1522. In 1581 they took place thrice weekly, on Tuesdays, Thursdays, and
Saturdays. Cf. Schering, p. 69.   [8] Gesner, p. 22.
[9] The town bore only half the cost (2,808 fl. 11 gr. 6 pf. was the total amount);
the remainder was supplied by contributions of money, goods, and labour.
Cf. Richter, p. 33.   [10] Sachse and Kemmerling print a picture of it.

on to the Thomaskirchhof, and fulfilled their purpose unaltered until Bach was a resident in them. Enlarged in 1732, they served the school till it migrated to its present quarters in 1877, and a generation later, on 7 April 1902, their demolition began.

The Cantorship of the school was older than the Reformation, and early in its history acquired distinction through the reputation of one of its holders, Georg Rhau, composer, theorist, and music printer, who in 1519 celebrated Luther's famous Leipzig disputation with Johann Eck by a Mass and *Te Deum* of his own composition. In the school's hierarchy the Cantor then ranked fourth, after the Praepositus, Prior, and Custos, with whom he shared the duty of imparting general instruction: Tobias Michael, Cantor a century later (1616), discharged the following tasks:

Praeter operas et labores musicos docet cantor Tertianos
Hora antemeridiana prima . . . Grammaticam latinam
   die Saturni vero . . . . Catechismum Lutheri latinum
Hora 12 meridiana . . . . Musicam
Hora 1 meridiana . . . . Syntaxin latinam

Rhau probably was succeeded by Michael Koszwick, author of *Compendiaria musicae artis editio*, published at Leipzig in 1514 and 1516. Seven Cantors followed him: Johannes Hermann, who provided melodies for Ludwig Helmbold's hymns, Wolfgang Jünger, Johann Bruckner, Ulrich Lange, Wolfgang Figulus, remembered for the hymn-tune 'Helft mir Gott's Güte preisen', Melchior Heger, the first Cantor to occupy the official lodging in the new building, and Valentin Otto. Otto's successor, Sethus Calvisius, was the first of a distinguished procession of Lutheran Cantors which included Johann Hermann Schein, compiler of the famous *Cantional*, and culminated in Bach himself.

The disastrous Thirty Years War was raging and Leipzig was in the hands of the Swedes when, in March 1634, the Council formulated the 'Vornewerte Schul-Ordnung' whose ten articles regulated the school until Bach's appointment. Its staff thenceforward consisted of the Rector and six colleagues (collegae ordinarii), graded thus in authority: Conrector, Cantor, Tertius, Quartus, Baccalaureus funerum, and Baccalaureus nosocomii, with the addition of two *collaboratores* for the lowest classes. Excepting the Rector and Conrector, each master taught four hours daily, the classes assembling and dispersing at the summons of a bell. None of the staff might leave the town without the ruling Burgomaster's permission, and all met monthly in the Rector's lodging to report their class's progress. Each of the seniors [1] in turn held

---

[1] Rector, Conrector, Cantor, Tertius. Cf. *Schulordnung*, 1723.

for one week the post of Inspector, being for that period respon-sible for discipline day and night, sharing the school meals, and sleeping on the premises in an apartment specially allocated to their use. The school rose at 4 a.m. in summer, at 5 a.m. in winter, and a quarter of an hour later met for morning prayers. At 10 a.m.[1] Mittagessen (*prandium*) was served, and during its continuance a portion of the Bible, or a chapter of history, was read. After the evening meal prayers were said at eight and the school retired to bed, the Inspector's last duty being to see that lights were extinguished in the dormitories. Regarding the *collaboratores*, the Baccalaureus funerum accompanied the school at the humbler funerals. A funeral 'mit der grossen halben Schule' called for the three upper classes and the Quintaner; one 'mit der kleinen halben Schule' was attended by the Primaner and Tertianer on Mondays and Tuesdays, and by the Secundaner and Quartaner on Wednes-days and Fridays. The Baccalaureus nosocomii, besides under-taking elementary tuition in the school, was employed in the Georgenhospital at the Ranstädter Thor.[2]

The 'Sänger-Chor', or foundation boarders, who formed the Alumneum, passed a test of general knowledge, and also received from the Cantor a certificate of musical proficiency, before being admitted. An undertaking that they would remain for a reasonable number of years was also demanded; for the school was not of the English cathedral pattern, a choir of boys associated in church with professional male singers. The Alumneum provided all four parts, as it does still, a fact illuminated by the ages at which foundationers were admitted. Bach took over from Kuhnau sixty-one singers, whose ages on admission were as follows:[3]

Age.				Number.
11	.	.	.	1
12	.	.	.	9
13	.	.	.	12
14	.	.	.	22
15	.	.	.	8
16	.	.	.	8
17	.	.	.	1

Of Bach's own entrants:[4]

Age.				Number.
9	.	.	.	1
11	.	.	.	5
12	.	.	.	12
13	.	.	.	44

---

[1] Changed to 11 a.m. in 1733. Cf. Gesner, p. 14.
[2] Sachse, *passim*.   [3] B.-J. 1907, p. 50.   [4] *Ibid.*

Age.				Number.
14	.	.	.	. 55
15	.	.	.	. 53
16	.	.	.	. 43
17	.	.	.	. 19
18	.	.	.	. 9
19	.	.	.	. 3
20	.	.	.	. 3
21	.	.	.	. 1

The number of foundationers did not vary from the seventeenth century: in 1634, as under Bach, the choir provided fifty-five singers.[1] Each class had its dormitory, regulated by a code of discipline. That of Sexta exhibited a tale of misdemeanours with the penalties their commission involved:

1. For losing the key or leaving it in the door . . 4 gr.
2. For failing to shut the door when the last to leave the room 2 gr.
3. For being sick (qui vomitat) . . . . 2 gr.
4. For swearing, loud, or improper speech . . . 6 pf.
5. For impertinent language, in Latin or German . . 6 pf.
6. For not getting up in the morning and missing prayers . 3 pf.
7. For not tidying the cubicle before 10 in summer and 12 in winter . . . . . . 6 pf.

Fines varied according to the standing of the offender. Theft was punished with a fine of 4 groschen in Quarta, of two in Quinta, of three in Septima. Noisy conduct entailed the loss of 3 pfennige in Tertia, while to speak German between morning prayers and Mittagessen, and after evening prayers, cost a Quintaner 3 pfennige and a Sextaner two. Quarrelling was fined at 6 pfennige, and more serious contentions at 2 groschen.[2]

The building that housed this historic foundation no longer stands. Till a quarter of a century ago, it stood venerable on a spot where everything had altered except itself and the church it served, facing the Kirchhof, in whose midst a fountain played from 1722 to 1816, when it was removed as an impediment to traffic.[3] The rear windows of the building looked out upon the Pleisse, the mill, Apel's garden, the Promenade, open country the modern town has quite engulfed. For the first eight years Bach lived in it the roof rose steeply above a three-story structure, beneath which three separate establishments had their own entrances on the Kirchhof. Nearest to the church was the Rector's lodging; the middle was occupied by classrooms and dormitories; and the southern wing housed the Cantor. But the building had

---

[1] 'Adjuvanten' were occasionally employed in choir and orchestra. Cf. Schering, p. 98.   [2] Sachse, p. 114.
[3] *Führer durch die Thomas-Kirche*, pp. 3, 4. See the illustration, No. 60.

long ceased to be adequate, and the need for enlargement was urgent. On his appointment to the Rectorship Gesner demanded its consideration; on 6 June 1730 the Council minuted [1] that the school was 'in grosser Unordnung', that the dormitories were inadequate to provide separate beds for all the foundationers, and that three classes were taught simultaneously in the *coenaculum*. It was resolved to add two stories to the building, and the work was begun at Easter 1731, the Rector, Cantor, and the scholars being provided with quarters elsewhere. The roof was stripped, the walls were heightened to provide an extra story and a mezzanine, and a curb-roof crowned the heightened structure. In little more than a year the work was completed, and the new building was formally opened on 5 June 1732. No other constructional changes were made until 1829, when the accommodation for Quarta and Quinta was recast.[2]

Rising more loftily on its ancient base, the school building resumed its threefold use. The middle section allotted to the school absorbed every floor from the basement to the roof, overflowed on the third into the Cantor's wing, and took in the whole of the fourth and fifth stories. The school door opened from the Thomaskirchhof upon a narrow hall, on the right of which a staircase rose steeply to the floor above. At its foot stood the so-called 'Kreuzköthe', a cupboard for the processional Cross used at funerals. To the left of the hall, a large five-windowed apartment accommodated the Primaner and served as the Aula on ceremonial occasions. Behind it, looking out from five windows upon the Promenade, was the 'Cönakel' (coenaculum) or dining-hall, served by the kitchen in the old building before the west door of the church, untouched by the renovation; dining-room and kitchen were joined by a passage which furnished a lavatory and conveniences. The dining-room was set with tables in two rows, and one for the Inspector for the week; from a desk or pulpit on the wall opposite the door the Bible, or a chapter of history, was read during meals. Above, on the first floor, Secunda, Sexta, and Quinta had their classrooms, the last two at the back of the building, the first above the Aula, but shorter by one window at the Cantor's end. All three rooms were entered through a windowless corridor from the landing. On the second story, a passage along the whole length of the section separated its two apartments, front and back, and at either end terminated in doors into the Cantor's and Rector's quarters respectively. For the Cantor the access had a peculiar convenience: the long, narrow apartment at the back,

---

[1] Bi. ii. 159.   [2] For my account of the interior of the school I follow Richter.

whose five windows overlooked the Promenade, was the practice-room, the only room in the school building, except that of the Primaner on the ground floor, which never varied in its usage. Here the mighty music conceived in the little room nearly below it was first heard, and from it the harmony of the great *Sanctus* reverberated down the dark passage, or mingled, as Veit's music once, with the mill-wheel's clatter outside. A platform for the instrumentalists stood against its southern wall, and here in after days hung Haussmann's portrait of Bach,[1] now in the Rathaus.[2] On the other side of the passage, looking out upon the Thomas-kirchhof, was the conference room, decorated with frescoes of the four seasons, frequented by the staff at their monthly meetings; later it was incorporated into the Rector's lodging. The third floor, added in 1731, was wholly allotted to the school, excepting in the Rector's wing. It provided the classrooms of the Tertianer and Quartaner and the apartments of the Inspector for the week. The fourth and fifth floors were entirely devoted to dormitories, whose cubicles generally accommodated two beds. Thus enlarged the buildings remained adequate for more than a century. The intro-duction of the Prussian nine-class system in 1867, however, created the need for larger accommodation; it was met by the migration of the school to the present buildings in the Schreber-strasse ten years later (1877).

Considerable repair was necessary before Bach took up his resi-dence in the south wing in 1723. Johann Kuhnau, his predecessor, had lived there more than twenty years, the father of eight children, of whom four daughters remained unmarried under his roof at his death.[3] Bach brought with him a family of five, the eldest, the only girl, not yet fifteen, and after Kuhnau's long tenancy much was needed for their accommodation. Kuhnau died on 5 June 1722, and throughout September, October, and November, Adam Jakob, mason, Johann David Schwan, joiner, Joh. Christian Schmied, carpenter, and a locksmith were employed by the Council at considerable cost to make the necessary repairs. The kitchen received a new oven, Eva Klemm was engaged for a week in scrubbing and cleaning, and in February 1723 the walls were whitewashed.[4] Thereafter till it was pulled down the Cantor's lodging was little altered.[5]

The front door which admitted Bach to his new quarters stood to the right of the single ground-floor window, and was reached

[1] The frontispiece to this volume.
[2] A copy hangs in the Singesaal of the present Alumneum.
[3] Mattheson, p. 157.   [4] Cf. Kroker.   [5] Richter, p. 48.

by two or three steps from the Kirchhof. A narrow hall within disclosed a staircase ascending to the floor above, and, on the left, a largish room whose single window looked out on the square. Another and somewhat smaller room behind, entered through the dividing wall, was lighted by a window opening on the passage from the square to the Promenade. The two rooms probably served as bedrooms for Wilhelm Friedemann, Carl Philipp, and their younger brothers; for, when the building was demolished, Greek and Latin exercises written by Friedemann were found in a recessed cupboard in the front room, along with the parts of a violin concerto (not by Bach), the libretto of a wedding Ode composed

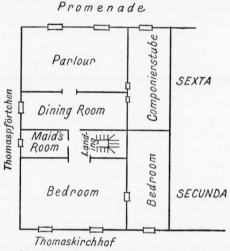

Plan of the Cantor's Lodging, First Floor.[1]

by him, and the title-page of the New Year cantata he offered to Prince Leopold before leaving Cöthen.[2] Behind these rooms the ground-floor space was occupied by a wash-house, accessible from within by a door beneath the stairway, from without by a side-door to the passage; it was lit by a window on that side and by two others looking out on the Promenade. On the first floor the Cantor's lodging took in the three end windows, back and front, and on the passage wall was lighted by two more. The latter served the dining-room and maid's room.[3] The three front win-

---

[1] Plans of each floor of the whole building are provided by Richter.
[2] Cf. B.C.T., pp. 545, 561. Both relics are now in the Eisenach Bach Museum. The wedding Ode, performed in 1725, bore the title 'Sein Segen fliesst'.
[3] A closet was placed here, whose wooden lid and foot-rest survived till the destruction of the building.

dows lighted a large and small bedroom. The rooms at the back have more intimate interest: the larger, entered from the dining-room and lighted by two windows, served Bach, as it served his successors to the time of Moritz Hauptmann, as a 'parlour', the scene of the happy family concerts in which he so much delighted. The narrow room next to it, with a single window overlooking the Promenade, was his study, the 'Componierstube', separated only by a lath-and-plaster partition from the juvenile Sextaner, little conscious that they neighboured an immortal.

Narrow stairs led from the first floor to the bedrooms above, two rooms, lighted by three windows, looking out on the front, and at the back, a third room, lighted by a single window in the end wall and two overlooking the Promenade. From the landing a door gave access to the corridor and practice-room in the school building. The Cantor's accommodation did not extend to the higher floors.

The constitution and discipline of the school during Bach's Cantorship are set out in two documents. The earlier was published on 13 November 1723 in fourteen chapters: *E. E. Hochw. Raths der Stadt Leipzig Ordnung der Schule zu S. Thomae.*[1] Even a concise synopsis of it affords a vivid picture of the circumstances of Bach's life during its last decades.

Cap. I. *Vom Amt des Rectoris.*

Besides his general and pedagogic duties, the Rector takes charge at night of the *clavis communis* (Haupt-Schlüssel), allows none to enter or leave the house unless for weighty reasons, and assures himself that all the scholars are within the building and in bed. He receives from each scholar on leaving for the University a fee, not exceeding two thalers, 'pro Testimonio als pro Oratiuncula'.

Cap. II. *Von dem Amt derer Praeceptorum insgemein.*

The titles 'Baccalaureus' and 'Collaborator' hitherto attached to the lowest masterships are suppressed in order to promote 'gute Harmonie und Ordnung'. The *Baccalaureus funerum* is henceforth styled Quartus, the *Baccalaureus nosocomii* Quintus, and the two *collaboratores* Sextus and Septimus respectively. The school teaching hours are four daily, excepting half-holidays, but the Rector and Cantor are exempt from this normal tale.

Cap. III. *Von dem Examine und Progressibus.*

Examinations are held half-yearly in the weeks following Quasimodo-geniti[2] and preceding Michaelmas, from 7–9 a.m. and 1–3 p.m. Representatives of the civic Council, the Superintendent, and the Pastor of the Thomaskirche attend them.

[1] The volume is a small quarto of 83 pages; its frontispiece is the picture of the school and church reproduced in illustration No. 60.
[2] First Sunday after Easter.

Cap. IV. *Von dem Amt des Wöchentlichen Inspectoris.*

The Rector, Conrector, Cantor, and Tertius act in turn as weekly Inspector. The Inspector conducts morning and evening prayers in German, and, 'zu Erweckung mehrerer Attention', no longer in Latin. He sees that the school is called at 6 a.m. in winter, at 5 a.m. in summer, and that fifteen minutes later all are assembled for prayers 'in das Auditorium hinunter'.[1] He says prayers again at 8 p.m., and is careful to note that none is absent and that no lights are taken into the dormitories. At meals he must see that there is 'kein Zechen in dem Vaporario', that grace is said in German before and after meat, and that the Bible or a history book is read during the repast. It is his duty to make sure that the scholars return in full number and at the proper hour from attending funerals, weddings, and especially the winter Currenden; particularly must he satisfy himself that none comes home 'mit dem Trunck überladen'. When the school attends church or funerals in a body he accompanies it to and from its duty. On Sunday the Cantor attends the first *coetus musicus* to church, the Conrector the *chorus secundus* to the other Hauptkirche, and the Sextus the third choir to the Neukirche. At the week-day early morning sermons the Cantor is on duty on Friday, the Rector on Tuesday, the Quintus on Thursday. At 'Betstunden' the Quartus attends. The Inspector holds the key of the Sanatorium [2] and visits the patients in it. Absence from his duty during the day entails a fine of four groschen, and at night of six.

Cap. V. *Vom Amt des Cantoris, so viel die Music betrifft.*

The Cantor instructs the *coetus superior*, leaving the *Incipienten* (beginners) to the Septimus; he teaches them collectively and individually. If the *coetus superior* is divided,[3] the Cantor attends the *chorus primus*, the Conrector the *chorus secundus*. On Sunday the *chorus primus* attends the two Hauptkirchen alternately, a Prefect and eight singers are on duty at the Neukirche, and a Prefect and four singers at the Peterskirche. In church and at funerals, if he is present, the Cantor starts the hymns, otherwise the Precentor of the church does so. He selects the hymns or motet to be sung at funerals. His fee for attending weddings is one Reichsthaler, and he must not demand more. The music and musical instruments are in his charge, as well as the general oversight of the organists and musicians of the Hauptkirchen. His practisings for the Christmas and spring [4] Currenden must not unduly interrupt the school curriculum.

Cap. VI. *Von Aufnehmung derer Knaben und deren Dimission.*

The sons of the burgesses may be admitted by the Rector to the lowest [5] classes to be taught to read, write, decline, and conjugate. But to the body of foundationers none may enter without the permission of the Council's Vorsteher, nor may be dismissed nor deprived of any emolument without similar sanction. If any of the *Externen* (day-boys) desires to be received into the upper classes, his name must be given to the

---

[1] *i.e.* in the practice room on the second floor. See note to Cap. **x**, *infra*.
[2] This apartment was in the old building immediately in front of the west door of the church.
[3] As, normally, it was.   [4] On St. Gregory's Day (12 March).
[5] These classes, attended by day-boys, who were not foundationers, and therefore were distinct from the *alumni*, were conducted, as has been shown above, in the top stories of the school building.

Vorsteher, and, provided he is musically adequate, he will be preferred to applicants from outside. A foundationer admitted as a descantist agrees to stay for five or six years.[1] The names of those who are expelled are posted on the school buildings and are intimated to the Town Clerk. Those who leave school with a good character are entitled to a *testimonium* from the Rector.

Cap. VII. *Vom Amt des Præceptoris Quarti.*

The Quartus, formerly Baccalaureus funerum, accompanies the 'smaller half' or 'quarter' of the school to funerals and starts the hymns, but if Betstunden are held in church the 'Leichen-Famulus' does that duty. He instructs the lower classes in the Bible, Catechism, reading and writing, accompanies them to church for the weekly Betstunden, and prepares them for the Sunday catechism.

Cap. VIII. *Von denen Leichen-Begängnissen und Schul-Accidentien.*

While it is the ancient custom for the school to attend funerals in the town, the ceremony must not take place before 3 p.m. when the entire *coetus scholasticus* attends, in order that school lessons be not hindered. If half the school attends, the first three Classes and the Quintaner represent it; if the smaller half, Prima with Tertia, or Secunda with Quarta, do so alternately. Scholars and masters proceed to the house of mourning a quarter of an hour before the time appointed for the funeral and at once begin their singing. The prayer of thanksgiving for the departed follows and is offered by the 'Leichen-Bitter'. The bearers then gather round the coffin and convey it to the place of interment. The funeral fee varies with the school representation, the masters' proportions being as follows:

	Whole School.	Larger half.	Smaller half.	Quarter.
Rector .	1 th.	15 gr.	6 gr.	1 gr. 6 pf.
Conrector	8 gr.	6 gr.	2 gr.	3 pf.
Cantor .	15 gr.	1 th.	4 gr.	6 pf.
Tertius .	8 gr.	6 gr.	2 gr.	3 pf.
Quartus .	8 gr.	5 gr.	4 gr.	2 gr. 3 pf.
Quintus .	5 gr.	4 gr.	2 gr.	3 pf.
Sextus .	2 gr.	2 gr.	2 gr.	—
Septimus	2 gr.	1 gr. 3 pf.	1 gr.	—
Total .	3 th.	2 th. 15 gr. 3 pf.	23 gr.	5 gr.

Money collected at the Currenden on St. Gregory's Day (12 March), St. Martin's Day (11 November), and between Michaelmas and Easter, is likewise divided among the staff and scholars in varying proportions.

Cap. IX. *Von der Schuldigkeit derer Schüler insgemein.*

The three upper classes converse in Latin among themselves and with their teachers. According to ancient usage, the Quintaner attend the Betstunden in church on Mondays, Tuesdays, Wednesdays, and Fridays; the Primaner attend morning sermon on Tuesdays; and all classes go to church for the Thursday and Friday morning sermon.[2]

---

[1] It appears from Gesner, p. 35, that a quarter's notice was required.
[2] Gesner (p. 6) required them to communicate three or four times a year.

Cap. X. *Wie die Schüler sonderlich in ihren auf der Schule befindlichen Cammern sich zu verhalten haben.*

The bell rings at 5 a.m. in summer and 6 a.m. in winter, when every scholar rises, washes, brushes his hair, and is ready at the quarter-hour [1] to attend prayers, bringing his Bible with him. Clothes, shoes, stockings, and linen must be clean and tidy. No lights may be used in the dormitories. Chamber utensils must not be broken or spilt or their contents be emptied from the windows. Before retiring to rest the lessons of the day should be recalled, with thanks to God for the knowledge acquired. The walls must not be disfigured with charcoal drawings or writing. Locks, windows, and keys that are broken, must be replaced at the delinquent's cost. Doors must be kept open in summer; noise and disorder are to be avoided. None may remain away at night without express permission. To such as absent themselves for two or three days '8 Tage des Tisches mangeln' on their return. Absence for a week entails the loss of free board altogether. Such as absent themselves for a month are expelled, unless they can explain their conduct satisfactorily. Before leaving the school, the scholar must state his reason in writing, give up the key of his cubicle to the Rector, and take away nothing that is not his own. He who runs away without explanation is posted on the notice-board and expelled with ignominy.

Cap. XI. *Wie die Alumni sich bey Tische zu bezeigen haben.*

Grace is said before and after morning and evening meals by the scholar whose turn it is to do so, the others repeating the words after him. During meals a Psalm, or chapter from the Bible, or another edifying book, is read.[2] Plates and spoons must not be removed from the table. The seniors are not to be helped more liberally than the rest: their preference causes discontent. A meal may not be taken outside school without permission.

Cap. XII. *Was sie bey Leichen-Begängnüssen zu beobachten haben.*

The prescribed uniform is a respectable black cloth suit and cloak,[3] and is imperative at funerals. The scholars follow at funerals in the order in which they sit in class, and their singing must display 'eine richtige Consonanz'.

Cap. XIII. *Ordnung des Chori Musici bey dem Gottes-Dienst.*

On Sundays the scholars assemble quietly in the *coenaculum*, and a quarter of an hour before the time for service proceed to church, where they remain seated on their benches at the back of the gallery till summoned to their singing-desks at the front. After the Cantata the Praecentor, Tenors, and Basses may remain at the balustrade at the front of the gallery. The rest return to their benches at the back and listen to the sermon and the prayers that follow it,[4] proceeding thereafter to the front to sing. Food may not be taken into church. To leave church without permission before the service is ended is punished with a birching. He

---

[1] Gesner (p. 13) extended this to half an hour. But the school was called at 5.30 a.m. in winter.
[2] Gesner (p. 5) introduced Bible readings in the Latin and Greek text.
[3] See the costume illustrated in the frontispiece to B.C.T.
[4] Cf. B.C.T., p. 39.

who absents himself from the choir for a month is struck from the list of 'Currend-Schüler'.

The *coetus musicus* is divided into four 'Cantoreien'. The first sings at weddings and on other occasions of a festal character, its earnings going into 'die verschlossene Büchse'. On the occasion of weddings and other festivities it is customary for special victuals to be provided for the choir's consumption, but money may be given instead, and will be credited to the fund out of which the scholars' meals are provided.

At Christmas time two extra Cantoreien are added to the four, and the town is divided into six districts for their Currenden. The *chorus primus* visits the school's patrons and Inspectors, and the six choirs follow a prescribed itinerary:

1. Thomaskirchhof, Burgstrasse, Thomasgässgen, Markt.
2. Catherinenstrasse, Grimmaische Gasse.
3. Peterstrasse, Altmarkt, Neumarkt.
4. Heustrasse, Neukirchhof, Fleischergasse, Barfüsser Gässgen, Brühl (as far as the Catherinenstrasse).
5. Reichsstrasse, Salzgässgen, Schustergässgen, Brühl (from Nikolaistrasse to Catherinenstrasse).
6. Nikolaistrasse and Kirchhof, Ritterstrasse, Brühl (from Nikolaistrasse to the Frauen-Collegium).

The money collected is handed to the Rector by the Prefects in charge. No member of the *chorus musicus* can be excluded from his share of the fund except for valid reasons. But six groschen towards the purchase of music are deducted from the first distribution he shares.

Cap. XIV. *Von der Schuldigkeit derer Praefectorum.*

The *Praefectus Inquilinorum*, or *General Praefectus*, exercises a general authority over the whole school, foundationers and day-boys alike. Unless he is incompetent in music, the oldest alumnus holds this position, otherwise the scholar next to him in seniority.

The *Praefecti Cubiculorum* [1] are eight in number, one for each of the 'Schul-Cammern'. They maintain order in the dormitories and report ill behaviour to the Rector and Inspector for the week.

The *Praefecti Coetuum* direct the Currenden and hand the money collected to the Rector.

The *Praefecti Chororum* are four in number and are appointed annually at Christmas by the Cantor, with the Vorsteher's approval. They control the choirs at funerals, and if the Cantor is absent act in his room.

The *Quaestores*: One in each class keeps the hour-glass, class register, chalks, and other apparatus, is responsible for order in the class, and hands delinquents to the Inspector for punishment.

The *Leichen-Famuli* keep the list of funerals to be attended, account for the money received for attendance at them, regulate the procession to and from the house of mourning, and see that the Cross is borne at its head.

The *Calefactor* rises before the others to heat the building, rouses them by ringing a bell, and fifteen minutes later rings again to call them to prayers. He lights the lamps on the walls and stairs and extinguishes them. He sees that windows, doors, and presses are shut, directs the

---

[1] Gesner (p. 29) calls them 'Decuriones'. It is clear from his *Gesetze* that the cubicles were also used as studies.

'Purganten', and keeps a store of firewood and sawdust. After meals he removes the cloth and spoons and sweeps out the room. He must not allow his duties to impede his studies [!]

The *Purganten* are responsible for cleaning the building and for removing dust and rubbish to the Thomaspförtchen. The rods and birches used for correction are in their charge.[1]

To this intimate picture Gesner's *Gesetze*[2] add a few details, with occasional sparks of humour. It is perceived that the restriction of youths of seventeen, eighteen, and even twenty, within boundaries which lacked every facility for recreation encouraged restiveness. The fact that penalties are prescribed for week-long absences presupposes that they occurred. Indeed, Gesner's rules permit an absent foundationer to find a deputy among the dayboys, who receives his free commons at meal-times till he returns.[3] His stern admonition to refrain from insobriety and tobacco-smoking as clearly indicates a community not wholly juvenile.[4] The Primaner late for a lesson is fined 6 pfennige, a Secundaner and Tertianer three, a Quartaner one.[5] Scholars are bidden to come to class with books, pen, ink, and clean paper, and to write out as much as can be remembered of the Sunday sermon.[6] A bad blunder in singing is punishable, an intentional mistake is severely corrected.[7] The discomforts of long services are revealed: the younger singers may return to school to hear a sermon read if the Inspector declares the cold in church beyond their endurance.[8] In cases of illness the doctor must not be called in till elementary remedies have failed to cure. The patient is then removed to the Sanatorium, where his meals, of better quality, are brought to him by a Tertianer. If the malady is obstinate, a woman is engaged at the Council's expense to nurse the patient.[9]

Gesner's *Gesetze*[10] sketch a normal day in the school's life. In summer time, the Calefactor, first to rise and last to bed, sounds the bell at 5 a.m., and half an hour later all are assembled for prayers in the *coenaculum*. After prayers some of the classes repair to their classrooms or cubicles till half-past six. Others attend the morning sermon in church[11] and return in time for the first hour of lessons at seven. Each class begins the day with a hymn, selecting one appropriate to the following Sunday or festival.

---

[1] They also administered corporal punishment at the orders of a master. Cf. Gesner, p. 32. See Kemmerling, p. 6, for pictures of the Thomaspförtchen.
[2] E. E. *Hochweisen Raths der Stadt Leipzig Gesetze der Schule zu S. Thomae* (1733).   [3] *Ibid.*, pp. 34, 35.   [4] *Ibid.*, p. 7.
[5] *Ibid.*, p. 19.   [6] *Ibid.*, p. 21.   [7] *Ibid.*, p. 23.
[8] *Ibid.*, p. 18.   [9] *Ibid.*, p. 33.   [10] *Ibid.*, pp. 12–16.
[11] The Calefactor was released from attendance at these week-day services (B.-J. 1907, p. 77).

A chapter of the Bible is read and, after it, a portion of the *Compendium theologicum*. Mittagessen is served at eleven. At noon the upper school meets the Cantor in the practice-room upstairs, while the rest repair to his assistant, an hour badly chosen for the digestion, remarks Gesner, but not to be evaded on that ground. Other lessons follow, and probably, in the afternoon, a funeral is attended. Abendessen is at 6 p.m., and by seven all are in their rooms, or, in winter time, to save light, at their tables in the *coenaculum*, reading, writing, or conning the next day's lessons under the eye of the Inspector. At eight prayers are said, and at nine all go to bed, first washing their bodies and brushing their clothes. Before yielding to slumber Gesner exhorts them to follow the example of Pythagoras, reflect on the day's happenings and lessons, and discover the path of prudence and godliness. The new building invited new rules: Gesner concludes with 'das vornehmste':

BEFÖRDERE DAS WOHL DER SCHULE.

CHAPTER VIII

DIRECTOR MUSICES

THE Leipzig Cantorship in Bach's hands broke from the traditions he inherited. He shared with his colleagues a common routine of pedagogic duty, though less heavily burdened than his predecessors. At an expenditure of 50 Rth. annually, he was released from the obligation to teach Latin in Tertia, and found a deputy in Carl Friedrich Petzold, the Tertius.[1] His evasion of

[1] The following unpublished letters from Superintendent Deyling to the Council relate to Bach's arrangement with Petzold:

Hochwürdige Magnifici, Hochedle, Beste und Hochgelahrte Hochgeehrteste Herren und Patroni.

Als Dieselben jüngsthin, ich sollte den neuen Cantorem zu S. Thomae Herrn Johann Sebastian Bachen zu seinem Amte, dem Herkommen gemäs, an und einweisen, untern 13 Maji a. c. an mich verordnet und E. E. Hochweiser Rath als Patronus den 31 ej. zu solcher Introduction angesetzet, habe ich derselben wegen anderer Amts-Verrichtung in eigener Persohn nicht beywohnen können, sondern meinem Vices dem Co-Inspectori Scholae Thomanae Herrn L. Weiss auftragen müssen. Ob er nun wohl diese Verrichtung übernommen, und *nomine* Consistorii den neuen Herrn Cantorem einweisen wollen, so ist ihm doch, laut beygehender Registraturen, nicht allein von dem Herrn Raths-Deputirten Wiederspruch geschehen, sondern es hat sich auch Nachmittags *nomine* Senatus der Herr Ober-Stadt-Schreiber Menser in meinem Hausse desswegen beschweret, und unter andrem sich vernehmen lassen, es wären dergleichen Vorstellungen und Praesentationes der Schul-Collegen von Seiten E. E. und Hochweisen Raths alle Zeit solitarie geschehen und hätte der Superintendens, samt dem Pastore Thomano, wenn sie zugegen gewesen, weiter nichts dabey gethan, als dass sie den neuen Schul-Collegen Glück gewünscht. Wenn auch überdiess die Herren Raths Deputirten gegen Herrn L. Weissen erinnert und mir zu vermelden gebethen, dass der neue Herr Cantor die Information in der Schule nicht abwarten werde, sondern mit dem Herrn Tertio sich desshalben verglichen habe, dass er gegen jährliche 50 Rthr. dergleichen Schul-Arbeit, an seiner statt über sich nehmen wolle, dieser auch darmit gar wohl zufrieden ist, als lasse ich mir meines Orts, in Betrachtung, dass der Herr Tertius ein gar geübter und fleissiger Schulmann ist, der die Jugend nicht versäumen wird, diesen Vorschlag, biss auf E. Hochlöbl. Consistorii Approbation, wohl gefallen. Was aber E. Edlen Hochweisen Raths Vorgehen anlanget, als wenn sie das *jus Collegas Scholae investiendi et introducendi solitarie et privative* hätten, davon findet sich auf hiesiger Superintendur keine Nachricht. Nach dem aber gleich wohl Ew. Hochlöbl. Consistorium solche Verrichtung mir committiret, und ich nicht absehen kan, wie *tacendo et nihil agendo* ein Superintendens einen Schul-Collegen zu seinem Amt einweisen könne, als habe meinen Hochzuehrenden Herren und Patronis ich solches gehorsamst einberichten und Dero Verordnung, wie es in Zukunfft in dergleichen Fällen gehalten werden soll, mir ausbitten wollen, der ich mit allem Respect beharre

Ihro Magnificenz und Hoch Edl. wie auch Hochehrw. Herren Gebets und Dienstergebenster

D. Salomon Deyling.

Leipzig, d. 29 Junii 1723.

The letter is among the Acta die Besetzung des Cantoramts bei der Schule

that duty by no means sprang from inability to fulfil it: Telemann, Graupner, and his other competitors, shared his disinclination to accept a post whose obligations made its holder primarily a teacher and choirmaster. Bach regarded it as equivalent to a Capell-meistership; at the bottom of his uneasy relations with the Council throughout his Leipzig career was his determination to fulfil its functions in that sense. As the years passed, he allowed his peda-gogic duties to sit more and more loosely on his shoulders, dele-gated his task as choirmaster to subordinate, though capable, hands, and devoted his time and genius to perfecting the musical forms German art had been patiently developing since the Reformation—the Oratorio, Passion, and Cantata. To emphasize his conception of the office, he almost invariably designated himself 'Director Musices', a title appropriate to the responsibilities he admitted.

Bach's deliberate interpretation of his duty imposed on him a heavy burden. There is every reason to accept the statement of his earliest biographers, that, over and above his Passions, Oratorios, motets, and secular concerted music, he completed five sets of cantatas, each of which covered the whole range of the ecclesiastical year. Of the 295 cantatas he must consequently have written, about thirty were in his portfolio when he came to Leipzig, and served him there. Thus, he composed at least 265 cantatas during the twenty-seven years of his Cantorship, and since he ceased to write in that form after 1744, this astonishing output was completed in little more than twenty years, at the rate, on the average, of one

zu St. Thomä zu Leipzig betr. erg. von dem Consistorio zu Leipzig in the Archiv des Sächs. Ministeriums für Volksbildung.

Deyling's second letter is as follows:
 Magnifici, Hochwürdige und Hochgelahrte insonders Hochgeehrteste Herren und Patroni,
 Als an dieselben untern 29ten Junii abgewichenen Jahres ich einberichtet, dass der neue Herr Cantor Thomanus allhier Herr Joh. Seb. Bach die Informa-tion in der Schule nicht abwarten werde, sondern den Herrn Tertium gegen eine gewisse Ergötzlichkeit die Schul-Labores an seiner statt über sich zu nehmen vermocht, habe ich nach der Zeit mehrere Erkundigung eingezogen, und befunden, dass erwähnter Herr Tertius die dem Cantori zukommende Schul-Information nicht allein würcklich übernommen, sondern dass auch der Cantor Bach, in dem Fall, wenn der Tertius wegen Krankheit oder anderer Hindernisse absens seyn müssen, die Classe besuchet, und denen Knaben ein Exercitium zu elaboriren dictiret. Welches zu eurer Hochgeehrtesten Herren und Patronen Nachricht gehörigermassen melden wollen, der ich allstets verharre
 Ihro Magnificenz und Hochedler wie auch Hochehrw. Herren Gebets und Dienstergebenster
 D. Deyling. m.pp.
Leipzig, d. 20 Febr. 1724.
The letter is among the Acta die Besetzung, &c. Sp. ii. 852 and Bi. (1st ed.) i. 442 print the Council's confirmation of Bach's arrangements, dated 22 March 1724.

cantata every month, a calculation significantly confirmed by the conditions of his Weimar situation.[1] Necessarily the burden was exceptionally heavy at the beginning of his Cantorship; during its first two years he is hardly visible apart from the work of his industrious pen. He had not been in office many weeks before the death of Oberpostmeister Käse's wife gave him his first commission to compose mourning music. Her Gedächtnispredigt was preached at Vespers on 18 July 1723 (Eighth Sunday after Trinity) by Superintendent Salomo Deyling, who took as his text Romans viii. 11, a chapter which provides the Epistle for the Day. The fact that Bach incorporated into it Johann Franck's funerary hymn makes it tolerably certain that his motet 'Jesu, meine Freude' was composed for the occasion.[2] For the preceding Second, Fourth, and Seventh Sundays after Trinity also he appears to have produced new cantatas,[3] and on Tuesday, 2 November 1723, took his choir to Störmthal, at the invitation of Statz Hilmor von Fullen, to open the organ lately built there by Zacharias Hildebrand, whose acquaintance he now made,[4] and to perform his cantata 'Höchsterwünschtes Freudenfest' (No. 194).[5] A few weeks later, at Vespers on Christmas Day, he produced in the Thomaskirche his Latin *Magnificat*, punctuating its score, as was usual, with Christmas hymns. Nor was this brilliant work the sole contribution to his first Christmas at Leipzig: he produced new cantatas on each of the three days of the festival : 'Christen, ätzet diesen Tag' (No. 63) was heard in the Nikolaikirche on Christmas Day, 'Dazu ist erschienen der Sohn Gottes' (No. 40) in the Thomaskirche on Christmas Monday, and 'Sehet, welch' eine Liebe' (No. 64) in the Nikolaikirche on Christmas Tuesday. It is not improbable that he also prepared their libretti.[6] New Year's Day 1724 he also distinguished by a new work, 'Herr Gott, dich loben wir' (No. 16).[7]

The year 1724 was as prolific. Bach produced new cantatas at Epiphany, the First and Fourth Sundays after Epiphany, the Feast of the Purification, Quinquagesima, Easter Day, Trinity Sunday, the Eleventh, Twelfth, and Thirteenth Sundays after Trinity, and perhaps the Third Sunday after Easter and Whit-Sunday also.[8] The Second Sunday after Trinity (25 June 1724) he spent at Gera,[9] where 'der berühmte Cantor und Capellmeister[10] Bach' opened

---

[1] *Supra*, p. 104.   [2] Cf. B.-J. 1912, p. 9.
[3] Nos. 76, 24, 186. Cf. B.C.T., pp. 318, 340, 364.   [4] Flade, p. 69.
[5] B.C.T., p. 297.   [6] *Ibid.*, pp. 69, 81, 91.   [7] *Ibid.*, p. 107.
[8] *Ibid.*, pp. 129, 137, 157, 164, 188, 219, 245, 279, 301, 398, 404, 411.
[9] B.-J. 1924, p. 125. The organ was burnt in 1780.
[10] So long as Prince Leopold lived Bach retained the honorary (' von Haus aus ') title. Thus, on 18 May 1727 he signed a *testimonium*: 'Joh. Sebast. Bach, Hochf.

the new organ in the Church of St. Johannes and St. Salvator,
receiving 30 gulden for his fee, 10 gulden for his journey, 17 gulden
8 groschen 8 pfennige for his board, and a liberal 7 gulden 8 groschen for his wine. Meanwhile, he had given his Leipzig superiors
a characteristic example of his independence. Since the introduction of 'die musicirte Passion' in 1721 it was customary to perform
it on Good Friday in the two churches alternately. As Bach's
'Johannespassion' was heard in the Thomaskirche in 1723, it was
the turn of the Nikolaikirche in 1724, whose authorities, seeing
there had been no performance in 1722, looked forward with
greater anticipation to the event.[1] Its organ was a fine one, but as
its choir-gallery was inadequate and the clavier in need of repair,
Bach ignored the rule and issued programmes announcing the performance in the Thomaskirche. The clergy of the sister church
protested, and upon the Council's undertaking to adapt its choir-
gallery to his requirements and repair the clavier, Bach recalled his
programmes and performed the Passion for the first time in the
Nikolaikirche.[2] But neither now nor in the future was he willing
to give this church the first performance of his own more elaborate
compositions.

For more than a year Bach's life moved without jars. His eldest
sons already were enjoying the school's educational facilities, and
on 22 December 1723 Wilhelm Friedemann matriculated at the
University. Anna Magdalena annually added a child to a household whose accommodation already was sorely taxed: in 1723 a
daughter, who did not long survive; in 1724 Gottfried Heinrich,
who died imbecile; in 1725 Christian Gottlieb, who died in
infancy; in 1726 Elisabeth Juliane Friederica, the only daughter who
married; and, after her, four younger children, not one of whom
survived infancy. As in the case of the elder family, the godparents of his younger children indicate Bach's high standing
in the professional society of the town. Among them were
Bürgermeister Gottfried Lange, Vorsteher of the Thomasschule,
at whose hands Bach received his office; the wife of Johann
Heinrich Ernesti, Rector of the Thomasschule; Christian Wilhelm
Ludwig, an official in the Excise; Johann Fr. Falckner, a lawyer;
Johann Ernst Kregel, a judge of the High Court; a daughter of
Archidiakonus Carpzov, and others.[3] The defective physique of
the first eight children of Bach's second marriage must be attri-

Anh. Cöthenischer Capellmeister u. Director Chori Musici Lipsiensis' (Liliencron, p. 295).   [1] B.C.T., p. 208.
[2] The Council's *Actum*, dated 3 April 1724, is printed in Bi. iv. 140; Sp. ii. 873.
[3] Cf. Sp. ii. 954.

buted in part to the congested quarters in which they lived. Of the five born after the school was enlarged only one died young, and two by their careers enhanced the reputation of their name. Meanwhile, Bach's tireless pen continued its activity. He graced the wedding of Christoph Friedrich Löfners, a Leipzig burgess, on 12 February 1725, with the cantata 'Sein Segen fliesst', whose music is lost.[1] He was already in touch with University undergraduate life, for, in the same year, the students of August Friedrich Müller, Professor in the Faculty of Philosophy, commissioned him to compose a complimentary cantata on the occasion of their teacher's nameday (3 August). The libretto, 'Der zufriedengestellte Aeolus',[2] was provided by the versatile Picander (Christian Friedrich Henrici), from whom a few weeks later Bach accepted the text for the cantata 'Bringet dem Herrn Ehre seines Namens', performed on the Seventeenth Sunday after Trinity (23 September).[3]

Bach's association with Picander on these two occasions makes it probable that for the Good Friday Passion in 1725 he set his *Erbauliche Gedancken auf den Grünen Donnerstag und Charfreytag über den Leidenden Jesum*, written in that year. The text[4] is modelled upon Brockes's, but is shorter than and inferior to its model. It ends, like the 'Matthäuspassion', written three years later, with a Chorus of Faithful Souls, which Picander repeated in the later work. The constructive superiority of the text over Bach's 'Johannespassion' is evident, but it cannot have satisfied the composer: the story of the Passion is too meagrely outlined, devotional emphasis is lacking, and Passion hymns are almost entirely excluded. The substitution of rhyming lines for the Bible text might be supposed a blemish in Bach's eyes had he not, in 1731, set another Passion of Picander's which has the same characteristic. His score has not survived, but it is eminently probable that Bach sought to please his public by producing a Passion of the popular Brockes type in 1725, the more so seeing it was the turn of the Thomaskirche; the church is unlikely to have waited until 1729 to hear his first Good Friday music after his appointment to the Cantorship.[5]

Meanwhile, Bach was involved in a controversy with the Univer-

[1] B.C.T., p. 545. La Mara, *Musikerbriefe*, i. 170, 172, prints two letters (Aug., and Sept. 1733) signed by Bach, Gesner, and Johann Schneider, organist of the Nikolaikirche, complaining to the authorities of the conduct of a Leipzig merchant, Johann Friedrich Eitelwein, who 'am 12ten Augusti dieses Jahres sich ausser Leipzig copuliren lassen, und sich daher befugt zu seyn glaubet, uns unssere diessfalls ausgemachte accidentia zu entziehen'. Eitelwein and his brother were in business 'am Marckte, unter Thomasii Hause' (D.J.F.L., p. 101).
[2] B.C.T., p. 575.   [3] *Ibid.*, pp. 10, 444.   [4] Printed in Sp. ii. 873.
[5] On this matter cf. the present writer's *Bach: The Passions*, Bk. i. 52; Bk. ii. 66.

sity, inherited from his predecessor, and closely related to the successful fulfilment of his office as he conceived it. It has been pointed out on an earlier page that the University afforded valuable musical material; the desirability of Bach's association with it was remarked when he received his appointment as Cantor. Kuhnau had experienced the advantages of this collaboration as 'Director Chori Musici' in the University, at a modest salary of 12 gulden. The office required him to direct the so-called 'alt Gottesdienst' in the Paulinerkirche on the three high festivals, the Reformation celebration, and certain academic occasions. In 1710, however, the Faculty of Theology instituted regular Sunday services in the church, the so-called 'neu Gottesdienst', and assigned its musical direction to other hands.[1] Kuhnau lodged a respectful protest (1 September 1710);[2] he declared his satisfaction and that of 'the whole community' at the provision of Sunday worship for the University's parishioners, but protested against his exclusion from it. He insisted that his duties as Thomascantor need not hinder him, and prayed for the restitution of his key. Disregarding his petition, the University appointed Johann Friedrich Fasch, a law student,[3] but, on receiving Kuhnau's promise to direct both the Old and New Service without increase of salary, eventually preferred him. Its action was not inspired solely by considerations of economy: it desired to demonstrate that the direction of its music was not *ex officio* the perquisite of the Stadtcantor. Telemann was granted it on his appointment to the Cantorship on 18 August 1722, but he was clearly informed that he received it on his merits and not as an admission of his claims as Cantor. His duties were to commence at Michaelmas, and, meanwhile, Görner was appointed to hold his place. After Telemann's withdrawal Graupner came forward, on whose retirement Görner, who held Bach of little account, advanced his personal claim to the position he was temporarily filling. On 3 April 1723, three weeks before Bach's appointment to the Cantorship, Görner's application was received; it was observed in his favour that he had filled the position agreeably and without charge, and the Directorship of both Services was conferred on him.

In severing the Old Service from the town Cantorate the Theological Faculty acted without consulting its Law colleagues. On the analogy of Telemann's appointment, Görner's duties as Director began in September, and at the Michaelmas (1723) University Council Bach challenged its action by demanding the stipend due

[1] Cf. Schering, p. 324.
[2] Printed in Sp. ii. 860.   [3] Bach's competitor in 1723.

to him in respect to the 'alt Gottesdienst'. Not yet aware of the dogged character of its petitioner, the Council replied (28 September 1723), that the situation was not his, that its duties had been assigned to Görner along with the direction of the New Service, and that Bach had no *jus prohibendi*. Unawed by the Council's legal terms, Bach repeated, that the 'alt Gottesdienst' and its stipend belonged to the Stadtcantor, and by his insistence at length brought home to the Council the irregularity of its action. Grudgingly he was restored to the direction of the Old Service, but without the salary of twelve florins, which had been transferred to Görner's more recent office. Bach again protested, and was successful in recovering half of his legal emolument.[1] But the dispute had now lasted for two years, and as no further concession was to be expected from the University, Bach carried his quarrel to the highest tribunal. On 14 September 1725 he stated the case to his sovereign: [2]

Potent and most gracious sovereign,

May it please your Majesty to be informed, with my most humble *submission*, that the *directorium* of the Old and New Service associated with the church of the illustrious University of this town, along with its salary and customary *accidentia*, was attached, in the time of my *antecessor*, to the Cantorate of St. Thomas's school. After his demise, and before a successor was appointed, the University post was bestowed on the organist of the Nikolaikirche, Görner by name. However, on my appointment to the Cantorship, the *directorium* of the so-called 'alt Gottesdienst' was restored to me, but without the stipend, which had been assigned to the above-named organist of the Nikolaikirche. I thereupon petitioned the worshipful Council of the University to restore the conditions which existed in the time of my predecessor, but I have been unable to recover more than half my lawful *salarium*, whose full amount is twelve gulden.

Meanwhile, may it please your Majesty, the worshipful University Council appointed me to direct the Old Service, and I fulfilled that duty, though the *salarium* paid to the director of the New Service properly belongs to the old foundation. I would not willingly enter upon a controversy with the organist of the Nikolaikirche regarding his right to the 'neu Gottesdienst', but I cannot submit to the loss of the *salarium* which belonged to my office long before the new *cultus* was instituted.

It is not usual for church *patroni* otherwise to dispose of, entirely withhold, or diminish revenues assigned to official posts. Yet for more than two years I have discharged the duties attaching to the Old Service without pay. Wherefore I make my humble suit and petition to your Majesty, to command the worshipful Council of the University to restore the old arrangement, and to confer on me control of both the Old and New

[1] The facts are set out by Prof. B. Fr. Richter in Monatsh. f. M.G., 1901, pp. 101–9, and B.-J. 1925, pp. 1–10.
[2] Dresden Staatsarchiv; Rescripte 1721–8. A facsimile of the letter is in 'Die Musik', Nov. 1912, Heft 3.

Services, in particular, the stipend of the Old Service, and the *accidentia* attached to both. And for this royal favour I shall remain always

Your Majesty's most obedient servant,

Johann Sebastian Bach.

Leipzig, 14 Sept. 1725.

To the most serene and potent Prince and Lord Augustus, King in Poland [&c., &c.], my most gracious King, Elector, and Sovereign.

Dresden acted with commendable promptness. Summoned to answer Bach's allegations, the University presented a document, which, however, he supposed inaccurate in particulars. On 3 November 1725 another letter took its way to Dresden: [1]

Potent and most gracious sovereign,

Concerning the matter in which I appeal as petitioner against the University as defendant, your Majesty has been graciously pleased to command, and the University has dutifully dispatched, a reply, at the same time acquainting me with the fact. I would therefore beg a further favour, that your Majesty will be pleased to cause a copy of the said reply to be communicated to me, and that no decision upon the cause at issue be pronounced until I have had opportunity to comment upon it. My observations shall be communicated with the least delay, and with lifelong *submission* I am

Your Majesty's most obedient servant,

Johann Sebastian Bach.

Leipzig, 3 November 1725.

[Endorsed as before.]

Bach spent Christmas in the composition of a lengthy reply to the University's statement, interesting in relation to the matter in dispute, and indicative of a mind singularly precise, practical, and orderly. He dispatched it on the last day of the year: [2]

Potent and most gracious sovereign,

With dutiful thanks I acknowledge your Majesty's goodness in causing me to be furnished with a copy of the University's reply to my complaint regarding the *directorium Musices* and the *salarium* belonging to the older of the two foundations withheld from me. I supposed that the University would immediately satisfy and accede to my reasonable demand without more ado, but I am disappointed to find that it raises objections, alleging the following statements in its defence:

1. That I claim the *directorium* of both the Old and New Service for the Stadtcantor, whereas the University can dispose of both *in libertate naturali*. But it cannot confute my statement that the *directorium* of the Old Service was assigned to me, and that, in virtue of an established *observanz*, an *honorarium* was attached to it.

2. They express astonishment at my allegation that I have performed my duty without emolument, declaring that the *Rationes Rectorales* show that for all *Quartal-Orationes*,[3] the three high festivals, and *Festum Reformationis Lutheri*, the due *honorarium* of 13 th. 10 gr. was assigned to me and that on every occasion I received it. Also,

[1] Archiv der Universität, Leipzig, Repert. II/III, Nr. 22.   [2] *Ibid.*

[3] The quarterly Academic congregations for conferment of degrees.

3. That I have not invariably been present in person at the *Quartal-Orationes*, but, as the *Registratur* shows, have delegated the direction of the motets to *praefecti*. Likewise,

4. That the Thomascantor's duties on Sundays and festivals put it beyond his ability to undertake the *directorium* of the music in the University church without causing confusion and *praejudiz*, seeing that at almost the hour at which it is held he has to direct the music in the Thomaskirche or Nikolaikirche. And again,

5. It is stated that, in respect to the *directorium Musices* of the New Service, my *antecessor* received an entirely new *gratial* of 12 florins. Again,

6. That the civic Council raised so many difficulties regarding the services of the Thomaskirche's choir and town's musicians, that the University was driven to rely on its own *studiosi* and to entrust the direction of the music to another *subjectum*, who could attend to it personally and associate on better terms with the *studiosi*, who refused to sing under the Cantor unless they were paid. And lastly,

7. That, during the long vacancy in the *officium* following the death of the late Cantor, the University conferred the *directorium Musices* of the New Service on Johann Gottlieb Görner, assigning to him a new *salarium* of 12 florins, an endowment altogether distinct from the *directorium* of the Old Service and a new *institutum* altogether.

It is easy, may it please your Majesty, to refute the University's *exceptiones*, for they are at variance with the facts.

1. In regard to the relation of the Old Service to the New, I did not assert that their *connexion* was imperative, but that it had existed. It is no business of mine to show cause why they should or should not be combined; that is a matter for the proper authority. What I did assert and set out in my dutiful representation was, that the *directorium* of the Old Service had been committed to me in accordance with previous custom. That being so, the *directorium* at *promotiones doctorales* and other solemn University *actus* in the Paulinerkirche, along with the *honorarium* attached thereto, cannot be taken from me, because the control of the music at all these ceremonies was distinctly associated with the Old Service before the new one was instituted. In the second place,

2. I am astonished at the University's statement that an *honorarium* of 13 th. 10 gr. was paid me, controverting my allegation that I fulfilled my duty without pay. For the *honorarium* is quite distinct from the *salarium* of 12 florins,[1] and, being a *gratial*, cannot have been given in lieu of it. Moreover, the *Rationes Rectorales*, which the University brings forward in evidence, prove conclusively that even the alleged *honorarium* of 13 th. 10 gr. has not been paid me in full, but that at each quarter the two *Bedelli*, as themselves can testify on oath, have paid me only 16 gr. 6 pf. instead of the 20 gr. 6 pf. set out in the *Rationes Rectorales*, while at the three high festivals, as well as at the *Festum Reformationis Lutheri*, I have received only 1 thaler instead of 2 th. 12 gr., that is, 6 th. 18 gr. (*sic*) instead of 13 th. 10 gr. yearly. Moreover, my *antecessores* Schelle [2] and Kuhnau—witness the attestations of their widows attached *sub lit.* A and B—never received more than that amount for the quarter and festival payments and never gave receipts for more, though the *extract* from the *Rationes Rectorales* names a larger *quantum*. Again,

---

[1] Or gulden. Bach seems to regard them as equivalent. Cf. *supra*, p. 62, note 4.
[2] Johann Schelle, Cantor 1676–1701.

3. The allegation that I frequently absented myself from the *Quartal-Orationes*, and that the *Registratur* of 25 October 1725 proves it, is not relevant: for the month and day named in the *Registratur* are subsequent to my complaint against the University, while up to that time nothing had been charged against me. My infrequent absences have been *ob impedimenta legitima*, for I have been obliged to travel abroad, particularly to Dresden, where I had business. Moreover, the *praefecti* are appointed to serve under the Cantor for that very purpose. My *antecessores* Schelle and Kuhnau never conducted the motets, but left the duty to *praefecti*.

4. Equally to be taken *in recessu* is the University's allegation, that it is not *compatible* for one person to direct the Cantata in both the town and University churches. Then how does Görner do so? His situation is even less *compatible* with the double duty. Being organist of the Nikolaikirche he cannot possibly function at the same time in the Paulinerkirche; for he has to play throughout the whole service till the closing hymn, whereas the Cantor is free after the Cantata and is not required to stay for the hymns that follow. The late Kuhnau certainly managed to discharge both offices without *praejudiz* or *confusion*; and when there is no *musica formalis* to direct the duty can quite conveniently be fulfilled by a *vicarius* or *praefectus*.

5. Regarding the twelve florins in dispute. The University will not venture to maintain that my *antecessor* Kuhnau received that sum as a *gratial* for the New Service, for it is incontrovertible that from time immemorial that sum was the *salarium* of the Old Service. To avoid the inconveniences attending the *separation* of the *directoria*, my *antecessor* undertook the New Service as well and did not ask a penny for his pains, much less receive the additional *gratial* of twelve florins of which they speak. Long before the New Service was instituted, Kuhnau and Schelle gave receipts for this sum of twelve florins, and, as the *attestata* of the widows of Kuhnau and Schelle *sub lit.* A *et* B show, the *salarium* was received for directing the Old Service. The University cannot refuse to produce these receipts. It follows that:

6. My allegation that the *salarium* is attached to the Old Service is not affected by the statement that the *studiosi* and the Cantor were not on good terms, and that the former were unwilling to assist unless they were paid. That cannot be proved or confuted. But there is no doubt that real music-lovers among them will always be ready to help, and I myself have never had any trouble with them; they are willing to assist me *gratis*, both singers and players. Next,

7. Touching the *directorium Musices* of the New Service, and Görner's position in regard to it: If the arrangement remains *in statu quo*, no one questions that the new office must be provided with a *salarium*, but from a new source. For the *salarium* of twelve florins hitherto paid him is not a new *institutum*, not a new fund to support a new office, but was diverted from the *directorium Musices* of the Old Service and attached to the new one during the vacancy in the Cantorate, when Görner received the *directorium*.

The facts set out above are familiar and *in notorietate* among all who have to do with the music in the town and University churches, and can be established by their depositions. In fact, I can adduce an illustration out of my own experience. Two years ago I took occasion to make a *remonstration* about the *directorium* to the then Rector Magnificus Junius. He said he could prove me wrong out of a book, very likely the *Liber*

Rationum Rectoralium, in which my eye fell on an entry showing that Schelle received twelve florins for the *directorium Musices;* indeed I showed the entry to Rector Magnificus Junius myself.

To conclude: On behalf of the University whose Rectorial functions he exercised, Dr. Ludovici last summer offered me half the full amount of twelve florins, and certainly would not have done so had he not been convinced that my position was a strong one. But the reduction of my *salarium* is as inequitable as its total withdrawal. I mentioned Dr. Ludovici's offer in my *Memorial,* but the University has not thought fit to reply to it in its counter-statement and passes it by altogether. Its silence supports my *praetension* and affords proof of the justice of my contention.

Whereas the University says I am entitled to a yearly sum of 3 th. 10 gr. for *Quartal-Orationes* in accordance with the *Rationes Rectorales sub* ⊙ *et* ☉, and for the three high and Reformation festivals to a further *honorarium* of ten thalers, in all 13 th. 10 gr. yearly, in accordance with established custom; and whereas I have held my situation in the University from Whitsuntide 1723 till now, a period of two years and three-quarters, I am entitled to 36 th. 18 gr. 6 pf., whereas I have received only 11 th. for as many festivals and 7 th. 13 gr. 6 pf. for eleven *Quartal-Orationes,* in all 18 th. 13 gr. 6 pf., leaving 18 th. 5 gr. still due to me. The normal *salarium* of 12 fl. is also owing for the same period of two years and three-quarters, in all 33 fl. more. As the University seems not unwilling to come to an arrangement with me, for it already has offered half the *salarium,* it cannot *eo ipso* regard my request as unreasonable and groundless, but must be supposed to admit it. Moreover, it disregards my contention in its dutiful reply to your Majesty, and so *tacite* accepts my facts, which it fails to controvert in a single particular. Wherefore I beg your Majesty and Electoral Sereneness at once to lay an injunction upon the University, both to restore its earlier practice and pay me 12 fl. annually for the Old Service, along with the *accidentia* for the *promotiones doctorales* and other *actus solemnes,* and also to make up the *honorarium* of 18 th. 5 gr. that is owing, and the residue of my ordinary *salarium* to the amount of 33 th., as well as to bear the costs of this application. Alternatively, if the University does not admit the correctness of the facts I have adduced, I pray that it be directed to produce the receipts given by Schelle and Kuhnau, both for the special *honorarium* and their usual *salarium.* So distinguished a favour I am ready to repay with life-long and devoted gratitude.

Your Majesty's most obedient servant,
Johann Sebastian Bach.

Leipzig, 31 December 1725.
[Endorsed as before.]

The Saxon Solomon decided the controversy promptly and with even-handed justice. A rescript dated 21 January 1726[1] announced

[1] The document, hitherto unprinted, is in the University's archives and reads as follows:

Von Gottes Gnaden Friedrich Augustus, König in Pohlen, Herzog zu Sachssen, Jülich, Cleve, Berg, Engern u. Westphalen, Churfürst.

Würdige, Hochgelahrte, liebe andächtige und getreue;

Uns ist gebührend vorgetragen und verlesen worden, was unserm, auf des Cantoris zu St. Thomä in Leipzig, Johann Sebastian Bachs, wegen des Directorii Musices bey dem sogenannten alten und neuen Gottesdienste in der Pauliner-

the King-Elector's ruling: the 'alt Gottesdienst' being of ancient foundation, its historical association with the town Cantorship was to be maintained; the 'neu Gottesdienst', not being governed by similar usage, was to be held subject to such regulations as the University saw fit to impose. Thus Bach won his case in regard to the Old Service and its perquisites, but failed to restore the association of the old and new directorates as under his predecessor. Görner retained the direction of the Sunday services in the Paulinerkirche, but in regard to the occasional *actus solemnes*, to which Bach referred in his second letter to the king, the sovereign's decision left room for doubt as to which of the two Directors should function, a problem which arose in 1727 in connexion with the public mourning for the Queen-Electress.

kirche allda, beschehenes unterthänigstes Suchen, vom 17. Sept. a[nno] p[raeterito] euch ertheilten Befehl zu folge, ihr unterm 29. Octobris solchen vorigen Jahres gehorsamst berichtet habt, Ihr aber erhaltet eingelegt, was vermeldter Cantor, nach vorheriger Communication besagten Berichts, darneben fernerweit vorgestellet und gebethen.

Nachdem Wir nun ersehen. dass das Directorium Musices beym alten Gottesdienste aus einem alten Geschäfte herrühre und mit dem neuen Gottesdienste keine Verwandtnis habe:

Als lassen Wir es bey der Bewanntnüs, und da ihr euch auch, ihm solch Directorium, *ratione* des alten Gottesdienstes, noch weiter zu überlassen, auch das darzugewidmete Accidens beständig zu reichen, euch anerbothen, es dabey und bey eurer, was den neuen Gottesdienst betrifft, gemachten absonderlichen Anstalt nicht unbillig zu bewenden;

Und ist demnach Unser Begehren hiermit, ihr wollet angeregtem eurem Erbiethen gebührend nachkommen: Im übrigen aber mehrbenannten Cantorem, gestellten Sachen nach, mit seinem Suchen abweisen. Daran geschieht Unser Meynung.

Datum Dresden am 21 Januarii 1726.

In Z. f. M. 1901, No. 40, p. 484, are four letters written by Bach (dated 14 Sept., 26 Sept., and 21 Oct. 1726) to the Council at Plauen, a town some sixty miles south of Leipzig, commending his pupil Georg Gottfried Wagner as Cantor. Wagner entered on his duties on 26 Jan. 1727 and died on 6 April 1756.

(1)

Worshipful and learned gentlemen, my gracious Patrons,

The agreeable *confidence* evinced in me by your condescending communication not only commands my obedient *obligation*, but also impels me to show my respect to your Worships by taking practical steps in the matter. The *affaire*, however, is not one to be dealt with hurriedly: some time may elapse before I can put my hands on a suitable *subjectum* having the qualifications your Worships require. Be assured I will not delay to supply the vacant Cantorship directly a competent *subjectum* is found. Nothing shall be wanting on my part to deserve the *confidence* reposed in my judgement, and to fill the vacancy expeditiously, taking every precaution against *desordres* and neglect.

I remain, worshipful and learned gentlemen,

Your obedient servant,

Joh. Sebast. Bach.

Leipzig, the 14th Sept. 1726.

(2)

Worshipful and learned gentlemen, my gracious Patrons,

Fulfilling the promise made in my last letter to your Worships, I have been

Meanwhile, we remark some abatement of the fertility that marked the first two years of Bach's Cantorship. Only twenty-one Cantatas can be approximately assigned to the years 1725-6-7,[1] a number which represents half his normal productiveness. He was active, however, in other fields. On 4 February 1726 Stadthauptmann Winckler's[2] wife was commemorated in a funeral sermon preached by Salomo Deyling from Isaiah xliii. 1 and 5, 'Fear not, for I have redeemed thee'. The text is treated in the motet 'Fürchte dich nicht, denn ich habe dich erlöset', doubtless performed at the commemorative service.[3] In the same year Bach began the series of Partitas or German Suites which he issued as Part I of the *Clavierübung* in 1731. He published the first of them at Leipzig in 1726 'in Verlegung des Autoris', the first of his instrumental compositions to be engraved. Nearly twenty years had passed since he last received a composition of his own in print, and an opportune event allowed him to associate his new work with

looking for a first-rate subject and have found one well versed *in humanioribus*, and especially in music. To afford you a slight *praegustum*: he is a good composer and has performed several *specimina* here with *applausus*. He is an efficient organist and clavier-player, can take a part on the violin, violoncello, and other instruments, has a pleasant, though not powerful, Bass voice, and is in my judgement generally competent to fill the vacant post. It now rests with your Worships to make your *ordre* known as to when and how the person in question shall fulfil his tests. I therefore await your commands and the opportunity to give further proof that I am *reellement* delighted to be of service. With due respect,

I remain, worshipful and learned gentlemen,
Your obedient servant,
Joh. Sebast. Bach.

Leipzig, the 26th Sept. 1726.

(3)

Worshipful and learned gentlemen, my gracious Patrons,

I presume that you have ere this received a respectful communication from the person recommended by me, Georg Gottfried Wagner, eldest son of the still surviving Cantor of Wurzen. From his youth until the present time he has resided mostly in Leipzig, where his character has been *honett*. He is an *alumnus* of the Thomasschule, wherein he acquired such a foundation in the humanities as enabled him to proceed *ad altiora studia* available to him here at the University, whose classes he attended with diligence and profit. I do not doubt that he has already informed you to this effect in his letter.

It now rests *pure* with your Worships to instruct the above-mentioned Herr Wagner how and when to submit himself for examination, and I await the favour of a further communication from you in order that I may be able to give renewed proof of the care and diligence I am ready to exercise in your behalf. Meanwhile, with profound consideration, I beg to subscribe myself

Your Worships' obedient servant,
Joh. Seb. Bach.

Leipzig, the 21st October 1726.   PS. Herr Wagner is a bachelor.

The text of Bach's fourth letter (15 Nov. 1726) is in the German edition (p. 360) of this work.

[1] Cf. B.C.T., *passim*.
[2] Probably Baumeister Hartmann Winckler, Inspector of the town arsenal in 1736 (D.J.F.L., p. 138).   [3] Cf. B.-J. 1912, p. 11.

an old friendship. After remaining a widower for more than two years, Prince Leopold of Cöthen on 2 June 1725 married as his second wife Charlotte Friederica Wilhelmine, daughter of Prince Wilhelm of Nassau-Siegen.[1] On 12 September 1726 she gave birth to Emanuel Ludwig, who lived barely two years and predeceased his father. The coincident arrival of his own offspring in print prompted Bach to offer it to the infant Prince, with the following dedication and verses:[2]

To the most excellent Prince Emanuel Ludwig, Crown Prince of Anhalt, Duke of Saxony, Enger, and Westphalia, Count of Ascania, Lord of Bernburg and Zerbst, &c., &c., these trifling musical firstfruits are dedicated with sincere devotion by Johann Sebastian Bach.

Serenest
          infant Prince,
                    whom swaddling bands encumber,
Although thy princely glance declares maturer age,
Forgive me if I dare to wake thee from thy slumber,
And humbly crave thy grace for this my playful page.

These firstfruits of my lyre to thee I dare to bring,
Thou Prince first born to feel a mother's royal kiss,
Hoping that she to thee the lay may sometime sing;
For of her womb thou art a firstfruit too, like this.

The wiseheads fain would scare us mortals with a warning
Because into the world we come with cries and tears,
As though they could foretell the evening from the morning,
And see our future clear beyond the veil of years.

But I will answer them and say, that as these chords
That round thy cradle swell are sweet and clear and pure,
So shall thy life flow on through all that earth affords
Of harmony and joy, calm, happy, and secure.

May I, most hopeful Prince, play for thy delectation,
When thousandfold thy powers exceed what men now mark!
I pray, for my own part, for constant inspiration,
And am,
          most noble Prince,
                    thy
                         humble servant,
                                   Bach.

A month later (30 November 1726) Bach visited Cöthen with members of his choir to offer homage to the infant's mother on her birthday; he performed the cantata 'Steigt freudig in die Luft',

[1] Bethge, p. 30.
[2] With some alterations I borrow this rendering from the English edition of Spitta, iii. 224. These verses were first published in the 'Magdeburger Zeitung'. Like Spitta, I have failed to discover their contributor; but their authenticity seems indubitable.

of which he made frequent use in after years.[1] Probably Anna
Magdalena accompanied her husband and sang once more in the
familiar Ludwigsbau.[2] Recently returned from Cöthen, Bach was
again invited to contribute to a function promoted by University undergraduates. On 11 December 1726 Dr. Gottlieb Kortte,
Professor of Roman Law, delivered his inaugural lecture, and
thereafter was offered a 'Gratulationscantate', 'Vereinigte Zwietracht der wechselnden Saiten',[3] written by an anonymous author.
As the occasion did not lie within Bach's duties as Director
Musices, his invitation to set the cantata to music indicates that,
whatever the attitude of their superiors, the *studiosi* preferred him
to Görner on occasions of this character. In the spring of 1727
Bach had his first opportunity to impress a more exalted auditor.
On 12 May the King-Elector Augustus II visited Leipzig, lodged
in Apel's House on the Marktplatz, and listened from its windows
to a birthday cantata written by Christian Friedrich Haupt and
set to music by Bach, who conducted it in person. Augustus
accepted a copy of the libretto, 'Entfernet euch, ihr heitern
Sterne',[4] whose fulsome banalities we would gladly exchange for
the music, which is lost, or, associated with another text, survives
elsewhere.

Augustus, known for his physical strength as 'the Strong', had
incurred the resentment of his Lutheran subjects by becoming a
Roman Catholic to receive the crown of Poland, which he had
worn since 1697. His wife Christiane Eberhardine, a Hohenzollern,
left him when he changed his religion, and had since lived in retirement at Pretzsch, near Wittenberg, where she died on 6 September
1727. Regarded with particular respect and affection by her people,
her death plunged Saxony into mourning prolonged over four
months, till Epiphany 1728. A fortnight (23 September) after her
death, Hans Carl von Kirchbach, a young noble, whose order was
invariably prominent in organizing Leipzig's demonstrations of
loyalty to the reigning house, approached the authorities of the
University, of which he was then a student,[5] craving permission
to deliver an Oration in the Paulinerkirche in commemoration of
the dead Queen. Expecting a command from Dresden for an
official ceremonial, the Deans of Faculties advised Kirchbach 'to

---

[1] Cf. B.C.T., p. 619.
[2] There is no record of any honorarium paid to Bach on this occasion. In July
1724 and December 1725 he and his wife had been summoned to Cöthen, and
received 60 th. on the first and 30 th. on the second occasion.
[3] B.C.T., p. 625.   [4] *Ibid.*, p. 588.
[5] Riemer, *Jahrbuch*, p. 218, calls him 'ein Studirender vom Adel'. He gave his
Oration in German between the two Parts of the 'Trauer-Ode'.

wait in patience'. Disregarding their advice, the young man appealed (3 October) to the King-Elector, requesting sanction for the delivery of a funeral Oration accompanied, as was customary, with mourning music. Coincidently (3 October) the University received from Dresden an order to that effect, and as Kirchbach's eagerness allowed it to obey without drawing upon a treasury not plenteously filled, he was permitted to proceed with his arrangements. He at once commissioned Gottsched to write the lyrics of a 'Trauer-Ode', and Bach to set it to music. Whether Bach was proposed by Kirchbach, as is probable, or suggested by Gottsched, the Oration had become a University celebration and Görner therefore entered the lists to battle for his rights. He insisted that Bach's intrusion prejudiced his title 'Director Chori Musici' and robbed him of legitimate income. He demanded that Kirchbach should either give him the commission to set the Ode, or alternatively pay the fee he ought to have been allowed to earn; in either case he asked for protection against a repetition of the slight. His protest found strong backing among the Professors, who perhaps had not forgiven Bach's recent pugnacity, and now (9 October) warned Kirchbach that the Thomascantor would not be permitted to take part in the commemoration. Kirchbach replied, that it was too late to vary his arrangements for a ceremony now only eight days distant; Bach, he added, had received his fee and for more than a week had been at work upon the score. Admitting the force of these objections, the University Concilium discovered a middle path of compromise: Kirchbach was told that Bach could finish his task and provide the music, but that Görner and his Collegium Musicum must perform it. As Kirchbach took no action, the commemoration being now six days ahead, Görner appeared on 11 October before the Concilium, with the draft of an agreement to restrain Bach in his pocket, insisting upon knowing definitely where he stood. The Bedellus was dispatched to Kirchbach's lodging with a peremptory order: either Görner must conduct the performance, or Bach's music could not be performed. The baited Kirchbach lost patience, and sent his reply: he had made a contract with Bach and would abide by it; if he continued to be harassed he would abandon the ceremony altogether. Perturbed at the threat, the Concilium invited him to meet Görner in its presence. He complied, but stoutly refused to cancel his contract with Bach, declaring himself willing to compensate Görner with a fee of 12 thalers. Görner accepted the solatium, but demanded Bach's signature to a document, already prepared, pledging him not to intrude on his domain in future. It was in these terms:

I do hereby admit that the illustrious University of Leipzig at first refused to allow the 'Trauer-Ode' composed by me to be performed in the Paulinerkirche on the occasion of the Oration pronounced by Herr von Kirchbach upon the recent edifying death of His Majesty's beloved spouse, but withdrew its veto upon these conditions:

That Herr von Kirchbach compensate the Director Chori Musici of the said University church; and

That I sign an agreement admitting the aforesaid permission to have been granted as a peculiar favour; that I bind myself not to regard it as a precedent or *actus professorius*; that I disclaim entirely the right at any time to act as Director in the said Church of St. Paul; and, most strictly, that in future I will enter into no agreement with any person to compose music for a similar occasion without the University's express approval and consent; and that I submit to the terms of the Electoral rescript given at Dresden on 21 January 1726.

Leipzig, 11 October 1727.   Signed

The University Clerk was dispatched to lay the document before Bach and obtain his signature. Mittagessen was over at the Thomasschule on 12 October when he invaded the Cantor's quarters. His plaintive sentence is very eloquent: 'I did my best from 11 till 12, but without success.' Bach showed the official irately to the door and saw him disappear dispirited across the Kirchhof. Returned to the University, he reported his failure to the Syndicus and was ordered to hand the unsigned document to Kirchbach, who might have greater success. Next day (13 October) it was delivered to Kirchbach's Italian servant and disappears from sight. Certainly it never received Bach's signature.[1] He tardily finished the score on 15 October, and two days later the Ode had its performance. Within the lofty church, thronged with mourners from far and near, a great catafalque exhibited the emblems of the departed Queen. As the civic and academic dignitaries entered in procession, the bells of all the churches clanged a solemn farewell, while the organist in the western gallery 'preambuled' and the University Bedelli distributed copies of Gottsched's text. The programme announced that the Ode had been 'set by Herr Capellmeister Bach in the Italian style', and Bach himself conducted it, seated in the gallery at a clavicembalo among the performers.[2] His victory was conspicuous.

Bach's biographer necessarily treads parochial paths, but they invite him to topics whose unravelling illuminates the conditions in which the master worked, and the usages to which his art conformed. Originally hymn-books were generally found only in the

[1] The narrative is based on Prof. B. Fr. Richter's paper in Monatsh. f. M. G., 1901, pp. 101–9, and B.-J. 1925, pp. 1–10.
[2] Bi. ii. 9, quoting Sicul's *Das thränende Leipzig* (1727). Bach's autograph dates the performance 'ao. 1727 d. 18 Oct.'

hands of the Pastor, Cantor, and choir.[1] Bach, for instance, owned Paul Wagner's eight-volumed Leipzig collection of over five thousand hymns, a cumbrous anthology inconvenient for congregational use. During his Cantorship, however, more convenient manuals were at the disposal of the Leipzig churches, and from them, for the most part, hymns in congregational use were drawn. Their selection to some extent followed a stereotyped rubric; for instance, the so-called 'Detemporelied' sung between the Epistle and Gospel, and the 'Kanzellied' sung on the preacher's entry into the pulpit. It was the Cantor's duty to select the other hymns, and he did so normally in consultation with the preacher, whose sermon, itself suggested by the Gospel for the Day, prescribed the hymns that preceded and followed it. The hymns sung during the administration of Holy Communion afforded the Cantor a freer choice. Kuhnau exercised the privilege of selection,[2] and Bach also, until in September 1728 his prerogative was challenged.

Hitherto the Cantor's choice of hymns was made from the collections of Gottfried Vopelius (1682) and Paul Wagner (1697), in so far as they conformed with the official Dresden *Neu-auffgelegtes Dressdnisches Gesangbuch* published in 1694, reissued in 1707, containing 440 hymns and 374 melodies. In Leipzig, as elsewhere, however, a growing body of church opinion demanded the admission of hymns excluded from the earlier compilations, and in 1729 was gratified by the publication of *Das vollständige und vermehrte Leipziger Gesang-Buch*, containing 530 pages of tuneless hymns. Reissued in 1740 and 1744, Bach found in it, with eight exceptions, all the hymns he used in his cantatas.[3] The book offered an augmented *corpus* of hymnody from which, even before it was in circulation, certain of the Leipzig clergy desired to draw hymns for congregational use. His cantatas reveal Bach's conservative and orthodox taste in hymns, and a refusal to surrender his prerogative of choice, or to sanction hymns of which he disapproved, brought him into conflict with the Consistorium. In the autumn of 1728 Gottlieb Gaudlitz, later Subdiakonus at St. Thomas's, and now acting as Diakonus-substitut in the Nikolaikirche, complained (7 September)[4] that Bach refused to perform the hymns he had selected for Sunday Vespers. The Consistorium supported Gaudlitz, and Deyling, as Superintendent, was instructed (8 September) to inform Bach that in future he must accept the hymns intimated to him.[5]

[1] Graff, p. 255.
[2] He writes on 4 Dec. 1704: 'Gleichwie ich die Lieder in allen 3 Kirchen anordne' (Sp. ii. 854).
[3] B.C.T., p. 13.   [4] The document is printed in Sp. ii. 869.
[5] Bi. ii. 230 prints the letter of the Consistorium.

Appealing direct to Caesar, as was his wont, Bach wrote to the civic Council:[1]

Most noble and learned Magnificences and *Patroni*,

You will recall, that on my *vocation* to the Cantorship of the Thomasschule I was directed to observe the traditional usages of public worship and to refrain from making innovations therein, on which condition you were pleased to promise me your high protection. Among these usages and traditions is the exclusive right to select the hymns preceding and following the sermon, a right vested in me and my *antecessores* in the Cantorship, though subject to the selection being *convenient* with the Gospel, Dresden usage, and the season. The honourable members of the *Ministerium* will not deny that hitherto *contradiction* has not been offered to that practice. Subdiakonus Gottlieb Gaudlitz, now serving the Nikolaikirche, however, recently attempted to alter it, proposing to substitute for those hymns appointed in accordance with usage others of his own choice. As I refused to accept them, in view of the serious consequences that might befall, he appealed to their Worships of the Consistorium, and obtained an injunction requiring me in future to perform the hymns selected by the preachers.

It appears to me that the innovation ought not to become operative without the knowledge of your Magnificences, the *Patroni* of the churches, the more so seeing that the Cantor's prerogative in the matter is of long standing. Indeed, in his complaint to the worshipful Consistorium, which I enclose, Herr Gaudlitz admits that on one or two occasions my consent as Cantor was sought for the hymns he had selected. Clearly, if the hymns are inordinately long[2], the service is unduly prolonged and thrown into confusion; and, moreover, other than Herr Gaudlitz, not one of the ministers favours the innovation. On these grounds I venture to approach your Magnificences as *Patroni* of the town churches, and to ask that my traditional right to order the hymns be upheld. With life-long devotion I remain

Your distinguished Magnificences' humble servant,
Johann Sebastian Bach.

Leipzig, 20 Sept. 1728.

Whether their Magnificences supported Bach is not known. But within the Consistorium his protest against undesirable hymns had approval. Prompted, no doubt, by the issue of the recent *Leipziger Gesang-Buch*, that body addressed Deyling on 16 February 1730 regarding 'nicht üblich gewesene Lieder' selected for use in church, expressing their disapprobation, and ordering their discontinuance.[3]

Bach's controversy with Gaudlitz found him already engaged upon the Good Friday music for 1729, when it was the turn of the Thomaskirche to hear it. Picander, now established as his collaborator, provided him with a *Text zur Passions-Music nach dem Evangelisten Matthäo*, leaving Bach himself to choose and distri-

---

[1] Leipzig. Stadtarchiv: Schul zu S. Thomae, Vol. IV. Stift 8, Bd. 2, fol. 410.
[2] The hymns of Paul Gerhardt and others frequently exceed thirty stanzas.
[3] The document is in Bi. ii. 231.

bute the Chorals.[1] His score was not completed when the death
of Prince Leopold, on 19 November 1728, called him to Cöthen to
pay a last tribute to his friend. Disinclined, or without leisure,
to compose an original work, he invited Picander to fit appropriate
words to completed movements of the 'Matthäuspassion'. Picander
made the adjustment cleverly, though it shocks us that music so
charged with spiritual emotion should have been adapted to a
sentiment less profound. At Cöthen, on 23 March 1729, the Prince's
remains were laid to rest among his forebears in the St. Jakobskirche, where, on the following day, the Gedächtnispredigt was
preached and Bach's 'Trauer-Music' was performed. His Leipzig
singers—his wife and eldest son are named—must already have
been familiar with the music in its original form, for Good Friday
was only three weeks distant. But the instrumentalists were drawn
from Halle, Merseburg, Zerbst, Dessau, and Güsten.[2] The score
was known to Forkel in 1802 but since has disappeared; it contained nine movements from the 'Matthäuspassion', along with the
opening Chorus of the 'Trauer-Ode' of 1727, and a new setting of
Psalm lxviii. 20, which probably formed the text of the funeral
sermon.[3] Thus ended a friendship upon which Bach could look
back with agreeable recollections. It deprived him of his honorary Capellmeistership, however, a title which it gratified him to
possess, and which was restored from elsewhere speedily.

Johann Gottfried Walther appears to assert in his *Musicalisches
Lexikon* (1732)[4] that Bach received appointment as Capellmeister
'von Haus aus' to the Duke of Sachsen-Weissenfels in 1723. In
the Genealogy Bach's brief paragraph outlining his career may also
bear that meaning. On the other hand, there is no instance of his
use of the title during his early Leipzig years, and while he held
a similar appointment to the Court of Anhalt-Cöthen it is improbable that he received it. But, as on Prince Leopold's death in
November 1728 the former dignity ceased, there would appear to
be significance in Bach's presence at Weissenfels on 23 February
1729, the occasion of Duke Christian's birthday, when forty-one

[1] Cf. the present writer's *Bach: The Passions*, Bk. II, p. 6.
[2] The date of the performance, hitherto not ascertained, is established by the
following entry in the Cöthen Cammerkasse at Zerbst: 'Denen anhero ver-
schriebenen Capellmeister Bachen, dessen Ehefrau und Sohn aus Leipzig, ingl.
denen Musicis aus Halle, Merseburg, Zerbst, Dessau, und Güsten, so den
23 März 1729, abends bei der Beisetzung, und am 24 März bei der Leichenpredigt, die Trauermusiken des Hochseligen Fürsten Leopold, Hochfürstl.
Durchl., machen geholfen, zur Abfertigung einschl. Kostgeldes, und dergl.
230 Thlr.'
[3] The text is printed in the present writer's *Bach: The Passions*, Bk. II, p. 7.
[4] 'An. 1723 nach des seel. Hrn. Kuhnauens Tode, Music-Director in Leipzig,
auch Hochfürstl. Sachsen-Weissenfelsischer Capell-Meister.'

noble guests assembled to do that potentate honour. 'Herr Capell Meister Bach' is named as lodging with 'Cammerdiener Ritter' during the festivity.[1] That he appeared at Weissenfels at such a moment, and was accorded a title recently lapsed elsewhere, clearly suggests that he was summoned to make a gesture of homage in return for an honour recently bestowed. He never visited Weissenfels again on a similar errand, and his titular office expired on the death of Duke Christian on 28 June 1736, when the Capelle was dispersed.[2] Meanwhile, as in 1716, Bach marked his visit with a performance of 'Was mir behagt',[3] a repetition attributable, either to the Duke's desire to hear it again, or to Bach's conviction that his patron had forgotten it.

On Good Friday (15 April) 1729 Bach produced the last and greatest of his Passions, the most noble and inspired treatment of its subject in the whole range of music, and also notable for its indication of the composer's reverent, subtle, and scholarly study of the Bible narrative. The score of the 'Matthäuspassion' is upon a scale the more remarkable in view of Bach's almost contemporary complaint of the inadequacy of his vocal and instrumental resources. To provide the two Choirs the work demands, he employed his *chorus primus* and *chorus secundus*; hence the directions *Coro primo* and *Coro secondo* in his score bear a particular and local meaning. While the former includes all the Bible narrative [4] and most of the Biblical characters, the latter provides only the two False Witnesses, while its Choruses are comparatively simple and within the competence of singers normally not called on to sing figural music. The Thomaskirche could provide the two organs the score prescribes. The larger, in the west gallery, a two-manual instrument,[5] had been in the church since 1525, was enlarged in 1670 and renovated in 1721; the smaller, and more ancient, stood beside the other until 1639, when it was removed to a gallery on the opposite wall, and was taken from the church altogether in 1740. Though inconveniently placed, it was certainly used in 1736, when the 'Matthäuspassion' was repeated; unless it was out of condition it was also played in 1729.[6] The two orchestras were

---

[1] Werner, p. 110. Inquiry at Weissenfels reveals Christian Siegmund Ritter, 'Laquai'.
[2] *Ibid.*, p. 56. Sp. ii. 703 incorrectly states that Bach frequently visited Weissenfels between 1723 and 1736. In fact, no other visit than that of 1729 is recorded in the minutes of the Capelle within that period. Nor is there any official record of Bach's appointment, though the fact that he held it is established.   [3] B.C.T., p. 635.   [4] Excepting one short passage in No. 39.
[5] Specifications of the Leipzig organs are in Sp. ii. 111; Pirro (3), p. 85; Bi. iv. 111; Schering, p. 108.
[6] B.C.T., p. 16. Cf. *Bach: The Passions*, Bk. II, p. 9.

partly composed of the town's musicians, partly of players in the Thomasschule, partly of University *studiosi* and members of Bach's Collegium Musicum, to whose conductorship he was opportunely appointed that year.[1] Few of those who heard the sublime work realized its devotional feeling, its technical majesty. Surely of this performance Gerber wrote three years later: 'Some high officials and well-born ladies in one of the galleries began to sing the first Choral with great devotion from their books. But as the theatrical music proceeded, they were thrown into the greatest wonderment, saying to each other, "What does it all mean?" while one old lady, a widow, exclaimed, "God help us! 'tis surely an Opera-comedy!"'[2]

Nothing is more striking than the contrast between Bach's pugnacity over the prerogatives of his office, and the buoyancy which floated his creative genius upon a sea of difficulties that must have submerged it, had not the call been irresistible and the inward voice compelling. Soon after the production of the 'Matthäuspassion' an incident brought vividly before him the impeding conditions in which he worked. The period was one of scholastic transition, in which the reasons were no longer tolerable which had permitted an earlier age to make musical ability the key to the higher classrooms. On the other hand, Bach was concerned to see that the foundationers possessed the musical qualifications necessary to enable the school to discharge the obligation which rested upon it. These conflicting standards clashed a few weeks after the performance of the 'Matthäuspassion', when, at the Easter examinations, nine foundationers passed out of the school. To fill the vacancies twenty-three candidates appeared, upon whose musical qualifications Bach reported in the following document:[3]

I. *Candidates possessed of musical qualifications.*

Sopranists:

1. Christoph[4] Friedrich Meissner, of Weissenfels, *aetatis* 13, has a good voice and excellent *profectus*.[5]
2. Johann Tobias Krebs, of Buttelstedt, *aetatis* 13, has a good strong voice and excellent *profectus*.
3. Samuel Kittler, of Belgern, *aetatis* 13, has a tolerably strong voice and good *profectus*.
4. Johann Heinrich Hillmeyer, of Geringswald, *aetatis* 13, has a strong voice and excellent *profectus*.

---

[1] It was founded by Telemann in 1705 as 'das grosse ordinaire Collegium Musicum' (Schering, p. 338).
[2] Quoted in Bi. ii. 58.
[3] Leipzig. Stadtarchiv: Schul zu S. Thomae, Vol. IV, Stift. VIII, Bd. 2, fol. 518.
[4] 'Ephraim' in B.-J. 1907, p. 69. Bach was acquainted with his family. Cf. Sp. ii. 955.   [5] *i.e.* proficiency.

5. Johann August Landvoigt, of Gaschwitz, *aetatis* 13, has a *passable* voice and tolerable *profectus*.
6. Johann Andreas Köpping, of Grossboden, *aetatis* 14, has a tolerably strong voice and *mediocre profectus*.
7. Johann Gottl. Krause, of Grossdeuben, *aetatis* 14, has a rather weak voice and moderate *profectus*.
8. Johann Georg Leg, of Leipzig, *aetatis* 13, has a somewhat weak voice and indifferent *profectus*.

Altists:

9. Johann Gottfried Neicke, of Grimma, *aetatis* 14, has a strong voice and passably good *profectus*.
10. Gottfried Christoph Hoffmann, of Nebra, *aetatis* 16, has a *passable* Alto voice; *profectus* backward.

II. *Candidates lacking musical qualifications.*

1. Johann Tobias Dietze.
2. Gottlob Michael Wintzer.
3. Johann David Bauer.
4. Johanna Margaretha Peile's son.
5. Gottlob Ernst Hausius.
6. Friedrich Wilhelm Ludwig.
7. Johann Gottlob Zeymer.
8. Johann Gottfried Berger.
9. Johann Gottfried Eschner.
10. Salomo Gottfried Greulich.
11. Michael Heinrich Kittler, of Prettin.

Joh. Sebast. Bach,
Direct. Musices and Cantor of
St. Thomas's.

[12.] Gottwald Petzold, of Aurich, *aetatis* 14, has an excellent voice and *passable profectus*.
[13.] Johann Christoph Schmid, of Bendeleben, *aetatis* 19, has a fairly strong Tenor voice and uses it very agreeably.

Their Magnificences received Bach's report—and disregarded it. Another foundation vacancy having occurred, they admitted ten youths—four Sopranos from Bach's approved list (Nos. 1–4), one Alto (No. 9), four whom he had declared useless (Nos. 1, 2, 7, 8), and one (Joachim Heinrich Feller, of Weimar) whom he had not examined at all.[1] With reason Bach wrote to his old friend Erdmann a year later: 'My masters here are strange folk, with very little concern for music in them.'[2] Perhaps he envied the apparently care-free career of Handel, who in June 1729 again visited Halle to see his aged and infirm mother. Being indisposed, Bach sent his eldest son Friedemann to invite Handel to Leipzig, an invitation Handel could or would not accept.[3] He either did not

[1] A list of *alumni* of Bach's period is in B.-J. 1907, pp. 68–76. The number of vacancies naturally varied. In 1723 there were seven; in 1724 ten; in 1725 four; in 1726 eleven; in 1727 ten; in 1728 five.
[2] *Infra*, p. 205.   [3] Forkel, p. 110.

reciprocate the esteem with which Bach regarded him, or behind the invitation suspected an intention to draw him into an ill-timed contest with his only peer.[1]

While the general conditions affecting his art, of which Bach complained, were beyond correction, the death of Rector Johann Heinrich Ernesti,[2] on 16 October 1729, promised improvement in the school's general discipline. A scholar of distinction, he had held his position as Rector since 1684, and that of 'Professor poeseos' in the University since 1691. In his later years he had shown himself singularly ill-fitted to control the institution of which he was the head: its discipline was lax, its staff at logger-heads, the Council ignorant or negligent of its urgent needs.[3] Bach's relations with the veteran, however, had been cordial: Frau Ernesti stood godmother to Gottfried Heinrich Bach in 1724; Fräulein Ernesti undertook the same responsibility for Regine Johanna Bach in 1728.[4] Duty and friendship alike therefore moved Bach to compose the motet 'Der Geist hilft unsrer Schwachheit auf' for performance a cappella in the Thomaskirche on the occasion of the Rector's Leichenpredigt; it was repeated in the Paulinerkirche with orchestral accompaniment to commemorate him as one of the University's hierarchy. After long delay the Council appointed (8 June 1730)[5] in Ernesti's room Johann Matthias Gesner, Bach's Weimar friend and sincere admirer, opportunely for Bach, whom his arrival found on the brink of an acrid controversy with the Council. Gesner's tactful discretion was no less beneficial to the school. Discipline was tightened by the drafting of new Gesetze,[6] the insanitary condition of the old building was forced upon the Council's notice, and a structure which had stood substantially unaltered for two hundred years at length submitted to enlargement. Meanwhile, the new Rector's installation coincided with the commemoration of a document of equal antiquity. Upon 25, 26, and 27 June 1730 Leipzig celebrated the second centenary of the Augsburg Confession, in morning and evening sermons preached on all three days.[7] The occasion called for special music and Bach provided it: on the first day he conducted his 'Singet dem Herrn ein neues Lied' (No. 190), on the 26th his 'Gott, man lobet dich in der Stille' (No. 120), and on the 27th his 'Wünschet Jerusalem Glück', the score of which is lost. All three cantatas were fashioned from old material, a fact of

---

[1] Forkel mentions the disappointment of Leipzig amateurs at the failure to arrange a meeting between the two masters. An earlier statement to that effect is in the *Music-Almanach* for 1789.   [2] Illus. No. 64.
[3] Sp. ii. 23.   [4] *Ibid.*, p. 954.   [5] *Ibid.*, p. 69.
[6] *Supra*, p. 174.   [7] Bi. i. 209 ; ii. 154.

which his congregations would not be conscious, but which indicates that for the moment his ardour was damped and his Muse unresponsive.

Seven years had passed since Bach's appointment to the Cantorship. He had maintained the music in the churches at least at its accustomed level, had produced upwards of fifty cantatas from his own pen, and on occasions of public ceremony, secular and ecclesiastical, had placed his skill at the service of the community. He had given his fellow-citizens two Passions unrivalled among their kind, and a *Magnificat* not less distinguished. His fame as an organist had not abated, though his official duties no longer associated him with that instrument, and in his controversy with the University he had upheld the prerogative of the Stadtcantor. But these activities counted little in the eyes of his employers, who, too little instructed to discern his genius, measured his service by their parochial requirements, and found him wanting. From the outset Bach, with permission, had evaded his pedagogic duty; even in musical instruction he had to some extent relieved himself of the drudgery of routine lessons. Invitations to open or report on organs in other towns took him from Leipzig more often than was agreeable to his masters, and increased their suspicion that his duties were neglected. His habitual failure to ask permission to absent himself added another stab of irritation. These murmurings found expression at the Council's meeting on 2 August 1730.[1] Hofrath Adrian Steger, with evident indignation, spoke of the Cantor as one who 'does nothing, refuses to explain his conduct, and neglects his singing lessons, not to mention other instances of his unsatisfactoriness'. There was general agreement that the Cantor's independence needed correction, and that his deputy Petzold was overloaded with work. The more lenient preferred to 'admonish' the delinquent and transfer his pedagogic duty from Petzold to Abraham Krügel. The proposal had little support; Syndicus Job insisted that Bach was 'incorrigible', and by a majority of seven votes to four it was resolved to impound his salary.[2] Undoubtedly he was a bad disciplinarian, prone to passionate outbreaks which made relations with his singers difficult, and but little deferential to those he served. On none of these charges was Bach concerned to defend

---

[1] The minute is printed in Bi. ii. 140; Sp. ii. 869.
[2] 'Besoldung'. The proposal affected Bach's regular income but not his irregular *beneficia*. However, the Rector's fees which had accrued during the vacancy were shared between Frau Ernesti, the Conrector, and the Tertius. Bach, whose periods of duty as Inspector had occurred once in three weeks instead of once in four, received nothing, in accordance with a resolution dated 6 Nov. 1730 (Sp. ii. 73). See his letter *infra*, p. 216.

himself. But the insinuation that the deficiencies of his choirs were due to himself was too ill-informed to pass without correction. He lost no time in exposing the conditions in which he worked, and on 23 August 1730 completed for the Council's digestion a document whose precise statement of elementary facts measures its author's contempt for the musical ignorance of those to whom it was addressed.

A short and much-needed statement of the requirements of church music. With some general reflections on its decline.[1]

To perform concerted music as it should be rendered, both singers and instrumentalists are required.

The singers are provided by the Thomasschule of this town and are of four kinds: Descantists, Altists, Tenors, Basses. If the choir is to accomplish what is required of it, it must include Concertists[2] as well as Ripienists. In *ordinaire* there are four Concertists in a choir, and as many as five, six, seven, or even eight, if they are grouped to sing *per choros*. The Ripienists must be at least eight in number, two to each part.

The instrumentalists also fall in different categories: violists, oboists, flautists, trumpeters, timpanist. N.B. Under the term violist are included viola, violoncello, and violone performers.

The *alumni Thomanae scholae* number fifty-five, who form the choirs of the four churches[3] and perform either figural music, motets, or simple hymns. In three of the churches, namely, the Thomaskirche, Nikolaikirche, and Neukirche, the choirs sing in parts; at the Peterskirche the choir leads the hymns, part-music is not sung there.

Each of the three part-singing choirs requires at least three Sopranists, three Altists, three Tenors, and as many Basses,[4] so that, if a chorister is unable to sing (as often happens, particularly at this time of year, as the prescriptions of the school *medicus*[5] prove), a double motet at any rate can be performed. (N.B. It would be much more convenient if the *coetus*[6] could be distributed to provide four *subjecta* to each part, giving sixteen voices to each choir.) It follows that thirty-six is the *numerus* of those who must be capable of part-singing.

The instrumental accompaniment requires the following players:

Violino I, 2 or even 3.
Violino II, 2 or 3.
Viola I, 2.

---

[1] Leipzig. Stadtbibl. Repert. III, 15⁰. [2] *i.e.* capable of singing solos.
[3] Cf. *supra*, p. 155.
[4] A note appended by Bach to his report on the candidates for admission (*supra*, p. 197) states that each of the three choirs had three singers in each part. In 1744–5 the four choirs were staffed as follows (B.-J. 1907, p. 77):

	I.	II.	III.	IV.
S. .	5	4	3	1
A. .	2	4	4	1
T. .	3	5	4	4
B. .	7	4	2	1

[5] In 1736 the school doctor was Johann Friedrich Crell; he resided 'auf der Reich-Strasse, in Freundens Hause' (D.J.F.L., p. 88).
[6] *i.e.* the whole body of *alumni*.

Viola II, 2.
Violoncello, 2.
Violone, 1.
Oboe, 2, or if necessary, 3.
Bassoon, 1 or 2.
Trumpet, 3.
Timpani, 1.

Summa: at least eighteen instrumentalists. N.B. In performances of church music flutes also are necessary (they are of two kinds, *à bec* and *traversieri*).[1] That adds at least two more players, or twenty in all. The *numerus* of professional players maintained for this duty is eight, namely, four wind, three strings, and one assistant. Discretion forbids me to offer an opinion on their competence and musicianship. I will merely remark that some of them are *emeriti*[2] and others not in such good *exercitium* as formerly. The following is a list of them:[3]

1st Trumpet, Herr Gottfried Reiche.[4]
2nd Trumpet, Herr Johann Cornelius Gentzmer (Gensmar).[5]
3rd Trumpet, *vacat*.
Timpani, *vacat*.
1st Violin, Herr Christian Rother.[5]
2nd Violin, Herr Heinrich Christian Beyer.
Viola, *vacat*.
Violoncello, *vacat*.
Violone, *vacat*.
1st Oboe, Herr Johann Caspar Gleditsch.[5]
2nd Oboe, Herr Johann Gottfried Kornagel.[5]
3rd Oboe or Taille, *vacat*.
Bassoon, Assistant.

Thus the following important *subjecta* for strengthening or filling essential parts, are lacking:

1st Violin, 2 players.
2nd Violin, 2 players.
Viola, 2 players.
Violoncello, 2 players.
Violone, 1 player.
Flute, 2 players.

The missing instrumental parts have so far been supplied, partly by *studiosi*,[6] chiefly by *alumni*. The former have shown themselves very willing to assist, since it affords them pleasure and used to provide a *stipendium* or *honorarium* as well. But of late the latter has not been forthcoming. The occasional *beneficia* which used to find their way into the

[1] The instruments of Bach's orchestra are discussed in the present writer's *Bach: The Cantatas and Oratorios*, Bk. II, p. 20.
[2] *i.e.* fit only for superannuation.
[3] Their Christian names are supplied from D.J.F.L., p. 79. In 1736 Ulrich Heinrich Ruhe held Reiche's place, and Johann Friedrich Caroli brought the number of string players to three; the total number of players was seven. Cf. B.-J. 1907, p. 32, for an article on the Leipzig town's musicians, and also Schering, chap. 9. A table of those in service under Bach is given on p. 206 *infra*.
[4] See an article on him in B.-J. 1918, p. 133, and Schering, *passim*.
[5] Cf. Schering, *passim*.   [6] *i.e.* University students.

pockets of the *chorus musicus* have gradually disappeared, and the readiness of the *studiosi* to assist disappeared with them: for no one cares to work for nothing. Moreover, since, owing to the lack of more expert *subjecta*, it has been necessary to take from the school the viola, violoncello, and violone players invariably, and the second violins usually, it will readily be understood that the singing choir is correspondingly weakened.

I have so far spoken of what is required for the Sunday music. Regarding festival music, which is performed in both churches, the lack of instrumentalists is even more serious, for in the *chorus secundus* I am obliged to use scholars otherwise available as instrumentalists.

Nor can I omit to point out, that owing to the *reception* in recent times of so many incompetent and untrained lads, the standard of musical proficiency has been lowered, and will continue to fall. For it is patent that a lad who knows nothing whatever of music, and cannot sing even a *secunda*, is *consequenter* no manner of use, for he has no natural gifts. Even entrants with some knowledge of the *principia* do not become serviceable as quickly as one could wish, and the others, after their *reception*, are put into the choir before there has been time to make them competent even to sing in time and tune. Moreover, every year singers of musical ability leave the school, whose places are taken by others not immediately serviceable, indeed, in most cases, of no use at all. Hence it is obvious that the *chorus musicus* must tend to deteriorate. In fact, it is known that my immediate *antecessores* Herren Schelle and Kuhnau were compelled to get help from the *studiosi* whenever a heavy work was performed, and obtained it the more readily because, *a parte* an honourable member of the Council, *stipendia* were provided for a vocal Bass, Tenor, and Alto, and for a few instrumentalists, particularly two string players, thus enlarging the resources for performing concerted music in church.

Now the present *status Musices* is quite different from what it was, its technique is so much more complex, and the public *gusto* so changed, that old-fashioned music sounds strangely in our ears. Greater care must therefore be taken to obtain *subjecta* capable of satisfying the modern *gustum* in music, and also instructed in its technique, to say nothing of the composer's desire to hear his works performed properly. Yet the *beneficia*, themselves inconsiderable, formerly available for the *chorus musicus* have been withdrawn. It is astonishing that German musicians should be expected to play *ex tempore* any music put before them, whether it comes from Italy, France, England, or Poland, just as if they were the *virtuosi* for whom it was written, men who therefore have had opportunity to study it, indeed almost to learn it by heart, enjoy (*quod notandum*) large salaries to reward their labour and diligence, and have leisure to study and master their parts. People do not bear this in mind, but leave our players in a position merely to do the best they can, the necessity to earn their daily bread allowing them little leisure to perfect their technique, still less to become *virtuosi*. A single *exempel* may be given: let any one visit Dresden and observe how the royal musicians there are paid. They have no anxiety regarding their livelihood, and consequently are relieved of *chagrin*; each man is able to cultivate his own instrument and to make himself a competent and agreeable performer on it. The lesson is obvious: the withdrawing of the *beneficia* formerly provided puts it out of my power to place the musical performances on a more satisfactory footing.

Finally I will set forth the *numerus* of the present *alumni*, stating the musical *profectus* of each, leaving over for future consideration the question whether concerted music can be properly performed under existing conditions, and, if not, what remedy can be found.

The present *coetus musicus* can be divided into three *classes*:

(1) Those who are quite efficient:[1] Johann David Petzold, Johann Gottl. Lange, Paul Christ. Stoll, *Praefecti*; Joh. Anton Frick, Gottfried Theodor Krause, Samuel Kittler, Adam Friedrich Pohlreuter, Joh. August Stein, Burckhard,[2] Philipp Christ. Siegler, Joh. Gottfried Nützer, David Salomo Reichardt, Joh. Ludwig Krebs, Joh. Tobias Krebs, Joh. Gottfried Schönemann, Samuel Gottl. Heder, and Joh. Ludwig Dietel.

(2) Motet singers, needing further training before they can take part in concerted music: Johann Michael Jenicke, Heinrich Wilhelm Ludwig, Fr. Wilhelm Ludwig, Ephraim Friedrich Meissner, Gottl. Heinrich Neicke, Joh. Gottfried Neicke, Joh. Heinrich Hillmeyer, Chr. Friedrich Steidel, Christ. Gottfried Hesse, Joh. Gottl. Haupt, Wilhelm Eusebius Suppe, Carl Friedrich Segnitz, Joh. Gottl. Thieme, Joh. Ephraim Keller, Christ. Sigismund Roeder, Samuel Ernst Ossan, Joh. Gottfr. Berger, Samuel Gottl.Lesche,Joh. Christ.Hauptmann, and Joh. Gottfried Sachse.

(3) Those named in this class are of no use whatever and are as follows: Joh. David Bauer, Joh. Gottfr. Gross, Carl Friedrich Eberhardt, Joh. Friedrich Braun, Joh. Heinrich Seymann, Joh. Tobias Dietze, Joh. Samuel Hebenstreit, Gottl. Michael Wintzer, Joh. Ephraim Oeser, Joh. Christ. Lepper, Gottl. Jakob Hausius, Joachim Heinrich Feller, Immanuel Crell, Joh. Gottl. Zeymer, Joh. Gottfried Guffer, Gottl. Friedrich Eichel, and Joh. Ephraim Zwicker.

Summa: 17 serviceable, 20 not yet serviceable, 17 useless.

Joh. Seb. Bach,
Director Musices.

Leipzig, 23 Aug. 1730.

Nothing came of Bach's remonstrance, and the Council's thunder reverberated as fruitlessly over his head. On 25 August 1730 Bürgermeister Dr. Born reported to the Council[3] a conversation with the Cantor, presumably regarding the complaints ventilated at its meeting three weeks before. The only conclusion minuted was a resolution to hand on to Abraham Krügel the work so far discharged on Bach's behalf by Petzold. Upon that finding the matter dropped. But in Bach's sensitive mind it rankled deeply; he contemplated resigning the Cantorship, and, scanning the horizon, remembered his school friend Erdmann, whom he had met at Weimar shortly before his appointment to Cöthen, and who was now settled at Danzig as Russian Agent. On 28 October 1730 he addressed to him one of the few intimate letters from his pen that has survived:[4]

Honoured Sir,
Pray excuse an old and faithful servant troubling you with this letter.

---

[1] I have added the Christian names from the list of *alumni* in B.-J. 1907, p. 66.
[2] Not named among the *alumni* in B.-J., *ibid*.
[3] The minute is printed in Dahms, p. 72.
[4] The original is in the Russian archives at Moscow.

It is nearly four years since you were good enough to answer the last I wrote to you, when you were pleased to desire news of me and my welfare. I will do my best to comply with your wish. You know my *fata* up to the *mutation* which took me to Cöthen as Capellmeister. Its gracious Prince loved and understood music, so that I expected to end my days there. But my *Serenissimus* married a Bernburg wife, and in consequence, so it seemed, his musical *inclination* abated, while his new Princess proved to be an *amusa*. So it pleased God to call me here as *director Musices* and Cantor of the Thomasschule. At first I found it not altogether agreeable to become a simple Cantor after having been a Capellmeister, and for that reason I forbore from coming to a *resolution* for three months. However, I received such *favorable* reports of the *situation*, that, having particularly in mind my sons' *studia*, and after invoking divine guidance, I at last made up my mind, came to Leipzig, performed my *Probe*, and received the post. And here, God willing, I have remained till now. But unfortunately I have discovered that (1) this situation is not as good as it was represented to be, (2) various *accidentia* relative to my *station* have been withdrawn, (3) living is expensive, and (4) my masters are strange folk with very little care for music in them. Consequently, I am subjected to constant annoyance, jealousy, and persecution. It is therefore in my mind, with God's assistance, to seek my *fortune* elsewhere. If your Honour knows of or should hear of a *convenable station* in your town, I beg you to let me have your valuable *recommendation*. Nothing will be wanting on my part to give *satisfaction*, show diligence, and justify your much esteemed support. My present *station* is worth about 700 thalers a year,[1] and if the death-rate is higher than *ordinairement* my *accidentia* increase in *proportion*; but Leipzig is a healthy place, and for the past year, as it happens, I have received about 100 kronen less than usual in funeral *accidentia*. The cost of living, too, is so *excessive* that I was better off in Thuringia on 400 thalers.[2]

And now I must tell you something of my domestic circumstances. My first wife died at Cöthen and I have married again. Of my first marriage are living three sons and a daughter, whom your Honour saw at Weimar and may be pleased to remember. Of my second marriage one son and two daughters are living. My eldest son is a *studiosus juris*, the other two[3] are at school here in the *prima* and *secunda classis*; my eldest daughter as yet is unmarried. My children by my second wife are still young; the eldest boy is six. All my children are born *musici*; from my own *familie*, I assure you, I can arrange a concert *vocaliter* and *instrumentaliter*; my wife, in particular, has a very clear soprano, and my eldest daughter can give a good account of herself too. I should trespass too

---

[1] Bach's income was derived mainly from *accidentia*. His fixed income was 87 th. 12 gr., with 13 th. 3 gr. for wood and light, 16 bushels of corn, and some small endowments. The residue was drawn from weddings and funerals, the fee for the latter varying, according to the school attendance, from 1 th. 18 gr. to 6 pf. The fees from this source were the Cantor's chief fund of revenue, and Bach himself states them as 100 thalers below the normal in 1729. The fee for a wedding was 2 th., and between 1735 and 1738 over 260 took place each year in the two churches. The Cantor, however, would not attend more than a fraction of them (cf. Bi. i. 181). He also shared the 'Musicgeld' collected at school processions.

[2] Cf. *supra*, p. 121.

[3] Carl Philipp Emanuel and Johann Gottfried Bernhard.

far on your forbearance were I to *incommode* your Honour further. I conclude therefore with my most devoted and life-long *respect*, declaring myself

Your Honour's most obedient servant,

Joh. Seb. Bach.

Leipzig, 28 Oct. 1730.

The letter expressed a passing mood, and the intention to seek employment elsewhere probably was not serious. Gesner was already settled in the Rector's lodging, tactful counsel was at hand, and Bach elected to remain.

THE following table of the Leipzig licensed musicians (Stadtpfeifer and Kunstgeiger) during Bach's Cantorate is compiled from Dr. Schering's article 'Die Leipziger Ratsmusik von 1650 bis 1775' in *Archiv. f. Musikwissenschaft*, 1921, Heft 1, pp. 17–53. I have corrected erroneous dates in it.

Name.	Kunst-geiger.	Stadt-pfeifer.	Instrument.[1]
Reiche, Gottfried	1700–6	1706–34	1st Trumpet.[1]
Beyer, Heinrich Christian	1706–48	—	2nd Violin.[1]
Rother, Christian	1707–8	1708–37	1st Violin.[1]
Meyer, Christian Ernst	1707–30	—	? 3rd Trumpet or 3rd Oboe.[3]
Gentzmer(Gensmar),Joh. Cornelius	1708–12	1712–51	2nd Trumpet.[1]
Gleditsch, Joh. Caspar	1712–19	1719–47	1st Oboe.[1]
Kornagel, Joh. Gottfried	1719–53	—	2nd Oboe.[1]
Caroli, Joh. Friedrich	1730–8	—	? 3rd Trumpet or 3rd Oboe.[3]
Ruhe, Ulrich Heinrich	—	1734–87	1st Trumpet or 1st Violin.[2]
Kirchhof, Joh. Friedrich	—	1737–69	Oboe or Flute.[2]
Oschatz, Joh. Christian	1738–47	1747–62	Oboe or 2nd Trumpet or Flute.[2]
Pfaffe, Carl Friedrich	1748–53	1753–73	Trumpet.[4]
Jonne, Andreas Christoph	1749–62	1761–84	? Violin.[5]

The trumpeters also played the horns and trombones. The oboists were responsible for all three kinds of the instrument. The strings were generally amateurs.

[1] Cf. *supra*, p. 202.
[2] So described in the "Tabula musicorum der Löbl. Grossen Konzertgesellschaft' (1746–8).
[3] Meyer held one of the posts described by Bach as vacant in August 1730. His successor Caroli, no doubt, succeeded to it. Probability indicates the Trumpet or Oboe as their principal instruments.
[4] Succeeded Gentzmer as Stadtpfeifer in 1753 (Schering, *ut supra*, p. 44). Gentzmer probably was 1st Trumpet after Reiche's death in 1734.
[5] Jonne apparently took Beyer's place.

CHAPTER IX

THE BATTLE OF THE PREFECTS

THE arrival of Johann Matthias Gesner[1] as Rector opened a new chapter in the school's history, and promised a restful oasis in the Cantor's indomitable contest with its authorities. Six years Bach's junior, Gesner brought with him wide pedagogic experience, ripe scholarship, and a generous humanity which smoothly effaced Ernesti's flaccid rule, eased magisterial jars, and tightened discipline with a velvet grip. Born near Ansbach in 1691, he had in 1715 become librarian and Conrector at Weimar, where he first admired Bach's genius. Returning in 1729 to Ansbach as Rector of the Gymnasium, he was swiftly called thence on 8 September 1730[2] to succeed Ernesti at Leipzig, his high reputation as a classicist permitting him, like his predecessor and successor, to aspire to the concurrent holding of a University Chair. The Council, however, forbade the association of the two offices, concluding that the school's disordered discipline demanded the Rector's undivided interest. The prohibition, though sensible, drove Gesner elsewhere after four years which impressed his character on every department of the school. Its *alumni* found him as friendly and approachable as he was firm in discipline. Indeed, amiability was the characteristic of him most vivid in the recollection of one of them,[3] who recalled him as slow to anger and punishment, affectionate and affable, eager to apprehend and encourage his pupils' bent, a sympathetic reader of their weekly diaries, and an interested listener to their music practices, a detail of their daily routine with which his predecessor and immediate successor did not concern themselves. Gesner, in fact, had a strong feeling for music, admitted the propriety of its place in the school curriculum, and afforded the Cantor hearty support and encouragement. The two men esteemed each other highly, and Bach never lost the admiration of his colleague.

Gesner early made it his business to smoothe Bach's relations with the irate Council. His intervention shifted from the Cantor's shoulders even the nominal obligation to give lessons outside his own subject. Instead, he was made responsible for the school's

[1] Illus. No. 65.　　　　　　　　[2] Bi. ii. 134.
[3] The appreciation occurs in a manuscript *Historia scholarum Lipsiensium* compiled by Joh. Fr. Köhler, Pastor of Taucha, near Leipzig, *circa* 1776.

attendance at the early morning week-day services, a duty heretofore restricted to Fridays; his practice hours also were somewhat expanded.[1] The death of the Conrector, Carl Friedrich Petzold, on 30 May 1731, afforded Gesner opportunity to remove another grievance. Bach's exclusion from the fees available for distribution during the Rectorial vacancy has already been remarked.[2] Gesner pleaded for the full restitution of his emoluments; hence the Cantor, equally with the Rector, Tertius, and Quartus, shared the fees accruing in the interval between Petzold's death and the appointment of his successor (Johann August Ernesti) some eight months later.[3] Relations between the two families consequently were close and cordial: Frau Gesner stood godmother to Bach's short-lived son Johann August Abraham in November 1733, and Bach acknowledged the favour in a

Canon a 2 perpetûm.

Leipzig, den 10. Januar
1734.

Dieses wollte seinem Hrn. Pathen
zum Andenken beyfügen
Joh. Seb. Bach.[4]

Gesner's energy achieved the long-needed enlargement of the school buildings [5] which his predecessor's obstinate lethargy had delayed. A resolution to add two stories to the overcrowded structure was taken on 6 June 1730,[6] three months before his appointment; but it was not until 18 April 1731, following the Easter celebrations, that the Council provided for the housing of its inmates [7] while the work was in progress. Accommodation for the school was reported [8] available until Michaelmas 'in dem ehemals Görischen, iezo Kochischen Hausse', the residence of Michael Koch, a member of the Council,[9] on the Marktplatz, at a rental of 60 thalers. Alternative quarters were suggested for Bach's use till the New Year 1732, 'entweder bey H. D. Dondorffen à 60 Thlr., oder bey den Herrn Appellations-Rath Packbuschen à 75 Thlr.' Dr. Salomon Friedrich Packbusch resided in the Petersstrasse.[10] Don-

---

[1] Sp. ii. 91, quoting the Rathsacten.   [2] *Supra*, p. 200.   [3] Sp. ii. 91.
[4] The autograph, originally in Gesner's possession, belonged in 1880 to Herr Karl Meinert of Frankfurt-a.-Main. Cf. Bi. ii. 233.
[5] *Supra*, p. 166.   [6] Bi. ii. 159.
[7] Gesner had not yet gone into residence in the Rector's wing.
[8] Leipz. Rathsakten, Schule zu S. Thomae, Fasc. II, Stift. VIII, Bd. 6.
[9] His name is found in D.J.F.L., p. 63, as 'Michael Koch, am Marckte, in seinem Hause'.
[10] In *ibid.*, pp. 3, 45, his address is given as 'in der Peters-Strasse, im Rechenbergischen Hause'.

dorff can be no other than Dr. Christoph Dondorff, 'Facult. Jurid. Assessor', who stood godfather to Johann Christoph Friedrich, the 'Bückeburg Bach', on 23 June 1732.[1] He resided in the Hainstrasse, where he owned a brewery.[2] Here probably Bach and his family took up their temporary quarters.[3]

So drastic a domestic upheaval necessarily reacted upon the official activities of Bach and his singers. It was the turn of the Thomaskirche to hear the Good Friday Passion in 1731, and Picander, with whom Bach collaborated when the 'Matthäuspassion' was produced in that church in 1729, provided him now with a libretto based on St. Mark's narrative. Incorporating with the Bible text a liberal provision of Chorals, and eight lyrical numbers, he constructed it with a view to making the slightest call upon the composer. It contains even fewer lyrical stanzas than the 'Johannespassion', and though St. Mark's narrative is as rich in incident as St. Matthew's, Picander was as reticent in his treatment of them as in his earlier text he was the reverse, being content to insert a Choral where before he had provided an original stanza for an Aria. Moreover, in passages suitable for concerted choral treatment St. Mark's narrative is far less rich than St. Matthew's: assuming that Bach treated them as in the 'Matthäuspassion', which contains them all, he needed to provide no more than ninety bars of music. Even Picander's infrequent lyrics were so constructed in form and rhythm as to enable Bach to adapt music already written: for five of them he utilized the 'Trauer-Ode' composed in 1727, and for the other three also almost certainly used old material.[4] Hence, the libretto and his treatment of it alike indicate Bach's disinclination to favour Leipzig with such a Passion as he had produced in 1723 and 1729. Uncordial relations with his civic superiors may have influenced him; but the chief reason is found in the disturbed conditions of school discipline. For the Good Friday performance in 1732 he found himself in similar circumstances. It was not his habit to give the first performance of his major works in the Nikolaikirche, and it is not improbable that, while he was a boarder in Dondorff's house in 1731, he copied out the earlier part of the 'Passion nach dem Evangelisten Lucas',

---

[1] Sp. ii. 955.

[2] D.J.F.L., p. 128, names among the twelve breweries in the town 'Herr D. Dondorffs Brau-Hauss auf der Hayn-Strasse', and among the doctors of law (p. 39) 'Gottlieb Wilhelm Dinckler, auf der Hayn-Strasse, in Hr. D. Dondorffs Hause'. Sp. ii. 10 says that Dondorff owned St. Thomas's mill and supposes that Bach resided there.

[3] The sum of 353 thalers was expended on the provision of beds in the requisitioned buildings.

[4] For Picander's text cf. the present writer's *Bach: The Passions*, Bk. II, p. 66.

P

published in 1898 by the Bachgesellschaft as his own composition and since rejected by every competent authority.[1] Like the
'Marcuspassion', it consists mainly of the Bible narrative and
Chorals; there are only eight lyrical movements in it. For that
reason its performance in 1732 is probable, in view of the circumstances in which Bach and his choir were placed. Between these
Good Friday Passions in 1731 and 1732 he appears to have largely
used cantatas already heard, or solo anthems in which the choir's
participation was limited to the concluding Choral. Thus, all three
cantatas[2] for the Whitsun Festival 1731 are revisions of earlier
works, as also is the Michaelmas cantata for that year,[3] while those
performed on the following Nineteenth to the Twenty-Second
Sundays after Trinity [4] are for a solo voice. Perhaps the unusual
addition of an organ *obbligato* to some of the cantatas written in
1731[5] also reveals the disturbing conditions in which their composer was placed.

In 1731 Bach announced himself in a field wherein his predecessor Kuhnau also had won applause. Annually since 1726 he had
engraved a Clavier Suite, designating it, in imitation of Kuhnau,
a Partita or Partie. These, with the addition of a sixth, he issued
in 1731 in a volume he himself distinguished as his 'Opus I'. For
its title he chose a word Kuhnau himself had used for a similar
publication in 1689,[6] designating his volume *Clavir Übung beste-
hend in Praeludien, Allemanden, Couranten, Sarabanden, Giguen,
Menuetten, und andern Galanterien; Denen Liebhabern zur Gemüths
Ergoezung verfertiget . . . Opus I. In Verlegung des Autoris. 1731.
Leipzig.*[7] Gesner's encouragement, his own leisure, and perhaps
an intention to counteract the recent strictures of his employers,
urged Bach to introduce himself to a larger audience than he had
so far addressed.[8] His success was immediate. Forkel,[9] repeating
Bach's sons, remarks that the Partitas attracted universal notice
and were in general demand: 'such compositions for the clavier
had not been seen or heard before, and any one who could play
them was sure of a success.' Their fame preceded Bach to Dres-

---

[1] Cf. *Bach: The Passions*, Bk. II, p. 77.   [2] Nos. 172, 173, 184.
[3] No. 149.   [4] Nos. 56, 49, 188, 55.
[5] *e.g.* Nos. 170 (Trinity VI), 27 (Trinity XVI), 169 (Trinity XVIII).
[6] A facsimile of Kuhnau's title-page is in Schering, p. 192. Cf. *ibid.*, p. 428.
[7] The volume was announced for sale 'in Commission bey Boetii seel. hinter-
lassener Tochter, unter dem Rath-hause'. In 1736 D.J.F.L., p. 89, names
among the Leipzig booksellers 'Joh. Theod. Boetii hinterlassene Tochter, im
Durchgange des Rathhauses'.
[8] Carl Philipp Emanuel, now aged seventeen, also published his Op. I in 1731,
a minuet for the clavier, which he himself engraved on copper. Cf. Wotquenne's
Verzeichnis, p. 35.   [9] Forkel, p. 116.

den, where he had many friends, especially Johann Adolph Hasse, Hofcapellmeister, and his wife, the celebrated Faustina, both of whom often visited Leipzig. Accompanied by his eldest son Friedemann,[1] Bach frequently attended the opera at Dresden, and, no doubt at Hasse's invitation, was present at the first performance of that composer's 'Cleofide' on 13 September 1731.[2] On the following day he gave an afternoon organ recital in the Sophienkirche, attended by Hasse and other luminaries of the Dresden firmament, who demonstrated their astonishment at his transcendent powers. A local poet, under the pseudonym Micrander, voiced it in the 'Dresdner Merkwürdigkeiten':[3]

A singing, rippling beck[4] to listening ears is pleasing,
As on through bosky dells or tow'ring rocks it flows.
But far more pleasant he whose nimble hand unceasing
So graciously his art on all who hear bestows.
'Tis said, Orpheus of old, his lute melodious sounding,
Could charm both beast and tree obedient to his will.
How much more wondrous Bach: for sure his powers astounding,
Whate'er and when he plays, grown men with wonder fill.

The Dresden recital breaks an interval of seven years during which there is no record of Bach's activity[5] in this particular field. Five months later, in February 1732, he visited Stöntzsch, some twenty miles south-west of Leipzig, to examine and display its organ, whose transposition to the west end of the church had permitted its enlargement by six stops.[6] In the following September (1732) Bach revisited Cassel, where in 1714 his performance on the Schloss organ had excited Prince Friedrich's admiration. On the present occasion[7] he was summoned to report on the large

[1] Forkel, p. 111.
[2] Martin Falck, *Wilhelm Friedemann Bach* (1919), p. 10.   [3] Bi. ii. 157.
[4] It is attempted to reproduce the play on the word 'Bach'. The original runs:
    Ein angenehmer Bach kann zwar das Ohr ergötzen,
    Wenn er in Sträuchern hin, durch hohe Felsen läuft,
    Allein den Bach muss man gewiss viel höher schätzen,
    Der mit so hurtger Hand gantz wunderbarlich greifft.
    Man sagt, dass wenn Orpheus die Laute sanft geschlagen,
    Hab' alle Thiere er in Wäldern zu sich bracht,
    Gewiss, man muss dies mehr von unserm Bache sagen,
    Weil er, sobald er spielt, ja alles staunen macht.
[5] Herr Hans Löffler (B.-J. 1925, p. 93) has usefully assembled the occasions on which Bach is known to have tested or opened church organs. None is recorded between his visits to Gera in 1724 (*supra*, p. 178) and to Dresden in 1731.
[6] *Neue Sächsische Kirchengalerie, Bd. XV. Die Ephorie Borna.* Hrsg. von den Geistlichen der Ephorie, p. 1091.
[7] The circumstances of Bach's visit are detailed by Dr. Heinz Ameln, *Der Aufenthalt J. S. Bachs in Kassel im Jahre 1732* (in 'Hessenland', Jhrg. XXXVIII, Heft 2, Cassel, Feb. 1926); Dr. Gustav Struck, *Joh. Seb. Bachs Kasseler Tage 1732* (in 'Der Chorleiter', Jhrg. VI, No. 2, Hildburghausen, 1 Feb. 1925); and

organ in the St. Martinskirche, built by Hans and Friedrich Scherer of Hamburg between the years 1610 and 1614, and recently enlarged by the Mühlhausen builder Nikolaus Becker, a work in progress since 1730. Accompanied by his wife, Bach arrived in Cassel on Sunday, 21 September 1732, and was accommodated in the 'Stadt Stockholm', a hostelry in the Mittelgasse, whose host, Herr Holtzschue, received eighty-four thalers to discharge his visitors' account.[1] The following days were spent in a close examination of the instrument, a task in which Bach was associated with Carl Möller, town and Court organist. On Sunday, 28 September,[2] he opened the organ at a public recital, which the 'Casselische Polizey- und Commerzienzeitung' (22 September) had already announced as an occasion of joy and encouragement for the whole community.[3] Bach's recompense was not inconsiderable: twenty-six thalers as journey money, fifty as his fee, two for the 'Porteurs' who carried him to and from his lodging, and one for a servant placed at his disposal.

Meanwhile, on Thursday in Whit-week (5 June) 1732, the renovated Thomasschule reopened its doors with speeches and the performance of a Cantata in the new Aula on the third floor. The Quartus, Johann Heinrich Winckler, had prepared a conventional libretto, whose character may be judged by its opening and closing lines:

> (Aria) Froher Tag, verlangte Stunden,
> Nun hat unsre Lust gefunden,
> Was sie fest und ruhig macht.
> Hier steht unser Schul-Gebäude,
> Hier erblicket Aug nur Freude,
> Kunst und Ordnung, Zier und Pracht.

. . . . . .

Dr. Karl Scherer, *Joh. Seb. Bachs Aufenthalt in Kassel* (in 'Mon. für Musikgeschichte', Jhrg. XXV, 1893, p. 129). The organ remained in use until 1896.
[1] Charles XII of Sweden slept in the inn on his journey northward in 1714.
[2] It is therefore improbable that Cantata 95,'Christus, der ist mein Leben', was performed at Leipzig on this Sunday (Trinity XVI), as Sp. ii. 292 suggests.
[3] 'Es ist die im hiesigen Stifft St. Martini, oder der so genannten grossen Kirche, grosse und kostbahre Orgel, woran beynahe 3. Jahr gearbeitet, endlich durch den Orgelbauer Herr Nicolaus Becker von Mühlhausen nach heutiger Art eingerichtet, und zu seiner Perfection gebracht worden. Nachdem dann nun dieses Werck auff Hohen Obrigkeitlichen Befehl durch den berühmten Organisten und Music Directorem Herrn Bach von Leipzig mit Zuziehung des hiesigen Hoff- und Stadt-Organisten Herrn Carl Möller examiniret werden wird, in ohngezweifelter Hoffnung, dass solche die erwünschte Probe erhält, so soll diese selbige künfftigen Sonntag geliebts Gott in öffentlicher Versammlunge vollkommen gespielet und mit einer Musicalischen harmonie inauguriret werden. Man wünschet, dass sothanes, zur Ehre Gottes hauptsächlich gereichendes Werck der gantzen Gemeinde und einem jeden insbesondere zur Auffmunterung gereichen möge.'

(Tutti) Ewiges Wesen, das alles erschafft,
   Segne die Väter mit daurender Kraft,
   Segne die Väter und Pfleger der Schule,
   Stärke die Häupter, die Leipzig verehrt,
   Schenke, was Hoffnung und Freude vermehrt,
   Gründe die Kinder zur Wohlfahrt der Sachsen,
   Lass sie stets grünen und blühen und wachsen.[1]

Bach's authorship of the music is stated on the title-page of the programme printed by Bernhard Christoph Breitkopf.[2] But the score has disappeared and, most probably, incorporated older material; certainly it was subsequently employed.[3] Complimentary speeches were delivered between the two Parts, and Gesner took the opportunity to emphasize the place of music in the school curriculum:

'Hic perfugium honestae paupertati aperit Amplissimus Ordo, si ea adjunctam sibi habeat sororem Bonam Mentem, et discendi cupiditatem. Hic ali jubet atque institui, qui nunc sanctissimo beatarum mentium munere, laudandi rerum omnium conditorem et parentem, fungantur, et cantus suavitate animos hominum ad divinarum rerum meditationem alliciant, qui denique boni viri et alteri saeculo profuturi evadant.'

Some were present who, as musicians, abundantly fulfilled their Rector's anticipation.[4]

The reopening of the school invited new regulations, which Gesner prepared and issued in 1733 through Bernhard Christoph Breitkopf, two small quarto pamphlets in Latin and German, of 32 and 39 pages respectively, whose twelve chapters bear the following titles:

Cap. I. Pietas erga Deum.
  II. Officia erga homines.
  III. Diei totius distributio.
  IV. Mores in templo, funeribus, et currenda.
  V. Mores in schola et studiis.
  VI. Musica.
  VII. Cibi capiendi ratio.
  VIII. Mores in cubiculis, frugalitas privata, et cura peculii.

[1] The complete text is in B.-G. XXXIV, p. li; Bi. iv. 172; Sp. ii. 889.
[2] The title-page is reproduced in B.-J. 1913, p. 75. Breitkopf's accounts suggest that 500 or 600 people were invited.
[3] Perhaps the opening movement was used later for the first Chorus of the Ascension Cantata 'Lobet Gott in seinen Reichen' (No. 11), while the first movement of the second Part ('Geist und Herze sind begierig') could be sung to the 'Domine Deus' of the Mass in F, as Arnold Schering points out in B.-J. 1921, p. 93. Bach used the music in 1733 for the cantata 'Frohes Volck, vergnügte Sachsen' (infra, p. 216).
[4] e.g. Joh. Ludwig Krebs, Joh. Ludwig Dietel, Christoph Nichelmann, Christian Fr. Schemelli, Gottl. Heinrich Neicke, and Joh. Heinrich Bach, of Oehringen.

IX. Praefectorum officia.

X. Aegrotorum cura.

XI. Proficiscentium officia aut discedentium.

XII. Externi.

The titles of the chapters distinguish the *Leges* or *Gesetze* of 1733 from the *Schulordnung* of 1723. The latter, imposed by the governing Council, was concerned with the administration of the institution, defined the duties of the members of its staff, and prescribed the curriculum. Gesner wrote for his scholars, aiming to revive the *esprit de corps* of a society whose standard had deteriorated under his predecessor's nerveless rule. That he should have found it necessary to denounce offences normally alien to a juvenile community declares the urgency of his appeal. Notable also, in view of Bach's imminent experience, was Gesner's attitude towards that branch of the curriculum for which the Cantor was responsible. In Chap. VI he reminds his readers that the provision of choirs in the town churches was the historical function of the school, a privilege, he bids them reflect, which linked them with the heavenly choirs above. He urges them to lose no opportunity to fit themselves for so honourable a duty, even to the sacrifice of their leisure. He warns them against prostituting their skill to unworthy purposes, counselling them to dedicate it to God's service, or to use it for innocent recreation. He recommends them to pay attention to their conductor's 'Wink und Takt', and imposes penalties of varying degree for accidental and wilful neglect to do so. Elsewhere [1] he again reminds them of the angels, whose pleasure is to sing God's praises, insisting that no lower ambition must inspire the true Thomaner.

Meanwhile, public events were happening whose reaction on Bach was considerable. Augustus II died on 1 February 1733, leaving Saxony to his son Augustus III, and a contest for the Polish crown from which that prince emerged victorious in 1736. The new sovereign, now in his thirty-seventh year, had followed his father into the Roman communion in 1712, and seven years later married the Archduchess Maria Josepha, daughter of Kaiser Joseph I. Unlike his father, he possessed neither talent nor inclination for affairs, preferring to pose as the Maecenas of music and painting. Meanwhile, Saxony plunged into public mourning, not abated till July 1733,[2] a period of five months during which figural music was not heard in the churches. That circumstance, and the new sovereign's character, inspired Bach with an ambition which, till its

---

[1] Cap. I, § 5.　　　[2] The rescript, dated 5 June 1733, is printed in Bi. ii. 163.

tardy attainment, he pursued with unflagging resolve. Relieved of the duty to provide Sunday cantatas and the Good Friday Passion,[1] he devoted the early months of 1733 to the preparation of a work for presentation to his sovereign, as a token of devotion, an indication of his skill, and a diploma for a post as Hofcomponist,[2] which he coveted. The value Bach placed upon a Court appointment has already been observed; but his application to the Dresden Court was prompted also by practical considerations which he admitted. The circumstances of the moment forbade him to offer a secular work, while a church cantata would be inappropriate; he therefore elected to convey his homage in a portion of their liturgies which Protestant and Catholic had in common, namely, the Lutheran 'Missa', or *Kyrie* and *Gloria in excelsis*.

Bach completed the score of the B minor Missa by the early summer of 1733, when opportunity occurred to convey it to Dresden. The incapacity of Christian Petzold (*d.* 2 July) rendered vacant the organistship of the Sophienkirche, in which Bach had astonished his hearers two years before. His eldest son Friedemann was now twenty-three years old, an organist already worthy of the name he bore. Urged, as is probable, by friends in Dresden, Bach proposed Friedemann for the vacancy, and on 7 June 1733[3] framed a formal application on his behalf. Other candidates offered themselves, but on 22 June Friedemann performed his Probe with such brilliance that he received the situation on the following day. On 11 July the organ key was handed to him, and, after examining and reporting on his instrument, he entered on his duties on 1 August.[4] Paternal solicitude brought Bach to Dresden with his son, whose quarters in the house of Hofrat Alius in the Wilsdruffer Gasse[5] he probably shared. Constitutionally indolent and as averse from putting words, as from expressing his musical thoughts, on paper, Friedemann's letters of 7 June and 1 August alike declare his father's composition. Bach, no doubt, was his active colleague, too, in the examination of the Sophienkirche

---

[1] Rost (*supra*, p. 159) states that no Good Friday performance was given in 1733; consequently the Thomaskirche's turn was postponed till 1734.
[2] Bach shared the title with others. See p. 242, note 4, *infra*.
[3] Herr Fr. Hoppe, in the 'Naumburger Heimat', No. 138, for 16 June 1927, reveals the new fact, that two months later Bach took a similar step on behalf of his second son Carl Philipp. Herr Hoppe prints a letter from the latter, dated 19 August 1733, addressed to the Bürgermeister and Council of Naumburg, submitting himself as a candidate for the vacant organistship in the Wenzelskirche. The letter bears evident signs of Bach's composition. The election took place on 15 Sept. 1733, when Joh. Christian Kluge, of Wiehe, obtained the appointment.   [4] Falck, pp. 11–16.   [5] *Ibid.*, p. 15.

organ, but was not hindered from completing the vocal and instrumental parts of the B minor Missa. On 27 July he conveyed them to the Electoral Schloss along with the following letter:[1]

Most gracious sovereign and illustrious Elector,

With profoundest *devotion* I offer your Majesty the accompanying insignificant example of my skill in *Musique*, begging in all humility that it may be received, not as its merits as a *composition* deserve, but with your Majesty's notorious generosity. At the same time, I solicit your Majesty's powerful *protection*. For some years past I have exercised the *directorium* of the music in the two principal churches in Leipzig, a situation in which I have been constantly exposed to undeserved affronts, even the confiscation of the *accidentia* due to me, annoyances not likely to recur should your Majesty be pleased to admit me to your Capelle and direct a *Praedicat* to be issued to that effect by the proper authority. Your Majesty's gracious response to my humble prayer will place me under an enduring obligation, and, with the most dutiful obedience and unflagging diligence, I shall show myself ready to fulfil your Majesty's commands to compose *Musique* for church or *orchestre*, devoting all my powers to your Majesty's service.

With constant loyalty I subscribe myself
Your Majesty's most devoted and obedient servant,
Johann Sebastian Bach.

Dresden, 27 July 1733.

Somewhat abrupt in form, Bach's petition was launched at an inopportune moment. Augustus was preoccupied by the situation in Poland, where, a few weeks earlier (May 1733), a strong anti-Saxon faction had declared against any sovereign but a native Pole. Augustus was still sounding the Austrian and Russian Courts when, on 10 September 1733, his rival, Stanislaus Leszczynski, was elected king at Warsaw. Feebly supported by France, Stanislaus was soon expelled from Poland, however, and withdrew from the field upon the surrender of Danzig, his last refuge, in June 1734. Amid these happenings Bach's gesture of homage passed unregarded. But opportunities to demonstrate his skill were conveniently afforded at a sequence of public celebrations which crowded the years 1733 and 1734. On 3 August 1733 Augustus's name-day was observed at Leipzig by the performance of Bach's cantata (Drama) 'Frohes Volck, vergnügte Sachsen', for which the facile Picander provided the libretto. Bach must have hastened from Dresden to direct its performance by his Collegium Musicum, and was at no pains to provide new music for the occasion: excepting the Recitatives, he revived the cantata sung at the reopening of the Thomasschule in 1732.[2] A month later (5 September 1733)

---

[1] Dresden: Sächs. Landesbibliothek, Musikhandschr. 1ᵐ.
[2] I infer this from the identical metres of the Arias and Tutti, and from frequent verbal coincidences. The libretto of 'Frohes Volck' is in B.-J. 1913, p. 80.

his singers and players celebrated the birthday of Augustus's lame and weakly heir, Prince Friedrich Christian,[1] in a more elaborate work. Picander again provided the libretto, 'Hercules auf dem Scheide-Wege'. Of Bach's music all but the Recitatives and concluding Chorus are familiar in the 'Christmas Oratorio', whose production took place a year later (1734).[2]

It has hitherto been concluded that the music of the 'Christmas Oratorio' is an adaptation of the secular cantata, an inference not unnatural in view of the fact that the latter work was the earlier in date of performance. But the conclusion cannot be maintained. Having recently adapted an old score to honour the father, whom he had urgent reasons to flatter, Bach is not likely to have been more punctilious in honouring the son. Moreover, on other similar occasions between September 1733 and Christmas 1734 it is observable that he was only at pains to provide original music when his sovereign was present in person. Thus it is inherently unlikely that the Hercules music was specially composed for Picander's libretto. But a collation of the two musical texts puts the matter beyond doubt. The opening Chorus of the Cantata is No. 36 of the Oratorio, whose words 'Loben' and 'Danken', rather than the Cantata's 'sorgen' and 'wachen', clearly inspired the florid phrases that carry them. No. 3 of the Cantata is No. 19 of the Oratorio, the two movements being in the keys of B flat and G respectively. Here there hardly can exist a doubt that the Oratorio's is the original key: not only is the lullaby more congruous to an alto voice, but the treatment of bar 52 almost positively declares the Cantata's text an adaptation. Compare the Oratorio's

Lieb - ster, ge - nies - se der Ruh,

with the Cantata's

Lieb - ster, und pfle - ge der Ruh

Bach would not choose any other than a descending note for his original treatment of the word 'Ruh'. The second part of the same movement yields another detail of evidence: Bach's pictorial idiom is too familiar to permit any doubt that its florid phrases

[1] Born 5 Sept. 1722; d. 17 Dec. 1763, little more than two months after his father.   [2] B.C.T., p. 75.

were originally inspired by the jubilant 'erfreuen' rather than the colourless 'Schranken'. The verbal test applied to No. 7 of the Cantata and its equivalent, No. 41 of the Oratorio, yields a similar, though less positive, conviction. The Oratorio (No. 4) version of the Cantata's No. 9, both in phrasing and mood, reveals the natural and original association of words and music. In No. 11 of the Cantata (No. 29 of the Oratorio) the awkwardness of the text is frequently evident in passages in which the association of words and music is natural in the Oratorio. If these glosses are sound, the 'Christmas Oratorio' was already composed, in whole or part, by the early autumn of 1733 when Bach drew upon it for his 'Hercules auf dem Scheide-Wege', and, as in the case of the 'Matthäuspassion', anticipated its production in its original form by putting some of it to another use.[1]

The persistence with which Bach's Collegium Musicum offered musical homage to Augustus III and his family in 1733 and 1734 must be attributed, in large degree, to Bach himself, who appears to have borne the expense of, or at least to have commissioned the publication of, the libretti of these complimentary cantatas. (Already his name is found in Bernhard Christoph Breitkopf's ledger for the libretto of Picander's Cantata 'Es lebe der König', performed by his Collegium on 3 August 1732 in honour of Augustus II's name-day.[2]) Having paid his homage to the new sovereign and his heir, and notwithstanding the imminent Christmas season, on 8 December 1733 Bach celebrated the birthday of the Queen-Electress Maria Josepha by the performance of his Cantata 'Tönet, ihr Pauken'. The title-page of its libretto bears no other name than Bach's, who perhaps was its author, a spirited text which did not omit to offer congratulations on the plight of Stanislaus and the French faction.[3] The music of four of its movements is also in the 'Christmas Oratorio',[4] and, on the test already applied to 'Hercules auf dem Scheide-Wege', was bor-

---

[1] It is established conclusively that the six Parts of the 'Christmas Oratorio' were performed consecutively in 1734 as the several parts of an 'Oratorium'. It is, however, not improbable that the Parts had had earlier and independent performance. It is observable, that whereas Bach attached the word 'Oratorium' to one of his compositions in 1734, he repeated the innovation in two closely contemporary works, the Easter 'Kommt, eilet', and the Ascension 'Lobet Gott in seinen Reichen'. We may perhaps infer the intention to please Dresden here. Cf. Kretzschmar, *Fuhrer durch den Konzertsaal*, II. Abeteilung, Bd. 2, p. 80. For a full discussion of the matter see the *Musical Times* for Oct.–Dec. 1930.

[2] The libretto is printed in B.-J. 1913, p. 77. Bach paid for 300 copies. Of 'Frohes Volck' and 'Hercules' he ordered 200 each. Cf. *ibid.*, pp. 80, 83.

[3] B.C.T., p. 620. A facsimile of the title-page is in B.-J. 1913, p. 85. Bach ordered 150 copies of the libretto.

[4] Nos. 1, 5, 7, 9 of the Cantata. Nos. 1, 15, 8, 24 of the Oratorio.

rowed from that work.[1] Little more than a month passed before the crowning of Augustus and his queen at Cracow called Bach and his forces again into loyal activity. For the occasion, on 17 January 1734, he revived an early Leipzig work, 'Der zufriedengestellte Aeolus',[2] whose text he probably himself adapted under the title 'Blast Lärmen, ihr Feinde'.[3] Seven months later, on 3 August 1734, he again revived old material to celebrate Augustus's name-day, using for the occasion, under the title 'Auf, schmetternde Töne', all but the Recitatives of 'Vereinigte Zwietracht', composed eight years before.[4]

By the autumn of 1734 the Polish situation shaped in Augustus's favour; he was not yet universally accepted, but had been crowned at Cracow. He therefore returned to Saxony, and early in October presented himself, with his consort, in Leipzig to afford the citizens opportunity to celebrate the anniversary (5 October) of his election to the Polish throne. The firing of cannons at midday and illuminations at nightfall in the houses and thoroughfares expressed civic loyalty. At nine o'clock six hundred students from the University congregated on the Marktplatz with torches, to support Bach's Collegium Musicum while it performed 'eine allerunterthänigste Abend-Music mit Trompeten und Pauken', Counts von Vitzthum, Hochberg, Flemming, and Dietrichstein, marshals of the ceremonial, being graciously permitted to kiss the sovereign's hand.[5] The entertainment cost 299 th. 22 gr., the larger part of which was expended on the torches. Bach and his musicians were remunerated with 50 thalers, and Johann Christian Clauder, the otherwise unknown author of the libretto 'Preise dein Glücke, gesegnetes Sachsen', received twelve.[6] The occasion called for Bach's fullest powers, if only to shame his prince's neglect of him. He had prepared a work to celebrate the sovereign's birthday on 7 October, but the commemoration of his election to the Polish throne had not been anticipated.[7] Bach was therefore compelled to employ old material. The 'Christmas Oratorio' provided one of the three Arias in 'Preise dein Glücke';[8] of its two

---

[1] A single example suffices: who can suppose that the virile Aria 'Grosser *Herr* und starker *König*' of the Oratorio was first conceived in association with the Cantata words 'Kron und Preis gekrönter *Damen*'?

[2] *Supra*, p. 180.

[3] B.C.T., p. 575. Bach ordered 150 copies of the libretto. Cf. B.-J. 1913, p. 84.

[4] *Supra*, p. 190.

[5] Contemporary accounts of the event are in Bi. ii. 168; B.C.T., p. 609; Riemer, p. 361.   [6] B.-J. 1925, p. 9.

[7] Bi. ii. 169 quotes Mittag's *Leben und Thaten Friedr. Augusti III* (1737), to the effect: 'da die Veranlassung dazu [*i.e.* for the celebration] kaum 3 Tage vorher gegeben worden', *i.e.* on the arrival of the royal pair in Leipzig.

[8] The soprano Aria 'Durch die von Eifer' is the Bass Aria 'Erleucht' auch

Choruses, the opening movement is familiar as the 'Osanna' of the Mass in B minor. It would be rash to assert that Bach was incapable of penning so stupendous a movement at three days' notice, but it is highly improbable that he did so. Hence the 'Osanna' must be supposed already available for adaptation to the secular use to which he put it. Its performance was darkened by a tragedy: Gottfried Reiche, senior of the town's musicians, a trumpeter of rare skill, was seized by a fatal stroke in the Stadt-pfeifergässlein on the following day; his death was attributed to his exertions in the preceding evening's performance and the effects of the 'Fackelrauch'.[1] The next evening (7 October) the royal birthday[2] was celebrated by Bach's Collegium in the Cantata 'Schleicht, spielende Wellen',[3] whose author, probably Picander, introduced flattering references to the King's Austrian consort. The sovereigns, both of whom were present, must have remarked the indefatigable homage of a composer who, two days before, had laid another garland at their feet. But his desire for the Court appointment remained unsatisfied. Still, he seems to have revived 'Was mir behagt', for Augustus's name-day in 1735, and 'Schleicht, spielende Wellen' for his birthday in 1736.[4]

Meanwhile Gesner had migrated to Göttingen to fill the University Chair denied him at Leipzig. He was succeeded by Johann August Ernesti,[5] who, since Petzold's death in 1731, had filled the position of Conrector. Of Thuringian stock, twenty-two years Bach's junior, he found himself Rector at the early age of twenty-seven. Distinguished as a theologian, philologist, and classicist, he represented a younger generation than his predecessor, and expressed a new outlook on education and culture. It aimed at releasing the schools and universities from the standards of the age in which they originated, from the classical trammels of the Renaissance, and the theological bonds of the Reformation, preferring their progressive secularization and modernization as educational agencies.[6] It challenged the tradition that the peculiar function of Stadt-Schulen, such as St. Thomas's, was to provide the musical apparatus of church worship, regarding that obligation as an impediment to a fuller and more practical culture. Bach already had met this spirit in 1729, over the vacant school places, and in Ernesti encountered it in so challenging a form, that

---

meine finstre Sinnen' (No. 47) of the Oratorio. The unnatural accent on 'Durch *die*' in the opening phrase suffices to show that the Oratorio's is the original text.
[1] B.-J. 1918, p. 137. Cf. Schering, p. 270.
[2] Augustus was born on 7 Oct. (O.S.) 1696.   [3] B.C.T., p. 609.
[4] B.-J. 1913, pp. 86, 88; Sp. ii. 824.   [5] Illus. No. 66.
[6] Cf. Fr. Paulsen, *German Education Past and Present*, tr. T. Lorenz, p. 95.

the harmony hitherto existing between Rector and Cantor was completely broken. Johann Friedrich Köhler [1] reveals the unhappy consequences. Ernesti lost no opportunity of publishing his opinion that music received prominence in the curriculum to which it was not entitled. 'So, you mean to be a pot-house fiddler,' [2] he would say to youths found practising an instrument in an idle hour. Bach, on his side, goaded to an antagonism as extreme, displayed his animosity towards those of his scholars who treated music negligently. The fires of controversy were laid, an outbreak imminent.

Ernesti's relations with Bach were not at first uncordial. He stood godfather to his son Johann August Abraham on 5 November 1733, and to Johann Christian, the 'English Bach', on 7 September 1735. [3] His installation as Rector on 18 November 1734 [4] was marked (21 November) by the performance of a 'Carmen' or cantata, 'Thomana sass annoch betrübt', a 'freudiger Willkomm' to which Bach contributed the music. The cost of 200 copies of its libretto was debited by Breitkopf to 'H. Landvogt auf der Thomas-Schule', [5] who can be identified with Johann August Landvoigt, the son of a Leipzig gardener, a senior *alumnus* in his twentieth year. [6] He may have been the author of the libretto, which offered at once a valediction to Gesner and a welcome to his successor. [7] No trace of Bach's score exists, but the metrical build of the Aria 'Himmel! und wie lange noch!' suggests that its music served later for the alto Aria 'Hochgelobter Gottes-Sohn' in the Easter Cantata 'Bleib' bei uns' (1736). Meanwhile, the early months of Ernesti's Rectorate passed without an open breach. Bach completed the Mass in B minor, [8] issued Part II of the *Clavierübung* (1735), [9] and acted as musical editor of Schemelli's *Musicalisches Gesangbuch* (1736), enriching it with matchless harmonies and some of his divinest melodies. [10] At Easter 1735 he found a new and

---

[1] *Supra*, p. 207, note 2.
[2] 'Bierfiedler'. For this class of unofficial and unprivileged musician see Schering, p. 286.   [3] Sp. ii. 955.
[4] Bi. ii. 233.   [5] B.-J. 1913, p. 86.   [6] Cf. B.-J. 1907, p. 70.
[7] Johann Heinrich Winckler, who had written the libretto for the opening of the Thomasschule in 1732, may also have provided one on this occasion. In 1732 not he but Gesner was debited with the cost of printing. Cf. B.-J. 1913, p. 74.
[8] The addition of the *Credo*, &c., converted the original Lutheran Missa into a complete Mass in the Roman use. Bach's motives in doing so are discussed in the present writer's *Bach: The Mass in B minor* (O.U.P. 1924).
[9] There is some evidence that he collaborated in Feb. 1735 with Balthasar Hoffmann of Merseburg in the cantata 'Schliesst die Gruft! ihr Trauerglocken'. Cf. B.C.T., p. 613; B.-J. 1913, p. 93.
[10] See Max Seiffert's *Seb. Bachs Gesänge zu G. Chr. Schemellis Musicalischem Gesangbuch* (1925), and C. S. Terry's *Bach's Original Hymn-Tunes* (1922).

welcome librettist in Frau Marianne von Ziegler, widow of an officer, whose literary deftness and sincerity afforded him pleasure and inspiration.[1] In the same period, perhaps, he visited Cöthen to inspect the enlarged organ of the St. Agnuskirche.[2] His second son Carl Philipp Emanuel already (1734) had left the parental roof-tree for Frankfurt, and in June 1735 he had the gratification of securing an appointment for his third son, Johann Gottfried Bernhard, in the city in which he spent the first year of his married life. The organistship of the Marienkirche at Mühlhausen was recently vacant through the death (6 April 1735) of Johann Gottfried Hetzehen, one of an old family of Mühlhausen musicians.[3] Probably Bach had not lost touch with the town, and his early association with it advanced the candidature of his son. On 2 May he wrote to Tobias Rothschier, 'Senior' of its governing Council:

Distinguished and learned gentlemen, worshipful Senior and esteemed Patron,
   It has just come to my knowledge that Herr Hetzehen, your town's organist, is dead, and that his post has not to this *datum* been filled. My youngest[4] son Johann Gottfried Bernhard Bach has for some time past shown himself so *habil* in *Music* that I hold him fully competent to enter for the vacancy. I therefore, with all deference and submission, beg your Worship to accord him your influential *intercession* for the position he aspires to, and to gratify my hopes by making my boy successful. You will in that case give me renewed opportunity to assure you, that for this, as for your former *faveur*, I am with unaltered regard your Worships', and in particular your most worshipful Senior's,
                                    Most obedient servant,
                                         Joh. Sebast. Bach,
                                    formerly organist of the Divi
                                    Blasiikirche, Mühlhausen.
Leipzig, 2 May 1735.
   To the distinguished and learned Herr Tobias Rothschier, member of the faculty of lawyers and most excellent Senior of the worshipful Council of Mühlhausen, at Mühlhausen.[5]

   Bach communicated also with the ruling Bürgermeister, Christian Petri, employing as his intermediary a member of the Hagedorn family, with which he was intimate at Mühlhausen.[6] A favourable response is indicated by the following letter:[7]

Your Magnificence, most noble, distinguished, and learned Bürgermeister, Senior, and gracious Patron,
   Herr Hagedorn's intimation of your gracious readiness once more to accord to an old and faithful servant a favour humbly requested obliges

[1] Her earliest libretto set by Bach was sung on the Third Sunday after Easter 1736 ('Ihr werdet weinen'). But cf. Sp. ii. 551.
[2] B.-J. 1925, p. 95.   [3] Thiele, p. 71.   [4] *i.e.* of his first marriage
[5] Mühlhäuser Stadtarchiv: Organista D. Blasii 1609–77, S. 47.
[6] *Supra*, p. 84.   [7] Mühlhäuser Stadtarchiv S. 65.

me forthwith to express to your Magnificence my most respectful thanks. It will be the dutiful pleasure of myself and my son to wait upon you personally to declare by word of mouth our respectful *obligation*, and at the same time to offer a small *specimen* of my son's musical *profectus*. We await your Magnificence's gracious directions and *ordre* to my son to present himself for the necessary test.

With profoundest *respect* and greeting I remain
Your Magnificence's most humble and obliged servant,
Johann Sebastian Bach.

Leipzig, 21 May 1735.

To his Magnificence the most noble, distinguished, and learned Herr Christian Petri, Bürgermeister and Senior, my most esteemed Patron, Mühlhausen. Franco p. tout.

Bach's paternal activity was rewarded. Entering comparatively late into the competition, Bernhard found rivals in the field, one of whom, Johann Nikolaus Götze, a native of Mühlhausen, Hetzehen's deputy during his last illness, was strongly supported in the congregational committee with which the nomination lay. It met on 21 May, and two days later added Bernhard's name to the roll of candidates. Götze's backers, declaring a contest unnecessary, demanded his appointment outright. Bach's correspondent, Bürgermeister Petri, however, opposed their intention to exclude the non-local musicians, upholding their right to be heard 'at their own charges'; he particularly insisted that young Bach should perform his Probe along with the other 'Auswärtige'. Early in June, accompanied by his father, Bernhard arrived, fulfilled the tests, and on the 16th of the month received the appointment. He held it for but a short time.[1]

The departure of his three talented sons left a void in Bach's household. They had not only participated in the family concerts it delighted him to direct, but lightened the drudgery of his official duty by copying the parts for his singers and players. Moreover, he was simultaneously bereft of his most dependable singers: Christian Friedrich Schemelli, afterwards Cantor at Zeitz, with whose father Bach collaborated in 1736, left the school in 1734; Johann Ludwig Dietel, afterwards Cantor at Falkenhain, followed in 1735; Johann Ludwig Krebs, Bach's favourite pupil, departed in the same year.[2] Among other seniors approaching the close of their schooldays was Gottfried Theodor Krause, a young man of twenty-two, whose father was Cantor at Herzberg, and whose younger brother had recently (1734) entered the school.[3]

---

[1] For his Mühlhausen career cf. *Mühlhäuser Geschichtsblätter*, Jhrg. XXI (1920–21), p. 71.
[2] The list of *alumni* is in B.-J. 1907, pp. 69–70. Bach's testimonial to Krebs, dated 24 August 1735, is in Sp. ii. 722; Bi. iv. 175. For Krebs, see B.-J. 1930, pp. 100–29.

He was proceeding to the University, and at the School Speeches on 20 April 1736 was selected by Ernesti as one of 'sex bonae spei adolescentes de commodis ex historia philosophica capiendis dicere jussi'.[1] Bach had a high opinion of him, and, exercising the power vested in him by the *Schulordnung* of 1723,[2] had made him head Prefect. His promotion had unforeseen consequences: it involved Bach in an acrimonious controversy with Ernesti, dislocated the discipline of the school, and was not composed for two years.

Krause unfolds the preliminaries of the battle in a letter addressed to the civic Council on 26 July 1736.[3] As senior Prefect he had received Bach's 'ernstlicher Befehl' to control the behaviour of 'die unter mir stehenden Kleinen', with power, should disorder show itself in church, to punish offenders in the Cantor's absence ('sie durch eine mir anständige Straffe ihres Amtes und Pflichten zu erinnern'). Finding admonition inadequate to maintain order, and that his charges' behaviour in church grew worse ('die üble und ungebührliche Aufführung dieser kleinen Schüler in denen Kirchen und bey anderen heiligen Verrichtungen immer mehr und mehr zunahm'), Krause threatened the more drastic measures sanctioned by Bach's instructions ('den mir von dem H. Cantore gegebenen Befehl'), particularly as the congregation was showing resentment at the choir's bad behaviour. Eventually its conduct at a wedding was so atrocious that he determined 'ein Exempel der allergeringsten und beynahe kindischen Straffe zu geben'. Punishment was resisted by lads grown bold under a milder rule, with the result that Krause laid on harder with the cane than was his intention ('die dadurch auffgebrachte Hitze meiner Jugend ihnen einen etwas härtere Straffe verursachet'). One of his victims alleged such severity that his back was cut and bleeding, though the school hairdresser and his assistant could discover no sign ('nicht die geringste Spur') of laceration. The victim, however, carried his tale to Ernesti, who intemperately ordered Krause himself to receive a thrashing before the whole school, a vindictive sentence on a young man of twenty-two, which, Krause alleged,

[1] 'Eandem ob causam, cum a quibusdam disciplinae nostrae alumnis, a nobis discessuris, pro more, oratiunculae habendae essent, ipsos de commodis ex historia philosophica capiendis dicere jussi. Dicent igitur hi:
  Gottfridus Theodorus Krause, Herzbergensis.
  Ioannes Andreas Koepping, Grosbothena-Misnicus.
  Christian. Gottfridus Hofmann, Nebra-Thuringus.
  Ioannes Augustus Landvoigt, Lipsiensis.
  David Dieze, Loebena-Misnicus.
  Theophilus Iacobus Hausius, Goelchauiensis-Misnicus.'
(Ernesti's *Schulprogramm* (1736), p. 15.)
[2] Cap. XIV, § 4.
[3] The letter is preserved in the Leipziger Rathsacten, Fasc. II, Sign. VIII, B. 6.

was to be regarded not so much as an act of correction as an attempt to inflict public ignominy ('mehr vor eine öffentliche Prostitution, als vor eine Verweisung meines Fehlers anzusehen war'). Krause implored Ernesti to spare him so degrading a punishment, but vainly: the Rector was adamant, indifferent even to the pleading of Bach, who took the blame on his own shoulders. Krause then begged permission to leave the school and demanded the customary certificate (Dimission). As Ernesti refused to grant it, Krause absconded to avoid a public caning ('eine so schimpffliche und den Fehler soweit übersteigende Straffe'). He quoted one of his masters, who declared that his school conduct had hitherto been exemplary, and that he had never before been punished ('ausser diesem einzigen Fehler, nichts begangen habe, worüber ich zu einiger Straffe hätte müssen gezogen werden'). But, implacable to the last, Ernesti refused Krause permission to remove his belongings ('meinen wenigen Hausrath'), and impounded a sum of thirty thalers ('die bisshero gesammlete Caution') standing to his account in the school ledger.

If Krause's statement is trustworthy, and it rings true, he was punished for exceeding the powers conferred upon Prefects under Cap. XIV, para. 4, of the *Schulordnung* of 1723, which, though it authorized them to maintain discipline in the Cantor's absence, did not license them to punish. Krause, whose appeal drew from the Council (31 July 1736) an order for the restitution of his 'Caution',[1] pleaded the Cantor's authority to justify his action, and so exposed the grounds of Ernesti's vindictiveness: Bach had asserted disciplinary powers which challenged the Rector's, and so brought a larger issue to the arena. Ernesti proceeded to deal with it as intemperately as he had treated Krause. At the period of Krause's absconding the second *Praefectus Chori* happened to bear the same name, Johann Gottl. Krause, son of the miller at Grossdeuben, and nine months older than his namesake.[2] His character was bad, and had been discussed by Bach and Ernesti in November 1735, when the two, returning from the wedding of

[1] 'Decr. E. E. Hochweiser Rath dieser Stadt verordnet hiermit, Dass Gottfr. Th. Kraussen gewesenen ersten Präfecto der hiesigen Thomas-Schule die Demselben zuständige und bisshero gesammlete Caution, ob es gleich sonst bey der hierüber ehemahlen erteilten Verordnung sein Bewenden habe, gestellten Sachen nach und wegen derer dabey vorwaltenden Umbstände abgefolget werden sollen.
Stadt-Decret beygedrückten (*sic*) uhrkundlich mit dem gewöhnlichen Sign. Leipzig, den 31 Juli 1736.
Vorstehende Verordnung ist dem Rectori auf der Thomas-Schule H. M. Ernesti und auch dem Voigt Joh. Mangolden zugestellet worden. Actum Leipzig d. 8 Aug. 1736. Christian Ludewig Mierisch, Oberstadtschr.' (Leipz. Rathsacten, Fasc. II, Sign. VIII, B. 6.)   [2] Cf. B.-J. 1907, p. 70.

Q

their colleague, the Tertius Abraham Krügel, were reminded of the approaching appointment of Prefects at Christmas. Among those whose seniority demanded consideration of their claims was the elder Krause. Bach strongly objected to him, and described him tersely as 'a dissolute fellow' ('ein liederlicher Hund'). Ernesti admitted that his character was not exemplary and that he was in debt, but was unwilling to pass him over, provided Bach was satisfied regarding his musical competence. As Bach was unwilling to declare him inefficient, Krause was appointed third Prefect at Christmas 1735, and at the time of his namesake's departure from the school was next below him in authority.[1]

Krause's rapid elevation to the second Prefectship had come about through the untimely resignation of Maximilian Nagel,[2] the first Prefect, at New Year 1736, and his performance of the duties of that responsible post was so inefficient[3] that Bach now opposed his appointment as first Prefect by Ernesti, as an infringement of his own prerogative, and on the ground that Krause lacked the necessary musical ability.[4] Satisfied that his position was impregnable on both points, Bach girded himself for battle. On 10 July 1736 he sent the second Prefect, Samuel Kittler,[5] to Ernesti, to intimate his appointment in Krause's room consequent on Krause's degradation to the second place, 'indem er [Bach] ihn nicht tüchtig zur ersten Praefectur befände'. Krause demanded the reasons for his supersession and was referred to Bach, whose temper mastered his discretion. Gleefully, and probably with some exaggeration of the actual words, Krause returned to Ernesti, to report that Bach had degraded him in order to demonstrate that the power of appointment was solely in the Cantor's hands. In fact, it was, though subject to the approval of the Vorsteher of the school,[6] whom Bach apparently had neglected to consult. That office was now held by deputy-Bürgermeister Christian Ludwig Stieglitz,[7] whom Ernesti two days later (12 July)

---

[1] These facts are drawn from Ernesti's letter dated 13 Sept. 1736, in Sp. ii. 904 and Bi. iv. 192.
[2] He belonged to Nürnberg, where his father was Cantor. He was twenty-two years old and left the school in 1736. Cf. B.-J. 1907, p. 70.
[3] Cf. Bach's letter of 15 Aug. *infra*.
[4] Ernesti (see his letter of 17 Aug. in Sp. ii. 898 and Bi. iv. 184) declares that Krause's record was good as third and second Prefect. Bach's opinion is expressed in his letters, and in regard to Krause's abilities is to be preferred.
[5] Kittler was the son of the smith at Belgern and was born 26 Nov. 1715. Cf. B.-J. 1907, p. 70.
[6] Cap. XIV, par. 4, of the *Schulordnung* of 1723 prescribed: 'Die vier Praefecti Chororum, welche der Cantor jährlich um Weynachten, jedoch mit Vorbewust und Genehmhaltung des Herrn Vorstehers, zu erwehlen hat.'
[7] D.J.F.L., p. 87.

informed of the circumstances. Finding Stieglitz willing to support him, Ernesti invited Bach to discuss the situation, and the mediation of the Conrector [1] arranged an amicable settlement: Bach undertook to reinstate Krause at the first singing practice ('er versprach den abgesetzten Praefectum in der ersten Singstunde wieder einzusetzen'), but for reasons not apparent did not do so. Upon Ernesti reminding him of his promise, Bach pleaded absence, but on his return to Leipzig at the end of the month still took no action. After waiting for ten days, Ernesti wrote to him (11 August) to threaten, that unless Krause was instantly restored he would himself reinstate him next morning. Faced with this ultimatum, Bach sat down to lay the circumstances before the Council: [2]

Magnifici, most noble, distinguished, worshipful, and learned gentlemen and Patrons,

I beg your Magnificences to allow me to inform you, that whereas your honourable Council's *Ordnung der Schule zu S. Thomae* declares it to be the Cantor's prerogative to select as Prefects those scholars whom he regards as fit and competent, having regard in their *election* to their possessing good and telling voices, and also to the circumstance (especially important in the case of the first Prefect), that in the Cantor's absence, or if he is ill, they must be competent to direct the *chorus musicus*, this prerogative has been exercised by successive Cantors until now without concurrence on the part of the Rectors. But the present Rector, Herr Johann August Ernesti, without consulting me and in spite of my objections, lately assumed the power of appointment himself,[3] promoted second Prefect Krause to be Prefect of the first Choir, and, notwithstanding my friendly remonstrations, refuses to withdraw. Since his action contravenes the *Ordnung*, is contrary to traditional usage, stands to the *prejudiz* of my *successores*, and is hurtful to the interests of the *chorus musicus*, I cannot allow it to pass unchallenged, and therefore respectfully petition your Worships to correct an irregular action that affects my *officium*. Knowing your benevolence and care for the welfare of the Thomasschule, and seeing that the Rector's presumptuous claim to appoint the Prefects must cause *disharmonie* and be detrimental to the scholars, I beg you to instruct Rector Ernesti to act for the future in accordance with the usages and practice of the school, namely, to leave the appointment of the Prefects in my hands, thereby affording your esteemed support to my *officium*. Counting on your Magnificences' distinguished countenance,

I remain with profound *respect*, etc.,

Joh. Sebast. Bach.

Leipzig, 12 August 1736.

To their Magnificences the most noble, distinguished, worshipful, and learned Bürgermeister and members of the eminent Leipzig Council, my distinguished masters and Patrons.

[1] Siegmund Friedrich Dressig.
[2] Leipzig. Stadtarchiv: Rathsacta, Schule zu S. Thomae, VII, B. 69, 70.
[3] Cap. XIV, par. 1 of the *Schulordnung* gave the first prefectship to 'der erste Alumnus', if he was competent in music.

Before the letter was in the hands of those to whom it was addressed, Ernesti carried the controversy to another degree of aggravation: fulfilling his threat, on Sunday, 12 August (Trinity XI), he reinstated Krause. At an early hour Bach called on Superintendent Deyling to put the matter before him. Returning to the Thomaskirche, his indignation boiled over at the sight of Krause functioning as Prefect with the *chorus primus*. Hastily ascending to the choir, he turned Krause out of the gallery and put up Kittler, whom he had brought from the Nikolaikirche, to conduct the hymns. The unedifying commotion in the gallery was observed from the nave, and Ernesti left the church to discover whether Bach was acting, as he was understood to allege, under higher authority. Deyling disavowed him, and so Ernesti informed Bach, who answered hotly: he would not budge an inch from his course, cost what it might ('er sich daran durchaus nicht kehre, es möchte kosten was es wolle'). A short hour intervened between Hauptgottesdienst and afternoon Vespers. Ernesti used it to give positive orders to Krause and Kittler to resume their former situations, at the same time forbidding the choir, under penalties, to sing under any one whom Bach might substitute for Krause.[1] His orders resulted in a disorderly scuffle at Vespers in the Nikolaikirche. Finding Krause again on duty with the first choir and defiant, Bach drove him out of the gallery ('hat er [ihn] mit grossen Schreyen und Lermen von dem Chor gejagt'). Ernesti's threats had so awed the choir, however, that none would act in his place, and Bach was compelled to invite his old pupil Krebs, who was present, to conduct the singing.[2] Kittler also felt the Cantor's wrath: as Inspector for the week, Bach took his evening meal with the school, and, when Kittler entered the room, drove him from the table ('vom Tische gejagt') for having obeyed the Rector.[3]

The quarrels of their seniors, so publicly advertised, no doubt afforded entertainment to the foundationers. Bach spent the night among them in the Inspector's quarters, and if reflection failed to mitigate his sense of the indignity offered him, it prompted him to state his grievance temperately in a further letter to the Council:[4]

---

[1] The fact appears from Bach's letter of 13 Aug.
[2] So Bach states in his letter of 13 Aug. Ernesti does not mention Krebs, but states that Bach 'dem *alumno* Claus befohlen, an statt des Praefecti zu singen', and that Claus apologized to him after the service for having disobeyed him. Johann Augustus Claus left the school in 1739 (B.-J. 1907, p. 70).
[3] Ernesti's letter of 17 Aug.
[4] Leipzig. Stadtarchiv: Rathsacta, Schule zu S. Thomae, VII, B. 69, 70.

Magnifici, most noble, distinguished, worshipful, and learned gentlemen and Patrons,

Only yesterday I addressed to your Magnificences a respectful *Memorial,* invoking your distinguished protection in regard to Herr Rector Ernesti's reprehensible attempt to appropriate my function, as Director of the *chorus musicus* and Cantor of the Thomasschule, in the appointment of Prefects. And now I find myself obliged to acquaint your Magnificences with the circumstance, that, although Herr Ernesti was informed that I had lodged a complaint with you and awaited your ruling, none the less, with scant *respect* to your honourable body, he yesterday ordered the *alumni,* under threat of *relegation* and *castigation,* that none should conduct the customary motet in Krause's place, or sing under any other conductor than Krause, whom I stated in my yesterday's *Memorial* to be incompetent to direct the *chorus musicus,* but whom none the less he wishes to force on me as first Prefect. Consequently, to my deep *despect* and *prostitution,* for fear of punishment not a single scholar would lead the singing, still less conduct the afternoon motet in the Nikolaikirche, and the *sacra* would have been seriously interrupted had not Krebs, a former Thomaner, undertaken at my request to do so instead of an *alumnus.* Thus, besides infringing my traditional right to appoint the Prefects, as I pointed out in my *Memorial,* the Rector *in modo procedendi* has seriously weakened, if indeed he has not wholly undermined, my authority over the scholars in the churches under my charge, and in the direction of the music for which I am responsible, authority conferred upon me by your honourable Council when I entered upon my *officium.* If high-handed action such as this is repeated, the *sacra* are in danger of interruption, the music sung in church will be injuriously affected, and the *alumneum* must deteriorate to such a degree that it may take years to recover its former efficiency. *Vi officii* I cannot remain silent, and there is *periculum in mora.* Wherefore most respectfully and earnestly I again beg your Magnificences strictly to admonish the Rector to cease to impede me in my duties, nor by threats of punishment to prevent the *alumni* from giving me the *obedience* due to me, but, as his duty is, to consider the welfare, rather than act to the disadvantage, of the school and *chorus musicus.* Counting on your gracious indulgence and *protection* in my *officium,* I remain with deepest *respect,*

Your Magnificences' most obedient servant,
Johann Sebastian Bach.

Leipzig, 13 August 1736.
To their Magnificences [as above].

Bach preferred to challenge Ernesti's action on the ground of constitutional practice and as an infringement of the Council's regulations. But the controversy, bruited abroad, threatened to turn upon Krause's ability and the justice of Bach's treatment of him. Indeed, Ernesti, whom Bach accused of partiality for the young man, roundly asserted his competence, adventurously challenging an expert's opinion to the contrary. Bach therefore deemed it necessary to acquaint the Council more fully with the matter. On 15 August he wrote the following addendum to his letter of 13 August:[1]

[1] Leipzig. Stadtarchiv: Rathsacta, Schule zu S. Thomae, VII B. 69, 70.

Fol. 5 P[ro] M[emoria].

The full and authentic history of *alumnus* Krause, and of the Rector's attempt to force him on me as first *praefectus*, is as follows:

A year ago Krause was in such bad odour, by reason of his dissolute habits and consequent debts, that the school authorities, after considering the circumstances, informed him that he merited expulsion for his bad behaviour, but that in consideration of his necessitous state (he admitted debts to the extent of twenty thalers), and provided he promised amendment, he would be permitted to remain another quarter, at the end of which he would be expelled, or not, according to his conduct in the interval. The Rector, who has always shown a marked predilection for Krause, asked me in the course of conversation [1] to make him Prefect, pointing out, when I objected that he was not competent, that Krause, as Prefect, would have a chance of getting out of debt, and so of removing from the school a load of *blame* that must otherwise go on increasing. He added, that Krause's schooldays were nearing their end, and that by the means suggested we should be able to get out of the difficulty with a good *manier*. I did not wish to disoblige the Rector, and so made Krause Prefect for the Neukirche (whose choir sings only hymns and motets; they have nothing to do with *Concert Musique*,[2] with which the organist alone is concerned): for, I reflected, his school period had only one more year to run, so that the likelihood of his having to direct the first or second choirs was remote. As it chanced, at last New Year's Currenden, Nagel of Nürnberg,[3] the *praefectus Chori I*, found his health did not permit him to continue in office, and so it became necessary to rearrange the Prefectships out of the usual season. Thus the second *praefectus* took Nagel's place and, consequently, Krause was promoted to the second choir. In that position he made frequent mistakes in beating time, as I was told by the Conrector, who is Inspector of the second choir, and when I made personal inquiries, members of the choir themselves told me that he could not beat time correctly. I tested his ability myself at a practice not long ago, when I found that he could not beat even the two ordinary measures accurately, namely, equal or $\frac{1}{4}$ time, and unequal or $\frac{3}{4}$ time, but turned $\frac{1}{4}$ into $\frac{3}{4}$ and *vice versa*, as the *alumni* can testify. It will therefore be understood, that, having convinced myself of his incompetence, I could not possibly accept Krause as first Prefect, for the music the first choir has to perform, to a large extent of my own composition, is infinitely more difficult and intricate than that rendered by the second, which sings figural music only at festival times, when I am careful to select works within its ability. I could give other grounds for my opinion of Krause's incompetence, but, I imagine, I have said enough to show the reasonableness of my complaint to your worshipful Council, and the justice of my call for immediate redress.

Joh. Seb. Bach.

Leipzig, 15 August 1736.

Ernesti as yet had made no formal statement of his version of the dispute. On 17 August he did so in a lengthy letter,[4] whose querulous and carping tone compares unfavourably with Bach's

[1] On the occasion of Krügel's wedding.   [2] *i.e.* figural music, cantatas, &c.
[3] *Supra*, p. 226.   [4] Sp. ii. 897; Bi. iv. 182.

concise and ingenuous representation of the facts. He challenged the *Schulordnung* on which Bach relied, insisted that the appointment of Prefects had never been made on the Cantor's sole authority and without the Rector's concurrence, quoting Cap. XIII, para. 8, of the *Ordnung* in proof of his contention. That clause, while it declared the Rector's assent necessary to the Cantor's grouping of the four choirs, explicitly charged the latter to appoint the Prefects, subject to his submission of their names to the Vorsteher, an obligation which, probably with truth, Ernesti declared Bach systematically to have disregarded. Ernesti insisted, moreover, that the Prefects' disciplinary powers emanated solely from himself, that the control of them was his prerogative, and that he was better qualified by opportunities of observation to know them efficient or the reverse. He defended his appointment of Krause as first Prefect on the ground, directly contradicted by Bach, that he had given satisfaction as second and third Prefect, and also because the *Schulordnung* (Cap. XIV, para. 1) decisively allotted the first Prefectship to the senior *alumnus*, unless he was deficient in musical ability. As to the two Krauses, Ernesti named, as his explanation of the misfortunes that had befallen them, the Cantor's inadequate fulfilment of the duties of his position, insinuating that Gottfried Theodor Krause would not have got into trouble if Bach had been in his place with the choir at the unfortunate wedding. He therefore begged the Council to admonish the Cantor to attend to his duties more closely ('dass er ... überhaupt sein Amt mit mehrern Fleiss abwarten möge'), and to uphold his own authority in the school, since a Rector without authority 'nicht allein ein unnützer, sondern auch schädlicher Mann ist'.

Both sides had made their appeal to the Council, which displayed no eagerness to pronounce judgement and compose the quarrel. Consequently, the unedifying scenes of the previous Sunday were repeated on 19 August (Trinity XII) and drew from Bach another letter of expostulation: [1]

Magnifici, most noble, distinguished, worshipful, and learned gentlemen and Patrons,

Your Magnificences will be graciously pleased to remember that a week ago I was obliged to bring to your notice the *desordres* during divine service caused by the action of Herr Ernesti, Rector of the Thomasschule. Similar disturbances happened again to-day, both morning and afternoon. I was obliged to conduct the motet myself, and afterwards to get a *studiosus* [2] to direct the singing, to prevent a commotion and *turbatio sacrorum*. Unless your Worships, my distinguished Patrons, hasten to accord me

---

[1] Leipzig. Stadtarchiv: Rathsacta, Schule zu S. Thomae, VII, B. 69, 70.
[2] *i.e.* a student at the University, probably Krebs.

your protection, matters will get worse and my authority over my singers go altogether. In present circumstances I cannot accept responsibility for the consequences if the disorders, which may prove *irreparable*, occur again. Therefore I am constrained most respectfully to beg your Magnificences at once to restrain the Rector, and, with your accustomed zeal for the common weal, to expedite the judgement I have prayed you to pronounce, thereby preventing an otherwise probable repetition of these scandalous scenes in church, disorders in school, the diminution of my authority as Cantor over the scholars, and other serious consequences.

I remain your Magnificences' most humble
Johann Sebastian Bach.

Leipzig, 19 August 1736.
To their Magnificences [as above].

The Council still withheld judgement, and Ernesti, perhaps at its invitation, replied on 13 September to Bach's damaging exposure of Krause's incompetence.[1] He did not scruple to insinuate that Bach's word was unreliable and his favour purchasable by bribery.[2] He dared to contradict Bach's statement that the first Prefect handled more difficult music than the second, and adduced the irrelevant instance of Nagel, who, though he was a violinist and not a singer, had satisfied Bach as first Prefect. He denied that he had originally asked for Krause's appointment as Prefect, and declared that the faults in time-beating which Bach instanced were of remote occurrence. As no independent authority exists to which the conflicting statements of Rector and Cantor can be referred, judgement must be pronounced on the correspondence, and, upon it, the verdict goes unhesitatingly to Bach: Ernesti's letters are tinged with pettiness and spite, and his venturesome contradiction of Bach on his own subject suggests that he was as uninstructed in it as he was generally self-sufficient and dogmatic.

Meanwhile, paternal anxiety increased Bach's load of care. It is a curious circumstance, that one who epitomized the integrity of his ancestry should have begotten two unsteady sons. The tragedy of his firstborn Wilhelm Friedemann was mercifully hidden from him, but the unstable courses of Gottfried Bernhard gave him anxiety till the young man's premature death in 1739. Bernhard had been little more than a year at Mühlhausen when he invited his father's assistance to procure him the organistship of the Jakobi- or Marktkirche at Sangerhausen, vacant in October 1736. Ignorant that Bernhard's debts were driving him from

[1] The letter is in Sp. ii. 904; Bi. iv. 192.
[2] 'Allein, gleichwie ich schon andere Proben anführen könnte, dass man sich auf seine *testimonia* hierinne nicht allezeit verlassen kann, und wohl eher ein alter *Species* Thaler einen Discantisten gemacht, der so wenig einer gewesen, als ich bin ...' As to Bach's *species* thalers, see *infra*, p. 270.

Mühlhausen, Bach put himself into communication with Johann Friedrich Klemm, a member of the Sangerhausen Council, an old acquaintance, whose father he had known at Leipzig:[1]

Distinguished and honourable Sir,

My *amitié* of many years standing with your deceased father emboldens me to hope that your Honour will continue it. Confident of your readiness to do so, I take the liberty of addressing you, for I understand that the organist of the Jakobikirche is dead, and so venture to solicit your Honour's *patrocinium* for a *subjectum* very near to me, and also to ask for information regarding the salary of the vacant post. Trusting that my request and the accompanying *annexum* may be favourably entertained, I remain, always with devoted gratitude,

Your Honour's obedient servant,
J. S. Bach.

Leipzig, 30 October 1736.

To Herr Klemm, a worthy member of the respected and worshipful Council of the town of Sangerhausen, my much esteemed Patron, at Sangerhausen.

Klemm declared his readiness to be of service, and three weeks later Bach wrote again:

Distinguished and honoured Sir,

Your favourable entertainment of the request I recently made to your Honour is apparent in every line of your condescending reply, and is the less surprising because I have in memory your auspicious condescension on an earlier occasion. You may rest assured that I shall let no opportunity pass to prove my lively regard. I should have expressed my acknowledgement by return of post, had I not thought to receive the further information your Honour promised to furnish. Your manifold occupations, no doubt, have prevented you from doing what you proposed, but my duty prompts me no longer to delay my reply.

I gather that, in consequence of your Honour's influential *recommendation* and *intercession* on behalf of the *subjectum* I have *in mente*, he will be called on to undergo his Probe with other candidates. I need therefore hesitate no longer to inform your Honour in secrecy that the *subjectum* in question is one of my sons. I have too much *confidence* in your Honour and your worshipful colleagues to fear that any candidate supported by you will be ill paid, even though you are at present unable to declare the amount of the salary. So, in God's good providence it may come about that you will be able to fulfil on behalf of a son of mine the goodwill you showed to my unworthy self some thirty years ago, when, too, the post of figural organist was vacant. Under the presidency of the late Bürgermeister Vollrath,[2] I then obtained the vote, though the higher powers advanced another candidate, and for that *raison* I had to abandon my good fortune.[3] Your Honour will not take it amiss that I refer to my *fata* on that occasion, for my *entrée* in this present correspondence has received so gracious an

---

[1] Bach's letters to the Klemm family are printed in Fr. Schmidt's article in 'Zeitschrift der I.M.G.', Jhrg. III (1902), pp. 351–60. Cf. 'Mühlhäuser Geschichtsblätter', Jhrg. XXI (1920–1), pp. 78–9. They are in the Preuss. Staatsbibliothek, Berlin, and were bought from the Sangerhausen archives for 3,000 marks in 1919.
[2] Johann Laurentius Vollrath, *d.* 7 June 1714.   [3] Cf. *supra*, p. 56.

ingress that I am fain to see the finger of God's providence in it. I beg your Honour to continue your gracious patronage to me and my family, and to be assured that, as the Most High is your rewarder, so with my family I shall remain always

Your obedient servant,

Leipzig, 18 Nov. 1736.　　　　　　　　　　　　Joh. Seb. Bach.

Three other candidates had entered the field when Gottfried Bernhard passed his *Probe* on 13 January 1737. He showed himself their superior, and on the following day received the appointment, subject to the production of testimonials of good conduct from Mühlhausen, to whose authorities (23 February 1737) he intimated his desire to leave their employment. The testimonials were forthcoming in March, and on 4 April 1737 the Leipzig Consistorium ratified the appointment. Bernhard held it briefly and abandoned it in circumstances that wrung Bach's paternal heart-strings.

Bach's second letter to Klemm coincided with a belated event which promised to dissipate the vexations that surrounded him. On 19 November 1736 his appointment as 'Hof-Compositeur' received the Electoral signature and seal at Dresden.[1] More than three years had passed since Bach first solicited it, an interval in which, not infrequently, he had devoted his skill to the glorification of his sovereign. His failure to receive the distinction earlier has been attributed to Augustus's concentration on the Polish War. A more probable impediment was the fact that in 1733, and until the summer of 1736, Bach was Capellmeister 'von Haus aus' to the Court of Sachsen-Weissenfels: the Elector would naturally be indisposed to employ a musician already bound in service to a lesser sovereign. On that hypothesis, the death of Duke Christian of Sachsen-Weissenfels on 28 June 1736, and the conferring of Bach's Dresden appointment five months later, are clearly related, for on Duke Christian's death the Weissenfels Capelle was disbanded.[2] The patent of Bach's dignity was committed to

---

[1] '*Decret* vor Johann Sebastian Bach, als *Compositeur* bey der Königlichen Hof *Capelle*.

Demnach Ihro Königliche Majestät in Pohlen und Churfürstliche Durchlaucht zu Sachsen p. t. Johann Sebastian Bachen, auf dessen beschehenes allerunterthänigstes Ansuchen, und umb seiner guten Geschickligkeit willen, das *Praedicat* als *Compositeur* bey dero Hof *Capelle* allergnädigst ertheilet: Als ist demselben darüber gegenwärtiges *Decret*, unter Ihro Königlichen Majestät höchsteigenhändigen Unterschrifft und vorgedruckten Königlichen Insiegel ausgefertiget worden. So geschehen und geben zu

Dressden, den 19 Nov. 1736.　　　　　　　　　　　　　A. R.

(L.S.)

G. W. Mentzel　　　　　　　　　　　　　　　　　　Gr. Brühl.'

(Dresden. Staatsarchiv, Abth. XVI. No. 1507.) See p. 242, note 4, *infra*.

[2] Werner, p. 56.

Carl Freiherr von Kayserling,[1] Russian envoy to the Dresden Court, whose instrumentality in securing it may be supposed. An invalid suffering from chronic insomnia, he employed a clavicenist named Johann Gottlieb Goldberg, a pupil of Bach's in 1733 and onwards, whose duty it was to play to him when he was wakeful. Probably while Bach was involved in controversy with Ernesti, the Count commissioned him to compose soothing music to relieve the tedium of sleepless nights. Taking as his theme a Sarabande in G copied into his wife's 'Notenbuch' in 1725, Bach produced the Variations popularly known as Goldberg's, though the Count, who never tired of hearing them, claimed them as 'my Variations' and paid the composer the generous fee of 100 louis d'or for them.[2] Kayserling received Bach's patent on 28 November 1736,[3] and either summoned him to Dresden to receive it, or took advantage of his presence in the capital to hand it to him. On 1 December 1736, the 'Dresdner Nachrichten'[4] records, between the hours of two and four, Bach gave a recital on the new Silbermann organ in the Frauenkirche, when Kayserling and other 'Proceres' were present and listened 'mit besonderer Admiration' to a player whose 'grosse Geschicklichkeit im Componiren' had just been recognized by his sovereign.

The coveted appointment failed to fulfil immediately the purpose for which Bach originally craved it. His letters to the Leipzig Council remained unanswered, and, shortly before his visit to Dresden, he drafted a statement of his case against Ernesti for submission to the Consistorium, an intention which his Court appointment caused him to recall, anticipating more august intervention in his behalf. Therein he was disappointed. At Dresden, no doubt, he had opportunity to ventilate his grievance, but he returned to Leipzig regretfully convinced that he must fight his battle single-handed. The November memorandum, accordingly, was drawn from its pigeon-hole, redated (12 February 1737), and forwarded to the Consistorium:[5]

Magnifici, most noble, worthy, worshipful, and learned gentlemen and Patrons,
    Some little time ago, Herr Johann August Ernesti, Rector of the Thomasschule, in spite of my objections, presumed to force on me an incompetent *subjectum* as *praefectus* of the first Choir, which consists of *alumni* of the school. As I would not, indeed could not, accept him, Herr

---

[1] Sp. ii. 488.   [2] Forkel, p. 118.   [3] Sp. ii. 488.
[4] Quoted in Bi. ii. 236. Cf. Flade, p. 86; Falck, p. 18; B.-J. 1925, p. 96.
[5] Leipzig. Stadtarchiv: Rathsacta, Schule zu S. Thomae, VII, B. 69, 70. The document was originally dated between 10 and 30 Nov. 1736; the day of the month is not decipherable owing to the erasure of the original and the superimposition of the later date.

Ernesti, under threat of *relegation*, forbade any *alumnus* to lead or conduct the motet other than the *praefectus* whom he had arbitrarily appointed. The threat was so effectual, that on the following Sunday afternoon at Vespers not a single *alumnus* could be induced to lead the singing or conduct the motet, for fear of the threatened punishment, and, had I not induced a University *studiosus* [1] to act, the *sacra* would have been seriously disturbed.

The Rector's action not only seriously affects and prejudices my *officium*, but tends to lessen the scholars' *respect* for me and my *reputation* among them. For, in terms of the worshipful Council's *Ordnung*, Cap. XIV, para. 4, it is my prerogative to select the *praefecti chororum* without the Rector's concurrence, a custom till now regularly followed by myself and my *antecessores*. And it is a reasonable custom: for the *praefecti* lead the choirs on my behalf, since I cannot be in all the churches at the same hour. And seeing that the inspection and control of the first choir is my own particular province, I ought to know better than other people what qualities its Prefect should possess. The Rector's order forbidding the scholars to sing under any but the *praefectus* chosen by himself is highly unreasonable and injurious in its consequences: if obedience is not to be rendered to me *ratione* my own sphere, the worst results are bound to follow. It is to prevent the Rector's action having these evil consequences that I am moved to take action.

I therefore very respectfully beg your Magnificences to protect me in my *officium*, and to let Herr Ernesti understand that he must in future abstain from molesting me, refrain from choosing *praefecti* without my consent and knowledge, and not again instruct the choir to show me no *parition*. Furthermore, I earnestly invite you to direct the Herr Superintendent, or one of the clergy of the Thomaskirche, to take suitable steps to instruct the scholars again to show me the *respect* and obedience due to me, and so make it possible for me to fulfil the duties of my position.

I trust that my reasonable desire will procure your Magnificences' assistance and protection, and I remain, with all *respect*,

Your most obedient

Johann Sebastian Bach,

Compositeur to His Polish Majesty's Capelle

and *Director Chori Musici* here.

Leipzig, 12 February 1737.

To their Magnificences [etc.], the members of the worshipful Consistorium in Leipzig, my worthy masters and esteemed Patrons.

Unknown to Bach, a week before he redated his letter, the civic Council delivered a cautious judgement which he could not regard as satisfactory. Dated 6 February 1737, the document [2] was withheld from publication for two months; Ernesti received it on 6 April, Bach on 10 April, Deyling on 20 April. It upheld Bach's contention regarding the nomination of Prefects, and, logically, should have condemned Ernesti's appointment of Krause as *ultra vires*. It shrank, however, from direct censure of the Rector, and, taking advantage of the fact that Krause was leaving the school at Easter (1737), permitted him to retain his prefectship till then.

[1] Probably Krebs.   [2] Sp. ii. 906.

Easter Day fell on 21 April; the decision was purposely held back until Krause's elimination from the controversy removed the necessity to pronounce judgement on his character and relations with his superiors. Meanwhile, on 13 February 1737, in ignorance of the Council's finding, the Consistorium passed on Bach's complaint to it and to the Superintendent, inviting the former to attend to it without delay, 'dass beim öffentlichen Gottesdienst kein Hinderniss und Aufsehen verursachet werde'.[1]

Easter had barely passed before Bach was assailed from another quarter. There had recently appeared at Hamburg (5 March 1737) a periodical, 'Der critische Musicus', whose editor, Johann Adolph Scheibe, was a native of Leipzig, his father the builder of the Paulinerkirche and Johanniskirche organs, and himself an unsuccessful candidate for the Thomaskirche organistship in 1729, when Görner secured the appointment. Bach was one of the judges on that occasion, and so incurred Scheibe's ill-will. He was an effective writer, inordinately self-esteemed, but of moderate practical ability. His ill-natured criticism of Bach was notorious before he left Leipzig, and Spitta conjectures[2] that Bach used his opportunity in 'Phöbus und Pan' to call Scheibe, in the character of Midas, an ass and a fool:

> Empty heads and swollen, lacking wit or gumption,
> Rightly feel the fool's cap sticking on their crown.
> He who's never seen a ship,
> Takes the rudder in his grip,
> And saileth the ocean inexpert, will drown!

The ridicule rankled, and Scheibe, settled at Hamburg, devoted the sixth issue (14 May 1737) of his periodical to an attack upon Bach, who, though not actually named, was clearly indicated:[3]

Herr —— —— is distinctly the most conspicuous musician in ——. He is an exceptional master of the clavier and organ, and as yet has met

---

[1] Sp. ii. p. 908.

[2] *Ibid.*, p. 476. The hypothesis is somewhat weakened by the fact that on 4 April 1731 Bach wrote the following testimonial in Scheibe's behalf (Liliencron, p. 292): 'Da Vorzeiger dieses, Herr Johann Adolph Scheibe, *LL. Studiosus* und der *Music* eifrigst geflissener, mich endes benandten ersuchet, Ihme wegen derer in Musicis habenden Wissenschafften einig *attestatum* zu ertheilen: als habe solches gar gerne thun, und zugleich bezeigen wollen, wie Er nicht alleine auff dem Claviere und Violine, sondern auch in *compositione* sich gar wohl habilitiret, und also nicht zweifle, dass er derjenigen *Function* woran Gott ihn etwanig ruffen mögte, vorzustehn in gnugsamen Stand sey.
Leipzig, d. 4 April 1731.   Joh. Sebast. Bach,
                                   Hochf. Sächs.-Weissenfels. Capellmeister
                                   Director Chori Musici Lipsiensis.'

[3] Schw. p. 165. Cf. a series of articles by Hans Tessmer, 'Joh. Seb. Bach im öffentlichen Schrifttum seiner Zeit', in 'Neue Musik-Zeitung', Hefte 11–18, 27 Feb.–19 June 1919, in particular Heft 13 of 13 April 1919.

only one man whose skill can compare with his own.[1] His technique is
astonishing; the dexterity with which he crosses fingers and feet is scarce
to be believed, so quick are his movements. Astonishing, too, are the
wide leaps he makes with them, never striking a wrong note nor violently
contorting his limbs, no matter how energetically they move.

This great man would be the wonder of the universe if his compositions
displayed more agreeable qualities, were less turgid and sophisticated,
more simple and natural in character. His music is exceedingly difficult
to play, because the efficiency of his own limbs sets his standard; he
expects singers and players to be as agile with voice and instrument as
he is with his fingers, which is impossible. Grace-notes and embellishments, such as a player instinctively supplies, he puts down in actual
symbols, a habit which not only sacrifices the harmonic beauty of his music
but also blurs its melodic line. All his parts, too, are equally melodic, so
that one cannot distinguish the principal tune among them. In short, he is
as a musician what Herr von Lohenstein [2] used to be as a poet: pomposity
diverts them both from a natural to an artificial style, changing what might
have been sublime into the obscure. In regard to both of them, we wonder
at an effort so laboured and, since nothing comes of it, so futile.

Not malice alone inspired Scheibe's criticism; he mistook Bach's
miraculous technique for artificiality, and was insensible of the
poetical feeling that controlled it. On that account Bach felt it
deeply, especially in the circumstances in which it appeared. The
anonymity of the attack prevented him from answering it in
person, but his friend Johann Abraham Birnbaum was ready to
break a lance in his behalf. In January 1738 he published a six-
leaved pamphlet dedicated to Bach 'mit vieler Ergebenheit',
in which, amid a good deal of not very effective criticism, he was
moved to protest indignantly against Scheibe's inclusion of Bach
among the 'Musicanten' of Leipzig. 'Der Herr Hof-Compositeur', he objected, 'ist ein grosser Componist, ein *Meister* der
Music, ein Virtuos auf der Orgel und dem Clavier, der seines
gleichen nicht hat, aber keineswegs ein Musicant.' [3] With vigour
rather than insight he met Scheibe's aesthetic criticisms, and
concluded with the hope that in future he would curb his inclination to find fault.[4] The controversy dragged on into 1739, on
Birnbaum's part with little understanding of the art of the man he
defended, and on Scheibe's side with belated recognition of the
bad taste that had initiated it.[5] Its significance is in the fact, that
instructed minds among Bach's contemporaries were as blind as

[1] *i.e.* Handel.
[2] D. C. von Lohenstein (1635–83) was the author of stilted dramas. His *Cleopatra*
is alleged to have been the earliest German tragedy.
[3] Bi. iv. 206 prints Birnbaum's pamphlet.
[4] 'den glücklichen Anfang eines neuen Lebens, das von aller unnöthigen
Tadelsucht völlig möge befreyt sein'.
[5] Cf. Hans Tessmer, *ut supra*.

their successors to the broad humanity and spontaneity of his alleged 'Schwülstigkeit'.

Meanwhile, the school controversy lingered on unresolved. Bach's representation to the Consistorium (12 February 1737) elicited no reply, and after an interval of several months was followed by another and final letter:[1]

Magnifici, most worthy, noble, learned, and worshipful gentlemen and Patrons,

Your Magnificences will be pleased to remember that on 12 February of this year I lodged a complaint against Herr Johann August Ernesti, Rector of the Thomasschule, for interfering with the functions of my *officium*, and telling the *alumni* to withhold their *parition* from me, to my consequent *prostitution*, and humbly craved your aid and protection. Since then the worshipful Council has sent me a decision (see Enclosure A),[2] which gives me no redress for the *prostitution* I have suffered, and indeed increases the injury I have endured.

In church, and in presence of the first choir, the Rector *publice* threatened with *relegation* and loss of their *caution* any who dared to show me *respect* or obey my orders, and I therefore have the right to demand that my dignity be vindicated as publicly. Moreover, the above-mentioned decision of the Council is based upon the 1723 *Ordnung*, which differs from the older one[3] in some respects, is prejudicial to my office and its *accidentia*, and has never been legally in force. The late Rector Ernesti opposed its publication, on the ground that it required the approval of your worshipful Consistorium,[4] whose *ratification*, so far as I know, has never been given. I am therefore unable to recognize regulations that prejudice my rights, for instance, their curtailing of my *accidentia*, and contend that the original *Ordnung* is still in force. The Council's decision referred to above, based as it is upon the new [1723] *Ordnung*, consequently does not settle the matter. I refer particularly to that part of the decision which declares it not competent for me to suspend a scholar once appointed to office, still less to deprive him of it.[5] For cases will occur where action on some point of school discipline must be taken *incontinenti*, pending a closer inquiry. In all *Trivialschulen*[6] the Cantor controls appointments in his own department, for otherwise the youngsters would become unmanageable, and he could not carry out his duties at all.

It has seemed necessary to inform your Magnificences on these points, and I now repeat my request to be supported in the exercise of my office and to receive the *respect* due to me in it; that Rector Ernesti be admonished not to interfere with me; that my dignity, which has been lowered, be forthwith restored in the eyes of the scholars; and that I receive your support in my opposition to the new school *Ordnung*, in so

---

[1] Leipzig. Stadtarchiv: Rathsacta, Schule zu S. Thomae, VII, B. 69, 70.

[2] The document is not extant.

[3] Bach refers to the *Schulordnung* of 1634.

[4] The elder Ernesti was conservatively set against any change. Cf. Sp. ii. 25.

[5] Regarding the Cantor's powers of punishment the 1634 *Schulordnung* is vaguer than its successor. Bach apparently appealed to general usage rather than to specific prescriptions.

[6] *i.e.* schools in which grammar, rhetoric, and dialectics (the Trivium) were taught.

far as it prejudices my office and impedes the fulfilment of my duties. For your assistance thus accorded I shall always remain with profound *respect*

Your Magnificences' most humble servant,
Johann Sebastian Bach.

Leipzig, 21 August 1737.

To their Magnificences [&c., as in former letters].

Bach's quarrel with the *Ordnung* of 1723 was an afterthought and belated. Upon the main point at issue between himself and Ernesti it supported his contention, and in his earlier communication to the Consistorium (12 February 1737) he invoked the very code he now repudiated. Nor in his letters to the Council had he appealed to the regulations of 1634. His present reason for doing so is not obscure: while the Council's decision affirmed his right to appoint the Prefects in terms of the *Ordnung* of 1723, it declared him incompetent to suspend or deprive a Prefect once appointed, an authority which, he asserted, the earlier code conferred upon him.[1] But his protest was intended to serve another purpose; he was aware of the jealous relations of the Council and Consistorium in regard to school government, and hoped to engage the latter in his quarrel by impugning the legality of a document which had not received its *imprimatur*. Therein he failed. A week later (28 August 1737) the Consistorium sent on his communication to the Council and requested its views within a fortnight.[2] That body gave the matter no attention until 4 October 1737, and then merely resolved to postpone it for a further period.[3] Driven to his last line of defence, Bach (18 October 1737) petitioned for his sovereign's intervention:[4]

To the most serene and potent King-Elector, my most gracious Sovereign.
Your Majesty's gracious condescension in conferring upon me the *praedicat* of *Compositeur* to your Majesty will command my life-long gratitude. Meanwhile, since I may now humbly but confidently invoke your Majesty's august *protection*, I appeal to it to release me from certain provocations that weigh upon me.

[1] I can find nothing in Caps. VI, VII, and XX of the *Schulordnung* of 1634 to support Bach's view that it gave him ampler powers than its successor. Cap. XX, para. 33, prescribes: 'Si quid gravius peccatum fuerit ab aliquo, arbitrio Rectoris puniatur, vel etiam ex Concentorum ordine ejiciatur.'
[2] Sp. ii. 910.
[3] 'Der Cantor bey der Schule zu S. Thomae Johann Sebastian Bach habe wegen des Rectoris daselbst H. M. Johann August Ernesti bey dem Consistorio allhier eine anderweitige Verwendung an den H. Superintendenten u. E. E. Rath extrahiret: ob und was zu antworten. *Concl.* Noch eine Zeit beyzulassen' (Protokolle in die Enge, VIII. 63).
[4] Leipzig. Stadtarchiv: Rathsacta, Schule zu S. Thomae, VII, B. 69, 70. On 28 Sept. 1737 Bach performed his secular Cantata 'Angenehmes Wiederau' at Wiederau. Cf. B.C.T., p. 567.

My predecessors in the Cantorship of the Thomasschule were authorized by traditional usage to appoint the *praefecti* of the *chori musici*, for the practical reason that they best knew who were the most competent *subjecta* for that duty. I exercised this prerogative myself for a long time without *contradiction*, until the present Rector, Herr Johann August Ernesti, presumed, without my concurrence, to appoint as Prefect a *subjectum* possessing inadequate musical ability. Knowing his incompetence, and the consequent effect on the performance of the music, I appointed a more able *subjectum* in his place. Thereupon, Rector Ernesti not only contested my action, but, to my great hurt and *prostitution*, assembled the scholars in *coetu publico* and forbade them *sub poena baculationis* to obey my orders. I endeavoured to establish my prerogative by appealing to the worshipful Council (Enclosure A), and also petitioned your Majesty's Consistorium here for *satisfaction* (Enclosure B); from the latter I have received no reply, while the former has given the decision herewith enclosed (Enclosure C). It deprives me, most gracious sovereign, of powers which I have hitherto freely enjoyed, and does so in pursuance of an *Ordnung* published in 1723 which I do not accept as valid, largely because it has not been confirmed by the Consistorium. With my most dutiful submission, I therefore appeal to your Majesty:

1. To direct the Council not to molest my *jure quaesito* prerogative of appointing the *praefecti chori musici*, but to uphold my due powers therein;

2. To be pleased graciously to order the Consistorium here to demand an apology from Rector Ernesti for the indignity put upon me, and to charge Superintendent Dr. Deyling to instruct the school *coetus* to show me the respect and obedience due to me.

I look forward to receiving your Majesty's exalted favour with undying gratitude, and with profound submission remain

Your Majesty's most obedient and dutiful servant,
Johann Sebastian Bach.

Leipzig, 18 October 1737.

To the most Serene and mighty Prince Friedrich August, King in Poland [&c., &c., &c.], my most gracious Sovereign, Elector, and Lord.

Dresden responded to the call of its Court official. On 17 December 1737 an injunction was issued to the Consistorium, to examine Bach's charges against the Rector and give him such satisfaction as he might be entitled to.[1] The document was received on 1 February 1738, and four days later (5 February) was communicated to Deyling and the Council, requesting their views within a fortnight.[2] The minutes of Council and Consistorium are silent as to what followed. The inclination of both bodies undoubtedly lay towards a compromise, and the visit of the sovereigns, on the occasion of Princess Amalia's marriage to Charles IV of Sicily on Jubilate Sunday, 27 April 1738, created a friendly atmosphere. As in 1734, the University provided an 'Abendmusic' on the Marktplatz at nine in the evening, when four noble

---

[1] The document is printed in Sp. ii. 910 and Bi. iv. 202.
[2] Sp. ii. 912; Bi. iv. 206.

youths were permitted to kiss hands.[1] Gottsched had prepared a libretto, 'Willkommen, ihr herrschenden Götter der Erde', which excelled in fulsome adulation and exaggerated compliment to the quartet of royalties.[2] But it had not been adopted without stirring the old controversy between Bach and Görner. As in 1727, the latter's supporters insisted upon his claim to function.[3] But the decision lay with the *studiosi* who provided the funds, and Bach's vogue with them assured his selection; we may suppose Gottsched himself not passive in the debate. Bach's score has not survived, though the music probably was used elsewhere; Birnbaum instanced it in his controversy with Scheibe as characteristic of its composer's genius, 'rührend, ausdrückend, natürlich, ordentlich, und nicht nach dem verderbten, sondern besten Geschmacke' (moving, expressive, natural, orderly, without extravagance, and in the best taste), adding that it was received 'mit durchgängigem Beyfall'.

Augustus apparently used his opportunity to terminate a controversy which his Hof-Compositeur, with characteristic doggedness, had waged for over two years, carrying it successively from che Council to the Consistorium, and from the Consistorium to the King. Whether Bach obtained full satisfaction is unknown. But royal favour, shining upon him in Leipzig itself, obliterated Ernesti's affront to his dignity, and made abundantly clear that he and his office could not be slighted with impunity. The fight on his part had been waged less for self than for his art and station, and for what remained to him of life he was not impeded.[4]

[1] The sovereigns commanded the performance, for which 91 *studiosi* provided 332 thalers 20 gr. One of the four nobles, Baron von Schmettau, delivered a congratulatory Ode in the Paulinerkirche earlier in the day (B.-J. 1925, p. 10). Breitkopf printed 700 copies of it at Schmettau's expense (B.-J. 1913, p. 90). The performance took place on Monday, 28 April, according to Riemer.
[2] The libretto is printed in B.-G. XXXIV, p. xlviii.
[3] Cf. B.-J. 1925, p. 10. Bach received 58 thalers, of which 8 were paid to the town's musicians.
[4] The title 'Hof-Compositeur' was not exclusively held by Bach. Besides Composers of French (Louis André, 1729–33) and Italian (Giovanni Alberto Ristori, 1729–50) Music, the Dresden Capelle included four Composers of Church Music contemporary with Bach—Johann Dismas Zelenka, 1735–45; Michael Breunich, 1745–54; Joh. Georg Schürer, 1748–86; and Tobias Butz, 1733–52. Bach's patent styled him simply 'Compositeur' (p. 234 *supra*), whereas he had particularly offered his skill in church and orchestral music (p. 216 *supra*). Probably his Oratorios and Masses can be associated with his appointment. Cf. Karl Pembaur, *Drei Jahrhunderte Kirchenmusik am Sächsischen Hofe* (1920), and the *Musical Times*, April 1932.

CHAPTER X

THE LAST YEARS

A RARE glimpse into an interior otherwise dimly visible is afforded in a series of letters written by one who lived with Bach from 1738 to 1742. Their author, Johann Elias Bach, was a grandson of Georg Christoph, Sebastian's father's elder brother. His father, Johann Valentin, was Cantor and musician at Schweinfurt; his elder brother, Johann Lorenz, has been mentioned earlier in these pages[1] as owner of a copy of the Genealogy. Johann Elias, thirty-three years old in 1738, and a divinity student in the University at Leipzig, lodged with his cousin in the Thomasschule and fulfilled responsible duties in his household. Of Bach's first marriage one daughter, a spinster of thirty, remained beneath the paternal roof-tree. Of the second marriage five children survived: Elisabeth Juliane Friederica (*b.* 1726), a daughter recently born (October 1737), and three sons—Gottfried Heinrich, aged fourteen, Johann Christoph Friedrich, later of Bückeburg, aged six, and Johann Christian, the 'English Bach', barely three.[2]

Johann Elias acted as tutor to the three boys, upon a formal contract to which his letters frequently refer.[3] Offered a situation elsewhere in 1741, he declines (21 October), among other reasons, 'because under my contract I cannot leave my cousin without giving him a quarter's notice'. Writing to his sister a few days earlier (3 October) he mentions the same obstruction. On 21 April 1739 he is preparing his 'two elder charges' to receive the Lord's Supper, and remarks in 1741 that his pupils need sound and careful tuition, 'especially the eldest of them', Gottfried Heinrich, a youth of weak intellect. His reverent affection for Bach is very apparent, and Bach thought highly of him. 'My cousin deems my stay here necessary for some time to come,' he writes on 21 April 1739. 'To tell the truth,' he declares (9 June 1741), 'there is no one who can take over my duties if I am absent.' His letters, too, are full of gentle tenderness for 'unsere Frau Muhme', so he names Anna Magdalena, whose ailing health caused him to reflect, after leaving Leipzig in 1742, that he had 'exchanged one *gymnasium*

---

[1] *Supra*, p. 4.   [2] Cf. Appendix II.
[3] *Die Briefentwürfe des Johann Elias Bach*, ed. Karl Pottgiesser, in 'Die Musik', 1912–13, pp. 3–19. The original letters are in the possession of Herr Oberlehrer Karl Freytag, Munich (Klugstrasse 124).

patientiae for another'. In April 1738 he writes to his mother, ' I should like to give some yellow carnations to our Frau Muhme; she loves the garden and would be so pleased to have them.' He makes a similar request on 23 August 1740, and a week later (2 September) declares that Anna Magdalena is awaiting the flowers 'with the expectancy of a young child over its *heiliger Christ*'. The flowers arrive, and (10 October 1740) he tells of the Frau Muhme's delight on receiving six beautiful plants, 'which have given her more pleasure even than children find in their Christmas gifts; she nurtures them as tenderly as a child lest harm befall them'. He adds another detail to the pleasant picture. Writing in June 1740 to Cantor Hiller in or near Halle, he says that Bach in Lent that year, newly returned from Halle, had spoken of a linnet which, under Hiller's tuition, sang like an accomplished artist. 'Frau Muhme is very fond of linnets', he tells Hiller, 'and bids me ask your Honour to let her buy the bird from you at a reasonable price, and to send it to her at a convenient opportunity.' Bach's pleasure also was his concern: on 5 October 1739 Elias desires his sister to send ten or twelve measures of sweet muscat wine by the carrier, 'to give our cousin pleasure, in return for the many benefits I have received in his house these two years past'.

Elias acted as Bach's secretary, and his letters reveal a friendly relationship between the Leipzig household and Joh. L. Schneider of Weissenfels, an invitation from whom to visit him Bach declines on 7 November 1739, owing to his medical adviser forbidding a journey in bad weather. In July 1741 Bach acknowledges a present of venison from him :

Worthy and distinguished Herr Consulent,
Though I was never in doubt concerning your Honour's inestimable good-will to me, you have been so gracious as to afford me another proof of it to-day. My household and myself acknowledge it with hearty gratitude, and hope for an opportunity to give practical proof of it. We have eaten your fine present of venison to the good health of your Honour, but would vastly prefer to have done so in your agreeable company. For the moment that hope is not fulfilled, but we look forward to no distant date when we may have the honour of welcoming you here in Leipzig.
With very respectful greeting to your excellent lady, and sincere esteem, I remain, most distinguished Herr Consulent,
Your obedient servant,
Joh. Sebast. Bach.
Leipzig, July 1741.

à Mons. Monsieur Jean Leberecht Schneider, Consulent de la Chambre des Finances de Son Altesse Sérénissime le Duc de Weissenfels, Weissenfels, p.p.

A letter from Anna Magdalena [1] reveals her affection for her old home (Schneider had invited her to Weissenfels): 'The pleasure I always look forward to on visiting my beloved Weissenfels, and in the company of your Honour and my relatives, transcends all other delights. But my ailing health has for some time past robbed me of those happy hours. The warnings of my family will not allow me to undertake a journey which, they declare, cannot improve my health and may gravely endanger it. So I can only beg your Honour not to take my non-compliance in ill part. It arises from no lack of esteem, which I still hold for you unchanged, but only out of regard for my health, which nature's laws oblige me to consider. Meanwhile, will not your Honour yield to the repeated prayer of my beloved husband ("meines Liebsten"), to which I add my own, and honour our house with your company at the Michaelmas Fair?'

Johann Elias is silent upon an event which laid a pall of gloom over Bach's household when he entered it. In the spring of 1738, Bernhard Bach, repeating his misconduct at Mühlhausen, absconded from Sangerhausen, where he had been irregular in his habits and owed money. Grief for his wayward son, and shame that the name he bore should be sullied by misconduct, weighed heavily on Bach, whose depression is evident in a letter to Bernhard's host at Sangerhausen: [2]

Honoured Herr Klemm,

You will not take it amiss that I have not till now answered your esteemed letter, for I only returned from Dresden two days ago. So loving and tender a father as yourself will understand the grief and sorrow with which I write this letter. I have not seen my, alas, undutiful boy since last year, when I enjoyed so many kindnesses at your hands. Your Honour will remember that I then paid what he owed for his board at Mühlhausen, discharged the bond which seems to have been the cause of his leaving that place, and left a sum of money to meet his other debts, hoping that for the future he would reform his *genus vitae*. You will therefore understand how pained and surprised I am to learn that he has again been borrowing money on all sides, has not in the least changed his *genus vitae*, and has absconded without giving me, so far, the slightest indication of his whereabouts. What can I do or say more, my warnings having failed, and my loving care and help having proved unavailing? I can only bear my cross in patience and commend my undutiful boy to God's mercy, never doubting that He will hear my sorrow-stricken prayer and in His good time bring my son to understand that the path of conversion leads to Him.

I have opened my heart to your Honour, and beg you not to associate me with my son's misconduct, but to accept my assurance that I have done all that a true father, whose children lie very close to his heart, is bound to do to advance their welfare. I recommended him to Sanger-

[1] Sept. 1741.   [2] *Supra*, p. 233.

hausen when the vacancy occurred, trusting that its more cultured society and distinguished Patrons would incite him to better behaviour. As the author of his promotion, I must once again thank your Honour, confident that you will not allow the *vacance* to be filled until we have discovered his whereabouts (God, Who sees all things, is my witness that since last year I have not set eyes upon him) and learn his future intentions, whether he resolves to change his courses, or intends to seek his fortune elsewhere. I shrink from troubling your Council on the matter, and only beg for *patience* until he returns or discloses his retreat. Already several creditors have written to me, whom I am not disposed to pay until, as I am entitled, I have come to an understanding with my son about his affairs, face to face or by letter. Meanwhile, I respectfully ask your Honour to discover his whereabouts and let me know, in order that, under God's providence, I may make a last effort to soften his hardened heart and bring him to his right senses. As he was so fortunate as to lodge in your house, may I ask your Honour whether he removed his few sticks of furniture, or if any of them remain behind? Awaiting your speedy reply and wishing you a happier holiday than I shall have, I remain, with humblest respects to your wife,

Your Honour's most obliged servant,

Joh. Seb. Bach.

Leipzig, 24 May 1738.

To Frau Klemm, who apparently had forwarded her lodger's unpaid account, Bach replied two days later:

Honoured Frau Klemm,
You will not imagine that I do not admit the claim forwarded in your esteemed letter if I say that, before settling it, I desire a written statement of his obligations in my, alas, undutiful son's handwriting, and at the same time would learn whether he means to return to your house again, taking my measures accordingly. God and my family are witnesses that he has not been here since my visit to Sangerhausen last year. Should you learn where he is, and be able to give me positive information, I shall be grateful and very ready to meet the consequent charges. Hoping soon to receive news from you, I remain, very honoured Frau Klemm,

Your most obliged servant,

Joh. Seb. Bach.

Leipzig, 26 May 1738.

No news of the fugitive having been received, the Sangerhausen Council (1 July 1738) reported his disappearance to the Consistorium at Leipzig, adding that he had neglected his duties, run into debt, absented himself from Sangerhausen, and for the past three months had not been heard from at all. While the Council desired the post to be declared vacant forthwith, Bach's influence perhaps obtained a respite for the truant: on 5 September 1738 Sangerhausen's authorities were instructed to make another effort to discover his hiding-place and to report again to the Consistorium. A month later (15 October 1738) the Council replied: they were still ignorant of their organist's movements and his father was no better informed. Bernhard, in fact, was no farther away than Jena, at whose University he matriculated on 28 January 1739[1] as a law student; he died there of fever on 27 May 1739.

Amid these distractions Bach accomplished a work whose plan links it with the 'Orgelbüchlein'. On 10 January 1739 Johann Elias writes to his step-brother, Cantor Koch of Ronneburg:[2] 'My cousin is anxious to publish some clavier pieces, eminently suitable for organists and exceptionally skilfully written. They fill eighty pages and should be ready for the Easter Fair. Can you find any subscribers for them at ——?[3] People who subscribe later will have to pay more.' On the following 28 September he informs Koch: ' My cousin's work is now engraved on copper and ready; copies are to be had at three thalers each.' The new work was the third Part of the *Clavierübung* and contained, its title-page declared, 'verschiedene Vorspiele über die Catechismus- und andere Gesaenge, vor die Orgel'. Bach's purpose in it was, to illustrate the Lutheran Catechism by Preludes treating the melodies of Luther's familiar hymns on the Commandments, Creed, Prayer, Baptism, Penitence, and Holy Communion, prefacing his exposition of Lutheran dogma with a triple invocation of the Trinity, a characteristic gesture of reverence. Less relevantly, he added a Prelude in E flat *pro organo pleno*, four Duetti for cembalo, and, to conclude, the Fugue in E flat known as ' St. Anne's '.[4]

Soon after the publication of the work, Friedemann Bach came over from Dresden in July 1739 for a month's holiday, bringing with him the celebrated lutanists Leopold Silvius Weiss and Johann Kropfgans.[5] There was much company in the Cantor's room overlooking the Pleisse during their stay, and 'something extra good in the way of music', Johann Elias informed his step-brother (11 August 1739). Not improbably Bach's compositions for the lute [6] date from this visit, whose relation to his invention of an instrument (Lautenclavicembalo) combining the qualities of the lute and harpsichord is apparent in the fact, that a few months later (1740) he commissioned Zacharias Hildebrand to build such an instrument to his specification.[7]

---

[1] The Matriculation Book contains no more than his name, place of birth, and date of matriculation. For Bernhard's Sangerhausen career, see Friedrich Schmidt's *Geschichte der Stadt Sangerhausen* (1906), i. 726.
[2] Joh. Wilhelm Koch, Cantor of Ronneburg; *d.* there 8 Nov. 1745.
[3] The price is not stated.   [4] Cf. T.B.C. iii. 66.   [5] Cf. Schering, p. 418.
[6] They are published (ed. E. D. Bruger) by Julius Zwissler, Wolfenbüttel (1925).
[7] Bach owned two of these instruments at the time of his death; each was priced at 30 thalers (*infra*, p. 271). The viola pomposa, a five-stringed instrument in size and compass approximate to a viola, was also his invention. He employed Johann Christian Hoffmann, of Leipzig, to build examples.

Friedemann's holiday coincided with the presence in Leipzig of Prince Augustus Ludwig of Anhalt-Cöthen. Bach's official relations with Cöthen had ceased on the death of Prince Leopold, but his earlier connexion with that Court, and also his official position in Leipzig, invited him to participate in an Abendmusic in honour of the Prince's name-day on 3 August 1739.[1] His Collegium Musicum, however, did not open until early October, though he was already preparing for its autumn season. On 28 September 1739 Johann Elias thanks his step-brother on the Cantor's behalf for a present 'which has been consumed to your good health. He [Bach] would like to retaliate properly, and begs you to excuse him for not sending you thanks in writing. The fact is, he is greatly pressed with work; his Collegium Musicum opens on Friday, and during the first week of the Michaelmas Fair he has to direct a performance in honour of his Majesty's birthday (7 October); it will be well worth hearing, I assure you, and if my brother can get away for the occasion he is not likely to regret it.' Unfortunately the composition Elias admired cannot be identified; it is improbable that it was written for the occasion. Nor at the moment was Bach disposed to put his pen at the service of his civic masters. Earlier in the year, in preparation for the Good Friday Passion (27 March 1739), he had, as usual, printed and circulated the libretto, but had thereafter received from the Council an order to withdraw it, on the ground that he had not observed the formality of submitting it for official authority. Bach treated the annoyance with cool contempt: he had acted, he replied, as on previous occasions; the work was an old one which had been performed before without objection, and he cared not a jot whether the performance took place at all; it was 'nur ein Onus' upon his shoulders, and he would therefore simply inform the Consistorium that the Council had forbidden it.[2] Bach's unconcern is partly accounted for by the fact that it was the turn of the Nikolaikirche to hear the Passion, and that, in accordance with his apparent custom, he had not proposed to produce a novelty in it. With similar indifference he observed the annual Ratswahl service on 31 August 1739, repeating his Cantata 'Wir danken dir, Gott' (No. 29), first performed on a similar occasion eight years before (1731). The service was held in the Nikolaikirche, the sermon was preached by Christian Gottlob Eichler from 1 Kings viii. 57, and an address was delivered to the Bürgerschaft by Hofrath Adrian

---

[1] Riemer, under dates 6 July and 3 Aug. 1739. The Prince was visiting Leipzig for a cure.

[2] Sp. ii. 868 quotes the Council's minute of 17 March 1739.

Steger, who, after half a century's service on the Council, now took the reins as Bürgermeister.[1]

It is evident from the letters of Johann Elias that in the last years of his life, at any rate, Bach lightly regarded the restrictions on his liberty imposed in 1723. He was frequently from home, displaying his ability as a player, advising on the construction and renovation of organs,[2] visiting his eldest sons, and fulfilling the ceremonial duties of his appointment at Dresden. The routine of his work in the Thomasschule suffered frequent interruption, and if the Council frowned, it had learnt by experience that the Cantor was not to be coerced. Early in 1740 it appointed an extra master to instruct the school in musical theory, probably on Bach's application, for he delivered a report on the candidates for the post.[3] He was rarely at pains to compose new music for his *chorus primus*: of his concerted church music but one Cantata[4] appears to have been written after 1740, and in the larger forms he had said his last word before that date. His interest was concentrated on instrumental music, particularly for the organ and clavier, and during the last ten years of his life he almost uninterruptedly employed himself in preparing the manuscripts of his organ works for the engraver. The publication of his vocal scores was beyond his range of expectancy, though they were in request. On 28 January 1741 Johann Elias refused his step-brother the loan of a Cantata for Bass Solo: 'My cousin regrets he cannot send it; he has lent the parts to the Bass singer Büchner, who has not returned them. He won't allow the score out of his hands, for he has lost several by lending them to other people.' If he made an exception he was careful to exact the cost of the postage,[5] and requests for printed copies, even from so intimate a relative as Johann Elias himself, met with a reminder of the published price.[6] Bach's business mind was as orderly as his counterpoint!

The summer of 1741 found Bach in Berlin, where his son Carl Philipp Emanuel had recently become accompanist to the new sovereign of Prussia, Frederick the Great. Only paternal anxiety, and the desire to see his son happily settled, can have induced Bach to journey at a time when Frederick was unchivalrously in arms against the Queen-Empress, in a contest that disagreeably involved

[1] B.C.T., p. 528.
[2] Bach visited Altenburg at this time (1739). Cf. B.-J. 1927, p. 103.
[3] It is dated 18 Jan. 1740. Cf. Sp. ii. 61.
[4] 'Du Friedefürst, Herr Jesu Christ' (No. 116), was written for the Twenty-fifth Sunday after Trinity, 22 Nov. 1744.
[5] On 28 Sept. 1739 Johann Elias acknowledges his step-brother's return of 'the Kirchenstück, together with ten [? groschen]'.
[6] Cf. Bach's letter of 6 Oct. 1748, *infra*, p. 256.

Saxony. Originally planned for June 1741,[1] Bach's visit was postponed until July, and, save that he lodged with Hofrath Dr.
Stahl,[2] no details of it have survived. It was disturbed, and probably shortened, by his wife's ill-health, of which Johann Elias
anxiously informed him. 'We rejoice to hear you are in good
health', he writes (5 August 1741), 'and wish that we were so here.
Our dear Frau Mama has been very unwell for a week or more, and
we are afraid that her violent haemorrhage [Wallungen des Geblüts]
may bring on low fever or some other ill consequence. We are
sorry to disturb your holiday with this disagreeable news, but it
would not be right to keep it from you, and we are certain that
our dear Herr Papa and cousin will not be angry with us.' Bach,
in fact, had already fixed the date of his departure when (9 August
1741) Johann Elias wrote again more urgently: 'We are in the
deepest anxiety over the growing weakness of our dear Frau
Mama. For a fortnight past she has had little more than an hour's
rest at night, being unable either to lie down or sit up. She was
so ill last night that I was called to her room, and to our deep
sorrow we really thought we must lose her. We therefore feel
bound to send on the news with the utmost urgency, so that you
may hasten your journey and relieve us all by your return.' Anna
Magdalena recovered; indeed, in the following February (1742)
she presented her husband with his last child, Regine Susanna,
who survived to receive the bounty of the public in her old age.

In 1742 Bach published the fourth and last Part of the *Clavierübung*, containing the variations written for Goldberg, to whose
employer, Kayserling, he paid a visit at Dresden in November
1741,[3] soon after his return from Berlin. The year witnessed the
production of a work of another kind. By the Treaty of Berlin
(July 1742) Prussia withdrew from the anti-Austrian coalition, and
her unwilling satellite Saxony followed her from the field. The
cessation of arms allowed Carl Heinrich von Dieskau, Kosputen,
and Altschönfels, Captain of the Leipzig Circle, to be invested with
the lands of Klein-Zschocher and Knauthain, near Leipzig, to
which he succeeded on his mother's death. Picander, who held
a post under him at Leipzig,[4] wrote the so-called Peasant Cantata

---

[1] This appears from Johann Elias's letter of 16 Aug. 1741 to a friend in Halle.
[2] Georg Ernst Stahl, physician in ordinary to Friedrich Wilhelm I. He lived
in Geheimrath Francke's house in the Friedrichswerder, and *d.* 14 May 1734.
Bach probably lodged with his widow.
[3] Johann Elias writes on 13 Jan. 1742: 'Two months ago I visited Dresden with
my cousin and received many undeserved courtesies in the house of the renowned
ambassador.'   [4] Von Dieskau was head of the 'Land-, Tranck-, Pfennig-
und Quatember-Steuer' of the Leipzig Circle. Cf. D.J.F.L., p. 10. Picander in
1736 held the post of 'Ober-Post-Commissarius' (*ibid.*, p. 14).

('Mer hahn en neue Oberkeet') for performance at the ceremony, which took place on 30 August 1742, giving it a local atmosphere by using the patois of Upper Saxony, while Bach introduced popular melodies, among them the familiar Sarabande 'Folies d'Espagne'.[1] In August 1745 the Prussians again took the field, crossed the frontier of Saxony, now a hostile neighbour, and in November were in Leipzig,[2] impressing its inhabitants to contribute food, drink, and money.[3] Dresden fell on 18 December. A week later, a treaty concluded there removed Frederick from the war and released Saxony from the Prussian heel. On this stormy canvas Bach is infrequently visible. In 1744 he was invited to test the organ in the Johanniskirche newly built by Johann Scheibe, the father of his Hamburg assailant, a relationship he did not allow to bias his verdict on the instrument, whose qualities he praised unreservedly.[4] In the same year he completed the second Part of the *Wohltemperirtes Clavier*, after an interval which suggests that it was devised for the instruction of his second family, as Part I had instructed the first.[5] In 1746 he was summoned to Zschortau, where Scheibe had completed another organ,[6] and a month later tested another in the Wenzelskirche at Naumburg, built by Zacharias Hildebrand of Leipzig. In his examination of this instrument he was associated with Gottfried Silbermann, the occasion having the further interest, that two years later (1748) Bach's recommendation secured the organistship of the church for his son-in-law Altnikol.[7]

These evidences of Bach's activity lend additional interest to the publication, probably in the same year (1746), of his 'Sechs Choräle von verschiedener Art auf einer Orgel mit 2 Clavieren und Pedal vorzuspielen'. Published by Johann Georg Schübler, of Zella, a small town near Gotha, the volume, the title-page announced, was retailed by the composer and his sons, Carl Philipp at Berlin and Wilhelm Friedemann at Halle, whither the latter had recently migrated from Dresden. All the six Preludes are based on familiar hymn melodies, and are distinguished from the rest

---

[1] It occurs in the eighth movement. For the figures of the dance, see Schering, p. 412.
[2] The town signed a capitulation on 30 Nov. (Beier, ii, p. 111).
[3] *Ibid.*, p. 112. [4] B.-J. 1925, p. 96; Schering, p. 257.
[5] An autograph is in the British Museum (Add. MS. 35021).
[6] Bach's certificate is dated 7 Aug. 1746. The document is in the British Museum (Add. MS. 33965, fol. 168). It is sealed with Bach's seal. See illustration No. 76. Cf. B.-J. 1911, p. 41.
[7] Bi. ii. 35 prints the certificate signed by Bach and Silbermann on 27 Sept. 1746. Cf. Flade, p. 145, and B.-J. 1906, p. 131. Bach's testimonials in favour of Altnikol are on p. 257, note 3, *infra*.

of Bach's organ music by the fact that five of them positively, and
the sixth with practical certainty, are arrangements of vocal
movements in his Cantatas.[1] His selection of them is an interesting
indication of his preferences, and also of the restricted currency he
anticipated for them in their vocal form.

Prussia being again accessible to a Saxon, Bach revisited Berlin
in the spring of 1747, to make the acquaintance of his daughter-in-
law Johanna Maria Dannemann, the child of a Berlin wine merchant, whom Carl Philipp had married in 1744. The wedding was
the first in Bach's family, and desire to visit the young couple was
increased by the arrival of his first grandchild, Johann August,
born to them on 30 November 1745. Bach picked up Friedemann
at Halle to take part in the family reunion. But the journey
brought him into more august company, in circumstances recorded
circumstantially by Forkel,[2] whose information, derived from
Friedemann, is not on that account to be deemed impeccable. He
declared his father to have been drawn northward by the urgent
invitation of Frederick, into whose presence at Potsdam he represented him to have hurried, travel-stained and weary, direct from
the coach. More probably, Bach alighted from his carriage at
Potsdam after but a short ride from Berlin, his presence there
having reached the king's ears through Carl Philipp, then in
attendance upon his sovereign. Excepting those evenings on
which the Opera House was open, a concert preceded the royal
evening meal, the king himself selecting the programme from his
conservative repertory, and even placing the parts on the orchestral
desks. On Sunday, 7 May 1747,[3] Bach arrived at Potsdam and
was announced to the sovereign, already surrounded by his
players. 'Gentlemen, Old Bach is here,' exclaimed Frederick;
the concert was abandoned, and in its place the king invited his
visitor to exhibit his skill on the new Silbermann claviers with
hammer action recently installed in the palace. Accompanied from
room to room by Frederick and his players, Bach tested them all
and, to the king's amazement, developed fugally a subject proposed by himself. The following day (Monday, 8 May) Bach gave
an organ recital in the garrison church (Heiliger Geist-Kirche) at
Potsdam, and in the evening, having been again summoned to the
palace, astounded the king by improvising a six-part fugue. From
Potsdam he returned to Berlin, where he inspected the new Opera
House and demonstrated his knowledge of acoustics. 'He took in

[1] T.B.C. iii. 70.   [2] Forkel, p. 23.
[3] The date is given in Spener's 'Zeitung', No. 56, for 11 May 1747. Quoted in
Bi. iii. 216. The Sunday was the fifth after Easter.

its good and bad qualities at a glance,' writes Forkel,[1] 'whereas others were able to do so only after experiment. He was shown the adjoining grand saloon, and ascended to the gallery that runs round it. Merely glancing at the roof, he remarked, "The architect has produced a novel effect here which, probably, neither he nor others suspected". The saloon is a parallelogram; if a person puts his face to the wall at one corner and whispers a few words, a listener at the corner diagonally opposite can hear them distinctly, though to others between them the words are inaudible. The effect is due to the arched roof, as Bach saw at a glance.'

Whatever Bach thought of Frederick's musicianship, a subject on which Carl Philipp had definite opinions, he could not fail to be gratified at his reception by the foremost figure in Europe. Measured by his opportunities, he was singularly averse from loading his scores with conventional and flattering dedications to august personages, and the treatment of his Missa in B minor and the Brandenburg Concerti would not encourage him to break his rule. But Frederick's dominating personality, the excellence of the fugal theme propounded for improvisation, and a father's desire to flatter a prince who could advance his son's career, all invited Bach to recall himself to the memory of his royal host by an example of his skill. On his return to Leipzig, unrewarded from Frederick's frugal exchequer,[2] Bach developed the royal theme with his profoundest skill, tactfully added a Sonata for flute, violin, and clavier, and dispatched his manuscript to Berlin on 7 July 1747 as a 'Musicalisches Opfer', with the following letter:

Most gracious Sovereign,

With humblest submission I have dedicated to your Majesty a Musical Offering, the most distinguished part of which is the work of your Majesty's own illustrious hand. With profound and agreeable duty I hold in mind your Majesty's gracious condescension when I visited Potsdam, in playing to me on the clavier the *thema* for a *fuge* which you commanded me there and then to develop in your royal presence. As in humble duty bound, I obeyed your Majesty's command. But I was not blind to the fact that, lacking opportunity to study the *thema*, my performance was not adequate to its excellence. However, I resolved to give a right royal *thema* the treatment it deserves, and to make it known to the whole world. That resolution I have fulfilled to the best of my ability, with the single and laudable desire to exalt, though in a minor sphere, the

[1] Forkel, p. 65.
[2] On inquiry at the Preuss. Haus-Archiv I am informed that neither in the 'Akten' nor in the 'Schatullrechnungen' is there record of any payment or gift to Bach. Perhaps the agate snuff-box mentioned on p. 271 *infra* was Frederick's gift. Nearly thirty years later, in conversation (23 July 1774) with Freiherr Gottfried van Swieten, who records the event (*Gespräche mit Friedrich dem Grossen*), Frederick 'sang mir mit lauter Stimme das Thema zu einer chromatischen Fuge vor. das er dem alten Bach gestellt hatte'.

fame of a potentate whose greatness, in the realm of music no less than in the arts of war and peace, is acclaimed and admired by all. I am bold to add this humble request—that your Majesty will condescend graciously to accept this little work and continue your favour to

Your Majesty's most obliged and humble servant,

The Author.

Leipzig, 7 July 1747.

Released from the necessity to augment the generous library of church music with which nearly twenty years of unremitting labour had endowed the Thomasschule, Bach surrendered himself with increasing zest to the theoretical problems of his art. Hence, he was drawn into a Society which till now had not attracted him. Its originator, Lorenz Christoph Mizler, graduated at Leipzig in 1734, when he dedicated his doctoral thesis, among others, to Bach, whose student he had been for composition and the clavier. Two years later (1736) he launched at Leipzig a critical periodical entitled 'Neu eröffnete musicalische Bibliothek', and in 1738 founded a Society for the Promotion of Musical Science (Societät der musicalischen Wissenschaften), whose statutes defined the conditions and objects of its membership.[1] Only those who held a musical position were eligible, though 'practical' musicians (*i.e.* those who were merely executants) were excluded. Formal meetings of the Society were not proposed, but members were invited to circulate their dissertations 'postfrey' among their fellows, none of whom was expected to retain a manuscript longer than one month. The contribution of 'theoretische Schriften' to the official 'Musicalische Bibliothek' was invited from members and also 'bekannte Componisten'; the publication of an Ode or Cantata was proposed to celebrate occasions of congratulation or mourning affecting the former, from whom one thaler was exacted at Easter and Michaelmas; the Society's library was at their disposal, and its walls were offered for their portraits, to be presented by themselves on their election. To Mizler's chagrin Bach at first held aloof from a Society of whose value he was doubtful. But Telemann was an early member, Handel was elected in 1745, and Carl Heinrich Graun, Frederick the Great's Capellmeister, was received in the next year. Their admission perhaps inclined Bach to accept nomination after his return from Berlin; in June 1747 he was elected. His portrait, painted by the Dresden Court painter Elias Gottlieb Haussmann,[2] was forthwith

---

[1] They are printed in Bi. iv. 229.
[2] See the frontispiece to this volume. On the dissolution of the Society, it became the possession of the Thomasschule and was hung in the Musicsaal. A replica hangs there to-day, and the original is in the old Rathaus.

presented; it shows him holding in his right hand a triple Canon
in six parts, subsequently published (1754) in the 'Musicalische
Bibliothek': [1]

For his diploma Bach presented the Society with a consummate
example of his skill, *Einige canonische Veränderungen über das
Weihnachtslied*: Vom Himmel hoch, da komm ich her, *vor die
Orgel mit 2 Clavieren und dem Pedal*. The work was engraved and
published by Balthasar Schmidt of Nürnberg, who perhaps had
been brought to Bach's notice by Carl Philipp Emanuel, whose
Concerto in D major he had recently (1745) published, and to
whom the latter sent his Concerto in B flat (1752) and Sinfonia in
E minor (1759).[2] Bach's delight in the stalwart Reformation tunes
is again apparent in this work, in which he set himself to demonstrate the whole art and theory of canon through the medium of
the Christmas melody. The Variations were an extravagantly
generous gift to an institution already moribund. The 'Musicalischer Almanach' for 1782 reveals that Mizler's Society had
enrolled only nineteen members in nearly half a century, of whom
but five were elected after Bach joined it; a few years later it died of
inanition,[3] having accomplished less than it planned, and attracted
but a few men of distinction into a fellowship of mediocrities.

The Berlin visit was Bach's last journey,[4] and he regarded it as
the culminating pinnacle of his career. Certainly the last three
years of his life yield little straw for biographical bricks.[5] Two

[1] B.-G. XLV (1), p. 138. A resolution by A. A. H. Redeker is in Hilgenfeldt,
Table 3.
[2] Wotquenne, Nos. 11, 25, 177. It is a moot point whether the Variations were
engraved in 1747 or subsequently. See generally, B.C.T. iii. 75.
[3] Bi. iii. 210.　　　　　　　　　[4] Forkel, p. 26.
[5] I may insert here an interesting receipt now in the Library of Congress,
Washington, U.S.A.: 'Dass mir Endes Gefertigter, von des Tit. Herrn Graffen
von Würben, Herrn Hoffmeister Ignatz Rath, anwiederumb vor das Clavier zu
leyhen vor hinein auf einen Monat vom 5ten October bis 5ten November ein
Thaler acht Groschen seynd bezahlet worden thue hiermit bescheinigen.
Leipzig d. 5ten October 1747. Joh. Sebast. Bach.' Clearly Bach was ready to

intimate letters to the faithful Johann Elias, now installed at Schweinfurt, his daughter's marriage, and the outbreak of an old controversy, are the meagre and only materials. Towards the end of 1748 Bach writes to Johann Elias: [1]

Worthy and respected cousin,

Time presses and I must endeavour to say much in few words, if only to acknowledge God's grace and bounty, both in the abundant vintage, and in regard to the now imminent wedding. You ask for a copy of the Prussian *fuge*; I cannot send you one, for *justement* to-day the edition is sold out. Only 100 copies were engraved, and most of them I gave away *gratis* to friends. However, between now and New Year's Fair more will be published, and if my cousin still desires an *exemplar* he should acquaint me with an opportunity to dispatch it, send me a thaler *post*, and it will be forwarded. I conclude with greeting from us all.

Your Honour's devoted
J. S. Bach.

Leipzig, 6 October 1748.

PS. My Berlin son now has two boys. The first was born about the time we, alas, suffered the Prussian *invasion*; the other is a fortnight old. [2]

Monsieur J. E. Bach, Chanteur et Inspecteur du Gymnase a Schweinfourth.

p. l'occasion.

The generous inclinations of Johann Elias had not abated; a cask of the Bavarian vintage accompanied his reply, a gift promptly acknowledged:

Worthy and respected cousin,

Your letter, received yesterday, brings me the good news that you and your dear wife are well, and for the delectable cask of wine that came with it accept my best thanks. Unfortunately the cask suffered a jar, or some other accident, on the journey, for on examination here it is found to be one-third empty and contains, the *Visitator* declares, only six *kannen*. It is regrettable that the smallest drop of so noble a gift of God should be wasted, but I am none the less heartily obliged by my worthy cousin's kind present. *Pro nunc* I am not *reellement* in a position to reciprocate; still, *quod differtur non aufertur*, and I hope to find an opportunity to discharge my obligation.

It is unfortunate that we live so far apart, for else I should give myself the pleasure of inviting her cousin to my daughter Lissgen's wedding, which takes place in January 1749, to the new Naumburg organist Herr Altnikol. However, though for that reason, and because of the inconvenient season, he cannot be present, I will ask him to assist them with his good wishes, and with the same I commend myself to my good

---

hire out the instruments in his collection; he exacted the rent in advance. An identical receipt dated 5 Dec. 1747 is in Sp. ii. 716.

A visit to Dresden at this period is suggested by the text of the secular cantata 'O angenehme Melodei'. Cf. B.C.T., p. 601.

[1] This letter and the following, of 2 Nov. 1748, are in the possession of Frau Helene Schöne. I am indebted to her son, Prof. Dr. Hermann Schöne, of Münster.

[2] Cf. Appendix II.

cousin's remembrance. With warmest greetings to you from all here, I remain

Your Honour's devoted and faithful cousin and
servant to command,
Joh. Seb. Bach.

Leipzig, 2 November 1748.

P.S. *Magister* Birnbaum was buried six weeks ago.

P.M. Though my good cousin offers to send me more of the same *liqueur*, I must decline on account of the heavy charges at this end. The carriage was 16 gr., delivery 2 gr., *Visitator* 2 gr., provincial excise 5 gr. 3 pfg., general excise 3 gr. So my cousin may calculate that the wine cost me nearly 5 gr. a measure, a too expensive present!

A Monsieur J. E. Bach, Chanteur et Inspecteur des Gymnasiastes de la Ville Imperialle à Schweinfourth, Franqué Coburg.

Of all Bach's children only Carl Philipp as yet had adventured on the sea of matrimony. But on 20 January 1749 Bach had the joy of giving his daughter Elisabeth Juliane Friederica to Johann Christoph Altnikol.[1] Eldest of the three surviving daughters of his second marriage, and barely twenty-three years old, she alone of all his children was married from the paternal roof, and before his death gave him a third grandchild, who bore his names. Her own is that of the pert Miss in the Coffee Cantata, in whose relations with choleric Schlendrian we perhaps catch a vision of the bride. A native of Berna in the Oberlausitz, the bridegroom had come to Leipzig in 1744 from Breslau, where he was a singer (*choralis*) in the church of St. Maria Magdalena and assisted at the organ.[2] He had become a pupil of Bach's, an assistant (Bass) in the Thomaskirche, and a few months before his marriage obtained the organ of the Wenzelskirche at Naumburg.[3] Bach esteemed him highly

---

[1] Altnikol's banns were published in the Wenzelskirche, Naumburg, on 26 December 1748. The wedding was solemnized ('Halbe-Brautmesse') by Archidiakonus Dr. Christoph Wolle in the Thomaskirche, Leipzig, on 20 Jan. 1749. Lieschen's married life was short. Altnikol died 25 July 1759, leaving his widow with two juvenile daughters (see Appendix II), with whom thereafter she returned to Leipzig, where both of them found husbands. Lieschen died at Leipzig 24 August 1781.

[2] B.-J. 1912, p. 147.

[3] Bach's interest in Altnikol, the son of Gottfried Altnikol, weaver, of Berna, Oberlausitz, is expressed in two letters recommending his candidature for the vacancy in the Wenzelskirche, Naumburg. The letters are among the Naumburg. Stadtarchiv, XXIV, 3, ff. 71, 88. I owe the text of them to Herr Stadtarchivar Friedrich Hoppe, of Naumburg.

Worshipful, learned, and distinguished Gentlemen,

I have the most agreeable recollection of the confidence shown in my unworthy self by your worshipful and learned Council, once when I was able to offer some small advice in connexion with the repair of your organ, advice which was graciously accepted, and again when I received a flattering commission to overhaul and test the instrument. The confidence you then reposed in me

and was rewarded by filial devotion during his last illness. Surely the wedding was graced by Bach's music, and though it lacked a cantata such as the wealthy commissioned the Cantor to write, it may be hazarded that the 'Drei Choräle zu Trauungen', extant in their original simplicity, were sung on the occasion; if so, their choice was Bach's, and indicates his preferences—Samuel Rodigast's 'Was Gott thut', Johann Jakob Schütz's 'Sei Lob und Ehr', and Martin Rinkart's 'Nun danket alle Gott', a trio of virile hymns set to noble melodies and enriched with Bach's matchless harmonies.

Grave signs of the malady to which Bach succumbed were not apparent till the spring of 1749. On 1 March of the year he dedicated, apparently to Johann Schmidt, the Thuringian organist at Zella, a Canon in seven parts on a *basso ostinato*:

emboldens me to trespass on your kindness in order to prefer a request. In the absence of my dear former pupil, Herr Johann Christoph Altnikol, now organist and schoolmaster at Greiffenberg, I venture on his behalf respectfully to beg for him the vacant post of organist in your gift. I am positive that your worshipful and learned Council will find in Herr Altnikol a man who will completely satisfy your requirements. He has for several years had to do with organs and their mechanism, is a good player and director, and fully competent to look after his instrument, qualities requisite in a good organist. He also displays an exceptional talent for composition, singing, and the violin. I am therefore convinced that your worshipful and learned Council will find no cause to regret the granting of my petition or the appointment of so worthy a *subjectum*. I should regard his preferment as a favour conferred on me, and subscribe myself

Your Worships' life-long and most obliged servant,

Joh. Sebastian Bach,

Royal and Electoral Court Composer.

Leipzig, 24 July 1748.

Bach's recommendation was instantly adopted. A week later he wrote to Oberbürgermeister Schaller:

Right worshipful and distinguished Councillor,

Accept my heartfelt thanks for your kind entertainment of my last letter, and equally for informing me through Treasurer Sonnenkalb that my respectful request has been conceded. I shall ever remember with lively pleasure this conspicuous favour. I venture to trouble your Worship further. On receiving early news of the Naumburg vacancy, before I could communicate with Herr Altnikol I took steps on his behalf, and instructed my former pupil to send in his application as quickly as possible to supplement my action. As your Worship is so good as to inform me, through Herr Sonnenkalb, that Herr Altnikol's personal application is now required, I have the greater pleasure in the fact that I anticipated the request, and am now in a position to forward the application which he has placed in my hands. If your Worship will be so good as to support it by your distinguished advocacy, it will give me life-long pleasure to subscribe myself

Your Worship's most obliged servant,

Joh. Seb. Bach.

Leipzig, 31 July 1748.

Altnikol's application is dated 27 July in Bi. iii. 227.

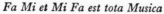

Fa Mi et Mi Fa est tota Musica

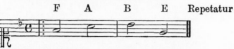

Domine Possessor
Fidelis Amici Beatum Esse Recordari
tibi haud ignotum: itaque
Bonae Artis Cultorem Habeas
verum amIcum Tuum.

Lipsiae d. 1 Martii 1749.

Even while he perpetrated this *jeu d'esprit* Bach was deeply involved in the preparation of his *Kunst der Fuge*,[1] a series of fugues and canons upon a single theme, developed with masterly ingenuity, posthumously published by his son Carl Philipp in 1750, and the direct outcome of his Berlin visit. The notoriety of that event, the interest roused by Frederick's 'königliches Thema', and the popularity, declared by his letter to Johann Elias,[2] of Bach's treatment of it, all summoned him to expound the principles of an art of which he was the profoundest master. So close is the relation between the Berlin visit and Bach's treatise, that the theme he selected for illustration is a shortened echo of the one whose excellence he had praised to the king:

Frederick the Great:

---

[1] A valuable study of the work, by Wolfgang Graeser, is in B.-J. 1924, pp. 1–104. See also articles by Dr. Alfred Heuss in 'Zeitschrift f. Musik' for Feb. 1927, and Heinrich Rietsch in B.-J. 1926, pp. 1–22. An orchestral version of the work, by Wolfgang Graesar, is published (1926) by Breitkopf and Härtel. See also Erich Schwebsch, *Die Kunst der Fuge* (1930), and D. J. Tovey's mongraph (1931).

Bach:

Bach did not complete the preparation of this remarkable work for the engraver,[1] for in the early summer of 1749 his ill health was so notorious that steps were actually taken to appoint his successor. Writing to Bürgermeister Jakob Born[2] on 2 June 1749, the all-powerful minister, Count Heinrich von Brühl, recommended his domestic Composer, Gottlob Harrer, demanding that he should forthwith be admitted to his Probe. Harrer carried the letter to Leipzig, and no time was lost in obeying its injunction. On 8 June Harrer conducted a composition 'with the greatest applause' in the Concert Hall of The Three Swans on the Brühl,[3] the head-quarters since 1743 of the new 'Leipziger Concert', with which Bach was not connected. Harrer's patron had demanded that he should be both tested and elected to Bach's office. It is therefore creditable to the Council that it took no further action regarding the appointment until after Bach's death.[4]

While Brühl and his nominee complacently anticipated his demise, Bach recovered to show interest in an old controversy unhappily revived. Since 1747 the Rectorship of the Freiberg Gymnasium was held by Johann Gottlieb Biedermann, who found there in office as Cantor since 1744 a distinguished pupil of Bach's, Johann Friedrich Doles; he succeeded to the Leipzig Cantorate in 1756. Meanwhile, he was entangled in meshes in which his master had already been involved: Doles celebrated the first centenary of the Peace of Westphalia (1748) with a Singspiel in the Freiberg Gewandhaus, with such success that Biedermann, assuming Ernesti's role, was moved to fulminate violently against

---

[1] Contrapunctus XIX is incomplete, and a concluding one was unwritten.

[2] The letter is in Bi. iii. 257.

[3] Riemer, p. 718: 'Den 8 [Juni 1749] ward auf Befehl E. E. Hochweisen Raths dieser Stadt, welche meistens zugegen waren, auf dem grossen musicalischen Concert Saale in drey Schwanen auf Brühl, durch Ihro Excell. des Geheimbden Raths u. Premier Ministers Grafen von Brühl Capell Director Herrn Gottlob Harrern Probe zum künfftigen Cantorat zu St. Thom., wenn der Capellmeister und Cantor Herr Seb. Bach versterben sollte, mit grösstem Applaus abgelegt.'

[4] There is some reason to think that in or about May 1749 Bach suffered a shock of paralysis, which would account for Count von Brühl's action. On 9 Aug. 1750, after Bach's death, Brühl again requested the Leipzig Council to appoint Harrer, who was then already installed. Brühl's letter is in Bi. iii. 259.

music as an interloper in the academic curriculum. He employed the School Programme for 12 May 1749 to vent his animus, alleged that music encouraged a low standard of character, and instanced Cato, Caligula, and Nero to support his thesis. His extravagance stirred a lively controversy, in which Mattheson, taking a hand, vigorously trounced him as an 'irriger Lehrer, schwermüthiger Verächter und gottloser Schänder der Tonkunst' (1750). The commotion reached the ears of Bach, probably through Doles, and revived the memory of his earlier duel with Ernesti. Unwilling, probably unable, to take the field in person, he invited Christoph Gottlieb Schröter,[1] of Nordhausen, to defend their maligned art. A fellow-member of Mizler's Society, Schröter framed a dignified rejoinder to Biedermann, and entrusted its publication to Bach, who, finding it entirely to his taste, expressed his appreciation of it (10 December 1749) to Georg Fr. Einicke of Frankenhausen,[2] who passed on the letter to Mattheson: 'Schröter's article is very well done, entirely to my *goût*, and will soon appear in print. . . .[3] Herr Mattheson's [*Panacea, als eine Zugabe zu seinem musicalischen*] *Mithridat* has made a big stir, I am told on good authority. If, as I expect, other *refutationes* follow, I have no doubt they will cleanse the author's [Biedermann's] dirty ear[4] and make it better able to listen to music.' In due course Schröter's article appeared (1750), under the title *Christliche Beurtheilung des von Herrn M. Biedermann Freybergischen Rectore im Monat May des 1749sten Jahres edirten Programmatis de Vita Musica.*[5] But in text and temper, Schröter discovered to his annoyance, his original draft had been seriously altered. He therefore (9 April 1750) expressed his disapproval to Einicke, desiring him to tell Bach, whom he held responsible, that he objected to the title under which his pamphlet was issued, and to the liberties which had been taken with his manuscript.[6] Bach replied (26 May 1750) briefly to

---

[1] Author of an important treatise on Thorough-Bass, published 1772.
[2] Only so much of Bach's letter survives as Mattheson, to whom Einicke sent it, published in the third 'Dosis' of his *Panacea*, p. 183: 'Die schröterische Recension ist wohl abgefasst, und nach meinem *gout*, wird auch nächstens gedruckt zum Vorschein kommen. . . . Herrn Matthesons Mithridat hat eine sehr starke *operation* verursachet, wie mir glaubwürdig zugeschrieben worden. Sollten noch einige *Refutationes*, wie ich vermuthe, nachfolgen, so zweifle nicht, es werde des Auctoris Dreckohr gereiniget, und zur Anhörung der Music geschickter gemacht werden.' [3] So in Mattheson.
[4] On Bach's word 'Dreckohr' Mattheson comments severely: 'Expression basse et dégoutante; indigne d'un Maître de Chapelle; pauvre allusion au mot: Rector.'
[5] Printed in Bi. iii. 236.
[6] Einicke communicated the letter to Mattheson, who prints it, *op. cit.*, p. 184: 'Herr Schröter . . . bat mich [Einicke] schriftlich, unterm 9 April 1750, dem Herrn Bach zu berichten: "dass die gewaltsame Veränderung seiner Recension ihm

Einicke: 'Please give my *compliment* to Herr Schröter, and say that I am not at present able to write to him, but when I can, I will satisfy him that I am not to blame for the alterations in his article; the culprit is the person who saw it through the press.'[1] Schröter was not pacified, and (5 June 1750) again demanded an explanation, insisting that 'Der Herr Capellmeister Bach bleibet *in culpa*'.[2] Death intervened, and Bach's promised letter was never written. He had, however, added a note to the chorus of ridicule that assailed Biedermann's 'Dreckohr'. Some time in the latter part of 1749, he took advantage of a performance of 'Phöbus und Pan' to confound the new Midas, changing Momus's invitation—

> Now, strike up, Phoebus, let the lyre be sounded!
> Thy song's the best acclaimed, and Pan's confounded.

to

> Now, strike up, Phoebus, strike with power resounding!
> Storm like Hortensius or Orbil's roaring!

Still unsatisfied with the lines, he substituted 'Birolius' for 'Orbil'. 'Birolius' is the anagram of Orbilius, Horace's schoolmaster, by which name Biedermann was indicated. Ernesti is Hortensius, of whose rival, Cicero, he was the editor.[3] Clearly the old wound rankled.

His letter to Einicke (26 May 1750) probably was the last Bach wrote or dictated. His eyesight had long been failing; from earliest youth he had taxed it beyond its normal service, with consequences Haussmann's picture so unmistakably discloses. Towards the end of 1749[4] his sight was so troublesome that, on the advice of friends, he consulted a specialist. For two or three years past, Germany had been toured by an English Opthalmiater—his own word—Chevalier John Taylor,[5] who at a later time treated Handel. Arriving at Cologne in February 1747, he was welcomed

---

sehr empfindlich gefallen sey. Ferner: Sein Trost hiebey wäre dieser, dass kein Leser, welcher seine Denk- und Schreib-Art, aus anderen Umständen, kennen gelernet, ihn für den Verfasser einer solchen Vermischung halten könne; des unglücklich gerathenen Rubrik: Christliche Beurtheilung . . . zu geschweigen. Denn obwohl sein flüchtiger Aufsatz nichts unchristliches in sich enthalte, so schicke sich doch solches Epitheton keinesweges zur vorhabenden Sache."'
[1] Mattheson, p. 184: 'An Hrn. Schrötern bitte mein *Compliment* zu machen, bis dass ich [Bach] selber im Stande bin zu schreiben, da ich mich, alsdenn, der Veränderung seiner Recension wegen, entschuldigen will, weil ich gar keine Schuld daran habe; sondern solche einzig demjenigen, der den Druck besorget hat, zu imputiren ist.'
[2] Bi. iii. 239.   [3] Sp. ii. 741.
[4] The Nekrolog states that the operation took place a full half-year before his death; and this accords with Taylor's movements.
[5] Taylor's account is in *The History of the Travels and Adventures of the Chevalier Taylor, Opthalmiater . . . written by himself*, vol. i (1761), pp. 14, 24.

at the Courts of the reigning princes, among them Prussia and Saxony, whence in December 1749 he moved to Vienna. He would appear to have examined Bach's eyesight before proceeding thither, and records the event in his extraordinary *History*:

I have seen a vast variety of singular animals, such as dromedaries, camels, etc., and particularly at Leipsic, where a celebrated master of music, who had already arrived to his 88th (*sic*) year, received his sight by my hands; it is with this very man that the famous Handel was first educated, and with whom I once thought to have had the same success, having all circumstances in his favour, motions of the pupil, light, etc., but, upon drawing the curtain, we found the bottom defective, from a paralytic disorder.

If Taylor can be relied on, Bach's condition was complicated by a shock of paralysis, whose incidence may be attributed to May 1749, and account for Count von Brühl's intervention on Harrer's behalf at that season. The operation probably took place in January 1750, when Taylor, summoned from Vienna to Mecklenburg, again visited Leipzig. At first it promised to be successful. But prolonged confinement in a darkened room told upon Bach's vitality, while the drugs and dressings ('schädliche Medicamente und Nebendinge'[1]) depressed him, and sapped a constitution till then singularly proof against illness.

Of the three sons of his second marriage, Johann Christoph Friedrich, now eighteen years old, early in 1750 took service under Count Wilhelm von Schaumburg-Lippe at Bückeburg, and was replaced in Bach's household by his last pupil, Johann Gottfried Müthel, afterwards organist at Riga; he may sometimes have assisted his weakening master up the familiar stairs to the choir gallery, intermittently to discharge his duty. When his eyesight permitted, Bach was re-reading and revising his organ compositions. In particular, he was selecting and preparing for the engraver the 'Achtzehn Choräle von verschiedener Art auf einer Orgel mit 2 Clavieren und Pedal vorzuspielen'—till the end the Reformation's heroic tunes filled his soul. Before the darkness closed upon him, fifteen of the Preludes were written out in his strong hand. A relapse followed; the dying man asked for Lissgen at Naumburg, who was mourning her son, his youngest grandchild, but recently dead. Altnikol, too, came at a summons and put on paper the master's last thoughts. Prelude XVI, 'Jesus Christus, unser Heiland', appears in his handwriting, and the XVIIth, too, 'Komm, Gott, Schöpfer, heiliger Geist'. The task was nearly done when, early in July, Bach dictated[2] the opening

[1] The words are those of the Nekrolog.
[2] Marpurg makes the statement in his Preface to the *Kunst der Fuge*.

bars of the last of the Eighteen, his inspired transformation of the Prelude 'Wenn wir in höchsten Nöthen sein', copied into the 'Orgelbüchlein' in the far-off days at Weimar. But no longer of Paul Eber's stanzas was he thinking. Death had never seemed terrible or forbidding to him, and now, facing eternity, he bade Altnikol head the movement with the title of another hymn, also associated with the melody, 'Vor deinen Thron tret ich hiemit', whose first and last verses were on his lips:

> Before Thy throne, my God, I stand,
> Myself, my all, are in Thy hand;
> Turn to me Thine approving face,
> Nor from me now withhold Thy grace.
>
> Grant that my end may worthy be,
> And that I wake Thy face to see,
> Thyself for evermore to know!
> Amen, Amen, God grant it so!

Abruptly the manuscript ends in the middle of the twenty-sixth bar; Bach had made his last music. But on 18 July he rallied; the blinds were drawn, and his eyes, so long vacant and unseeing, rested on the familiar walls and the faces of his loved ones.[1] It was for the last time: within a few hours he was stricken unconscious by an apoplexy, and for ten days lay in high fever, tended by two skilful physicians. Sounds entered faintly to where he lay awaiting his call: the voices of his scholars at play round the old fountain in the Thomaskirchhof, the traffic along the Promenade, the water-wheel of the old mill, the organ in the church hard-by. The city was darkening and hushed when the end came: at a quarter to nine on Tuesday evening, 28 July 1750, Bach breathed his 'Adsum'.[2]

For more than two centuries Leipzig had buried her dead round the Johanniskirche beyond the east wall of the town. Here Bach was laid to rest on Friday, 31 July. The day was the second of the three 'Busstage' instituted in 1710 and annually observed;[3] from six o'clock in the morning, when the bells of St. Thomas's were tolled, onwards to the conclusion of Vespers, church services were continuous. So, at a very early hour the school assembled before the Cantor's lodging and, headed by the cross-bearer, accom-

---

[1] 'Zehn Tage vor seinem Tode schien es sich gähling mit seinen Augen zu bessern; so dass er einsmals des Morgens ganz gut wieder sehen und auch das Licht wieder vertragen konnte' (Nekrolog, in B.-J. 1920, p. 20).
[2] 'Allein wenige Stunden darauf, wurde er von einem Schlagflusse überfallen; auf diesen erfolgte ein hitziges Fieber, an welchem er, ungeachtet aller möglichen Sorgfalt zweyer der geschicktesten Leipziger Aerzte, am 28 Julius 1750, des Abends nach einem Viertel auf 9 Uhr, im sechs und sechzigsten Jahre seines Alters, auf das Verdienst seines Erlösers sanft und seelig verschied' (Nekrolog, *ibid.*, p. 21). The symptoms point to Chronic Interstitial Nephritis, a form of 'Bright's Disease'. Failing vision due to Albuminuric Retinitis is a common complication.　　　　　　[3] Graff, p. 229.

panied the Leichenwagen conveying their dead Cantor to his grave near the south wall of the church.[1] As was customary, the event was announced from the pulpit of the Thomaskirche:

'There has passed to his rest, and now sleeps blessedly in God,' said the minister, 'the right worthy and esteemed Herr Johann Sebastian Bach, Composer to his Majesty the King in Poland and Prince-Elector of Saxony, Capellmeister to his Highness of Anhalt-Cöthen,[2] and Cantor of St. Thomas's School on the Thomaskirchhof. With the rites of Christian usage his body has this day been committed to the earth.'[3]

No memorial to Bach's memory was erected, and more than a century passed before a tablet on the outer wall of the Johannis-kirche marked approximately the site of his grave; its exact locality had long been forgotten.[4]

Bach's vacant office was filled with unusual expedition. On 7 August Burgomasters Born and Stieglitz and other members of Council met to consider the situation created by the Cantor's death. No minute of regret, no appreciation of him was recorded. With disparaging intention he was referred to as 'der Cantor an der Thomas-Schule, oder vielmehr der Capell-Director Bach', while Stieglitz, in words that illuminate the background of Bach's artistic life for near a generation, exclaimed: 'The school needs a Cantor, not a Capellmeister.'[5] Carl Philipp Emanuel Bach was anxious to succeed his father; Görner, August Friedrich Graun of Merseburg, and Bach's favourite, Johann Ludwig Krebs, were also in the field. The meeting hardly discussed their merits, and Gottlob Harrer was unanimously preferred.

---

[1] The entry in the Leichenbuch runs: '1750. Freytag den 31 Julii. Ein Mann 67 Jahr. Hr. Johann Sebastian Bach, Cantor an der Thomas Schule, starb ♂. 4 K[inder]. accid[entia] 2 Thlr. 14 gr.' The burial fee was on the reduced scale for those officially connected with the church and school. A memorandum now in the Leipzig Stadtbibliothek reads: 'Ein Mann, 67 J. Hr. Johann Sebastian Bach, Capellmeister und Cantor an der Schule zu St. Thomas, auf der Thomas-Schule, wurde mit dem Leichenwagen begraben den 30 Juli 1750' (Bi. iii. 253; Sp. ii. 760). The date 30 July may indicate that Bach's body was then removed to the Johanniskirche for interment on the following morning.

[2] Bach, in fact, received no appointment at Cöthen from Augustus Ludwig, Prince Leopold's successor.

[3] 'Es ist in Gott sanfft und seelig entschlafen der Wohl Edle und Hochachtbare Herr Johann Sebastian Bach, Sr. Königl. Maj. in Pohl. und Churfürstl. Durchl. zu Sachsen Hoff Componist, wie auch Hochfürstl. Anhalt-Cöthenscher Capell-meister und Cantor an der Schule zu St. Thomae allhier am Thomas Kirchhofe; Dessen entseelter Leichnamb ist heutiges Tages Christlichem Gebrauche nach zur Erden bestattet worden.' Appended is the note: 'Ist am anderen Buss-Tage als den 31 Julii 1750 abgekündiget worden.'

[4] For the discovery of Bach's resting-place see infra, p. 279.

[5] 'Die Schule brauche einen Cantoren und keinen Capellmeister, ohnerechtet er auch die Music verstehen müsse.' Bi. iii. 260 prints the minute, but mistakes both the date and the occasion of the meeting. Harrer was elected on 7 August, signed the customary 'Revers' (supra, p. 146) on 17 August, and passed his Consistorial tests on 20 August. For Harrer, see B.-J. 1931, pp. 112–46.

It is not the purpose of these pages to appreciate Bach's genius, to measure his stature among his peers, or establish his place in the history of his art. Nor, enlightened by a belated revelation of his majesty, would it be reasonable to blame a generation to which that illumination was not vouchsafed. In the last decade of his life he probably was out of touch with the community he served. From about 1740 he ceased to direct his Collegium Musicum, and was succeeded in its conductorship by Carl Gotthelf Gerlach.[1] With the Leipzig Concert, established in 1743 on foundations strange to him and his traditions, he was not actively associated. In his latest years even his duties as Cantor were perfunctorily performed, though Ernesti exhibited little generosity in his exclusion of any reference to him from his annual speech on 4 May 1751.[2] Hence, his passing invited brief and infrequent notices in contemporary periodicals. Abraham Krügel[3] wrote a few lines tinged with sincerity in the 'Nützliche Nachrichten' for 1750: 'The shock of an operation for eye trouble carried off this man, whose musical genius has won him undying fame, and whose sons inherit his distinction.'[4] Riemer briefly outlined his career, repeating the fiction, probably accepted by Bach himself, that his family was of Magyar origin.[5] In Berlin his death was announced tersely in Spener's 'Zeitung', of 3 August 1750, as due to 'the unfortunate effects of a severe operation to his eyes performed by an English oculist'. The writer added: 'The loss of this uncommonly able man will be deeply mourned by all true lovers of music.'[6] More critical, though imperfect, appreciations of Bach's genius were offered by his fellow-artists. Telemann, his successful competitor in 1723, published a generous 'Sonnet auf weyland Herrn Capellmeister Bach', which incidentally introduced a compliment to his godson at Berlin:[7]

Lasst Welschland immer viel von Virtuosen sagen,
   Die durch die Klingekunst sich dort berühmt gemacht:
Auf deutschen Boden sind sie gleichfals zu erfragen,
   Wo man des Beyfalls sich nicht minder fähig acht't.

---

[1] B-J. 1913, pp. 89, 96, suggests 1737 for Gerlach's appointment (but cf. *supra*, p. 248). For other musicians of this name see Flade, p. 74.
[2] Bi. iii. 254.   [3] Sp. ii. 761.
[4] 'Eine übel ausgeschlagene Augen-Cur raubte diesen Mann der Welt, welcher sich durch seine ungemeine Kunst in der Music einen unsterblichen Ruhm erworben hat, und welcher solche Söhne hinterlässt, die gleichergestalt in der Music berühmt sind' (Bi. iii. 255).
[5] *Chronik*, p. 751. Like Krügel, he gives the time of Bach's death as 'Abends um 8 Uhr'.
[6] 'an den unglücklichen Folgen der sehr schlecht gerathenen Augen-Operation eines bekannten engl. Oculisten verstorben. Der Verlust dieses ungemein geschickten Mannes wird von allen wahren Kennern der Music ungemein bedauert' (Dahms, p. 99).   [7] *Ibid.*, p. 120. Cf. Bi. iii. 256.

Erblichner Bach! Dir hat allein dein Orgelschlagen
  Das edle Vorzugswort des Grossen längst gebracht;
Und was für Kunst Dein Kiel aufs Notenblatt getragen,
  Das ward mit höchster Lust, auch oft mit Neid betracht't.
So schlaf! Dein Name bleibt vom Untergange frey:
  Die Schüler Deiner Zucht, und ihrer Schüler Reih',
Bereiten für Dein Haupt des Nachruhms Ehrenkrone;
  Auch Deiner Kinder Hand setzt ihren Schmuck daran,
Doch was insonderheit Dich schätzbar machen kann,
  Das zeiget uns Berlin in einem würdgen Sohne.

Mattheson and Marpurg, the foremost critics of their day, praised the technical mastery of the *Kunst der Fuge*; the former named it to support his boast that Germany was the true home of the fugue and organ music[1]; the other[2] recalled Bach's 'erstaunende Fertigkeit im Erfinden und Extemporisiren', and found in his music an incomparable depth and sincerity. Mizler, desiring a fuller commemoration of his Society's distinguished member, committed to Carl Philipp Emanuel Bach and Johann Friedrich Agricola, Bach's former pupil, the preparation of an obituary article (Nekrolog), published belatedly (1754) in the Society's 'Musicalische Bibliothek', Band IV, Theil 1.[3] Concise, inadequate, it none the less sufficed for a hundred years. It afforded the earliest catalogue of Bach's compositions, emphasized their inventiveness, originality, and gift of melody,[4] their author's remarkable ability in score reading, his ear so accurate that he could detect the smallest error amid a flood of sound, his reliability and 'accuracy' as a conductor, and his preference to adopt quick *tempi*. But its praise was chiefly lavished on its object as an instrumentalist: 'Our Bach was the greatest organ- and clavier-player that has ever lived' ('der stärkste Orgel- und Clavierspieler den man jemals gehabt hat'), his feet more agile than the hands of other players. It recalled his technical knowledge of organ construction, his revolution in the method of tuning the clavier, his inventiveness in the construction of musical instruments, qualities which supported the eulogy of him as a man 'der der Music, seinem Vaterlande, und seinem Geschlechte, zu gantz ausnehmender Ehre gereichet'.

As an Appendix to this appreciation, the Society, fulfilling its regulations, published an Ode or 'Singgedicht' from the pen of one of its members, Dr. Georg Wenzky, or Venzky, Rector at Prenzlau,

---

[1] Sp. ii. 684.   [2] In his Preface to the *Kunst der Fuge*.
[3] Reprinted in B.-J. 1920.
  'Seine Melodien waren ... erfindungsreich, und keinem andern Componisten ähnlich.'

Brandenburg.[1] Its opening Chorus bids the Muses mute their strings, and continues :

> Hört was euch das Gerüchte bringt:
> Hört was für Klagen Leipzig singt.
> Es wird euch stören:
> Doch müst ihrs hören.

In a Recitative Leipzig tells her tragic news :

> Der grosse Bach, der unsre Stadt,
> Ja der Europens weite Reiche
> Erhob, und wenig seiner Stärcke hat,
> Ist leider! eine Leiche.

Before the coffin, crowned with bays, pass Bach's fellow-musicians (Die Componisten oder Tonmeister), who hail him in an Aria:

> Wo eilst du hin? Verehrungswerter Bach!
>
> . . . .
> Gott lasse deinen Geist auf deinen Brüdern ruh'n,
> Damit sie ihre Kunst in voller Reife sehen,
> Und seine Majestät nach Würdigkeit erhöhen.

The amateur lovers of music (Freunde der Tonkunst) next recall Bach's qualities, the rich variousness of his nature, his loftiness of aim, the compelling appeal of his music, concluding, with a gust of emotion:

> O dass wir diesen Held der Virtuosen missen!
> Doch werden wir an seinen Meisterstücken,
> Die er uns hinterlässt
> Als einen edlen Rest,
> Uns desto mehr erquicken.

Bach's fellow-members of the Musicalische Gesellschaft next bewail their 'Verherrlichter', who comforts the mourners with an assurance that he is happy 'mid the choirs of heaven, whither he bids them follow him to the home of unending joy and music that transcends his own:

> O köntet ihr die reinen Töne hören,
> Die unser Chor zu Gottes Lob anstimmt,
> O köntet ihr das Musiciren hören,
> Das hier kein Ende nimmt!
>
> . . . . . .
> Drum tröstet euch
> Und folget mir. Was man an mir verloren
> Das hört man treflicher in unsern Toren.

---

[1] He immediately preceded Handel in his election to the Society. Cf. Bi. iii. 210. His 'Singgedicht' is printed in B.-J. 1920, p. 26; Bi. iv. 236; Dahms, p. 102.

CONCLUSION

BACH died intestate. His estate consequently passed, as to one-third, to his widow, now approaching her fiftieth year, and, as to two-thirds, to his surviving children, nine in number: of his first marriage, Wilhelm Friedemann, Carl Philipp Emanuel, and Catharina Dorothea, a spinster of forty-two; and of the second marriage, Gottfried Heinrich, Elisabeth Juliane Friederica Altnikol, Johann Christoph Friedrich, Johann Christian, Johanna Caroline, and Regine Susanna. The last four being under age, though Johann Christoph Friedrich was already in service at Bückeburg, Anna Magdalena invited the University (17 October 1750) to appoint a guardian for them. Four days later (21 October), amending her request, and asserting her inclination not to marry again, she begged that her husband's sometime rival and colleague Görner might be her 'co-tutor' in the imminent distribution of his estate among her own children.[1] For the half-witted Gottfried Heinrich, Gottlob Sigismund Hesemann, a law student in the University, agreed to act, while Friedemann Bach, more conveniently placed at Halle, became attorney for his brother Carl Philipp, and curator for his sister Catharina. Dr. Friedrich Heinrich Graf[2] filled the office of curator in the widow's behalf. The inventory on which the distribution was made furnishes the interior of Bach's home.

An Inventory of the Effects of Johann Sebastian Bach, late Cantor of the Thomasschule, Leipzig, deceased 28 July 1750[3]

CAP. I.

	Th. Gr. Pfg.
1 share in the 'Ursula Erbstollen' mine at Klein-Voigtsberg	60
Facit	60

---

[1] Sp. ii. 976 prints both letters.
[2] He was promoted Licentiate in the Law Faculty in 1733; Doctor in or before 1736. He lived then 'auf der Haynstrasse im Grafischen Hause' (D.J.F.L., p. 41). He stood godfather to Bach's youngest child, Regine Susanna, in 1742. It may be observed that Anna Magdalena spent her last years in the Hainstrasse.
[3] Sächs. Hauptstaatsarchiv Dresden, Amtsgericht Leipzig, No. 3.

CAP. II.
Cash

(a) *Gold.*

		Th.	Gr.	Pfg.
1 treble ducat		8	6	
4 double ducats		22		
1 ditto, show piece		5	12	
28 single ducats		77		
41 ducats	*Facit*	112	18	

(b) *Silver gulden and half-gulden.*
a. Thalers.

		Th.	Gr.	
77 *species* thalers		102	16	
24 *alte* gulden		16		
1 half-gulden			8	
	Facit	119		

b. Show-pieces.

No. 1. 1 triple *species* thaler . . .		4	
2. 1 double ditto . . .		2	16
3. 2 *species* thalers, at 1 Rth. 12 gr. . .		3	
4. 1 double *species* thaler . . .		2	16
5. 1 *species* thaler		1	8
6. 2 *species* thalers with rings . . .		2	16
7. 2 square *species* thalers . . .		2	16
8. 4 *species* thalers		5	8
9. 2 gulden		1	8
10. 1 piece			4
	Facit	25	20

CAP. III.
Outstanding Credits

Bond of Frau Krebs [1]		58	
Ditto Unruh		4	
Ditto Haase		3	
	Facit	65	

CAP. IV
Loose Cash

Loose cash out of which certain *debitores passivi* named in Cap. I and II have been paid . . .	36	
	Facit	36

[1] Johanna Christina Krebs, godmother of Regine Johanna Bach (*b.* 1728), was Anna Magdalena Bach's sister.

CAP. V

Silver plate and objects of value

				Th.	Gr.	Pfg.
1 pair of candlesticks,	32 *loth* at 12 gr.	.	.	16		
1 ditto,	27 ,, at 12 gr.	.	.	13	12	
1 set of 6 cups,	63 ,, at 11 gr.	.	.	28	7	
1 smaller ditto,	10 ,, at 12 gr.	.	.	5		
1 set of cut ditto,	12 ,, at 13 gr.	.	.	6	12	
1 still smaller ditto,	10 ,, at 11 gr.	.	.	4	14	
1 goblet with lid,	28 ,, at 13 gr.	.	.	15	4	
1 large coffee pot,	36 ,, at 13 gr.	.	.	19	12	
1 smaller ditto,	20 ,, at 13 gr.	.	.	10	20	
1 large teapot,	28 ,, at 13 gr.	.	.	15	4	
1 sugar basin and spoon,	26 ,, at 12 gr.	.	.	13		
1 smaller ditto,	14 ,, at 12 gr.	.	.	7		
1 snuff-box with spoon,	12 ,, at 16 gr.	.	.	8		
1 ditto engraved,	8 ,, at 16 gr.	.	.	5	8	
1 ditto inlaid .	.	.	.	1	8	
2 salt cellars,	11 *loth* at 12 gr.	.	.	5	12	
1 coffee salver,	11 ,, at 12 gr.	.	.	5	12	
2 dozen knives, forks, and spoons in case, 48 *loth* at 12 gr.				24		
1 engraved knife and spoon in case, 9 *loth* at 10 gr.			.	3	18	
1 gold ring .	.	.	.	2		
1 ditto .	.	.	.	1	12	
1 agate snuff-box mounted in gold	.	.	.	40		

Facit 251 11

CAP. VI

Musical Instruments

1 veneered Clavier, which the family desires to retain, if possible .	.	.	.	.	80	
1 Clavier .	.	.	.	.	50	
1 ditto .	.	.	.	.	50	
1 ditto .	.	.	.	.	50	
1 smaller ditto .	.	.	.	.	20	
1 Lautenclavicembalo .	.	.	.	.	30	
1 ditto .	.	.	.	.	30	
1 violin, by Stainer .	.	.	.	.	8	
1 ditto, in bad condition .	.	.	.	.	2	
1 violino piccolo, ditto .	.	.	.	.	1	8
1 viola .	.	.	.	.	5	
1 ditto .	.	.	.	.	5	
1 ditto .	.	.	.	.		16
1 violoncello piccolo [Bassettgen]	.		.	6		
1 violoncello .	.	.	.	.	6	
1 ditto .	.	.	.	.		16
1 viola da gamba .	.	.	.	.	3	
1 lute .	.	,	.	.	21	
1 small spinet .	.	.	.	.	3	

Facit 371 16

CAP. VII
Tinware

	Th.	Gr.	Pfg.
1 large dish	1	8	
1 smaller ditto		16	
1 ditto		16	
1 still smaller ditto		8	
1 ditto		8	
1 small dish		6	
1 ditto		6	
1 still smaller ditto		4	
1 ditto		4	
1 ditto		4	
1 washbasin		8	
2 dozen plates, each ¾℔, at 4 gr. the pound . .	3		
4 jugs with tin handles	1	8	
Facit	9		

CAP. VIII
Copper and Brass

	Th.	Gr.	Pfg.
2 dishcovers with iron handles	3		
2 pr. of brass candlesticks	2		
1 brass coffee-pot		16	
1 smaller ditto		16	
1 still smaller ditto		6	
1 brass coffee-tray		16	
1 copper kettle		8	
1 smaller ditto		8	
Facit	7	22	

CAP. IX
Clothes and the like

	Th.	Gr.	Pfg.
1 silver-hilted sword	12		
1 silver-mounted stick	1	8	
1 pr. of silver shoe-buckles		16	
1 coat of *Gros du Tour*, turned	8		
1 funeral cloak of *Drap des Dames* . . .	5		
1 cloth coat	6		
Facit	32		

CAP. X
At the wash

11 linen shirts	—	—	

CAP. XI

House furniture   Th. Gr. Pfg.

	Th.	Gr.	Pfg.
1 toilet wardrobe	14		
1 washstand	2		
1 clothes press	2		
1 doz. black-leather covered chairs . . .	2		
½ doz. leather covered ditto	2		
1 writing table with drawers	3		
6 tables	2		
7 wooden bedsteads	2	8	
Facit	29	8	

CAP. XII

Theological Books [1]

In Folio

	Th.	Gr.	Pfg.
Abraham Calovius, *Biblia illustrata V. et N. Test.* 5 Bde. (1719), 3 vols.	2		
Martin Luther, *Opera,* 7 vols. (1539) . . .	5		
Opera, 8 vols. (1556) . . .	4		
Tischreden oder Colloquia Doct. Mart. Luthers (1566 or 1722)		16	
Comment. über den Psalm. 3ter *Theil* (1566) . .		16	
Martin Chemnitz, *Examen Concilii Tridentini* (1566 and 1707) [2]		16	
Postilla oder Ausslegung der Evangelien. . . . Gedr. durch weil. M. Ch. Sampt einer Vorrede des Herrn D. Polycarpi Leyseri (1593) . . .		1	
Heinrich Müller, ?*Evangelische Schluss-Kette und Kraft-Kern, oder Predigten über die Evangelia* (1622 and 1734)		1	
Johann Tauler, *Geistl. Predigten auff alle Sonn- u. Feyer-tage* (1720)		4	
Christoph Scheibler, *Aurifodina theologica. Geistl. Gold-grube nebst Trauer-, Leichen- u. Busspredigten.* 2 *Theile* (1727), 3 vols.	1	8	
Heinrich Bünting, *Itinerarium Sacrae Scripturae* (1579 and 1718)		8	
Johannes Olearius, *Erklährung der Bibel A. u. N. Testaments.* 5 Theile (1678–81), 2 vols. [3] . .	2		
Flavius Josephus, *Opera.* ? Ed. Arnoldus Peraxylus Arlenius (1544)	2		

In Quarto

	Th.	Gr.	Pfg.
August Pfeiffer, *Apostolische Christen-Schule oder Erklärung der Episteln* (1728) . . .	1		

[1] An attempt is made here to indicate the works and editions on Bach's bookshelves. The cryptic and unilluminating entries in the Inventory have therefore been unravelled and extended. I have failed to trace the few works to which no date is attached in this catalogue. Since this work was published, Dr. H. Preuss has contributed an article entitled 'Bachs Bibliothek' to the 'Zahn-Festgabe' (Werner Scholl, Leipzig: 1928).

[2] The Inventory wrongly attributes this work to Luther.

[3] The Inventory has: 'Haupt Schlüssel der gantzen Heil. Schrifft, 3B.'

Th. Gr. Pfg.

Gazophylacium oder Evangelische Schatzkammerpostille
    (1714)   16
Nuptialia oder Haus- u. Eheschule (1702)   .   .   4
Evangelischer Augapfel oder Erklärung der Augspurgi-
    schen Confession (1710)   .   .   .   16
Kern und Safft der Heil. Schrift in Erklärung der
    Hauptsprüche (1718)   1
Heinrich Müller, Evangelisches Preservatif wider den Scha-
    den Josefs in allen 3 Ständen (1741)   .   .   16
    Apostolische Schluss-Kette (1663)   .   .   1
Johann Müller, Atheismus devictus (1685 and 1710)   .   4
    Judaismus oder Judenthumb (1644 and 1707)   .   16
Nikolaus Stenger, ? Postilla evangelica, or ? Postilla cre-
    dendorum et faciendorum (1661)   .   .   1
    Grundfeste der Augspurg-Confession (1649)   .   .   16
Martin Geyer, Zeit und Ewigkeit (1702 and 1738)   .   16
Johann Jakob Rambach, Betrachtung über den Rath Gottes
    von der Schlechtigkeit der Menschen. 2 Theile
    (1737)   16
    Betrachtung ¹   1
Martin Luther, Hauss-Postille   16
—— Frober, Psalm   4
Unterschiedene Predigten [Sermons by various authors]   4
J. C. Adami, Güldener Apfel in silberner Schaal oder Be-
    trachtung des Hohen Liedes Salomonis (1708)   .   4
Joh. Matth. Meyfart, Christliche Erinnerung von der auss
    den Evangelischen Hohen Schulen in Teutschland
    an manchen Orten entwichenen Ordnung und ehr-
    baren Sitten (1636)   4
Joh. Christoph Haynisch, Offenbarung Johannis .   .   4
—— Jauckler, Richtschnur der Christl. Lehre   .   .   1

In Octavo

August Hermann Francke, Predigten und Traktätlein.
    4 Bde. (1723)   8
August Pfeiffer, Evangelische Christenschule (1724)   .   8
    Anticalvinismus oder Unterredung von der Reformirten
        Religion (1729)   8
    Lutherthum vor Luthern oder das alte Evangelische
        durchs Lutherthum erneuerte Christenthum (1713)   8
—Antimelancholicus oder Melancholievertreiber. 2 Theile
    (1706, 1710)   8
Joh. Jakob Rambach, Betrachtung der Thränen und Seuffzer
    Jesu Christi in 2 Predigten (1725)   .   .   8
Heinrich Müller, Göttliche Liebes-Flamme Oder Auffmun-
    terung zur Liebe Gottes (1676) .   .   .   8
    ?Die geistlichen Erquickstunden des Herrn Heinrich
        Müllers (1691)   8
    Menschlich Getichte . . . aus blossem Rahtschluss
        Gottes (1657)   4

¹ The particular 'Betrachtung' cannot be identified.

Th. Gr. Pfg.

	Th.	Gr.	Pfg.
Johann Müller, *Lutherus defensus, d. i. Gründliche Nieder-legung dessen, was die Bäpstler D. Lutheri Persohn fürwerfen* (1634 or 1706) . . .		8	
Johann Gerhard, *Schola pietatis oder Übung der Gottselig-keit* (1736), 5 vols.		12	
Erdmann Neumeister, *Tisch des Herrn über 1. Corinth. xi. 23–32 nebst Bebels Bericht von der Messe* (1723)		8	
?*Die Lehre von der Heil. Tauffe* (1731) . .		8	
Phil. Jakob Spener, *Gerechter Eifer wider das Antichrist-liche Pabstthum* (1714) . . .		8	
Egidius Hunnius, *Reinigkeit der Glaubenslehre* .		4	
Franz Klinge, *Treuhertzige Warnung für Abfall von der Lutherischen zur Papistischen Lehre* (1700 and 1717)		4	
Johann Arndt, *Vom wahren Christenthum* (1606–9 or later edition)		8	
Paul Wagner, *Andächtiger Seelen Brand- und Gantz-Opfer. Das ist vollständiges Gesangbuch in acht unter-schiedlichen Theilen* (1697), 8 vols. . .	1		
Facit		38	17

The Inventory clearly is not complete. Bach's wardrobe surely contained more than three coats, eleven shirts, and a pair of shoe-buckles! His household furniture must have included other articles than are here set down. Not a single score of his own composi-tions, nor any of his laborious transcripts of other composers, are named. His library, too, improbably consisted exclusively of theological works, though their preponderance indicates his pre-ference as a reader. The Inventory, in fact, discloses only that part of Bach's estate admitted to distribution after particular claims on it had been sifted and satisfied. The two eldest sons, Friedemann and Carl Philipp, declaring their father's scores their personal property, withdrew them from the general estate.[1] Their youngest half-brother, Johann Christian, as successfully asserted his ownership of three claviers, a present, he declared, from his father before he died. His mother, Hesemann, and Alt-nikol bore him out in the assertion, and though the children of the first family were dubious, the claim was admitted.[2] Bach's por-trait of his father is not included, and it is obvious that many other articles were omitted. But enough remains to permit us to decorate the interior of Bach's home: the dining-room, solidly furnished with heavy black leather-seated chairs, a brave show of silver plate, and on the wall the painting of Ambrosius Bach; the study or 'Componierstube', with books, writing-table, and leather-covered

[1] Forkel, p. 139.
[2] This appears from the deed of 11 November 1750 (*infra*). Cf. Sp. ii. 968.

chairs; and the kitchen, bright with burnished copper and brass. The library shelves contained some eighty theological books, including Luther and the Lutheran pillars of the seventeenth and eighteenth centuries, in particular those stalwart champions, Heinrich Müller of Rostock and August Pfeiffer of Leipzig. His possession of Bünting's *Itinerarium* declares Bach's search for vivid and authentic pictures of Bible scenes and characters, and Josephus bears the same testimony. Bach's acquaintance with Lutheran hymnody was wide and intimate, and though he found in Paul Wagner's volumes nearly all his texts, it is difficult to believe that Vopelius, Schein, and other Leipzig manuals were not in his possession. We miss, also, the Cantata texts of Neumeister, Salomo Franck, and Picander, on which he drew so largely. Still, incomplete as the catalogue appears to be, it suffices to declare its owner a student of theology, a stout disciple of Luther, and a man of sincere religious feeling.

The scheme of distribution was completed and signed by the participants on 11 November 1750. Anna Magdalena received the mining share (Cap. I), burdened with the obligation to pay two-thirds of the interest on it to the other heirs. Her sister's bond (Cap. III) also was assigned to her at two-thirds (38 th. 16 gr.) of its value, as well as those of Unruh and Haase, assets of doubtful value, since neither debtor could be found. The items catalogued in Cap. V were distributed according to their valuation; perhaps Anna Magdalena received the articles she most prized: the pair of candlesticks, the engraved cup, the large coffee-pot, the teapot, two snuff-boxes, and the coffee-tray. The gold-mounted agate snuff-box was left in her keeping to find a purchaser, its value and character declaring it appropriate to a collector or connoisseur rather than workaday musicians. The instruments (Cap. VI) were also placed in her charge for similar treatment. Friedemann took his father's ceremonial silver-hilted sword, and the eleven shirts were magnanimously divided among the three youngest sons, 'with the consent of the elders'! The coins and books were distributed by lot according to their valuation, Regine Susanna, a child of eight, becoming the owner of Luther's eight-volumed *Opera*. Each participant contributed *pro rata* to the payment of Bach's debts, which, after deducting cash in hand (Cap. IV), amounted to 116 th. 21 gr. 6 pfg.

Like her children, Anna Magdalena, no doubt, withdrew from the general estate articles she declared her own by her husband's gift; the incompleteness of the inventory of his household furniture is probably explained by the fact. Her resources, lamentably small, were pitifully augmented by the payment to her of 21 th. 21 gr., due to Bach for salary at the time of his death, and an equal amount for the surrender of her claim to occupy the Cantor's quarters in the Thomasschule for six months thereafter.[1] Her own children as yet were unable to maintain her, while her stepsons do not appear to have admitted an obligation to do so.[2] Yet, her indigence was notorious: on 19 May 1752 the civic Council paid her 40 th. 'in view of her poverty', and as the sum also covered the purchase of 'certain pieces of music',[3] she was seemingly reduced to selling her husband's manuscripts. In her last years she resided as an 'Almosenfrau',[4] in the Hainstrasse, where she died on 27 February 1760. She was given a 'solenne' funeral[5] in the burial-ground which had received her 'Liebster' ten years before, where he lay in a grave whose locality already was fading from the memory of the community he served. Nothing more vividly declares its unappreciation of him than its cold neglect of his widow.

Anna Magdalena was the first of Bach's household to follow him to the grave. Gottfried Heinrich, whom his only married sister had received at Naumburg, died there three years later (12 February 1763). The other sons, in widely separated spheres, added distinction to the family name till near the end of the century. Johann Christian, the 'English Bach', died in 1782, Friedemann, brilliant but wayward, in 1784, Carl Philipp, steady and prosperous, in 1788, Johann Christoph Friedrich in 1795. Of Bach's daughters, his eldest, Catharina Dorothea, died in 1774, his youngest but one in 1781. Of all his family only Regine Susanna, the youngest, entered the nineteenth century, forgotten by all until Rochlitz published an arresting 'Appeal' in the 'Allgemeine Leipziger Musikzeitung' for May 1800: 'The family of Bach is extinct [6] but for a single daughter of the great Sebastian. And that daughter, now no longer young, is —— starving!' [7] He was not unheeded: in December 1800 Regine Susanna published a touching acknowledgement of 96 th. 5 gr. received from the public through Rochlitz

---

[1] Her letter of 15 Aug. 1750 begging the boon is in Bi. iii. 264.
[2] Carl Philipp, however, undertook the education of Johann Christian.
[3] 'einiger überreichten Musicalien' (Bi. iii. 266). Can these have been the parts of the Church Cantatas now in the Bibliothek of the Thomasschule?
[4] Under the Leipzig Council an 'Almosen-Amt' was constituted to relieve the needy and prevent beggars from frequenting the streets. Six 'Armen-Vögte' were employed for the latter purpose, while a seventh visited the Almosen in their homes. Anna Magdalena perhaps lodged in Graf's house in the Hainstrasse (*supra*, p. 269 n.).
[5] *Der Bär* (1929–30), p. 168.
[6] Literally, the statement is untrue. Cf. Appendix II.   [7] Quoted in Bi. iii. 267.

and Breitkopf and Härtel. The appeal was heard and answered from farther afield: on 19 May 1801 Rochlitz announced generous contributions from Vienna, including Beethoven's promise of a manuscript for publication to augment the fund.[1] 'With tears of happiness' Regine Susanna acknowledged (20 May 1801) the bounty which relieved her remaining years.[2] She died at Leipzig in 1809, four years before Wagner first saw the light in the same city.

Bach's male issue did not survive beyond the second generation. Wilhelm Friedemann's two sons died in infancy; Carl Philipp's younger son died unmarried in 1778, the elder, without issue, in 1789. Of the sons of Bach's second marriage, only Johann Christoph Friedrich of Bückeburg had male issue, a son, Wilhelm Friedrich Ernst, born in 1759, who became cembalist to the beloved Queen Luise of Prussia. Upon her death in 1810 he passed into retirement, forgotten beyond the circle of his friends, until he presented himself at the unveiling of the memorial erected to his grandfather's memory at Leipzig on 23 April 1843 by the enthusiasm of Mendelssohn. Schumann's 'Neue Zeitschrift für Musik' (4 May 1843), after describing the event, added: 'Honour was paid not only to Bach but also to his sole surviving grandson, a man of 84, still full of energy, with snow-white hair and expressive features. No one knew of his existence, not even Mendelssohn, who had lived so long in Berlin and, he supposed, had followed every trace of Bach he could discover. Yet his grandson had resided there for over forty years. No information was obtained regarding his circumstances, except that he had filled the office of Capellmeister to the consort of King Friedrich Wilhelm III, and enjoys a pension which maintains him in comfort.'[3] He died on 25 December 1845 and Bach's direct male lineage with him.[4]

The second centenary of Bach's birth in 1885 appealed to a

---

[1] Beethoven does not appear to have fulfilled his promise. Dr. Hitzig tells me that there is no record in the archives of Breitkopf and Härtel of the receipt of any manuscript from him. See 'Die Musik', Nov. 1912, Heft 3, p. 160.
[2] Her letters are in Bi. iii. 268. See Der Bär (1929–30), pp. 167 f.
[3] The 'Allgemeine Musikalische Zeitung' for 10 May 1843 notices the event more briefly. It is not referred to in Mendelssohn's letters and appears to have excited no interest outside Germany.
[4] Whether Bach's lineage survives on the spindle side is more difficult to decide. One of the two grand-daughters of his first marriage (see Appendix II), Carl P. E. Bach's daughter, died a spinster at Hamburg in 1804; the other, Friedemann's daughter, was married late in life and had two daughters. Of Bach's second marriage four grand-daughters have been traced. One of them (Juliane Wihelmine Prüfer) had no issue; one (Dorothea Charlotte Magdalena Bach) was unmarried; two (Auguste Magdalena Ahlefeldt and Anna Philippina Friederica Colson) had issue. The former's certainly terminated on the death

generation no longer indifferent and undiscerning. The Bach-gesellschaft had been launched in 1850, with a membership representing almost the whole civilized globe, and it seemed imperative to repair a former generation's neglect by honouring his neglected grave. Its precise site was unknown, but tradition placed it six paces from the south door of the Johanniskirche. The ground, however, had long been put to secular use,[1] and as a closer association was impossible, the civic Council erected a tablet on the south wall of the church, between the south door and the nearest altar window, bearing the inscription:[2]

> AUF DIESER SEITE
>
> DES EHEMALIGEN JOHANNISKIRCHHOFES
>
> WURDE
>
> JOHANN SEBASTIAN BACH
>
> AM 31 JULI 1750 BEGRABEN

Nine years later, the reconstruction of the church involved the demolition of its walls and the inclusion within the enlarged building of ground hitherto outside it. The removal of material, and excavation for the new foundations, afforded opportunity to search for Bach's grave, and work was begun forthwith upon the plot in which tradition located it. A further clue was afforded by the knowledge that Bach was buried in an oak coffin,[3] a detail of value seeing that, of 1400 persons buried in 1750, he was one of only twelve coffined in that wood. After three days' fruitless digging three oak coffins were exposed on 22 October 1894, one of which contained the almost perfect skeleton of an elderly male, well-proportioned, not large of stature, with massive skull, receding forehead, shallow eye-sockets, and heavy jaws. The skull was forthwith compared with Haussmann's and other portraits,[4] a col-

of her grand-daughter in 1818. The latter's was apparently extinct in 1852. After that date Bach's only known descendants were the grandchildren of his Bückeburg son. They had no issue and the last of them died in 1871. See Appendix II.

[1] 'Musicalisches Wochenblatt', No. 27 (27 June 1895), p. 339.
[2] His, p. 3. The tablet was placed in the vault of the church containing Bach's sarcophagus.
[3] The register of the Johannishospital for 1750 has the entry: '4 thlr. zahlte der Todtengräber Müller wegen Herrn Johann Sebastian Bach's eichenem Sarg' (His, p. 4).
[4] Besides Haussmann's picture, the portraits used for the collation were: one in the possession of the firm of Peters; and a copper-plate by S. G. Kütner executed in 1774. In fact neither has original value; the copper-plate was

lation which revealed striking physiognomical similarities. The sculptor Karl Seffner was commissioned to model a head upon a cast of the skull, and after an exhaustive and scientific investigation the remains were admitted to be those of Bach.[1] Enclosed within a massive and unpretentious limestone sarcophagus tersely inscribed:

JOHANN SEBASTIAN BACH
1685–1750

they were placed beneath the altar of the church in their present mortuary. *Ruhe sanfte, sanfte ruh' !*

rudely executed from Haussmann's portrait, and from it, about 1800, the Peters portrait was painted. An oil portrait by C. F. R. Lisiewsky, painted in 1777, is in the Joachimsthal Gymnasium (figured in Reimann, p. 64). Bach's pupil Kittel owned a portrait at Erfurt which has since disappeared, but is perhaps the picture discovered by Dr. Fritz Volbach in 1904 (figured in Parry, frontispiece, and Forkel, p. 92). Cf. Volbach's paper in 'Die Musik', Jhrg. IX, Oct.–Dec. 1909, p. 107; also His, p. 10. A contemporary pencil sketch of Bach is reproduced in Zor. frontispiece. Herr Manfred Gorke has recently announced his possession of another portrait of Bach, formerly C. P. E. Bach's. It is by Haussman and is autographed. It was executed shortly before Bach's appointment to Leipzig in 1723.

[1] The subject is exhaustively treated by His.

INDEX

I. PERSONS

WORKS

Hagedorn, Anna Dorothea, 84, 99.
Hagedorn, Georg Christian, 222.
Hahn, Michael, 40.
Hammerschmidt, Andreas, 37, 38, 40.
Handel, Georg Friedrich, 67, 101, 114, 129, 134, 198, 238, 254, 262.
Hanff, Johann Nikolaus, 40.
Harbordt, Wilhelm Andreas, 119, 120, 121.
Harrer, Gottlob, 260, 263, 265.
Hasse, Johann Adolph, 122, 211, 218.
Haupt, Christian Friedrich, 190.
Haupt, Johann Gottl., 204.
Hauptmann, Johann Christ., 204.
Hauptmann, Moritz, 169.
Haus, Gottlob Ernst, 198.
Haus, Gottl. Jakob, 204.
Haus, Theophilus Jacobus, 224.
Haussmann, Elias Gottlieb, 167, 254, 262.
Hays (de la Haye), Henri de, 50.
Hebenstreit, Johann Samuel, 204.
Heder, Samuel Gottl., 204.
Heger, Melchior, 163.
Heider, Justus (? Jobst), 40, 42.
Heindorff, Ernst Dietrich, 40, 64.
Heineccius, Joh. Michael, 101, 102, 105.
Heinichen, Johann David, 118, 143.
Heininger (Heiniger), Johann Christoph, 92, 93, 94.
Heitmann, Johann Joachim, 130 ff.
Helmbold, Ludwig, 76, 163.
Henrici, Christian Friedrich, 153, 180, 194, 209, 216, 217, 218, 220, 250.
Herbst, Johann Andreas, 40.
Herda, Elias, 27, 29.
Hermann, Johannes, 163.
Herthum, Christoph, 12, 59, 63, 68.
Hertzog, Johann Georg, 131, 133.
Hesemann, Gottlob Sigismund, 269, 275.
Hesse, Christ. Gottfried, 204.
Hetzehen, Johann Gottfried, 222.
Hickethier, Johann Lorenz, 50.
Hildebrand, Johann, 40.
Hildebrand, Johann Heinrich, 46.
Hildebrand, Zacharias, 178, 247, 251.
Hiller, Cantor, 244.
Hillmeyer, Johann Heinrich, 197, 204.
Hindorff, Johann Christian, 106.
Hochberg, Count von, 219.
Hofe, Dorothea von, 24, 98.
Hoffmann, Anna Sophie, 81.
Hoffmann, Balthasar, 221.
Hoffmann, Christian Gottfried, 224.
Hoffmann, Christoph, 8.
Hoffmann, Gottfried Christoph, 198.
Hoffmann, Johann Christian, 247.

Hoffmann, Johann Georg, 92, 93, 94.
Homilius, Gottfried August, 162.
Homilius, Johann Hieronymus, 162.
Horn, Johann Caspar, 38, 40.
Hucke, Georg, 40.
Hudemann, Ludwig Fr., 259.
Hülsemann, Martin Georg, 43.
Huhn, Christian Gottfried, 159.
Hutter, Leonhard, 28, 44.

Ihle, Paul, 4.

Jakob, Adam, 167.
Jakobi, Daniel, 40.
Jakobi, Michael, 40.
Jeep, Johann, 38.
Jenicke, Johann Michael, 204.
Job, Syndicus, 200.
Joffe, Guillaume, 50.
Johann Ernst, Duke, of Sachsen-Weimar, 56 ff., 85, 87.
Johann Ernst, the younger, Prince, of Sachsen-Weimar, 57, 103, 106.
Johann Georg, Duke, of Sachsen-Weissenfels, 56.
Johann Wilhelm, Duke, of Sachsen-Weimar, 57.
Jünger, Wolfgang, 163.
Jungk, Nikolaus, 122.
Jungknickel, Johann, 40.
Junius, Rector Ulrich, 185.

Käse, Frau, 178.
Kaldenbach, Christoph, 40.
Kannewürs, Sophie Elisabeth, 13.
Kappelar, Laurens, see Cappeller.
Kapsberger, Johann Hieronymus, 40.
Kaufmann, Georg Friedrich, 142, 143, 145, 147.
Kayserling, Carl Freiherr von, 235, 250.
Keiser, Gottfried, 40.
Keiser, Reinhard, 48.
Keller, Johann Christian, 141.
Keller, Johann Ephraim, 204.
Kempis, Nikolaus à, 38.
Kerll, Johann Caspar, 25, 40.
Keul, Barbara Margaretha, 21.
Kiesewetter, Johann Christoph, 26, 88.
Kindermann, Johann Erasmus, 40.
Kirchbach, Carl von, 190 ff.
Kirnberger, Johann Philipp, 99.
Kittel, Johann Christian, 4, 279.
Kittler, Michael Heinrich, 198.
Kittler, Samuel, 197, 204, 226, 228.
Klemm, Eva, 167.
Klemm, Johann Friedrich, 233 ff., 245 ff.

II. PLACES

2. GRÄFENRODA

3. WECHMAR, VEIT BACH'S MILL

4. WECHMAR, HANS BACH'S HOUSE

5. ARNSTADT, TOWER AND RUINS OF SCHLOSS NEIDECK

6. ARNSTADT, CASPAR BACH'S HOUSE

7. ARNSTADT, HEINRICH BACH'S HOUSE

8. ARNSTADT, JOHANN CHRISTOPH BACH'S HOUSE

9. EISENACH, SITE OF JOHANN AMBROSIUS BACH'S HOUSE
(*Lutherstrasse 35, now a Friseur's shop*)

1c. EISENACH, THE GYMNASIUM

11. JOHANN AMBROSIUS BACH

12. OHRDRUF, JOHANN CHRISTOPH BACH'S HOUSE

13. OHRDRUF, THE MICHAELISKIRCHE

14. LÜNEBURG, FROM THE KALKBERG

15. LÜNEBURG, THE MICHAELISKIRCHE, FROM AUF DEM MEERE

16. LÜNEBURG, THE MICHAELISKIRCHE, *c.* 1705

17. LÜNEBURG, THE MICHAELISKLOSTER

18. LÜNEBURG, SITE OF THE OLD MICHAELISKLOSTER

19. LÜNEBURG, THE JOHANNISKIRCHE, ORGAN GALLERY

20. HAMBURG, THE CATHARINENKIRCHE

21. CELLE, THE SCHLOSS

22. CELLE, THE SCHLOSS CHAPEL

23. CELLE, THE SCHLOSSTHEATER

24. ARNSTADT, THE BONIFACIUSKIRCHE, EAST END

25. ARNSTADT, THE BONIFACIUSKIRCHE, WEST END

26. ARNSTADT, THE GOLDEN CROWN

27. ARNSTADT, THE BONIFACIUSKIRCHE, ORGAN GALLERY

28. ARNSTADT, KEYBOARD AND PEDALS OF BACH'S ORGAN

29. LÜBECK, THE MARIENKIRCHE, ORGAN GALLERY

30. MÜHLHAUSEN IN THE EIGHTEENTH CENTURY

31. MÜHLHAUSEN, THE KIRCHE DIVI BLASII

32. MÜHLHAUSEN, THE KIRCHE DIVI BLASII

33. MÜHLHAUSEN, THE MARIENKIRCHE

34. DORNHEIM, THE CHURCH

35. DORNHEIM, THE CHURCH

36. BACH'S MARRIAGE, THE ARNSTADT REGISTER

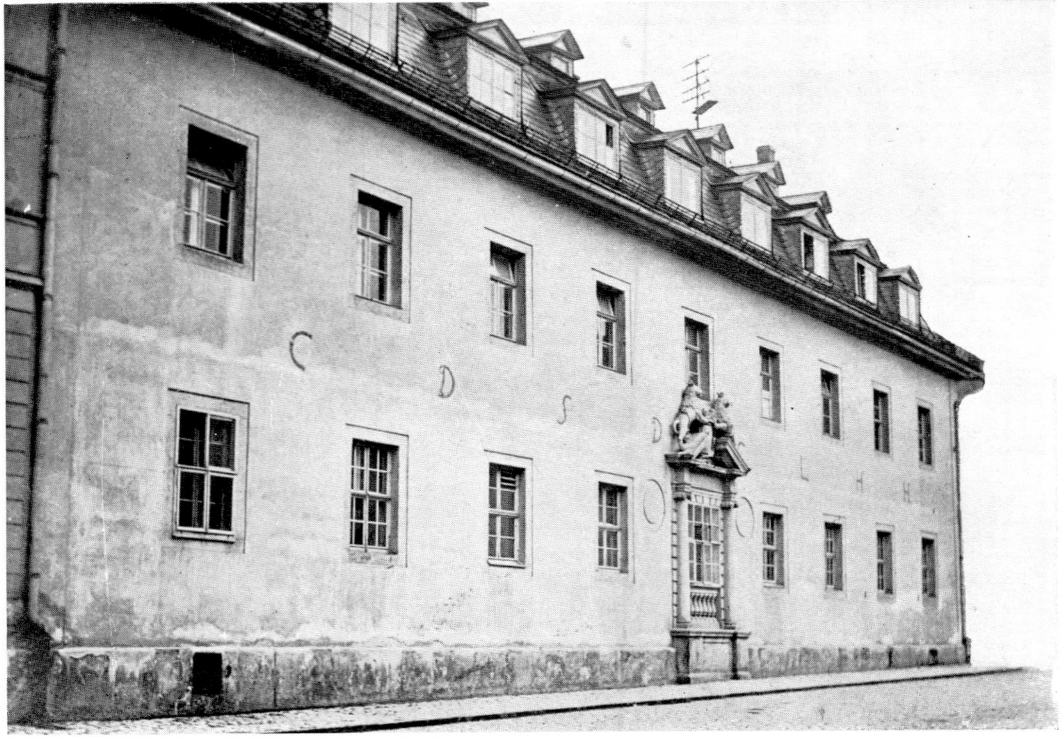

37. WEIMAR, GELBES SCHLOSS, NORTH FRONT

38. WEIMAR, GELBES SCHLOSS, WINDOW ON NORTH FRONT

39. WEIMAR, GELBES SCHLOSS, WEST FRONT

40. WEIMAR, SCHLOSSTHURM AND BASTILLE

41. WEIMAR, WILHELMSBURG

42. WEIMAR, PARKHOTEL ERBPRINZ

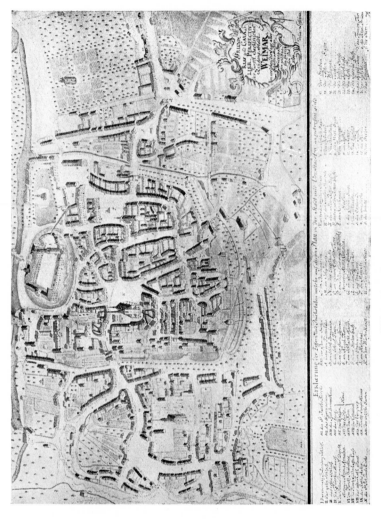

43. WEIMAR, LOSSIUS'S PLAN, 1786

44. WILHELM ERNST, HERZOG VON SACHSEN-WEIMAR

45. JOHANN ERNST, HERZOG VON SACHSEN-WEIMAR

46. WEIMAR, HIMMELSBURG

Cöthen nach Merian im Jahre 1650.

47. CÖTHEN, GENERAL VIEW, 1650

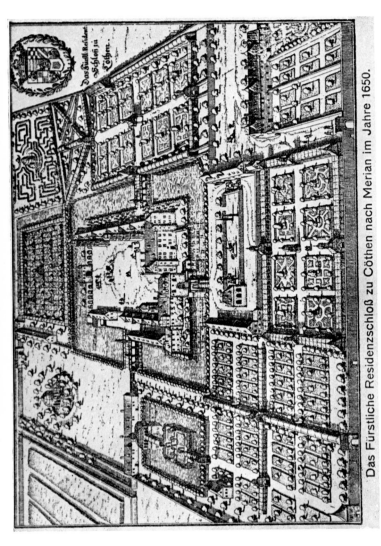

Das Fürstliche Residenzschloß zu Cöthen nach Merian im Jahre 1650.

48. CÖTHEN, THE SCHLOSS, 1650

49. CÖTHEN, THE SCHLOSS, WEST WING

50. CÖTHEN, THE SCHLOSS, LUDWIGSBAU, SOUTH-WEST ANGLE

51. CÖTHEN, THE SCHLOSS QUADRANGLE AND LUDWIGSBAU

52. CÖTHEN, THE BACHDENKMAL, RATHAUS, AND ST. JAKOBSKIRCHE

53. LEOPOLD, FÜRST VON ANHALT-CÖTHEN

54. FRIEDERICA HENRIETTA, FÜRSTIN VON ANHALT-CÖTHEN

55. CÖTHEN, THE SCHLOSS, AS IN BACH'S TIME

56. CÖTHEN, SCHALAUNISCHE STRASSE, NOS. 29 AND 30

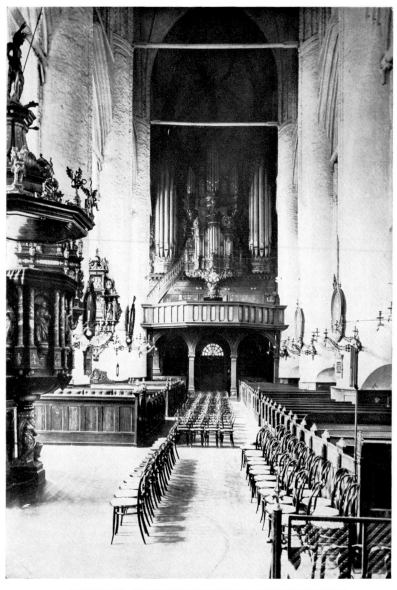

57. HAMBURG, CATHARINENKIRCHE, ORGAN GALLERY

58. LEIPZIG, MATTH. SUETTER'S PLAN

59. LEIPZIG, FROM THE NORTH, 1736

1. Die St Thomas Kirche. 2. Die Thomas Schule.
3. Der Steinerne Wasser=Kasten.

60. LEIPZIG, THE THOMASKIRCHE AND THOMASSCHULE, 1723

Mit vieler Verbesserung erbauete Thomas-Schule Ao 1732

61. LEIPZIG, THE THOMASSCHULE, AFTER ENLARGEMENT, 1732

62. LEIPZIG, THE THOMASSCHULE, FROM THE WEST, 1877

63. LEIPZIG, THE THOMASKIRCHE, BEFORE RESTORATION IN 1885

64. JOHANN HEINRICH ERNESTI

65. JOHANN MATTHIAS GESNER

66. JOHANN AUGUST ERNESTI

Die St Nicolai Kirch in LEIPZIG,
Mitt umligenden Gebeuren.

1. Die Niclas Schule sampt anstosenden Pfar Häußern,
2. Das Grosß Fürsten Collegium.

67. LEIPZIG, THE NIKOLAIKIRCHE

68. LEIPZIG, THE NIKOLAISCHULE

69. LEIPZIG, ORGAN GALLERY OF THE NIKOLAIKIRCHE, 1785

Das PAULINER COLLEGIUM in LEIPZIG.

1. Das Collegium.
2. Der Hoff.
3. Der Schöpff brunen.
4. Die Pauliner Kirch.
5. Der Creutz oder Durch gang.
6. Durchgang in die Grimische Gasse.
7. Wohn Häuser.

G. Bodenehr del. et Sculp.
Cum Gr. et Priv. S. C. Majest.

70. LEIPZIG, THE PAULINER COLLEGIUM

Die Pauliner Kirch
und der näbeft
darangelegene Hortg medicg.

71. LEIPZIG, THE PAULINERKIRCHE AND HORTUS MEDICUS

72. LEIPZIG, THE PAULINERKIRCHE, ORGAN GALLERY

S. Johannus Kirche mit dem neu gebauten Thurn

73. LEIPZIG, THE JOHANNISKIRCHE AND FRIEDHOF

74. WEISSENFELS. THE SCHLOSS, c. 1680

75. WEISSENFELS, THE SCHLOSS CHAPEL

76. BACH'S SEAL AND SIGNATURE, 7 AUGUST 1746